D0146116

GOD AND THE LAND

GOD AND THE LAND

The Metaphysics of Farming
in Hesiod and Vergil

STEPHANIE A. NELSON

With a Translation of Hesiod's
Works and Days
by
DAVID GRENE

New York   Oxford
OXFORD UNIVERSITY PRESS
1998

Oxford University Press

Oxford   New York

Athens   Auckland   Bangkok   Bogota   Bombay   Buenos Aires
Calcutta   Cape Town   Dar es Salaam   Delhi   Florence   Hong Kong
Istanbul   Karachi   Kuala Lumpur   Madras   Madrid   Melbourne
Mexico City   Nairobi   Paris   Singapore   Taipei   Tokyo   Toronto   Warsaw

and associated companies in
Berlin   Ibadan

Copyright © 1998 by Oxford University Press

Published by Oxford University Press, Inc.
198 Madison Avenue, New York, New York 10016

Oxford is a registered trademark of Oxford University Press

Library of Congress Cataloging-in-Publication Data
Nelson, Stephanie A. (Stephanie Anne), 1958–
God and the land : the metaphysics of farming in Hesiod and Vergil
with a translation of Hesiod's Works and days by David Grene / by
Stephanie Nelson
p.   cm.
Includes bibliographical references and index.
ISBN 0–19–511740–9
1. Hesiod. Works and days.   2. Didactic poetry, Classical—
History and criticism.   3. Didactic poetry, Greek—Translations into
English.   4. Mythology, Classical, in literature.   5. Agriculture—Greece—
Poetry.   6. Agriculture in Literature.   7. Gods, Greek, in literature.
8. Gods, Roman, in literature.   9. Metaphysics in literature.   10. Virgil, Georgica.
I. Hesiod. Works and days. English. 1998   II. Title.
PA4009.07N45 1998
881'.01—dc21   97–13801

1 3 5 7 9 8 6 4 2

Printed in the United States of America
on acid-free paper

PREFACE:
MAN, GOD, NATURE—
AND FARMING

In Plato's *Parmenides* the young Socrates is disconcerted by Parmenides' challenge: if there are forms of beauty and goodness, are there also forms of mud and hair? When Socrates admits his perplexity, Parmenides replies that he is still young; when he is older he will not, in his pursuit of understanding, despise even these (*Parmenides* 130b–e). Farming is like that. Farming is a matter of dirt and dung. It is not the kind of thing we look to to find the meaning of human life. It is too ordinary, too inescapably a part of life to be interesting. We know that it has to be done, but see no reason to pay much attention to it.

But it is just because farming is inescapably a part of human life that it may provide a clue to what is most basically human, and so a clue to our place within the cosmos. Or, at least, so Vergil and Hesiod believed. The latter stands, with Homer, at the very beginning of Greek thought. The former devoted himself to a vision of Rome seen *sub specie aeternitatis*. Although the two poets, in their lives, their times, and their temperaments, had little in common, they shared a sense that it is in the grime of reality that its deepest metaphysical layers are found.

This book is based on that idea. Its premise is that our view of farming, whether we are aware of it or not, implies a particular understanding of nature, of the cosmos, and of the divine, and of our own relation, as human beings, to the physical world, to other human beings, and to God. Human beliefs, like nature, are interdependent. They do not live in compartments. As a factory in Gary, Indiana, cannot operate in isolation from the pine forests of Canada or the monsoons in India, our attitude toward a modern combine harvester, or toward a free range egg, is linked to our sense of God, of nature, and of ourselves. This book is not directly about current issues, but it addresses them nonetheless. Hesiod's vision of farming is of a piece with his vision of the cosmos. So is Vergil's, very different, vision. As we explore theirs we cannot help but reflect on our own as well.

It is a question which requires exploration. The vision of an Amish farmer, who sees his care of the land as a sacred duty, who believes that simplicity and honesty, not competition, must underlie human relations, and who sees these two aspects of his life as determining his relation to God, is unified. So also is a view that sees nature as plastic in human hands, human relations as necessarily founded upon competition and the urge of individual needs, and our relation to God as personal and independent of society or the physical world. There now appears to be a movement towards the first vision. The increasing popularity of environmental causes, of organic and health food movements, and of recycling, point to a growing belief that we cannot force nature into whatever mold we please. We must learn nature's ways, not force nature to learn ours. But farming continues to be seen through the second vision. While we do not believe that nature should, nor even can, be endlessly exploited, we continue to believe that a farm, to be modern and efficient, must be run as a factory. While we no longer believe that society benefits from a focus on machines rather than human beings, we continue to feel pride, open or disguised, that modern Western agricultural methods require constantly fewer farmers to produce constantly more food. While we no longer feel that ethics is a concern of churches and philosophy departments rather than of the real world, we continue to act as if the march of progress must continue, whether it is a good thing or a bad thing.

Farms that are more dependent on fossil fuels than on human labor, and that rely on pesticides, herbicides, and chemical fertilizers rather than on the interrelation of animals, varied crops, and types of soil for their survival, are a relatively new development in the history of human civilization. As such they cannot simply be an economic necessity. Rather, I believe, the view that our society requires "modern" farming methods is as much a part of our particular vision of the world as Hesiod's and Vergil's views of farming were part of theirs. In our case it is part of a vision that is radically split. We are living in a society that looks forward to the day when we can, even in the suburbs, purchase mass-produced "natural" foods from huge organic supermarkets. We are living in a contradiction of terms.

Sometimes we best come to understand ourselves by attempting to understand others. The two authors I examine in this book, Hesiod and Vergil, are very different. So is their usefulness here. Hesiod is valuable because he is so unlike us. The vision within which he sees God, human beings, and nature as forming a simple whole is striking because of its unfamiliarity, and in being so striking it forces us to reflect on our own divided sense of the world. Vergil, in contrast, is valuable because his vision is so like our own. His is a world divided, one in which human beings often seem terribly alienated from the universe that they inhabit. He is modern even to the extent of turning to a simpler past in order to explore the complexity of his own world. In examining Hesiod as a way of exploring ourselves we are only doing for our own time what Vergil, by basing the *Georgics* upon the *Works and Days*, already did for his.

Neither poet will help us by examining the relative merits of organic and nonorganic farming. That is not the way in which their concerns speak to us. The concerns we share lie rather in the connection between farming and the deeper questions of whether we feel ourselves alienated from the physical, moral, or spiritual world around us, or in harmony with it. It is on this understanding that our sense of what farming is, and what it should strive to be, ultimately is based. Immediate questions of current policy must, of course, be answered on an immediate level, as they mostly are. But it is, I believe, exactly because this immediate level tends to usurp all of our attention that our sense of farming has come to be divided from our sense of nature. We must occasionally learn from poets as well as from environmental reports. It is only then that we can address, in all its depth and complexity, the relative merits of organic and nonorganic farming

A farm, like a garden or an orchard, is a part of nature that human beings take as their own, to try and direct towards ends profitable to themselves. With the land that the farmer encloses comes its inhabitants, animals and plants, invited and uninvited, domestic and wild, friendly to the farmer's ends and hostile to them. The impersonal forces of nature are part of the farm as well, externally in the climate and conditions of farming, internally in the processes of generation and growth, of disease, accident, and death, of crops and animals. Together, the crops and the weeds, the cattle and the birds and the insects, the rain and the wind and the soil and the sun, and the farmer, form a whole. It is a whole which is both a crucial element of human life and a microcosm and image of the greater whole within which we, as human beings, live.

The kind of farm which both Hesiod and Vergil imply in their poems is the farm which has persisted throughout most of human history, and which persists today throughout much of the world. It is small, varied, and largely, but not completely, self-subsistent. It is worked by a family, perhaps with one or two servants, hired or slave. Its goal is primarily the raising of grain, but it contains also trees—for Hesiod and Vergil, as in the Mediterranean generally, primarily vines and olives; and animals—hens, pigs, goats, or sheep; a cow, perhaps; one or several of oxen, horses, donkeys, mules, or camels for work and hauling. Most of what the family, the servants, and the animals eat comes from the farm. The rest must be purchased by the sale of any available surplus. The oxen plow and manure the fields which produce their fodder; goats or sheep, tended by children raised on their milk, graze whatever margins are left; pigs or poultry gather what they can and recycle any household scraps, until they become household scraps themselves. The success of the farm is measured by how completely its elements work together, how well they manage to resist the hostile forces of disease, drought, storm, weeds, insects, or wild animals that threaten the farm, and how well they use and adapt themselves to the natural and the economic and political forces that make the difference between affluence and poverty.

Both Hesiod and Vergil saw in such a farm a basic element of human life and a microcosm of the place of man in the world. For Hesiod this is, most probably, the kind of farm he knew and worked. For Vergil, although it may well have been the farm he knew as a boy in Mantua, this was not contemporary Italian farming. Hesiod chooses this as the farm he knew; Vergil chooses it first because it is the farm of the *Works and Days*, but secondly because he finds it more expressive of what is basic in farming than the huge, slave-run, monoculture farms of his own time. For what is essentially true of the farm of the *Georgics* is also true of the farms of Augustan Italy. The farms of the twentieth-century American Midwest may lack horses or oxen, cattle or hogs, poultry, or even a garden, but farming is still, in essence, an interaction of farmer and weather, crops, insects, and weeds, of the economic and political forces which affect the farm from the human side, and of the conditions of soil and climate which affect it from the side of nature. So with the farms of Augustan Italy. Vergil chose the farm of the *Georgics* partly as a contrast to the farms he knew. He chose it even more because it expresses their essence.

The advantage of the small farm of the *Works and Days* and the *Georgics* is not that it is simpler than the large farms that we, as Vergil, are familiar with, but that it is more complicated. As such it reveals more clearly our relation to nature, to other human beings, and to God. As it contains more elements it reveals more clearly the complex interaction of human beings and nature implied by a farm. As it supplies most of the farmer's needs it gives the farmer independence, although it itself depends upon society, as surely as society depends upon the farm. It thus brings out the complexity of human relations implied by a farm. And as, on this kind of small farm, human beings live lives largely unmediated by the institutions established to soften our struggle with the cosmos, this farm, as a microcosm, provides a clue to our relation to the macrocosm that we most often call God.

Farmers attempt to direct the creatures and forces which make up their farms. They cannot create them, and can, at best, only partly control them. Their relationship with nature is thus both cooperative and hostile. Nature is what farmers nourish, and what they attempt to destroy. It is the force that causes the corn to grow, and the insects, disease, and storms that destroy the corn. This complexity, inherent in the farmer's relation to nature, appears in the word itself.[1] At one extreme, "nature" can mean what is untouched by human beings. This sense of nature calls up visions of mountain streams bearing no mark of human contact. In regard to this "nature" human beings can be only spectators, or destroyers. Our farms are not, in this sense of the word, part of nature; they are rather intrusions upon her. But "nature" can also include human beings, and define them, for we, just as any other element of the cosmos, have a "nature" and belong to the "natural" world. And then again "nature" may be seen as plastic, governed by "laws of nature" which we are capable of understanding, and so employing, the province of the "natural" sciences. This "nature" does not exclude human beings, but exists as the material given into our hands. Our farms do not intrude upon it; they use it.

Farming tells us about the place of human beings within nature in each of the many senses of the word. It also tells us about the nature of human beings. Our nature is to be social, to live not independently, but in relation to other human beings. Farming, and the possibility of a production of food in surplus, is necessary for a society where not all members are to produce food. Society requires farming. Conversely, farming requires society, both as a market, and for its guarantee that what you sow you may also reap. Farming is thus the place where nature and culture meet. It is our life within nature, but a life so unique to us that it has given us the word "culture," by which we distinguish ourselves from nature. The farm connects nature and culture, and it is dependent upon both. It can be destroyed by storm or drought. It can as easily be destroyed by revolution, or by the stock market.

Farming is both our alliance with nature, and our war against her. This ambivalence brings us to the third factor here examined, God. Farmers may be seen as embattled beings, attempting to carve out a small area of peace in a violent and irrational

cosmos. They may also be seen as beings endowed with the reason needed to comple-
ment and guide nature into the ways best for both. And they may be seen as beings
who, tempted to control, must learn, instead, to cooperate. It is our sense of the ultimate reality, and not simply our experience of farming, that determines which view
we take. Our vision of farming and of what farming implies about our place in the cosmos cannot be divorced from the sense we make of the cosmos itself and of the principle, if any, which governs it. How we see farming depends finally on how we see God.
This is what Hesiod and Vergil understood, and what we can learn from them.

I would like first to address the general reader. The next section of this Preface is
addressed to professional Classicists. This book attempts to serve two masters. As a
scholarly book it is produced for Classical scholars, who know the works in question
and who are interested in the relation of any new argument to previous scholarship.
On the other hand, there is, I believe, a large and growing readership for a book of this
kind among those not versed in current Hesiodic and Vergilian scholarship. These
readers are of two kinds. On the one hand, as academic studies have become increasingly specialized, it has become increasingly difficult for scholars in related fields to follow the current research in Classics. The *Work and Days* and the *Georgics* are as relevant
to scholars involved in the Law, the History of Religions, Anthropology, Philosophy,
or Comparative Literature as they are to Classicists. In writing this book I have tried
to keep the needs of non-Classical scholars in mind.

I have also tried to remember that Hesiod and Vergil themselves composed not
for scholars but for the general audience of their day. To me this means that my two
masters are not necessarily at odds. Scholarship is not an end in itself; it is rather a
means to help us better understand works like the *Georgics* and the *Works and Days*, a
means that can, and should, be used to help not only scholars, but any interested
reader.

Changes of time and place, differences of language, and the loss of assumptions
once shared by author and audience can obscure a literary text just as the grime of centuries can dull a painting. The *Works and Days* and the *Georgics* have suffered, in this
regard, more than many other Western texts, much more than, for example, the *Iliad*
or the *Aeneid*. Hesiod is liable to appear to a modern audience disjointed, a potpourri
of vaguely related proverbs and stories, while the point of Vergil's detailed description
of farming may be mysterious to an audience that does not see farming through the
eyes of an ancient Roman. These are, consequently, works particularly appropriate to
my purpose here, which is to clarify the text, not to replace it. This is also why my commentary accompanies a translation of the *Works and Days*.

Where my arguments differ from usual interpretations of these poems will be seen
below. As will be apparent, my aim is not to overturn the work of other scholars, but
to reveal a perspective that unites their views. My strongest hope is that this commentary will serve both to introduce these poems to readers unfamiliar with them, and
to enrich them for those reading them once more.

It is hard, however, to address two audiences. I have tried to solve this problem
by compartmentalizing elements of interest only to scholars, or only to general readers. Discussion of purely scholarly questions has been confined to the notes, while the
notes have been confined, in turn, to scholarship. As I have tried to include nothing

in the notes which is necessary for a general reader I have felt free to place them at the back of the book. On the other hand, in the introduction to the book, and in the first two sections of the first chapter, I have assumed a reader who knows nothing of Hesiod, his time, or his method of composition, and have attempted to include all material necessary for an understanding of the poet and his society. Here Hesiod's antiquity has come to my aid; these sections are short because very little is known. A parallel section, giving general information about Vergil, will be found at the opening of Chapter 3. Aside from a discussion of Hesiod's implicit claim to be a farmer, scholars will find very little in these sections that they did not already know, while general readers should find everything necessary to an understanding of the argument of the book.

As I do not assume a reader who knows even who Hesiod is, I obviously cannot assume one who has a detailed knowledge of his poem. Here I have been exceptionally fortunate. David Grene's translation, unique, in particular, because of its sensitivity to Hesiod's feeling for farming, has long been needed. It fills the additional need, here, of a text to accompany my analysis of the poem.

I have also used Grene's translation of the *Works and Days* in the body of the book. I have, however, in some places altered the translation when my treatment of a particular point needs to be brought out more explicitly than the metrical demands of a formal translation allow. When I have done so I have included a footnote which explains the reasons for the alteration. My occasional alterations, at the price, I am afraid, of poetry, weigh less heavily upon my conscience because of the accompanying translation. The *Georgics* has already found, in C. Day Lewis, a translator to do it justice, although this translation is unfortunately out of print. Assuming, therefore, that readers are using no one single translation of either the *Theogony* or the *Georgics*, I have translated these references myself.

Above all, I hope that I have made these two poems not only accessible, but even inviting. If Classics is not to die altogether, it must find a way to engage people who are personally, not professionally, interested in ideas. This is not to give these texts an artificial existence. It is only to keep alive the flame that was kindled a long time ago, when they were first composed.

The above describes what this book has to offer to readers who are not professional Classicists. For what this book contributes to Classical scholarship I can best start by quoting M. L. West's summary of the *Works and Days*:

> To anyone who expects an orderly and systematic progression of ideas, [the *Works and Days*] is liable to appear a bewildering text. The same themes recur several times in different places, connections between neighbouring sections are often difficult to grasp, trains of thought are interrupted by seemingly irrelevant remarks, the didactic intention is here and there suspended in favour of pure description; and taken as a whole, the variety of contents is so great that it is hardly possible to describe the subject of the poem in a single phrase.[2]

The argument of this book is that West is, in this respect, wrong. The *Works and Days* is as unified a work of literature as the *Iliad* or the *Odyssey*. If it is harder for us to grasp its unity it is because we have been looking in the wrong direction.

The unity of the *Works and Days* cannot, I believe, be found where scholars have most recently been looking for it, through a search for a more subtle and intricate structure to the poem. The structure of the poem is just as it appears to be, as scholars have so often pointed out, episodic. What we have missed is the connection of the episodes. We have done so because when scholars ceased to view the *Works and Days* as simply an agricultural handbook, and began to recognize the subtlety of Hesiod's religious and ethical conceptions, they inadvertently threw out farming altogether. It is certainly true that the aim of the *Works and Days* is not to teach farming. It does not follow that the poem is not about farming at all. Not only is it about farming, it is precisely farming that serves as the keystone of the work, holding together all the rest and making of the various episodes a whole. But to see this we must see farming as Hesiod saw it, not as a business for profit, but as a way of life determined for man by Zeus, whose implications are as deeply ethical and religious as they are practical. It is only by adopting this stance towards farming that we can grasp the unity of the *Works and Days*.

The reason why scholars have missed the basic importance of farming to the *Works and Days* is indicated by scholarship's approach to the farming section of the poem, which is, largely, to ignore it.[3] Having accepted that the section contains practical advice on farming scholars have felt free to turn to the poem's more enticing sections on myth, on justice, or even on social advice. Scholars have managed to disregard almost half of Hesiod's poem because, I believe, they tend to share consciously or unconsciously the premise that underlies West's approach to the *Works and Days*, that Hesiod is not a completely competent poet. I hold, in contrast, that Hesiod is fully competent as a poet, and that the reason that his poem has been misunderstood is that work that has long been accepted on archaic Greek social and ethical attitudes, and, anthropologically, on peasant views of the world, has not been adequately applied to Hesiod.[4] The scholarly aim of this work, therefore, lies only partially in a new interpretation of the *Works and Days*. It is far more to bring together ideas not new in themselves, but new when consistently applied to Hesiod. In so doing the unity that Hesiod saw in his work, and that he assumed his contemporaries would see, becomes transparent.

Hesiod has been misread because he has been considered naive in his poetic techniques. No one has ever made this mistake about Vergil. But Hesiod's supposed naïveté, and Vergil's undoubted sophistication, have led, ironically, to much the same misreading. Vergil, unlike Hesiod, dedicates his entire poem to farming, explicitly noting the *Works and Days* as its model. Scholars have taken this to be merely Vergil's ostensible topic, and his ostensible model.[5] Having jettisoned the simplistic belief that the poem was commissioned by Augustus in order to call Romans back to their farms, scholars have come to ignore the importance of farming to the poem altogether.[6] Once more, the baby has most emphatically disappeared with the bath-water. My aim in reading the *Georgics* is thus not so much to engage in novel interpretations of particular passages, as to point out how the extensive work which has now been done on the *Georgics* deepens, rather than refutes, an understanding of the poem as genuinely a response to Hesiod, and genuinely a work on farming.

My focus leads to omissions that many scholars may find surprising. I do not attempt to examine the influence of the Near East, or of the oral tradition, on Hesiod, both of which have been and are being fully explored elsewhere. Nor am I particularly concerned with Vergil's use of allusion, even to the *Works and Days*. Although I have used particularly striking cases of allusion to illustrate main points, most of Vergil's allusions appear to be directed at authors other than Hesiod, as Farrell has quite conclusively demonstrated. Scholars interested in allusion should be able to find all that they need in his work.[7] Nor have I, in general, attempted to summarize the scholarly debates on either Hesiod or Vergil. For scholars who wish to recapitulate these debates I have included, in the notes, references to works that do this. For my own part I have used the notes to engage actively in debate only in those cases where my particular interpretation of the text appeared to require it. Otherwise footnotes are intended to substantiate my interpretations, to give credit to the original interpretations of other scholars, and to indicate possible alternate interpretations. My aim is not to define and classify the schools of Hesiodic or Vergilian scholarship. It is to respond to the texts with what I believe is a new vision, and with gratitude for the help of the generations of scholars that have gone before me.

My approach in this book is one I think of as modified reader-response or performance criticism. What I have tried to do, whenever possible, is to follow not only the text, but also the shifting moods of the text, treating the poem not as an argument or a logical presentation but as a work of art designed to call forth in us sometimes even contradictory emotions. As the poet modulates his voice it is, I believe, the modulations of tone, even more than the literal statement of fact, that the poet expects us to respond to. Within such a reading the context of any line, passage, or section of the poem is clearly critical. I have therefore attempted, overall, to follow the structure of the poems themselves. Where the structure of my own argument has made it necessary for me to deviate from this, I have tried at least to sketch in the context of the line or passage. Finally, I should warn the reader that this approach necessarily involves, to some extent, an unworthy version of the same modulation of tone used by the poet. When I make a point strongly only to modify it, with certainty only to end by undercutting it, or with doubt only to allow it finally to prevail, I hope the reader will understand that what I am trying to do is to reflect the strength, the certainty, and the doubt of the poets who originally experienced these poems.

I myself am more of a Classicist than a farmer. But twelve years on a small dairy farm in Ireland, half a year at a time, have made me look at farming with different eyes. Among other things that I have learned (the good and bad points of barbed wire, for example), I came to see how two great poems could locate their center of gravity in a topic as mundane as farming. The fact that the owner of the farm, David Grene, is as good a farmer as he is a Classical scholar, has given me much encouragement in this project. His is truly an understanding of farming in its deepest sense. That understanding has done much for this book. I hope that what it has helped bring to fruition is no more a book devoted only to academics than it is one devoted only to farmers. What we seek is an understanding, not only of Hesiod and Vergil, but through Hesiod and Vergil, of our own understanding of God and the land.

Chicago, Illinois   S.N.
September 1997

ACKNOWLEDGMENTS

I would like to thank first the members of my dissertation committee at the University of Chicago who helped enormously in my first preparation of this work: James Redfield, Ralph Johnson, Wendy Doniger, and, in particular, the late Arthur Adkins, whose care and concern at every stage of my work was outdone only by the example of his own enormous bravery and good humor. Despite his struggle with Parkinson's Disease, and the increasing difficulties that he faced in pursuing his own, seminal, work, Professor Adkins did as much or more for me, and for all of his students, than any other teacher that I have met. He is very deeply missed by all of us.

I would also like to thank the Triopian Foundation, the Bentley Fellowship, and, in particular, the Mary Isabel Sibley Fellowship of Phi Beta Kappa, for their help at a crucial time in my career. Without the aid of institutions such as these, the transition from graduate student to author would be nearly impossible. As my aim is to fulfill Chaucer's final description of his scholar, "And gladly wolde he lerne and gladly teche," I begin by imitating the earlier lines: "And bisily gan for the soules preye / Of hem that yaf him wherwith to scoleye." I am very grateful.

Finally, I would like to thank my family and friends, in particular David Tracy, Kathie Heed, Fred Coe, Mark Wielga, and my father, David Nelson, who have (sometimes intentionally and sometimes not) examined the manuscript from a non-professional perspective—the perspective that I believe, in the end, comes closest to the heart of the poems.

In the end, however, the man to whom this book is most indebted is David Grene. From David I have learned the most important things I know about farming, about Greek, and about literature. Whatever part of this book is not already his own is, with my whole heart, dedicated to him.

CONTENTS

Abbreviations   xvii

Geneaological Table   2

Translator's Note: Hesiod's Works and Days   5

HESIOD'S *WORKS AND DAYS*   9
    Translated by David Grene

INTRODUCTION: HESIOD, POET AND FARMER   31

    Hesiod's Time   33
    Hesiod's Town and Country   34
    Hesiod—Or Was He?   36

1. THE COMPOSITION OF HESIOD'S POEMS   41

    The Composition of the *Theogony*   44
    The Composition of the *Works and Days*   46
    The Farmer's Year   48

2. THE MYTHIC BACKGROUND   59

    Hesiod's Outlook   59
    Pandora and the Nature of Hardship   64
    The Five Ages: The History of Hardship   68
    Hesiod's Fable and the Justice of Zeus   77

3. THE COMPOSITION OF THE *GEORGICS*: VERGIL'S FARM   82

Roman Farming   88
Vergil's Works and Days   91
Vergil and the Animals   94

4. GOD   98

The Divine Order   98
Zeus and His Children   104
The Theology of Farming   107
The Gods of the *Georgics*   110
The Georgic of Force   113
The Georgic of Understanding   117

5. THE HUMAN CONTEXT   125

Justice, Perception, and Farming   125
The Balance of Justice   130
The Place of Justice   135
Force and Order: Vergil and Caesar   138
The Third Georgic: The Problem of the Individual   141
The Fourth Georgic: The Promise of the Whole   146

6. THE PLACE OF NATURE   152

The City, the Farm, and Nature   152
Orpheus and Aristaeus   155
Hesiod and the Balance of Nature   162

Notes   171
Bibliography   231
Index   247

ABBREVIATIONS

PB	Aeschylus, *Prometheus Bound*
Rust.	Varro, *De Re Rustica*
Th.	Hesiod, *Theogony*
WD	Hesiod, *Works and Days*
West	M. L. West, *Hesiod: "Works and Days."* Oxford: Clarendon Press, 1978
West, *Hesiod*	M. L. West, *Hesiod: "Theogony," "Works and Days."* Oxford: Oxford University Press, 1988.
West, *Th.*	M. L. West, *Hesiod: "Theogony."* Oxford: Clarendon Press, 1966

GOD AND THE LAND

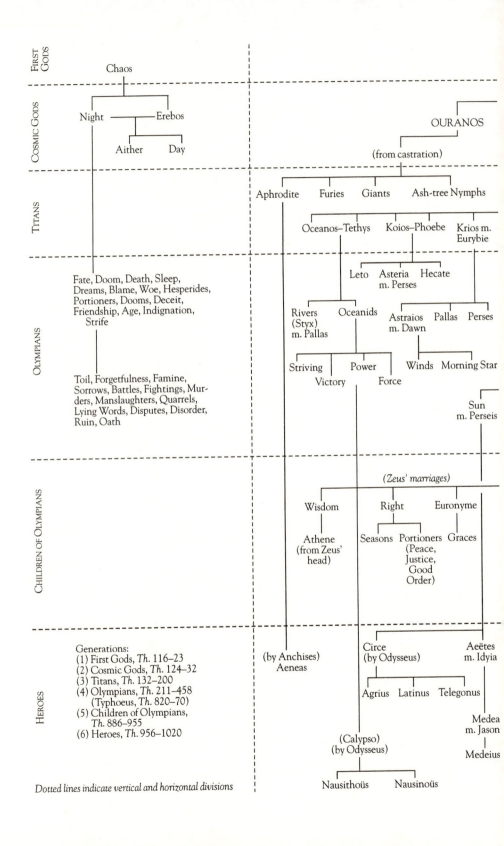

FIRST GODS

Chaos

COSMIC GODS

Night ——— Erebos

OURANOS

Aither   Day

(from castration)

TITANS

Aphrodite   Furies   Giants   Ash-tree Nymphs

Oceanos–Tethys   Koios–Phoebe   Krios m. Eurybie

OLYMPIANS

Fate, Doom, Death, Sleep, Dreams, Blame, Woe, Hesperides, Portioners, Dooms, Deceit, Friendship, Age, Indignation, Strife

Leto   Asteria   Hecate
        m. Perses

Rivers (Styx) m. Pallas   Oceanids   Astraios m. Dawn   Pallas   Perses

Toil, Forgetfulness, Famine, Sorrows, Battles, Fightings, Murders, Manslaughters, Quarrels, Lying Words, Disputes, Disorder, Ruin, Oath

Striving   Power   Winds   Morning Star
Victory   Force

Sun m. Perseis

CHILDREN OF OLYMPIANS

(Zeus' marriages)

Wisdom   Right   Euronyme

Athene (from Zeus' head)   Seasons   Portioners (Peace, Justice, Good Order)   Graces

HEROES

Generations:
(1) First Gods, *Th.* 116–23
(2) Cosmic Gods, *Th.* 124–32
(3) Titans, *Th.* 132–200
(4) Olympians, *Th.* 211–458
    (Typhoeus, *Th.* 820–70)
(5) Children of Olympians, *Th.* 886–955
(6) Heroes, *Th.* 956–1020

(by Anchises) Aeneas

Circe (by Odysseus)   Aeëtes m. Idyia

Agrius   Latinus   Telegonus

Medea m. Jason

Medeius

(Calypso) (by Odysseus)

Dotted lines indicate vertical and horizontal divisions

Nausithoüs   Nausinoüs

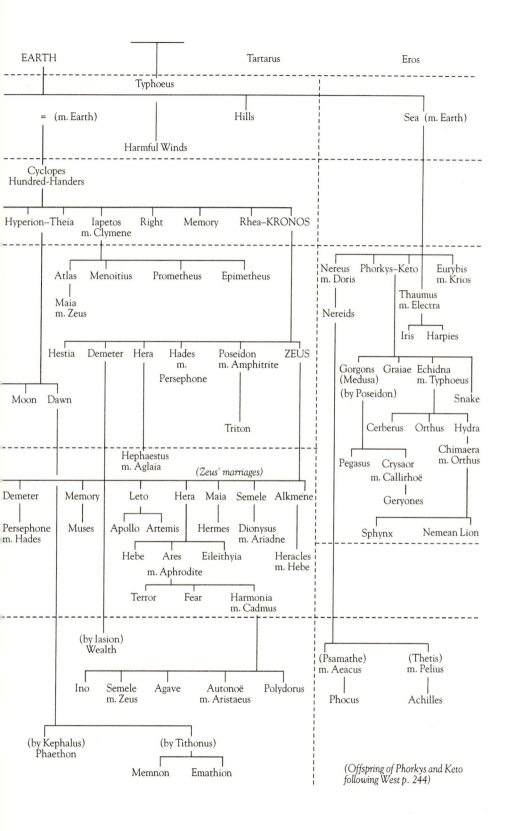

EARTH   Tartarus   Eros

Typhoeus

= (m. Earth)   Hills   Sea (m. Earth)

Harmful Winds

Cyclopes
Hundred-Handers

Hyperion–Theia   Iapetos   Right   Memory   Rhea–KRONOS
         m. Clymene

Nereus   Phorkys–Keto   Eurybis
m. Doris   m. Krios

Atlas   Menoitius   Prometheus   Epimetheus

Thaumus
m. Electra

Maia
m. Zeus

Nereids

Iris   Harpies

Hestia   Demeter   Hera   Hades   Poseidon   ZEUS
                 m.   m. Amphitrite
             Persephone

Gorgons   Graiae   Echidna
(Medusa)   m. Typhoeus

Moon   Dawn

(by Poseidon)   Snake

Triton

Cerberus   Orthus   Hydra

Hephaestus
m. Aglaia   *(Zeus' marriages)*

Chimaera
m. Orthus

Pegasus   Crysaor
         m. Callirhoë

Demeter   Memory   Leto   Hera   Maia   Semele   Alkmene

Geryones

Persephone   Muses   Apollo   Artemis   Hermes   Dionysus
m. Hades   m. Ariadne

Sphynx   Nemean Lion

Hebe   Ares   Eileithyia   Heracles
                             m. Hebe
     m. Aphrodite

Terror   Fear   Harmonia
                m. Cadmus

(by Iasion)
Wealth

Ino   Semele   Agave   Autonoë   Polydorus
     m. Zeus   m. Aristaeus

(Psamathe)   (Thetis)
m. Aeacus   m. Pelius

Phocus   Achilles

(by Kephalus)   (by Tithonus)
Phaethon

Memnon   Emathion

(Offspring of Phorkys and Keto
following West p. 244)

TRANSLATOR'S NOTE: HESIOD'S
WORKS AND DAYS

I had wanted for a long time to do a translation of the *Works and Days* but had been deterred by some of the special features of the poem that make for difficulties in translating it. When Stephanie Nelson asked me to do a poetic version, so that, at least on the Greek side of her book on the *Works and Days* and Vergil's *Georgics*, the reader might have between the covers an English translation to refer to, the temptation proved too much for my misgivings. This was especially true because the manuscript of the book, which I knew well, seemed to present the Hesiodic poem in much the same fashion as I saw it. I thought that the translation might give some further illumination to the argument of the book and the book to the translation.

All the same, let me lay before the reader, especially the Greekless reader, some of the difficulties, as I see them, of making an English translation of Hesiod's *Works and Days*. Some of the trouble comes from the likeness to Homer and the remarkable difference. Both Homer and Hesiod wrote highly stylized poems, in a literary language—a version of Ionic—which was almost certainly never spoken. It is designed for literature, and especially for the hexameter line. After Homer and Hesiod it was used by the pre-Socratic philosophers and by Herodotus—in prose. The translation must take account of this formalized style. Again, the later Greeks, from the fifth century on, put Hesiod and Homer together as the beginners of their Greek culture, jointly, and they comment much less on the differences between the two. Aristophanes in the *Frogs* declares that both of them gave the Greeks much of their technical knowledge—Homer of how to train men of war, Hesiod of how to farm (1130 ff.). This certainly looks rather like some sort of comic absurdity. Perhaps both authors do contribute "useful" technical information, but it is very far-fetched to claim that drill and formations in war are really even much a byproduct of Homer as seen in the fifth century. I believe also that the ostensible didacticism of Hesiod in teaching his brother

5

Perses how to farm is not seriously didactic. This is one of the points on which I agree with Stephanie Nelson.

Another very significant statement about the *two* poets comes from Herodotus when he says that it is pointless to ask whether the Greek gods were eternal or where they came from, because everything the Greeks know about the gods has been given them by Homer and Hesiod (2.53), again as the two originators without distinction between them. Certainly both Homer and Hesiod are writers with the deepest commitment to religion. The *Iliad* and the *Odyssey* both live altogether in the context of man and God and their interaction. But what we learn from Homer—in the sense in which Herodotus speaks of what we *know* about the Greek gods—is not from the dubious quotation of the worship of Athene at Troy but from such passages as the encounter of Achilles and Priam at the end of the *Iliad*, which is quite certainly fictionalized. As, it seems to me, most of the accounts of conversations between the gods are fictionalized. What we get from Homer, from a religious perspective, is something uncommonly like a tragic sense of man in his world of gods, fate, and himself.

It may be that when Herodotus mentions both Homer and Hesiod as the source of our information about the Greek gods he is thinking, in Hesiod's case, mostly of the *Theogony*, the "birth of the gods." But he was certainly also thinking of the *Works and Days*, with its competing myths of the origin of men and gods, and Hesiod's description of contemporary farming as the creation of Zeus, with farming as the natural field for Zeus' judgment of men's success or failure. Again, Nelson's emphasis on the religious and moral side of the *Works and Days* seems to me especially valuable.

In these various ways it is the similarity of Homer and Hesiod that stands out. But when one comes to try to render Hesiod into English for English readers, it is the amazing difference that strikes one. I do not believe that Hesiod in the *Works and Days* is truly didactic, any more than Homer is directly didactic as historian or as theologian. There is in Hesiod's poem a loving intensity of detail—true enough. But there are such gaps of more or less importance in the general instruction as makes it overwhelmingly unlikely that the whole represents a serious effort at instruction on "how to do it." When he does get to the account of the farmer's year one can see that the description of farming practice is the occasion of the poetry and the heart of it. It is not there as part of a lesson. For whatever reason, Hesiod has decided that his approach to farming will be in the form of a personal story of himself and his brother Perses who had cheated him in a lawsuit arising from his father's will. The farming descriptions are ostensibly to teach Perses how to do the job right—on the assumption that Perses never really knew how to farm properly. It is a flimsy enough pretext, but the pretext does not matter much. (There are recent theories that this *sort* of poem is based on Wisdom literature and the precedents in Mesopotamia.) At any rate, Hesiod's feeling about farming, with all its elaborate intensity, had to be conveyed by him in this personal setting. Homer worked on stories arising from the Trojan War. Often later Greeks see him as a poetic historian. It is now rightly stressed that the evidence of the details indicates that Homer did not in fact know much about how that war was fought. He certainly inherited characters and scenes involving these characters that had been the subject of many other minstrels before his time. But at a certain moment he wrote a big, overarching story that combined much of the current stories and created characters that are fictionalized versions of what his tradition had given him. I would suggest that Hesiod, from whatever source, came to feel that *his* sort of epic poem would concern farming. Under his hand it acquired its special personality from a story that was either his own or something specially close to his understanding. It may very well be, also, that his generalizations came to him through peasant proverbial sayings which he now turned into hexameters. In Homer the original material, with whatever formal ground for its exposure—that of the revelation of history or homecoming—is surely infused by special personal elements, but they are untraceable by us. What is remarkable about the Hesiodic *Works and Days* is that the personal *voice* is there all the time. And the difficulty of rendering this in English, as far as the poem as a whole goes, is to keep the sense of formality; which demands a certain dignified directness and simplicity with the complexity, and indeed turbulence, of the personal insight and inspiration. Hesiod seems relatively easy to render until one tries it. The inner language, not just the Ionic form of it, is extremely difficult and rich in ambiguity. That's where the hardest task lies for the translator of this poem.

Also, the rhythm and musicality of Hesiod is very personal to him. I do not think he can be rendered adequately in prose because of that. And blank verse always carries any English reader back to drama, in fact to Shakespeare. So willy-nilly I believe one has to try Hesiod's own meter, the hexameter. It is a somewhat different meter in English from what it is in Greek, but all the same the verse with its break in the middle had much in common in both languages. I have been enough haunted by the individual Hesiodic verses to try it.

Line numbers in the translation refer to the Greek text of M. L. West, rather than to the translated lines. Any differences have been noted in the footnotes.

D. G.

HESIOD'S *WORKS AND DAYS*

Translated by David Grene

Muses from Pieria, celebrators in song, 1
come hither to me, and tell of Zeus,
sing of him, your own father.

It is through Zeus that mortal men
become famous or fail of fame.
It is through mighty Zeus
they are spoken of or left in silence.

Lightly he makes a man strong and lightly maims one who *is* strong.
Lightly he lessens the famous and will exalt the obscure.
Lightly he straightens the crooked and lightly withers the proud.
He is Zeus, the high lord of thunder, whose home is the highest.
Hear, see, give ear; straighten court judgments with justice.
This is your part. I would wish to speak very truth to Perses. 10

There is no single breed of Strife, but on earth there are two of her.
One of the two you have but to see and you will praise her at once,
the other draws only blame; the hearts of the two are different.
The one increases vile war and enmity; she is cruel.
No mortal loves her! Only under Necessity
through designs of the Immortals do they honor her, this harsh Strife.

The other is the elder—black night was her mother;
and the Son of Cronos whose throne is on high, who lives in heaven,

set her in earth in its roots; and for men she is far better.
This is the one that rouses even the shiftless to work;   20
for a man may look at another, a rich man, in haste to plow,
and to plant, set his house in good order;
and the shiftless, looking, longs for work.
So neighbor is jealous of neighbor hastening towards wealth.
This strife is good for men.
And potter has a grudge against potter, joiner against joiner,
and beggar envies beggar, and singer, singer.

    Perses, put all these things away in your heart;
do not let the evil-delighted strife keep your mind from work—
as you watchfully eye for quarrels, listening in the marketplace.
Scant is the seasonableness of quarrels and marketplaces   30
for the man without a year's sustenance, reaped in due season, lying
safe in his house, a harvest, born of earth, the grain of Demeter.
When you have a sufficiency of this, promote quarrels
and squabbling over other men's goods.
But in your case there will be no second
doing of this; let us settle the quarrel once, now, and forever,
with straightness of judgments, those best judgments
that come from Zeus.

Already we divided the estate, but you plundered and bore off much else
gratifying mightily the kings,
gift-gobblers, very willing, to render this kind of justice—
Fools they are—not to know how much better the half than the whole is   40
and what great blessing there is in mallow and asphodel.

    For the gods have steadfastly hidden his livelihood from mankind.
You could easily work a day's space and so for a year have a living
with never a hand's turn of work.
At once you could hang up your steering oar over the smoking hearth,
and the work of oxen and drudging mules would be ended.
But Zeus in the wrath of his heart hid our living from us
because Prometheus of crooked counsels cheated him.
So Zeus contrived against men destructive sorrows.
He hid fire; but in turn the crafty son of Iapetus   50
stole it from cunning Zeus for men, hiding fire in the narthex stem,
unknown to Zeus, whose joy is in the thunderbolt.

Now, in his anger, cloud-gathering Zeus spoke to Prometheus:
"Son of Iapetus, whose cunning excels all others',
you are glad now you have stolen fire and have cheated
my mind; but it shall be to yourself
great mischief and also to men of the days that are still to be.

To them to match their gaining of fire I shall give
an evil in which they will all joy,
welcoming each in his heart his own ill.

So he spoke and laughed outright, the Father of gods and men,
and he bade the famous Hephaestus with all speed make a fusion   60
of earth with water and therein set a human voice
and a human strength, but in countenance making
her like the immortal goddesses, a fair desirable maid.
He bade Athene teach her work weaving the embroidered web,
and golden Aphrodite to pour on her head
grace and painful lust and anxious desires
that wear out the limbs; he bade Hermes, the Killer of Argos, instill in her
the cunning mind of a bitch and a knavish disposition.

So he commanded and they obeyed, Zeus son of Cronos, the King.
And thus from the earth the strong Smith shaped   70
the likeness of a modest maiden
according to Zeus' designs.

And the goddess, golden-eyed Athene, girdled her, adorned her
and those Graces, the goddesses, and Queen Persuasion
put on her body golden necklaces and about her
the fair tressed Seasons wove a mantle of spring-time flowers.
All of these things, a glory of the body, Pallas Athene
fitted to her. But in her breast the Conductor, the Killer of Argos
set lies and dissimulation in words and knavish spirit;
he worked by design of Zeus, the deep thunderer; and a voice
the herald of the gods put into her and the name that he gave this woman   80
was Pandora, All-gift, for all that live
in Olympus had given her as a gift, as a bane
to men that live by bread.
Now when he had completed this mischief, sheer and bewildering,
the Father sent the distinguished killer of Argos, the quick
messenger of the gods, to Afterthought bearing a gift for him;
and Afterthought never bethought him how Prometheus-Forethought had said:
"Never accept a gift, that comes from Olympian Zeus;
send it back lest in some way some ill come about
to mortal men." But Afterthought took it
and—only when he had taken the evil thing—understood.

For at first the tribes of men lived   90
free of troubles, free of difficult labors, free
from painful diseases that give men their deaths.
But the Woman with her own hands took away
the great lid from the jar and scattered. And for mankind she devised

bitter sufferings. All that remained in the unbreakable walls
of the jar was Hope—she remained beneath the lips of the jar;
she did not fly out for, before that, the Woman
clapped to the lid of the jar,
by design of aegis-bearing Zeus, who gathers the clouds.
But other ten thousand evils have gone wandering among men;   100
the earth is full of these ills, and the sea is full,
And diseases by day and every night, too,
come of themselves, and bring
to mortal men trouble—in silence, for Zeus has stolen their voice.
So true it is there is no way
to escape from the purpose of Zeus.

There is another story—if you like I will tell you its substance,
well, and skillfully; and you lay it up in your heart.
It tells how the gods and mortal men spring from the same beginnings.

It was of gold at the very first that the breed of men who use speech
were made by the Immortals who live in Olympus.   110
They were in the time of Cronos, when he was king in Heaven.
They lived like gods, their hearts undisturbed by cares,
without labour, without misery. Upon them
there came no wretched old age, their hands and their feet were the same
always. They found their joy in feasts,
free of every trouble; and died like those conquered by sleep.
All good things were theirs.
The grain-growing earth bore them crops, full, ungrudgingly
of its own accord. At their will
they leisurely did their work in the midst of their many blessings   120
And when the earth hid this breed in its depths,
they are Spirits, by the plans of great Zeus;
good, they are still on earth's face and are guardians of mortal men.   123
They are givers of wealth; this too they obtained as their kingly function.[1] 126

Then those who hold their home in Olympus made another breed to
    follow.
It was of silver and far worse than the other.
Neither in form nor in mind were they like the golden
but a child among them, for a hundred years by the side of his good
    mother   130
was raised, playing, great fool, in his home.
And when he grew up and came to his young man's measure,
they lived but a little while, and through their folly had pains as well,
for they could not hold off from each other
their reckless violence, nor were they willing to serve the Immortals
nor on the holy altars of the Blessed to offer sacrifice,

as is right for men according
to their several customs. But these, again,
Zeus, son of Cronos laid in earth, angry because they did not give
honors to the blessed gods who hold Olympus.
And when this breed, too, the earth concealed,   140
they are called by mortal men Blessed-Ones-Under-the-Earth;[2]
they are the second, truly; but honor attends them, also.

   Then Zeus the Father made yet another breed among mortal men;
it was of bronze, and it equaled the silver in nothing.
He made them of ash-trees, a breed terrible and monstrous;
what they thought of were groaning deeds of the War-God and acts
          of outrage.
They ate no bread, their spirits, harsh-thinking, adamantine;
there was no yielding to pressure in them. Their power was huge
and from their shoulders grew their hands, defying
any grapple, over their thick limbs.
Bronze was their armour and bronze were their homes,   150
and with bronze, too, they worked; there was no black iron.
By their own hands were they conquered, and went to the moldering
home of chilly Death. They had no names;
but for all their terribleness black Death laid hold of them,
and they left the bright light of the sun.

   And when this breed, too, the earth concealed,
yet another, the fourth, on the earth that feeds many,
Zeus son of Cronos created, and it was far juster and better.
It was the breed divine, of the men who were heroes;
they are called demi-gods and were the race before us   160
over the boundless earth.
Some of them evil War and the dreadful battle cry
killed at Thebes of the Seven Gates, in the country of Cadmus,
fighting for the flocks of the sons of Oedipus.
And others, too, in their ships, over the sea's great gulf
the war, having brought to Troy, for the sake of fair-tressed Helen—
some of them there the fated end of Death enfolded,
But to others Zeus son of Cronos gave a livelihood and a homeland;
far from men he settled them in the distant limits of earth,
and there they live, their hearts untroubled by care   170
in the Islands of the Blessed, by the deep eddying Ocean,
fortunate heroes, for whom thrice yearly the honey-sweet harvest
blooms, borne by the earth, the giver of corn.

   But, thereafter—I would I were not among the fifth men
but rather had died before or been born at a later time.
For now indeed is the race of iron, and never a day's space

shall they cease from toiling and wretchedness, nor have a night without
continuity of destruction; the gods will give them
gnawing anxious cares.
Yet even in their evils there shall be a mixture of good.
Zeus will destroy these also, this race of mortal men,   180
when even at their birth they shall be grey at the temples;
when father shall not be at one with his children nor they with him,
nor guest with host nor friend with friend nor brother
shall be friendly as before. These people shall dishonor
their parents, even at the moment of aging; they will fault them
with words of abuse. Cruel, they will know nothing of the gods' vengeance;
nor will they give to their parents in age a return for the cost of their
    rearing,[3]   188
nor shall oath-keeping have any grace among them, nor yet justice nor
    good.   190
Rather shall they honor the wreaker of evil, the man
who is Insolence; justice shall be in their hands only,
and shame shall be no more. The evil man
shall injure the better, speaking
with crooked lies and swear with an oath to top them.
Envy shall attend all wretched mankind, envy
malicious in voice, delighting in ill, with a face of hatred.
And on that day to Olympus, away from the broad wayed earth,
to join the tribe of Immortals, and to leave men behind,
Shame and Retribution go. But misery and pain   200
are left for mortal men; there shall be no cure for ill.

    Here is a fable for the kings, although they are knowing themselves.
This is what the hawk said when he spoke to the dapplenecked songbird:
high up in the clouds the hawk gripped her with talons and took her;
pitifully she screamed, pierced by the nails cramped in her.
But the hawk overmastering spoke to her and this was his word:
"You fool, why have you screamed so? He that has you is far stronger
and you go where I shall bring you, even if you are a songster;
if I will, I will make a meal of you, or I will let you go.
He is witless who seeks to contend with rivals stronger than he is;   210
he loses the fight and besides suffers pain and shame together."
So said the hawk, swift-flying, bird with long outstretched wings.

    Perses, you listen to Justice; do not magnify your Insolence.
For Insolence is bad in a man of insignificance;
not even a great man can carry her, but she is a heavy burden
to him when he has met his disasters. The other road that leads
to Justice is better to travel by, for Justice in the end
comes out over Insolence. He is a fool who only
understands when he suffers.

Oath runs quickly alongside judgments that are crooked.
There is a clamor, as Justice is dragged away where men lead her,   220
men who gobble up gifts, giving judgments with crooked Justice.
But Justice follows weeping to the city and haunts of the people,
wearing a mantle of mist, bringing evil to those of mankind
who shall drive her out, and have not rendered her straightly.
But those who give straight decisions to strangers and citizens
and in no way transgress the limits of Justice—
their city blooms and the folk blossom in it.
Peace, that rears the young men, is in their land, nor against them
does loud-voiced Zeus set savage war as witness of his judgment,
nor ever does famine attend them, those men that deal in straight justice,
nor yet infatuate blindness; at their feasts   230
they eat their land's crops, on which they spent their care.
For them the land gives a generous crop; in the mountains the top
        of the oak tree
bears acorns, and its middle, the honey bees.
Their woolly sheep are weighted down with heavy fleeces.
Their women give birth to children like their parents.
With all good things, utterly, they prosper, nor do they voyage on ships
but the grain-giving earth yields them its fruits.

But those given over to wicked outrage and cruel deeds,
against them the son of Cronos, loud-voiced Zeus
set as witness of his judgment, retribution.
Often, too, the whole city shares in what befalls a bad man—   240
a sinner, a contriver of reckless mischief.
Upon such men the son of Cronos sends from heaven a great disaster,
a famine and with it a plague; the people die.
The women bear no children, the homes dwindle,
through the plans of Zeus of Olympus. In other places, again,
the son of Cronos destroyed a great army of theirs,
or their forts; or their ships on the sea he took from them.

You kings take heed yourselves, too, of this your giving of justice;
for near at hand among men are the Immortals that take heed   250
of those who with crooked judgments grind one another down,
and do not think of the anger of God.
Thirty thousand there are on the earth that feeds many,
Immortals, guardians for Zeus of mortal men,
to watch over the judges' decisions, and their deeds of cruelty;
these put on a mantle of mist and travel
everywhere over the land.
There is also the Maiden Justice, daughter of Zeus;
revered and valued she is in the sight of the Olympian gods,
and whenever someone injures her by crookedly scorning her,

immediately she takes her place beside Zeus her father, the son
    of Cronos,
and complains, bemoaning the mind of the men of injustice, so that   260
the people may pay for the reckless sins of the kings,
in perverting the course of justice in suits, by crooked speeches,
thinking thoughts that are ruin.
Watch these things, you kings, and straighten your speeches,
you gobblers of gifts, and forget utterly your crooked decisions.
A man working ill to another works ill to himself,
and wicked counsel is wickedest to the wicked giver.

The eye of Zeus sees all, takes note of all,
and, if he please, he watches this too unerringly—
what kind of justice this is which the city contains in itself.

Were that not so, I would not be just myself   270
nor would I have my son so—for it is a bad thing
to be just if the unjust should get more justice than the just man;
but I do not believe that yet Zeus of Counsel will make such an ending.

Perses, do you lay up these things in your mind;
and listen to Justice, forgetting entirely violence.
For this is the Rule for men that the son of Cronos has given—
for the fish and the beasts and the winged birds,
that they should devour one another, for they have no Justice among
    them—
but to man he has given Justice and she proves to be far the best;
for if a man, of his knowledge, wills to speak justly, to *him*   280
Loud-Voiced Zeus grants prosperity;
but to him who will lie by witnesses, swearing falsely,
consciously, and injuring Justice shall fall to sin past cure,
his generation after him is left weaker;
but the generation of the just-swearing man remains better than before.

    What I say to you, great fool Perses, is said from good will.
Badness is there and, easily, for crowds to choose it;
but for Goodness the gods immortal have placed sweat in its way.
The road is long and sheer that leads to it, and rough   290
at the first; but when you are come to the high point, then thereafter
it is easy—but still it is hard enough.

That man is best who knows of himself all matters,
when he has taken notice which is better in past and future;
but good also is he who obeys the man who speaks wisely;
but he who is neither wise himself nor will hear another
and lay it up in his mind—that man is surely useless.

But, Perses, do you remember all that I urge—and work,
work Perses, stock of Zeus, that hunger may hate you,
and Demeter love you, fair-garlanded, revered,   300
and fill your granary with grain for livelihood.
For the man who won't work, you notice, has hunger as constant
    companion.
The gods are angry with such a man, and men too, when he lives
    without working,
in temper like stingless drones
who eat, but won't work, wearing out the fruit of the bees' labor;
let it be dear to you to arrange your work in due measure,
that your granaries may be filled with seasonable grain.
It is from the work they do that men become flockmasters
and rich, and, as they work, they are much dearer to the Immortals;   310
so shall you be to mortals, too, for surely they hate the unworking.
There is no shame in working, but the shame is in not working;
if you work, your workless fellow will very soon envy you
as you grow rich, for virtue and esteem both attend on riches.
Whatever your fortune in life, it is better to work, if only
you can turn your sinful thoughts away from another's possessions,
and to your own work; take heed of your livelihood, as I advise.
There is an evil shame that attends on the needy man;
for shame greatly injures men, and benefits them also greatly;
shame goes with the want of prosperity, but confidence with prosperity.

Riches are not for grabbing; when God gives them they are far better;   320
for even if, with violent hand, you win a great fortune,
or take it as booty with your tongue, as happens so often,
when profit deceives men's minds and shamelessness drives out shame,
such a man the gods easily maim, and make meager his household,
and only for a moment in time does prosperity attend him.

Such, too, is the lot of one who wrongs suppliant or stranger
or, again, whoso goes to the bed of his brother's wife,
in secret lust committing acts that contrary right;
or the one who in thoughtlessness wrongs someone's orphan children   330
or taunts an old father, standing on old age's cruel threshold,
with him Zeus himself is angry and in the end for his deeds of injustice
imposes a bitter requital.

No—from such acts keep your sinful mind at a distance,
and to the best of your power make sacrifice to the Immortals,
purely and cleanly and burn the glorious thighbones after.

And at other times with libations and sacrifice propitiate
the gods, when you go to your rest, and when the sacred light comes,

that they may have toward you a heart and a mind that is gracious,   340
that you may buy another's farm, rather than he buy yours.

Invite your friend to supper, but let your enemy be;
most of all invite him who is your nearest neighbor.
For if anything untoward happen on your estate,
your neighbor comes ungirdled, but your kin only after they are girdled.
A bad neighbor is a calamity as great as a good one is a blessing.
A man who has won a good neighbor has surely won good value.
An ox would never be lost if your neighbor had not been a bad one.
Take good measure from your neighbor, and give him again good
      measure
with just the same measure—or better, if you can do so;   350
that when you need him again you can rely on finding him.
Make no ill profits, ill profits are just so much loss.

Love one that loves you, meet him that is ready to meet you.
Give to the one who gives; do not give to the ungiver.
One gives to the giver of gifts, but he that gives no gifts gets none.
Give is good, Grab is bad; the gift that Grab gives is death.

The man who, of sheer good will, gives, although the gift be a great one,
rejoices in his gift, and delights in the depth of his spirit;
but the one who takes from another, because shamelessness is his master,
though the thing itself be small, the frost seizes his very heart.   360
For if you place a small thing on the top of something small,
and do so often enough, there will soon be a big thing in being.
He who carries to add to what is there shall keep fiery hunger away;
and no one is ever vexed by what is stored in his house.
(It is best that it should be at home; what is abroad is endangered.)
It is good to have store to choose from, but a pain to the spirit to lack
what you have not; that is something I bid you take heed of.

When the barrel is at its beginning, and at its end, too, drink your fill;
spare when you are in the middle; sparing is base in the dregs.

Let the wages you promised a friend be secure for him; but for a brother   370
get a witness as well, though you do it with a laugh.
Trust and distrust alike, you will find, have been men's destruction.
Let not a big-arsed woman cheat your mind with wheedling chatter,
while she is poking about your barn.
One who has trusted a woman has trusted a highway robber.

May you have an only son to support his father's house,
for that is how wealth will grow in your halls;
and pray that he die old having left behind another son.

Yet easily Zeus will grant large wealth for more than one;
when more men are at work, there is more work done and the increase   380
is greater. So if the spirit within you yearns for wealth, do thus,
and work, piling work on work.

   At the rising of the Pleiades, daughters of Atlas, begin
your harvest, and your plowing at their setting.
For forty days and forty nights they are hidden,
and again as the year comes round they appear at the very first
when the iron is being sharpened.
This is the rule of the land, both for those who live near the sea,
and those that live in the rich land, far from the foamy sea,
in the wooded glens.   390

Naked, sow the seed, plow with your oxen, naked,
and, naked, harvest the crop if you wish to do all of the tasks
of Demeter at proper season—and so in *their* proper season,
shall your crops increase, that not in want
in the days to come you may crouch
a beggar at another's homestead, and still get nothing;
just as you came to me; but I shall give you no more,
nor measure out more to you; work, you stupid Perses,
work at the tasks that the gods have set for men to do,
that you and your wife and your children in the sorrow of your heart
do not go begging a livelihood, from your neighbors—who will not care.   400

For twice or even thrice you may readily gain your wish,
but if you harrass them further you will have no success,
and you will talk at length, altogether vainly;
the range of your words will be useless. What I bid you is, consider
the settlement of your debts and how to stave off hunger.

First of all get you a woman and an ox for the plow; the woman
not wedded but bought, one that can follow the cattle.
And in your house make all your gear ready
that you not ask another, to be denied and left without,
and the season goes by and so much the less work done.
Do not postpone till tomorrow nor till the next day;   410
for there is no filling a barn if a man scamps his work,
or keeps postponing; it is effort that makes the work grow,
and the postponing man wrestles with disaster.

   When the heat of the sharp sunbeams ceases its sweaty warmth,
and the autumn rain has fallen from mighty Zeus
and men's skins are turned lighter—for this is when the Dog Star
hangs only briefly in daytime on the heads of men reared for doom,

but shares most of its time with night—
then is the timber you cut with the ax freest from the worm;   420
it has dropped its leaves on the ground, and its branching has ceased;
cut your wood then and remember the timeliness of your work.

Cut three foot for a mortar, and three cubits for a pestle,
and seven for an axle—that would suit very well.
If you cut eight foot of wood, cut off some of that for a mallet,
and for a ten palm wagon cut three span for a wheel.
There are many bent timbers; take home, when you find it, a plowtree—
of holm oak, after a search of hill and field both.
This is the strongest of any for plowing with oxen,
once Athene's servant has fitted it to the plowstock   430
and also, with wooden pegs, secured it to the pole.

See that you have two plows, having worked them up at home,
one of a single block of wood and the other jointed;
far better to have two of them, for, if you break one,
put the other on your oxen.
Ox poles of bay or elm are freest from the woodworm.
Your plowstock should be of oak and of holm oak your plowtree.

Get you two nine-year oxen, males; with this measure of youth
the strength they possess is greatest, and such a pair best for the work.

Such a pair is not apt to fight in the furrow and break your plow,
and so leave the work, there and then, undone;   440
and let a man of forty follow that team of plow oxen,
when he has eaten his loaf of four pieces or eight half pieces;
such a one will heed his work and drive his furrow straight,
not looking around for his fellows but keeping his mind on his work;
there should also be another, not a whit younger,
he will be the better as such to sow seed and avoid oversowing;
for a younger man is excited to look round at the other young men.

Take heed when you hear the voice of the crane, as she cries her yearly cry,
from high up in the clouds;
she gives you the signal for plowing, and shows the season in winter   450
when the rain comes; and she bites the heart of the oxless man;
then is the time, with your oxen indoors, to fodder them fat and sleek;
it is so easy to say, "Lend me a team and a wagon,"
but the answer is easy, too, "The oxen have work to do."
The man whose riches are all in his head may say he has built him a
        wagon—
the fool, he doesn't know this: a wagon needs a hundred timbers;
you had better take care, beforehand, to have those timbers at home.

But when, at the very first, plowing shows itself to mortals
then drive on your servants and yourself, all of you,
and plow, wet and dry, in accord with the plowing season;   460
you must hurry, to be very early, that your fields may be full of seed.
The plowland you must work first in spring; if you plow it again in the summer
the land will not play you false.
Fallow land that is plowed should be sown when it is still light;
fallow will save your children from ruin, fallow delightful.

Pray to Zeus-Under-Earth and to Demeter the Holy
that the sacred corn of Demeter be heavy when ready for harvest;
pray as you first begin plowing, a hand on top of the top of the plowstilt
and with your goad come down on the backs of the oxen straining
at the peg at the plowpole's middle; and let a small boy behind you   470
make work for the birds with his mattock, covering up the seeds.
For men, thrift is as much the best as unthrift is the worst.
That is the way your ears, in their ripeness, will droop to earth,
if the Olympian himself shall later give a good end to the harvest;
you may then brush the spiders from your buckets, and I am sure
that you will be glad to have your choice from a livelihood stored within;
and you will come in good trim to a white spring, and you will not
fix your eyes in entreaty on others, but another will need your help.

But if you plow the good earth at the turning of the solstice,
you will harvest your crop sitting down, your hand holding but a little   480
when you tie the stalks, with ears at both ends, yourself all coated in dust
with little occasion for gladness; a basket will suffice you
to carry your corn home; few will look your way with wonder.
But sometimes the mind of Zeus, aegis-bearing, is one way
and sometimes another; for mortal men it is hard to fathom.
For, even if you plow late, there might be a cure for your lateness;
when the cuckoo cries his first "cuckoo" in the leaves of the oak-tree,
and it makes mortal men glad over the boundless earth,
at that time Zeus may rain for two days' length, unceasingly,
to the depth of your ox's foot neither more nor falling short of it;
when this happens the man who plowed late may rival him that plowed
    early.   490

Keep all this well in your mind—let the grayness of spring when it comes
not go unheeded by you, nor unheeded the rain in due season.

In wintertime pass by the seats at the forge where men chatter in warmth,
when the cold keeps a man from his work.
Then may one who shuns rest increase greatly the good of his household,
lest the helplessness of a bad winter grasp you, together with poverty,
and you pinch, with a hand grown thin, a big leg swollen with hunger.

A man who does no work, waiting on hope that is empty,
short of livelihood, has a power of bad things to say to his spirit.
Hope is no good companion for a needy man sitting inside   500
and no secure means to live.

While it is still midsummer, tell your servants, "It will not be so
always—make huts for yourselves."

  The month Lenaion, dreadful days all, that would skin the hide from
      an ox—
beware that month, and its frosts that rage terribly
under the breath of the North Wind, that comes from horse-rearing Thrace,
and blowing on the wide sea churns it up.
The land and the forest groan, and many a towering oak
and many a stout ash tree in the mountain glens
come crashing down to the earth, that feeds many,   510
under attack of the North Wind,
and the whole immense forest roars.
The wild creatures shiver and put their tails under their bellies.
Even through those with fur-coverèd skin, yes, even through these,
through all their shaggy breasts the North Wind blasts its way;
through the hide of the ox it goes and the hide cannot stop it;
and it blows through the goat's long hair, but not through sheep's fleeces
for the layers of the wool are too many.

It makes the old man run like a hoop,
but it does not go through the soft skin of the girl
who stays with her loving mother inside of the house, not knowing   520
yet the works of Aphrodite, the Golden;
well she has bathed her tender skin, and anointed it with smooth oil,
and shall lay herself down to sleep in her house, in an innermost corner,
on a winter's day, when No-Bone the octopus gnaws
his own foot in his fireless home, and his miserable haunts.
The sun shows him no place to hasten to for his food,
for the sun roams his way to the folk and state of the black men
and shines tardily on the Pan-Greeks.
The horned and unhorned wild creatures that make their beds in the forest
painfully grinding their teeth flee through the wooded thicket.   530
This was the thought in the mind of them all, as they seek for shelter,
to gain the depths of their caves and the hollow of the rock.
Then are all men like Three Foot
whose back is broken forward and his head gazes towards the ground;
like him they travel along dodging the white flakes of snow.

Then, for your skin make a covering, as I will tell you how—
a soft cloak and a tunic that reaches right down to your feet,

and have full plenty of wool woven on a small warp.
Put this on yourself, that your hairs may not be in movement,   540
nor stand upright and shiver, rising all over your body;
and, on your feet, tie fitted shoes from the skin of a slaughtered ox,
and cover them on the inside with flocks of felting.

When the cold comes in due season stitch together the skins of kids,
first-born kids, with a cowhide strap, to give shelter against the rain
for your back; and on your head above put a cap made of felting
to avoid your ears getting wet.
For the dawn comes very cold when the North Wind has fallen on it,
and at dawn on the earth, from the starry heaven, a mist,
fertile for grain, is stretched over the fields of the wealthy,
drawing its water up from the ever-flowing rivers,   550
lifted high over the earth by the blast of the wind, bringing sometimes
rain, towards evening time, and sometimes a windstorm
when the North Wind from Thrace drives many clouds in rout.
Before this, get you home as soon as your work is finished
that the black cloud in the sky may not envelop you,
and soak you to the skin and drench your clothes as well;
no, avoid this; for this month is hardest of all to deal with,
this winter month—it is hard on cattle and hard on men.
Give half rations to your oxen, to your men rather more than half,
for the nights then are long and that can be a help.   560
Watching all this, till finally the year comes to its end,
balance equally night and day, until again the land,
mother of all, bring forth all the mingled fruits of her bearing.

But when Zeus has brought to pass the sixty days of winter
after the turn of the sun, when the dog star, Arcturus,
leaving the sacred stream of the Ocean, first shows his rising
at the edge between light and darkness
and after him the swallow, Pandion's daughter, shrillvoiced,
comes to call men to the dawn, as the new spring comes into being—
before this, prune your vines, for in this way it is better.   570

But when the House-Carrier climbs from the ground to the plant,
                                                             avoiding
the Pleiades, then is no longer the season for digging round vines—
no, but for sharpening blades, wakening your work-people;
no more sitting in shade, and no more sleeping till daybreak,
for this is the season of harvest, when the sun parches your skin;
this is the hour of hurry and gather your harvest homewards,
though you rise before dawn to do it—to win safe what ensures your life.
Daybreak takes a third of a day's work as its share,
daybreak pushes man on his road, pushes him, too, in his work,

daybreak at her appearance has set many a man on his travels;   580
it is daybreak that lifts the yoke on the neck of many an ox.

   When the thistle blows and the musical cicada
sits on its stem and sheds the stridency of its song,
in its fullness, from under its wings, in the season of wearisome summer,
then are the goats fattest, then the wine at its best,
the women most full of lust, and the men, you note, at their feeblest
when Sirius sets a dryness in head and knees,
when the flesh is baked dry with the heat in it—that then is the moment
for the shade of the rock and the Bibline wine,
for the milk-baked cake, and the milk, when the goats are drying off,   590
and the meat of the heifer that grazed in the woods and had not yet
       calved
and the meat from first-born kids, and to top it, flaming wine,
as you sit in the shade, your heart fed to its fullness with food,
your face turned towards Zeus' brisk wind, and the spring-well ever
       flowing,
so clear, unmuddied; pour three parts of its water
into your drink—but for the fourth part, in with the wine!

   For your servants—bid them thresh the holy grain of Demeter
when, at his first appearing, Orion has shown his strength;
they should thresh in a wind-swept place, and on a well-rolled surface,
and carry the grain, with a scoop, heedfully, in buckets,   600
and when you have all your livelihood safely locked in your house,
my advice to you is: turn your hired man out of doors,
and get you a maid-servant, not one with a child,
for a servant with a calf underneath her causes trouble.
Feed a sharp-toothed watch dog—and do not stint his food—
lest the man—the Day-Sleeper—rob you of your possessions.
Get your fodder inside, and the chaff, that you may have plenty
for your oxen and mules. Then, after that, your servants
may relieve their poor legs; and do you take the yoke from your oxen.
But when Orion and Sirius come to the middle of heaven,
and when the red-fingered Dawn looks upon Arcturus,   610
Perses, cut off all your grapes, and bring them homeward,
and for ten days and ten nights display them to the sun,
and for five more, shade them; in the sixth pour them into buckets,
the gifts of Dionysus, the joyful. But when the Pleiades sink
and with them the Hyades, and with both the strength of Orion,
then again be mindful of plowing, in its due season,
and let your year go underground, in its fullness.

   But if a desire possess you for a rough stormy voyage,
just when the Pleiades shrink from the savage strength of Orion,   620

and fall on the dark misty sea,
at that very time is when the blasts of all winds rage,
then do not keep any longer your ships on the wine-dark sea,
remembering as I bid you the working of your land.
Pull your ship to the land and guard it on every side
with stones to hold it from the force of the winds blowing wetly;
take out the plug from the boat that Zeus' rain may not rot it.
Put all your gear in the house in ready condition,
folding, in their due order, the wings of the seafaring ship.
But for yourself, wait a proper time for your voyage,   630
till that should come,
and *then* draw your quick ship seaward, stow in her a suitable cargo,
to win you a profit to carry homewards,
even as our father, great fool Perses, yours and mine,
was used to sail on ships, through lack of a decent living,
the father who one day came here, having traveled a great sea-journey,
leaving in his black ship Aeolian Cyme behind.

It was not riches he sought to avoid, nor yet wealth or prosperity,
but evil poverty—and it's Zeus that gives that to men.
He landed near to Helicon, in a miserable village,
Ascra, in winter bad, in summertime oppressive, at no time ever good.   640

And you Perses, remember seasonableness, in all kinds of work and always
and most of all in seafaring.
Give your praise to a small boat, but put your freight in a big one.
The bigger the freight, the bigger will be gain added to gain,
if only the winds refrain their cruel blasts.

But if it is towards trade that you have turned your sinful mind,
because you would escape debts and the ugliness of hunger,
I will tell you myself the measure of the sobbing sea,
although I have learned nothing of seafaring nor of ships,
for I never yet sailed in a ship over the broad sea,   650
save only to Euboea, from Aulis where once the Greeks,
waited the length of a winter and gathered their host together,
as they went from holy Greece to Troy, mother of beautiful women.
There I had crossed to Chalcis, to the funeral games of Amphidamus,
a master in war, where his sons offered many prizes, declared
beforehand in the great-souled hero's honor; and there I may say
I won with my poem the prize, a tripod with earshaped handles;
I dedicated this to the Muses of Helicon,
where they first set my feet on the path of tuneful song;
that indeed is all I know by experience of crafted ships;   660
but even so I will tell of the mind of aegis-bearing Zeus,
for the Muses have taught me the singing of songs without limitation.

For the fifty days after the summer solstice,
when the summer is drawing to an end, in the season of wearying heat,
then is man's sailing time, his proper time; then you will not
break your ship upon rocks, nor the sea kill the men in it—
unless with his fullest intent Poseidon the Earth-Shaker
or Zeus, King of the Immortals, will your destruction outright,
for with them lies the fulfillment of all things, good and bad.   670
At that season the winds are clear to be judged, and the sea harmless;
you may cheerfully trust the winds and draw your ship seaward,
and stow your cargo in her;
but hurry to make your way home, with all the speed you may;
do not wait for the new wine to come, nor the rain in autumn
at the advance of winter, and the dreadful blasts of the South Wind
which stirs the sea to action accompanying Zeus' rain,
in its autumn plenty, and renders the sea a terror.

Another sailing time there is for men—in the spring of the year;
when the leaves on the tip of the fig tree, of the size of a crow's footfall,   680
show themselves—then the sea can carry your boat.
This is the springtime sailing. For myself, I have no praise for it;
it is not to my heart;
it is a moment snatched; it is hard to avoid its danger;
but men do these things because wisdom is not in their minds;
for possessions are the life of unhappy mortal men.
It is a terrible thing to die with the waves around you;
indeed I would have you think of all this in your heart as I tell it;
do not put in hollow ships all that supports your life,
but leave the most part behind and ship the lesser in freight.   690
For it is a terrible thing to meet disaster among the waves,
and terrible, too, to put on a wagon a load beyond its bearing,
and shatter your axle and ruin your cargo.
Keep watch on measure; in all things best is the when and how much.

    At the right time of your life bring home a wife to your house.
You should be thirty years old; not many more years or less;
that is the right time for marriage.
Let the woman grow ripe for four seasons
and marry in the fifth.
Marry a virgin that she might learn the right habits of life from you;
the very best is to marry the woman who lives beside you,   700
and look carefully at everything, that your marriage may not be for
        neighbors
an occasion for their delight.
There is no better prize for a man to win than a wife
if so be that she is a good one, and none worse if she is bad,
one ever alert for a meal; she will burn the strong man

with no torch; she'll bring him to a still raw old age.
Be well and truly careful of the anger of the blessed gods.

Do not make a friend the equal of a brother, or if you do,
let you not be the first to do injury to him;
do not lie to him to please him, but if he is the first to say
the word or do the act that vexes your heart, remember   710
and pay him back twice over; but if he again would lead you
back into friendship, and is willing to give compensation,
accept him; the man who keeps constantly changing his friends
is worthless; let not your mind do shame to your appearance.

Do not be called a friend of many nor yet of none,
nor a comrade of evil-doers, nor a taunter of the good.

Do not dare to insult a man for deadly heart-chilling poverty,
for poverty lies in the gift of the gods that are forever.

The best treasure of the tongue among mortals is its sparing,
and when it runs in measure that is its greatest grace.   720
If you use a bad word to someone you will soon hear a worse yourself.

Do not rudely avoid a dinner where there are many guests
and the cost is common to all; there the grace is greatest
and the cost least.

Let not your hands be unwashed when you pour a libation
of flaming wine to Zeus or the other immortal gods,
for they will not hear you; they will spit your prayers away.
Do not piss standing upright with your face to the sun;
but only after sunset, remember, and until its rising again.
Do not piss either on the road or off of it, as you walk,
nor stripped of clothes; the Blessed Ones own the nights.   730
The pious man who is wise will do it sitting
or go to the wall of his well-enclosed courtyard.
When your sexual parts are smeared with sperm do not let them be seen
close to the hearth of your house; you must draw back from it.

When you come from a burying, a thing of ill-omened words,
do not sow your seed—but after a feast of the gods.[4]   736

Do not piss into the waters of rivers that flow to the sea   757
nor into the springs; avoid this very carefully;   758
neither shit into them; that would be far from well for you.   759

Never let your feet cross the beautifully flowing water   737

of the rivers that are for ever, till you pray looking into the fair stream   738
after washing your hands, in the beautiful whitish water.   739
He who crosses the river unwashed of hands, of his evil,   740
with him the gods are angry and after they give him sorrows.   741

On the rich feast of the Gods do not cut the Dry from the Green,
from your Five Branch, with gleaming iron;[5]
nor put the jug above the mixing bowl of those drinking;
for a deadly fate stands over this.

When you are building a house do not leave the roof rough,
lest the croaking crow find a perch on it and cry, "Caw, caw."

Do not take from pots unconsecrated, either to eat or to wash;
upon these acts, too, there lies a penalty.
Do not let a twelve-year-old child sit on the sacred floor,   750
for it is better not; and it makes a man less than a man;
nor set there a twelve-month child—this case is the same as the other.
Nor let a man wash his skin in the water a woman has washed in;
for a time, too, on him there shall be
a penalty of misery.

If you happen upon a sacrifice, as it is burning, do not   755
find fault with the mystery; with that, too, the god is vexed.   756

Do, as I say, avoid an ill report from your fellows,   760
for there *is* ill report among men—very easy it is to raise it,
but hard to endure and difficult to shed it,
for no report which many men voice dies entirely;
it is itself a kind of god.

   Days come from Zeus; heedfully and properly for each one,
tell your men about them. The thirtieth is the month's best day
to oversee the work, and to share out the provisions,
when people judge truly and celebrate it rightly.
For these are the days that come from Zeus of Counsel.

To begin with, the first and the fourth and the seventh are holy days,   770
for, on the first, Leto bore Apollo of the sword of gold;
and also the eighth and the ninth; these two days of the month,
as it wanes, are especially good for the doing of man's work.[6]
The eleventh and twelfth are both of them good,
for shearing sheep or gleaning a welcome harvest,
but the twelfth is far better than the eleventh, of the two days,
for on that day the spider, the air-borne, weaves its web

at the full time of the day when the Cunning One gathers its heap;
that is the day the woman shall raise her loom
and set her work forward.

Avoid the thirteenth day of the starting month for beginning   780
of the sowing—but it is best for the plants, to get them bedded in.
The sixth day of the middle month is very unsuited to plants,
but a good day for a man's birth; for a daughter it is not favorable,
neither at first for her birth nor yet for her gaining of marriage.
Nor is the first sixth day of the month for the birth of a girl
suitable, but for castration of kids and woolly sheep,
and a genial day for building the pen to encompass the flock.
It is a good day, too, for the birth of a man—but he is likely to be
one whose speech is mocking words, and lies and crooked sayings
and secret seductiveness.
On the eighth day of the month cut the boar and the bellowing bull,   790
and on the twelfth the mules enduring of labor.[7]
On the full day, the great twentieth, beget a learned man
for his will be a mind that is deeply closed in caution.
The tenth is best for a man's birth, but the middle fourth for a girl,
and on that day, too, lay your hand on your sheep, to gentle them,
and your sleek oxen with shambling gait, and your sharp-toothed dog,
and your mules that patiently bear their work; but be wary in your mind
to avoid the first of the waning month and also the first of its rising,
with their pains that gnaw the heart; this is a deadly fulfilling day.

On the fourth of the month bring a wife to your house, once you judged
    the bird omens   800
that are best, set over this deed.
Avoid the fifths, for bitterer are they and harsh,
for on the fifth day, they say, the Furies were busy with Oath,
with his birth; Strife bore him to be a bane
to such as are false to their oaths.
On the seventh day of the middle, cast the holy corn of Demeter
on the well-rolled threshing floor; pay a heedful watching eye.
Let the carpenter cut the planks for the house, and the many timbers
for the making of ships, such as fit all the needs of the ships.
But for the *narrow* ship begin to fit frames on the fourth.
The middle ninth is a better day towards afternoon,   810
but the very first is quite free from any ill for men;
it is an excellent day to plant and for birth as well,
either of man or woman; never a wholly bad day.
Few know that three nines of the month is the best for beginning a cask,
and placing the yoke on the neck

of oxen and drudging mules and the horses quick of foot,
and drawing to the wine-dark sea the many-thwarted ship.
But few men call by its true name this day of the month.

Open your cask on the fourth; it is a holy day,
beyond all others, at noon time. Few know that the twenty-first   820
is best at dawn, but it grows worse towards evening.

These are the days that are a great blessing for men on earth;
the others are variable, not fraught with fate, bringing nothing to pass.
One praises one day, and one another, but few know;
"Sometimes a day is a stepmother, and sometimes a mother."

Well with God and prosperous who knows well all these things,
and does his work and keeps clear of blame by the immortal gods,
judging the omens by birds and avoiding all highness of heart.

INTRODUCTION: HESIOD, POET AND FARMER

Greek civilization was founded, as the Greeks themselves believed, by two poets, Hesiod and Homer.[1] This was very fortunate for Greece, but somewhat unlucky for Hesiod. Homer is a hard act to follow. Like Ben Jonson, who had the misfortune to live in Shakespearean England, Hesiod was born an also-ran; the shadow of Homer has, from the very beginning, obscured his unique virtues. Unfortunately, Hesiod's poems, which are very unlike Homer's, completely resist a "Homeric" approach, revealing their beauty only when taken on their own terms. This is what fortune has denied them. From Herodotus to the latest critical work, it is a rare reference to Hesiod which does not position him in relation to Homer. In contrast, few studies of Homer have felt it necessary to point out that he was a near-contemporary of Hesiod's.

Of these two poets' works, four have come down to us entire: the *Iliad* and the *Odyssey*, attributed to Homer; and the *Theogony* and *Works and Days*, attributed to Hesiod. The authenticity of these poems, as works composed in Greece sometime between 800 and 600 BC is not doubted. The authenticity of the poets is. Fashions change in Classical scholarship, as they do in anything else. The nineteenth-century tendency to see the works of Homer as compilations gave way to a search for unity in the poems. That search then gave way to discussions of the newly-discovered oral nature of the poems, a discussion now yielding to new searches for unity. In all of this Hesiodic scholarship has tended to trail behind Homeric.[2] Like a reluctantly acknowledged younger sibling, Hesiod can be fiercely defended, but is seldom appealed to in his own right.

As Homer and "Homer," the rivals for authorship of the *Iliad* and *Odyssey* continue to do battle, Hesiod has moved from person to persona, and occasionally back again. The author of the *Theogony* and *Works and Days* may be a single poet, two poets, or a collection of poets. He may be the poet described by the poems themselves, or he may be using this identity as his literary persona. I myself believe that he is who he says

31

he is. But the issue is not as critical as it might seem. With Hesiod, just as much as with Vergil, it is poetry and not autobiography that we are dealing with. As we admire a self-portrait by Rembrandt or Van Gogh for the painting itself, and not for its likeness to the painter, the "Hesiod" we are interested in examining is the "Hesiod" that the poet intended us to see, the "Hesiod" presented in the poems. We may wonder about the poet, as we may find ourselves particularly interested in Van Gogh's bandaged ear, or as we might wonder why Shakespeare gave Hamlet the name of his own dead son. The question is, nonetheless, incidental to our main concern. The poet we truly care about lives inside of the poems.

The *Theogony* and the *Works and Days* have always been attributed to Hesiod, along with other works and fragments, notably the *Shield of Heracles* and the *Catalogue of Women*. We also possess a varied assortment of biographical information. Unfortunately the information which tradition has handed down to us ranges from the improbable to the incredible. That Hesiod was, as he implies, a farmer on the poor land of Mount Helicon, is quite credible. That he engaged in a poetic contest with Homer, as *The Contest of Homer and Hesiod* informs us, is not.[3] That his father's name was Dion stems transparently from a misreading of a line in the *Works and Days*. Nothing in the tradition, including the existence of Hesiod and his authorship of the *Theogony* and *Works and Days*, can be accounted certain. What we have are the poems. What we can conclude about their author can come only from them, from the limited information we have about the period during which they were composed, and from our own sense of what is likely.

Unlike any other poetry that survives from this period, and particularly unlike the Homeric epics, the *Theogony* and the *Works and Days* themselves tell us about their author. This information makes discovering who Hesiod was both simpler and more complex. It is simpler because we can thereby sketch a rough biography. It is more complex because it is impossible for us to know whether what we are told is true. It is not even necessarily clear that the author, or authors, of the poems meant to leave us with the impression that one man named Hesiod composed both poems. And if he, or they, did so intend, we still cannot forget that the information we are given, is given not as history or biography, but as part of the poem. The persona of the author is as much an element of a poem as is the poem's subject. And like the poem's subject, it can be either true or fictional.

The *Theogony* tells us that while Hesiod, so named, was pasturing his sheep on Mount Helicon, the Muses came to him and gave him the gift of poetry. Also, says the poet, "they gave me a rod, a branch of flourishing laurel, and breathed into me a divine voice" (καί μοι σκῆπτρον ἔδον δάφνης ἐριθηλέος ὄζον / δρέψασαι, θηητόν· ἐνέπνευ-σαν δέ μοι αὐδὴν / θέσπιν *Th.* 30–32). The statement seems to imply, although the conclusion is not a necessary one, that Hesiod and the poet are one and the same person. This is all that the *Theogony* tells us about its author.

The *Works and Days* contains a greater wealth of information. The poem is addressed to a man named Perses, who, we learn, is the poet's brother. When the two came to divide the family holding which was their inheritance, Perses, the poet claims, snatched more than his fair share, by gratifying the "gift-gobbling kings" who judge this sort of case (*WD* 35–39). It turns out that Perses' gain was short lived, for the poet refers to (and rejects) an attempt by the now impoverished Perses to beg money from his more prosperous brother (*WD* 396–97). We also learn that their father had been a trader from Cyme in Asia Minor before his poverty drove him to settle in the small town of Ascra, near Mount Helicon; a place, the poet grumbles, "in winter bad, in summertime oppressive, at no time ever good." (χεῖμα κακῇ, θέρει ἀργαλέῃ, οὐδέ ποτ' ἐσθλῇ *WD* 639–40). And we learn that the only time Hesiod has been to sea was to cross over from Aulis, in Boeotia, to the island of Euboea (a distance just under half a mile). There he won a tripod in a poetry contest, which he dedicated to the Muses of Mount Helicon in the place where they had first taught him song (*WD* 650–60). This last is a local touch, since the more usual home of the Muses is on Olympus, and seems to refer back to the episode described in the *Theogony*. This is all that the poet of the *Works and Days* tells us about himself. For the rest we find out, in passing remarks, that he believes that hard work is the only road to success, that he doesn't trust women very far, and that he doesn't like sailing at all.

From these fragments it is possible to reconstruct a hypothetical life for a real human being. Hesiod's (as we may call him for the sake of convenience) father, having acquired a probably unoccupied plot of land on the foothills of Mount Helicon, set up a smallholding with crops and some sheep. The sheep would be sent up to the mountain to graze in summer, when heat and drought had burnt the grass in the low-lying areas. Then, as now, a young son whose work could be spared would be sent with them.[4] While up on Helicon, Hesiod passed the time by reciting to himself the poetry which would have provided the main amusement of local festivals. He discovered a talent at it, and when the words began to flow spontaneously from his lips, he realized that the Muses had favored him with their gift. But there was not much of a living in poetry, and so Hesiod worked the farm with his father and brother, practicing his poetry when he had a chance, performing in local festivals, or even, occasionally, at more important affairs, such as the games in Euboea. Bit by bit he put together the *Theogony*. After his father's death and the lawsuit with his brother, Hesiod continued to work the part of the farm left to him, cherishing a grudge. But the grudge turned into poetry.[5] As Hesiod worked on it the poem developed a life of its own, moving away from mere indignation towards an exploration of all of human life. It was a warning to Perses of how he couldn't get away with it, an explanation of what he ought to do instead, a discussion of the will of Zeus, and a revelation of how, as Perses' laziness and cheating shows us the wrong and disastrous course, farming shows us the place where human beings fit into the cosmos. This was Hesiod's masterpiece. It became the *Works and Days*.

Hesiod's Time

Herodotus, the Greek historian of the fifth century BC, believed that Homer and Hesiod lived about 400 years before his time, that is, around 850 BC.[6] Modern scholars, looking at Hesiod's knowledge of Delphi and of geography, to his reference to the games in Euboea for Amphidamus, who may have been killed in the Lelantine War of, perhaps, 730–700 BC, and to his imitators, are inclined to date him about one hundred to one hundred and fifty years later.[7] Most scholars think that Homer lived anywhere from fifty to one hundred years earlier than Hesiod, and almost all are agreed that the heroic Mycenaean age, the subject of the Homeric epics, had come to a close about 1200 BC The Mycenaean period had been a time of great, almost feudal lords, who, having taken over predominance from the earlier Minoan civilization of Crete, presided over and protected societies of their dependents. They themselves were linked by the personal ties which served for trade and diplomacy. Their greatest exploit was the Trojan War. It was also their last.

Why the Mycenaean age came to a close is still an open question. The most common explanation is the Dorian Invasion, the conquest of Greece by a band of Indo-European invaders from the north. As the invaders took control, the political organization of the Mycenaean age was destroyed. What followed was a Dark Age, a time when writing was lost, trade dwindled, the arts went into decline, and the great kingdoms of the Mycenaeans dwindled into petty lordships over isolated estates. It is at the end of this period that we find Hesiod and Homer. The Dark Age merges into a period of intense colonization. In the ninth and eighth centuries Greeks move from the mainland to Asia Minor, to the Balkans, to Sicily, to the coast of Africa, and throughout the Mediterranean world. As the Greeks settle new colonies, trade revives, and with trade the arts of pottery and weaving. The acquisition of wealth through trade gives a new impetus to the creation of less necessary objects, such as statues and jewelry. Hesiod's father becomes a trader, seeking wealth in the new spurt of trade between mainland Greece and towns such as Aeolian Cyme in Asia Minor. He was one of the ones that failed.

And culture revives. The earliest specimen we have of Greek alphabetic writing is generally dated to some time before 700 BC. Whether Hesiod or Homer availed themselves of the new invention we cannot know.[8] But Greece was coming into its greatest period; the city-state which we think of as Greek was on the horizon; written laws were about to take over from the oral pronouncements of Hesiod's "gift-gobbling kings;" and Greek influence was about to spread through the Mediterranean world. Hesiod, on his little farm in the backwoods of Boeotia, had no reason to think that the future would be much different from the present. The Greeks of the fifth century would look back to his time as we do, as the dawn of Greek civilization.

Hesiod's Town and Country

Most of what we can say about Hesiod's society is speculation based upon Hesiod's own poems. We may supplement these hints with Homeric descriptions, but here we are on much shakier ground. Hesiod sets the *Works and Days* firmly in his own place and time. The Homeric poems describe a time long before Homer's, a time when "one man could lift a stone such that it would take two men to lift now" (*Iliad* 20.285–87, for example). It is impossible for us to know for certain which details of the Homeric poems Homer draws from his own experience, and which he draws from tradition, or from his own imagination of what those times, so long ago, were like.

The petty lords and major landowners whom Hesiod refers to as the "kings" are not the great lords of Mycenean times. They seem rather to have played the role in eighth-century Greek society that the English squire was to play later in the English countryside. There is, however, an important difference. Hesiod's kings had not even a nominal government over them. They were thus both judges and lawgivers, although only as a group, and over limited territories. The kings managed the assemblies in the *agora*, the marketplace where people gathered to buy and sell or merely to gossip, and where disputes were decided. The kings also, presumably, determined the position of the community in peace or war. For Hesiod the contrast between himself and the kings would be marked. He scratched a living from a patch of mountainside, from which he could look down into the fertile valley which gave Boeotia its reputation as one of the richest farming areas of Greece. That land was owned by the kings. Ascra, Hesiod's local town, was only a hamlet. The local big town, a few miles away, was Thespiae. It was here that the kings probably heard the case between Hesiod and Perses, a case that they, according to Hesiod, decided wrongly.

The only references to Hesiod's own time in the *Theogony* occur in the Proem. Here Hesiod describes how he was inspired, and how the people gather and admire when a good king, also inspired by the Muses, renders judgment (*Th.* 79–103). This king is doing well what the "gift-gobbling" kings of the *Works and Days* do badly, deciding a lawsuit. Our one explicit description of this process comes from the case depicted on Achilles' shield in the *Iliad*. Here two men, disputing the restitution which must be made for a killing, rush for arbitration to the elders of the city seated in the marketplace. The people clamor in support of one or the other of them. Heralds keep the people in order. Two talents of gold lie on the ground, either as the amount disputed, or as a reward for the best decision (*Iliad* 18.497–508).

According to this description, cases were voluntarily submitted to the judges by the parties involved, a supposition corroborated by Herodotus' account of Deioces, who made himself king of Persia by deciding his neighbors disputes fairly (1.96–98). If acceptance of the judges' decision was, for Hesiod, compulsory, it would seem to be only newly so. According to the description in the *Theogony*, the kings do not make their judgment on the basis of written laws, which did not yet exist, but on their knowledge of the *themistes*, the oral code handed down from one generation of nobles to the next, which determined what was, and what was not, acceptable.[9] The aim of the decision, as Hesiod describes it, is not to act in accordance with the law, but to persuade with soft words, and "end even a great quarrel wisely" (*Th.* 86–90).

Hesiod may have been a poor man in comparison with the kings. But he was not a serf.[10] The *Works and Days* declares itself to be advice and a warning, not only to Perses, but also to the kings. Hesiod's favorite epithets for the kings, "gift-gobbling" and "fools," hardly imply a man cowering in fear before his betters. The Mycenaean age appears to have been a time when small landholders had their land from their lord, and so were dependent on him not only for protection, but also for their very livelihood. Hesiod has far more independence. His land is his own. His pair of oxen is his own.[11] He can hope, if his crops flourish, to gain more. He also need fear, if his crops do badly, the loss of what he has.

Despite archaeological evidence that money was not in use in Greece at this time, a line of the *Works and Days* carries all the implications of a society well used to buying and selling, not only produce, but even land. Propitiate the gods, Hesiod says, so that they might be gracious, "that you may buy another's farm, rather than he buy yours" (WD 341). This aim, and fear, motivates most of the advice of the Works and Days. We should not read back into Hesiod's society the independence and individual possibilities of winning or losing wealth of the later Greek city-states. We would also be wrong, however, not to see the opening up of these possibilities in the Works and Days.[12]

The section of the Works and Days that deals with farming does not deal only with farming. It deals with farming and sailing. The reason to sail, if one is a Greek farmer, is that Greece is a mountainous country surrounded by the sea. If you want to transport goods, you had better get a boat. Hesiod, in other words, assumes that a plausible adjunct to farming is selling, or trading, one's own goods oneself. The fact that Hesiod, who hates sailing, includes this section, is evidence of how very common marketing one's produce must have been.

What Hesiod would have traded in we do not know. Perhaps grain, perhaps wine, perhaps even an occasional small animal. What is significant is that the farm he is discussing, although it largely provides for itself, is not simply a subsistence farm. Judging from Hesiod's picture the farm is neither outstandingly large nor particularly small. As far as we can tell this probably means a farm of 6 to 10 acres.[13] Hesiod himself, and his family, seem to do the major amount of the work. A man hired to do plowing and sowing is also mentioned, a servant-girl, preferably without children, and an indeterminate number of slaves to do work both in the household and in the field. How large the household is depends, presumably, on how prosperous it is, and, in the sort of relation Hesiod loves to point out, vice versa: the larger the household is the more workers there are to make it prosperous.

The farm centers on the growing of crops. Tillage would have provided most of the food for the household. Hesiod declares that until one has enough grain stored away for a year, one had better not waste time gossiping in the marketplace. A team of oxen works the ground and pulls Hesiod's wagon. He mentions both horses and mules, although he does not give the impression that he himself uses them. He provides fodder, probably hay, for the working animals. He also, of course, has a vineyard, and makes his own wine. Although he mentions olive trees or oil only once, he probably had these as well. He makes most of his own tools, gathering wood from around the place, and from the forests up on the mountain, but there is a blacksmith nearby and a carpenter fastens his plow together. Hesiod's summer picnic, after the crops are in, includes the possibility of a heifer who proved not in calf and firstling kids. Besides the goats and a cow there are, of course, the sheep he spent his youth with, and whose wool provides his winter clothing. And a dog for keeping off thieves. Such is the composition of Hesiod's farm. It is nothing to compare with the kings in Thespiae, but it is prosperous enough.

Hesiod—Or Was He?

This then would have been Hesiod's life, a life very much like that of peasant farmers throughout history, and throughout much of the world today. Although the information which Hesiod gives us about himself is abundant only when compared to other poems of the time, the *Works and Days* is an intensely personal poem. The sentiments, the beliefs, even the quirks, of an individual, and a somewhat crotchety one, pervade the poem. They are strikingly similar to those of many a small farmer.[14] Hesiod's emphatic belief in the necessity of hard work and thrift, his dislike of violence, war, and heroism, his distrust of government and of people who hang about town gossiping and looking out for the main chance, his hatred of the sea, his disinclination to run risks, his suspicion, and his implicit belief that virtue lives on the farm, are easily paralleled. They are also attitudes almost diametrically opposed to the emotional and risk-loving character, devoted to gossip, to company, and to politics, which elsewhere seems stereotypically Greek. Of course the fact that Hesiod seems more like a small farmer, even of the twentieth century, than like our idea of his contemporaries, is no proof that Hesiod was what the poems imply—a small farmer. But it is suggestive.

It does not ultimately matter whether Hesiod was a farmer or not, any more than it matters whether the *Theogony* and the *Works and Days* were written by Hesiod, a poet or poets who adopted the persona of Hesiod, or by poets unknown who accidentally came to be identified as "Hesiod." It is the poems that matter. But poems are composed by people, and I believe, against the current fashion, that the person who composed these two poems was, in fact, a farmer. The hypothesis that he was a farmer, and as such felt as other farmers have about justice, the land, God, and neighbors, unravels many of the difficulties of the *Works and Days*. Most importantly it explains why a poet would have chosen farming as his unifying theme. If Hesiod *was* a farmer it does not take much to figure why he chose farming as the keystone of his poem. If he was not, it is difficult to see why he would have chosen so unusual a topic.

In its most radical form the argument against Hesiod the farmer claims that the autobiographical material of the *Theogony* and the *Works and Days* serves as a literary device to unite the work of many poets composing within a common tradition.[15] A less radical view sees "Hesiod" as a single poet using the persona of the Ascrean peasant farmer as an element in his poetry, either a single persona which covers both the *Works and Days* and the *Theogony*, or a separate persona for each.[16] In either case we must ask: if "Hesiod" was not a farmer, why is he portrayed as one? If we picture a single persona for both poems it is difficult to see why the small peasant farmer from the backwoods of Boeotia is an appropriate expositor of the genealogy of the gods. In fact, as the autobiographical material of the *Theogony* is confined to Hesiod's meeting with the Muses, it could be argued that Hesiod himself took this view.[17] If, on the other hand, we assume two different personae, the problem is simply transferred to the *Works and Days*. Why does the poet of the *Works and Days*, a poem which declares that its intention is to educate kings, picture himself as a small farmer?

Hesiod's picture of himself was not likely to excite admiration. The Greeks were remarkably free from the idea that the sweat of one's brow is ennobling. Hesiod himself, despite the more romantic view of some commentators, sees work as simply a necessary evil.[18] The siblings of "Painful Toil" (*Th.* 226) in the *Theogony* include features of life that Hesiod sees as closely related: Famine, Sorrows, Murders, Lies, and Ruin (*Th.* 226–32). Nor did Greek literature tend to idealize country life in preference to the life of the city. When Achilles declares that he would rather be a hired hand on a poor man's farm than king of all the perished dead (*Odyssey* 11.489–91), he is clearly imagining the worst fate that could befall a man. Plato declares in the *Laws* that the citizens should own farms. They are also to own slaves to work them (*Laws* 847e ff.). An ordinary Greek would have found the independence and status implied in owning land eminently desirable. He would have found the idea that it was desirable to *work* one's land ridiculous.[19]

Hesiod's choice of a persona cannot be seen as self-aggrandizement. Nor, on the other hand, can it be seen as self-abasement. The suggestion that this humblest of personae has been chosen ironically, as evidence of the poet's power to humble kings, is belied by the poem itself. Far from stressing his humble circumstances, Hesiod, quite naturally, creates the impression that he is fairly well off. The farm he describes includes oxen and more than sufficient tools, servants, and slaves, and a sufficient surplus for at least a pleasant summer picnic, complete with imported wine. It is Perses who comes begging to Hesiod, not Hesiod to Perses (*WD* 396–97). The Hesiod pictured in the *Works and Days* would, in fact, be deeply offended at being described as "the least of men, the most socially marginal of men."[20]

Hesiod's account of himself has also been attacked on the grounds that it is occasionally fuzzy, and perhaps contradictory. Some details of Hesiod's life, his father's backward migration from the prosperous Aeolian Cyme to Ascra, Perses' shifting circumstances, and the unclear status of the trial, do indeed seem anomalous. But, if anything, this argues against their being deliberately constructed. These details may well not be probable enough for fiction.[21] They are, however, quite possible enough for real life.

There appears to be no particular reason for the poet of the *Theogony* or the *Works and Days* to choose the persona of a small but far from destitute farmer, unless he was just that. This supposition explains another curious detail of the poems. Although Hesiod more than implies that he is a farmer, he never directly says so. He spends far more time on the details of his poetic inspiration and success than on the details of his farm. Rather than implying that Hesiod was a professional poet rather than a farmer, this seems to imply the reverse. A farmer among farmers would certainly boast of the particular talent that was his claim to fame. A prosperous poet who was adopting farming as a persona would not. A peasant of eighth-century Boeotia would hardly have felt the need to identify himself as a farmer. One would expect a poet, assuming the fictitious identity of a farmer, to identify himself as such.

Poetry is to Hesiod glorious and noteworthy. Farming is his ordinary life. And so he treats them. For, although it is poetry that Hesiod brags of, it is farming that remains faithfully in the background of the *Works and Days*.[22] As the poem opens, the goddess Strife stirs on an idle man to work when he sees his neighbor, "a rich man, in haste to plow, / and to plant, set his house in good order" (πλούσιον, ὅς σπεύδει μὲν ἀρώμεναι ἠδέ φυτεύειν / οἶκον τ᾽ εὖ θέσθαι *WD* 22–23). The neighbor is, it is assumed, a farmer. Similarly, there is no time for quarrelling, Hesiod says, "for the man without a year's sustenance, reaped in due season, lying / safe in his house, a harvest, born of earth, the grain of Demeter" (ὧτινι μὴ βίος ἔνδον ἐπηετανὸς κατάκειται / ὡραῖος, τὸν γαῖα φέρει, Δημήτερος ἀκτήν *WD* 31–32). Hesiod's section on farming is followed by a section on sailing, as practiced by a farmer.[23] Similarly Hesiod's social advice ("An ox would never be lost if your neighbour had not been a bad one" οὐδ᾽ ἂν βοῦς ἀπόλοιτ᾽, εἰ μὴ γείτων κακὸς εἴη *WD* 348), his taboos, and his account of lucky and unlucky days assume, rather than declare, that farming is man's regular occupation. Hesiod's penultimate piece of advice in the *Works and Days* is that the twenty-seventh is the best day for breaking oxen (*WD* 815–16). The kings were no doubt glad to hear it.

Hesiod's sense of farming is not confined to one section, one subject, or one trope of the *Works and Days*. It is all-pervasive.[24] This omnipresence cannot be explained by the economic conditions of the times.[25] Farming was not the only, nor even the most successful, way to make a living in eighth-century Boeotia, as Hesiod's own references to pottery, smithing, carpentry, and, above all, commerce make clear. Rather, farming was simply a given of Greek life. It was neither glamorous nor oppressed, a life neither more virtuous, nor less, than the common run of lives. As a result, no writer from Homer to Xenophon sees any reason to choose farming in particular as his topic. Hesiod is the one exception. He cares very deeply about farming. He sees in it the clue to the nature of human life. It is certainly not necessary for Hesiod to be a farmer to feel this. We need look no farther than Vergil to find a writer deeply sensitive to farming, who is not himself a farmer. Nor is anything in the pages that follow changed if we choose to believe that Hesiod himself never held a plow. Nonetheless, there is a time when the simplest explanation is the best one, and the simplest explanation for Hesiod's deep and all-pervasive concern with farming is that he was, in fact, a farmer.

1

THE COMPOSITION OF HESIOD'S POEMS

The discovery of tablets inscribed with the writing known as Linear B proved that the Greeks of the Minoan and Mycenaean ages were literate. There is no further evidence of writing in Greece until around the time of Homer and Hesiod. Homer's description of the "baleful signs" unwittingly carried by the hero Bellerophon (*Iliad* 6.168) suggests a tradition more familiar with spells than with alphabets. And yet Homer's poems describe a time nearly five hundred years before his own. It is difficult to see how, in the absence of written records, this is possible. The explanation appears to lie in the existence of an oral tradition that gradually developed its own "epic language," combining elements of various dialects and developing standard epithets and descriptions of common acts, such as sacrifice, or setting sail. The language passed from one poet to another, each poet adopting what he found useful and further modifying it. In this way the epic tongue spread throughout Greece, and down through the centuries which separated the epic poets from the heroes they celebrated.

It seems incredible that poems of the unity, complexity, and sheer length of the *Iliad*, the *Odyssey*, the *Theogony*, or the *Works and Days*, could be composed entirely without the ability to fix one section of the poem in writing before commencing on another. Such a judgment may reveal no more than our own dependence on writing. It may also be that Homer, or Hesiod, or both, did have access to writing, either dictating their work, or themselves writing it down. But a tradition of poetry which has lasted four hundred years, and created one of the world's greatest poetic languages, does not die overnight, even with the discovery of a force as potent as writing. However these poems were recorded, they were conceived, and communicated, orally.[1] Whether Homer and Hesiod knew of writing or not, it was in the poet's voice that poetry lived for them, and not in his pen.

41

For all of that, Homer's method of composition has made much less difference to our understanding of his poems than one might have supposed. The discovery of the oral tradition explained features that were strange to us, the mixture of dialects, the identical passages, the standard epithets. All these can now be seen as part of a poetry neither memorized, nor created *ab nihilo*, but improvised, like a jazz performance. But the response of readers who have had, for more than two thousand years, no notion of an oral tradition, remains authentic. The human stories of Achilles and Odysseus are able now, as they have always been, to touch us directly, despite the ages between ourselves and Homer, and despite the differences between his world and ours. Like sunshine through a dusty window, the human emotions shine through, only slightly blurred by Homer's assumption of traditions that we have lost.

Hesiod has not fared as well as Homer. Particularly the *Works and Days*, but also the *Theogony*, can seem to a casual reader a mishmash of barely related information. The fault lies not with the reader, nor with Hesiod, but with the discrepancy between the assumptions and connections Hesiod and his audience made, and our own. In composing the *Iliad* and the *Odyssey* Homer made use of a compositional device known to all men in all places and times—he told a story. Hesiod wrote a different kind of poetry, one more dependent on the vision of the world, and on the understanding of poetry, that he shared with his audience. What Hesiod has to say is as universal as the stories of the *Iliad* and the *Odyssey*. *How* he says it, however, requires more explication.

The poems Hesiod wanted to write could not be composed around a plot. It is essentially this which makes Hesiod's poetry difficult. What Hesiod is saying in any given section of the poem is perfectly clear. It is why one section follows another that can be difficult to see. In other words, it is the unity of the works which is in question. Unfortunately, exactly that unity is critical to an appreciation of the poems. In a work organized primarily as a collection, Hesiod's fragmentary *Catalogue of Women*, for example, or Ovid's *Metamorphoses*, *The Arabian Nights*, or *The Canterbury Tales*, the beauty of any part can be appreciated even when it has been separated from the whole. This is not true, in general, of Hesiod. Here each part of the poem gains its meaning precisely from its place within the whole. As, in a painting, no individual figure can be said to be well or badly painted except with reference to the whole, so also in Hesiod. No part of the work can be truly appreciated without a sense of the whole of which it is part. To understand that whole we will have to try to understand how Hesiod saw his world. First, however, we can look at a simpler question: how Hesiod and his audience understood a poem to be put together.

Because of the nature of an oral tradition originality, in our sense of the word, is not only not valuable, it is nearly impossible. The words that make up an oral poet's work, the descriptions, the phrases, even entire scenes, are no more unique to the poet than the painter's canvas, brush, or paint is unique to him. What matters is not the episodes but what one does with them. Hesiod happily incorporates myths, proverbs, fables, or traditional stories in his poems. These are, from his point of view, simply the materials from which the poem is to be made.[2] The work of the poet is composition, literally a "putting together." For Hesiod what was to be put together was not individual words, or even lines, but blocks of material, ranging from proverbs of two lines to myths of over a hundred.

From these blocks of material Hesiod composed the larger sections which combine to form the poems themselves. Hesiod's poems, like Homer's, are too long for a single performance. What Hesiod must have performed are sections of the poems. These would not necessarily strike him, or his audience, as excerpts. For Hesiod these sections, designed to be performed in a single sitting, would have been the basic units of poetry. They would have been composed individually, each, like the Homeric Hymns, with a structure and unity of its own. Such, presumably, were the vast majority of the poems composed at the time. The larger poem was the innovation, and with it the notion that such a context gave each individual composition a deeper meaning. Once the idea of the whole was conceived, the smaller sections could then be composed with it in mind. The end result is like a collage, or a patchwork quilt. Both the whole created by the sections, and each section on its own, has its own integrity. The meaning of the whole is both built from, and contributes to, the meaning of each of the constituent parts. It is not, however, merely the same meaning writ large.

The two major devices that Hesiod uses to mark off, organize, and unify the various sections of his poems are repetition and ring-composition. Both are common in oral poetry. A poet composing in a ring structure will mark off the close of a particular segment with a repetition of the section's opening image or idea. Thus Hesiod opens and closes the Prometheus episode of the *Theogony* with a description of Prometheus rendered immobile by the bonds of Zeus. These rings, marking off sections, often occur within even larger rings, giving a structure not of A B A but of A B C B A.[3] The Prometheus myth, for example, constitutes one section of the essential story of the *Theogony*, the rise of Zeus. This central story is itself marked off by the ring formed by Hesiod's initial Hymn to the Muses, which includes a description of their birth, and his repetition of this story near the poem's conclusion. The opening and closing of the *Theogony* are thus set as a frame, in ring-composition, around the various rings that make up the poem's central story.

Repetition marks off a poem's sections, serving as the oral equivalent of chapter headings. It also emphasizes the ideas central to these sections, and to the poem as a whole. In this way it becomes a unifying as well as an organizing device. Through the repetition of ideas and images, often signaled by a repetition of key words, Hesiod is able to point out the themes which underlie the various, and apparently miscellaneous, topics he treats. Both the *Theogony* and the *Works and Days* employ these devices in order to bring out their central concepts. In the *Theogony* Hesiod's central theme is the rise of Zeus and the new order that Zeus brings into the cosmos. In telling this story certain patterns emerge: the wise counsel of Mother Earth, a violent father's suppression of his children, Zeus' distribution of powers to the gods, Zeus' relationship to his children. With these images come key ideas, such as force and intelligence, and key words, such as "perception" (νόος), "portion" (μοῖρα), and "honor" (τιμή) which mark the themes underlying Hesiod's repeated images. In the *Works and Days* the key words and images become both more pronounced and more complex. Justice, hard work, reciprocity, understanding, due measure, and right season run throughout the poem, and throughout the various topics Hesiod addresses. With these themes, and these key terms, Hesiod points out the unity of his poem. He also points out the poem's subject, which is no less than the way human life must be lived within the order of Zeus.

The epic language that the young Hesiod picked up at the festivals of Ascra and Thespiae and practiced as he pastured his father's sheep was about heroes and epic wars. But Hesiod had no great love of heroes and epic wars. He had a new use for the ancient poetry. First, it was to tell the story of the gods, but not in particular episodes, as he had heard them. Hesiod saw that the episodes could be, instead, the bits and pieces of a greater whole, and that he could put these pieces together to show how the myths, when one saw them rightly, explain the nature of Zeus' order. Later, after his quarrel with Perses, he had an even greater inspiration. He could use his poetry not to describe the lives of gods or heroes, but to describe human life as ordinary people live it. He could use it to show that justice and farming mark out the life that Zeus has ordained for man. The tools Hesiod used were the ancient ones. The way in which he used them was all his own.

The Composition of the *Theogony*

Hesiod's poem, the *Theogony*, describes just what the title declares, the birth of the gods. In Hesiod's hands this story turns into an account of the gradual emergence of Zeus and of his divine and cosmic order. This one story is told in two different ways. In the narrative of the poem Zeus, as an actor, imposes his order on the universe. As the poem proceeds Zeus conquers, through force or deceit, his father Cronos, his cousin Prometheus, his uncles the Titans, Typhoeus, the last son of Earth, and finally his wife Wisdom. In the genealogies, however, the order of Zeus appears in the universe without Zeus' intervention. It is, rather, a natural completion, an order which develops spontaneously out of the universe rather than one imposed upon it. Hesiod has constructed the *Theogony* by alternating between these two modes of discourse. A section which describes the genealogy of a generation of gods is followed by the myths which narrate that generation's history. This section of narrative is then followed by the genealogy of the next generation, which is followed, in its turn, by its story, and so on.[4] Thus, for example, the genealogy which leads to the birth of the Titans is followed by the story that ushers the Titans into prominence, the castration of Ouranos, while the genealogy which leads to the birth of the Olympians is followed by the deception of Cronos and the succession of the Olympians to his throne. Narrative leads us to genealogy, and genealogy to narrative, in a roughly chronological pattern.

In a human history such a combination of genealogy and narrative subordinates genealogy to narrative. The genealogical table at the back of a history of England serves primarily to identify the characters in the story. This is not the case in a history of the gods. In the first place, the existence of any particular god is in itself an important fact about the universe. In the second, an account of the genealogy of the Greek gods is also an account of the development of the cosmic order. The children of any king of England are, like himself, human beings. The children of the gods of the *Theogony* are most often not beings like themselves. The first children of the primal deity Earth are features of nature, Heaven, Hills, and the Sea. Her next children are the Titans, violent and coarse, but gods with wills and shadowy personalities, akin to the partially anthropomorphic monsters born after them. From the Titans are born two new kinds of beings, the gentler nymphs of the rivers and seas, and finally the Olympians, the culmination of the line. These are gods who have not only will, but also intelligence; not only power, but also beauty. The overall regularity of the pattern reveals a development from primal gods to Olympians, and, preeminent among the latter, to Zeus.[5] This is a change in the divine order which occurs independently of the narrative. It is not done; it simply happens.[6]

Zeus' development out of the old order occurs both vertically, through the development of the line from Earth to Ouranos to the Titans to Zeus, and horizontally, through the distinction of three major lines of gods.[7] Vertically, Hesiod's gods are transformed largely through evolution. Horizontally, they develop into three distinct kinds of gods, the evil abstractions which stem from Chaos through Night, the main line of anthropomorphic gods which stem from Earth and Ouranos, and the line from Sea, which through Ceto develops into the monsters. Just as Zeus comes, through evolution, to dominate the central line of the gods, Zeus' offspring come to dominate the other two lines. Zeus transforms the central line of the gods simply by being born; he transforms the other two through the children born of him.

In the simpler of the two cases, the line of monsters descended from Pontos are killed off by Zeus' heroic children, Heracles, Bellerophon, and Perseus. The monsters that descend from the ever changing sea are monstrous because they are hybrids: the Harpies, "lovely-haired," like women, but with wings like birds; Pegasus, the winged horse; Echidna, half nymph and half snake; Chimera, composed of lion, goat, snake and dragon; the Sphinx, a lion with an eagle's wings and the face of a woman. The children Zeus begets are another kind of hybrid, one that will conclude Hesiod's poem and lead into all the future history of the earth. They are half-god and half-human, the heroes from whom the kings of ancient Greece traced their descent. As became thematic in the case of Heracles, the suppression of the monsters by the heroes is not merely another battle. It is a passage from a world of pre-civilization, a world that blends gods and animals, to the world we know, the world where it is the human that paramountly manifests the divine. This is the world as Hesiod understands it, a cosmos made a cosmos because it is informed by the order of Zeus.[8]

The monsters are replaced by heroes. The evil abstractions which descend, on the other side, from Chaos and Night, are absorbed into Zeus' order. This happens through the birth of their good counterparts, the children and companions of Zeus. Thus Zeus' children, Peace, Good Order, and Justice, are born to complement the children of Strife, Battles, Disorder, and Oath, the avenger of perjury; Memory joins Forgetfulness; the Graces, goddesses of reciprocal good will, join Deceit, and Lying Words, and Disputes, and, most remarkably, a new set of Fates or "Portioners" (Moirai) is born to replace the old Fates, the children of Night.[9] As their good counterparts are born, the evil abstractions which once had a portion, or sphere of influence, of their own, now become only the negative side of a double portion. This new two-sided role is, once more, determined by Zeus' children. In this way both of the alternate lines of genealogy have come to be dominated by Zeus, who is himself the culmination of the central line. The genealogies of the Theogony, which appear at first (and perhaps second) glance to be incoherent, in fact blossom spontaneously into a quite complex order of their own. The culmination and the focal point of this order is, necessarily, Zeus himself.

The genealogies of the *Theogony* reveal that a new order has developed in the universe. The narrative explains how the old gods, who, as gods, can neither conveniently die, nor simply disappear, became part of the new order. Hesiod makes the difficulty work for him. The narrative of the *Theogony* brings out the two basic and underlying themes of the poem, force and intelligence. The final union of these qualities in Zeus is the essence of Hesiod's theology.[10] The story is told in six stages:

1. The castration of Ouranos by Cronos (*Th.* 154–210)
2. The deception of Cronos by Earth and Zeus (*Th.* 459–506)
3. The deception of Prometheus by Zeus (*Th.* 512–616)
4. The victory of the new gods over the Titans (*Th.* 617–731)
5. The defeat of Typhoeus by Zeus (*Th.* 820–68)
6. Zeus' swallowing of Wisdom (*Th.* 886–900)

Hesiod uses his ordering of the myths to reveal Zeus' growing dominance, from no involvement (naturally enough) in the castration of his grandfather Ouranos, to a vague peripheral involvement in the deception of his father Cronos, to a shared involvement in the defeat of the Titans, to total responsibility for the defeats of Typhoeus and Wisdom. He uses the myths, simultaneously, to highlight the two themes of force and intelligence. In this way the myths explore the nature, as well as reveal the fact, of Zeus' order.[11] As the *Theogony* progresses both force and intelligence are attributed, and more and more particularly attributed, to Zeus himself. We are first introduced to a Zeus who has achieved his supremacy through force: "in strength having conquered Cronos, his father" (κάρτεϊ νικήσας πατέρα Κρόνον *Th.* 71–73).[12] From this point the narrative of the *Theogony* alternates victories by deceit, over Prometheus and Wisdom, with the central victories through force, over the Titans and Typhoeus. Zeus' final victory is his swallowing of his wife Wisdom, which prevents the birth of the son destined to overcome him. This victory, which ensures the permanence of Zeus' reign, also puts an end to the continual overthrow of cunning through force, and of force through cunning. Once Zeus has violently conquered the other gods, and swallowed Wisdom, he has, quite literally, united force and intelligence inside himself.

The Composition of the *Works and Days*

Because the *Theogony* tends to be read by scholars interested in mythology, and the *Works and Days* by scholars interested in Greek ethical thought, the two are seldom read together. This is a shame. Hesiod's vision in the *Works and Days*, and particularly his connection of justice and farming, rests on his understanding of the world order, and that understanding is best explored through the *Theogony*.[13] As the *Theogony* is

Hesiod's attempt to find the meaning which underlies mythology, the *Works and Days* is Hesiod's attempt to discover the underlying truth behind the facts of everyday life. This truth can also be called "the will of Zeus." The poems are similar in composition and in overall outlook. Their most profound congruence, however, lies in Hesiod's vision of the order of Zeus.

The primary difficulty of the *Works and Days*, far more than of the *Theogony*, lies in grasping the unity of the poem.[14] Despite a tendency in scholars to see the poem as a diatribe on justice clumsily attached to a farmer's manual, the *Works and Days* falls, I believe, more naturally into three sections; first, a section of myths, second, a section on justice and farming, and finally, the taboos and the lucky and unlucky days.[15] Three themes, marked by the key words "measure" ($\mu\acute{\epsilon}\tau\rho\text{o}\nu$), "perception" ($\nu\acute{o}\text{o}\varsigma$), and "due season" ($\acute{\omega}\rho\alpha\hat{\iota}\text{o}\varsigma$), run throughout these sections and unify them, showing us the need for perception, the importance of right measure and due season, and the necessary balance of good and evil in human life. These themes run throughout the poem as they run, in Hesiod's vision, throughout human life.[16] Together with the various sections of the poem that deal with the various aspects of life, they form the warp and woof through which Hesiod creates the overall design of the *Works and Days*.

Most of the individual episodes of the *Works and Days* are easily distinguished. The myth of Prometheus and Pandora, the myth of the Five Ages, the fable of the Hawk and the Nightingale, the sections on farming and sailing, and the lucky and unlucky days, stand out immediately as distinct units within the poem. The section addressed to Perses and the kings, with its insistent repetition of its key word and theme, justice, is also easily distinguished, as is the poem's opening with a description of two goddesses, Good Strife and Evil Strife, goddesses who do not appear outside of this section. With the exception of two sections of loosely connected aphorisms, these episodes account for the entire poem.

The *Works and Days* often leaves the impression that it is a collection of loosely associated aphorisms. The impression arises largely from a feeling, more appropriate to written than to oral literature, that what is truly Hesiod's in the poem is what is left when we remove the "borrowed" material discussed above.[17] What is left is, quite correctly, the two sections of the poem which are aphoristic or "freewheeling." It is not critics' perception of these particular sections that is misleading, but rather the idea that we should distinguish "Hesiod's" part of the poem from what he has borrowed. The aphoristic sections of the *Works and Days* are no more, and no less, Hesiod's own than any other part of the poem. Rather than assimilating the entire poem, with its carefully marked-off episodes, to these sections, we would do better to see these as themselves episodes within the larger work, playing their particular role in the overall construction of the poem.

Hesiod's first aphoristic section centers around the idea of honest hard work. In so doing it complements both the section on justice and the section on farming. The second aphoristic section focuses on social and religious concerns and so is linked to both the farming section and the section on lucky and unlucky days. If we look at Hesiod's aphoristic sections in this way the poem, overall, appears thus (the sections overlapping where they are linked by themes that apply equally well to what precedes and to what follows):[18]

1. The Goddesses Strife (*WD* 1–46)

2. The Pandora Myth[19] (*WD* 42–108)
3. The Five Ages Myth[20] (*WD* 106–201)
4. The Fable of the Hawk and the Nightingale (*WD* 202–12)

5. Justice in the Courts (*WD* 212–97)
6. Hard Work and Honesty (*WD* 286–382)
7. Farming and Sailing (*WD* 381–694)

8. Social Advice and Religious Taboos (*WD* 694–764)
9. Lucky and Unlucky Days (*WD* 765–828)

Hesiod's opening section describes first the two goddesses Strife and then Hesiod and Perses, their respective followers. In so doing it provides an image of the opposition which is to inform the entire poem, between idleness and cheating on the one hand, and justice, hard work, and farming on the other. The next large section of the poem is clearly the matched myths of Pandora and the Five Ages, together with their concluding fable. Here Hesiod explores, in mythic terms, the hardship which Zeus' order has determined for human beings. This hardship, Zeus' determination that human beings cannot gain a living for nothing, is the double condition placed upon human life—justice and work.[21] It is this hardship which has made a choice between the goddesses Strife necessary. The section thus provides, as it were, the theological background for the poem, exploring in mythic terms the necessity that underlies the central section on justice and farming.[22]

This section follows. Having shown us the establishment of Zeus' order in myth, Hesiod shows it to us as it exists in society and on the farm. Hesiod's remaining and final section, on social advice, religious taboos, and lucky and unlucky days, then sums up his theme by revealing, in the smallest details of Zeus' order, the same truths that have held throughout, that human life is and must be a balance of good and evil, and that understanding, due season, and right measure are the ways, and the only ways, in which we may live successfully within the order of Zeus.

The Farmer's Year

Hesiod's description of the farmer's year is the heart of the *Works and Days*. As an illustration of the basic truths of Zeus' order it reveals, in the seasons themselves—winter and summer, spring and fall, seedtime and harvest—the balance of good and evil in human life. The farmer's life, as explored by Hesiod, *is* the life of understanding, due season, and right measure. It is by these that the farmer stands or falls. It is this that Hesiod's dramatic recreation of the farmer's year shows us, not by telling us that it is so, but by making us live the fact. We are not asked to note the unity of the farmer and his world; we are asked to experience it.

But, important as Hesiod's description of farming is, why it is important *here* may not be so evident. There are two reasons. Hesiod's section on farming is built up through the juxtaposition of vignettes, each describing a season and its task. It is thus a model, in small, of Hesiod's overall method of composition.[23] Even more importantly, it is a model of the sophistication of the method. For Hesiod the discrete moments of fall or summer, plowing or vintage, are both discrete moments and inseparable parts of a whole, united by the overall rhythm of the year. Hesiod shows us this by using the themes and patterns that run throughout to unite the blocks of material that make up the section. The forms dictated by his art have thus been made to serve Hesiod's particular ends. Out of what might have been the limitations of his description, Hesiod has created its greatness.

Hesiod's description of farming is also, however, a model of the pitfalls into which his method of composition can lead commentators. Scholars have, sometimes consciously and sometimes not, treated Hesiod's poetry as if it were trying to be prose. In the case of the farming section this view has both reinforced, and been reinforced by, another common assumption, that the section is intended to teach the farmer, one by one, each of his various tasks.[24] Having assumed that this is Hesiod's purpose, scholars have either overlooked cases where this clearly is not happening, or treated them as evidence of Hesiod's unsophisticated poetic technique.[25] Hesiod's selection of tasks is spotty; the advice he gives is often elementary; his organization is erratic. But these anomalies appear to be "mistakes," or "infelicities," only if we assume that Hesiod's aim is instruction. If, instead, we allow the section itself to inform us of its intent, we find that Hesiod's "lapses" serve a distinctly dramatic end.[26]

The first anomaly of the farming section is Hesiod's total unconcern with the importance of any given task. Thirty-three lines describe preparations for the fall plowing and sowing (WD 414–47); six describe the sowing itself (WD 465–71). The sixty-line description of winter (WD 504–63) surveys the reactions of cattle, sheep, deer, the young girl inside the house, and even an octopus, to the cold north wind. The only advice it contains is to feed the oxen on half rations and avoid getting wet (WD 557, 560–61). More lines describe a summer picnic (WD 582–96) than are given to the harvest (WD 571–81), to the vintage (WD 609–14), or to the threshing (WD 597–600).

Nor is Hesiod's description of a farmer's work all-inclusive. The tools that Hesiod's farmer prepares, a mortar, pestle, mallet, wagon, and plow, are all for the grain crop. No tools for the vineyard are mentioned.[27] Hesiod refers to sheep, goats and cattle.[28] They presumably tend to themselves, for Hesiod never mentions any tasks that concern them. The vines are mentioned twice, at pruning time and at the vintage. These vines, unlike most, do not require preparing the ground, planting, cultivating, or staking. The olive tree, a staple of Greek agriculture, a third of what has been called the "Mediterranean triad" of olives, vines, and grain, is never mentioned.[29] Hesiod's focus is on the crops, and yet he mentions the need to let the land lie fallow, which is the basis of his system of farming, only in passing.[30] As at WD 473, where the grain is pictured as "bowing to the ground in fullness" (ὧδέ κεν ἀδροσύνῃ στάχυες νεύοιεν ἔραζε), Hesiod the farmer decided whether the grain was ready for harvesting by looking at the grain. Hesiod the poet judges by the more picturesque behavior of a snail (WD 571–72).

As to his organization, Hesiod deliberately creates the impression that he is following the course of the farmer's year, describing the farmer's tasks, one by one, as each follows in its season.[31] The impression is illusory. Hesiod's "chronology" is, in fact, highly impressionistic. Hesiod twice tells us that the farmer's year begins and ends in the spring.[32] This is only natural, since in a Mediterranean climate the growth of crops depends on the winter rainfall, and so both the new breaking of fallow land and the harvest from the previous fall's sowing occur in spring. The farming section of the *Works and Days*, however, begins and ends in the fall, one of the few times when farm tasks are not particularly pressing, so much so, in fact, that Hesiod tells us in his appended section on sailing and trade that this is a good season for sailing, if one feels driven to do so.

Hesiod's description of fall includes both the breaking of fallow and (three times) the harvest (*WD* 462–64 and 473–92). Both of these tasks, as Hesiod's mention of the "gray spring" of harvest-time reminds us (*WD* 491–92), occur not in the fall but in the spring. Hesiod's chronologically correct harvest should be followed by the threshing, a task which requires some haste, as the harvested but unthreshed grain lies under the threat of both weather and pests.[33] Hesiod interposes a gratuitous summer picnic. Finally, Hesiod overlaps his description, beginning in September and ending in the November of the following year. With the new fall appears a new task as well, Hesiod's first mention of the vintage. We can only wonder what happened to the vintage of the previous fall.

Hesiod has a vivid description of sowing, but no advice on what to sow. He tells us that a pair of nine-year-old oxen are best for pulling the plow, but not where to get them, what to do if they fall sick, or when to discard them. He describes picnicking off the meat of a heifer that did not calve, but not what to do with the heifer that did. Moreover, not only is it unlikely that Hesiod would want to teach Perses how to farm the farm he stole from Hesiod, it is even more unlikely that Perses would need to learn. The farmers of Boeotia were farmers because their fathers had been farmers before them. There is nothing in Hesiod's advice that anyone from such a background would not already have known.[34] Hesiod himself misleads us into seeing the section as instruction, a difficulty that will be considered below. Nonetheless, whatever this description of farming is, it is not a farmer's manual.[35]

Hesiod introduces his description of the farmer's year with a passage (*WD* 383–413) that locates the section in the context of the overall poem. The introduction blends the figure of Perses, the warnings against idleness, and the importance of due season into Hesiod's first vivid description of what it feels like to be a farmer. Perses, the need for work, and due season, will reappear again, explicitly, at the end of Hesiod's description of farming, when he turns to sailing. As Hesiod uses these passages to frame the farmer's year, I am using them, and their vision of farming, to frame this book. They will be discussed not here but in the final chapter, when we consider Hesiod's vision of nature.

Hesiod's farmer's year is a poem within a poem. During its course the voices we have become accustomed to, the voices that encourage justice and industry, and that chastise idleness and cheating, the voices addressed to Perses, are almost entirely silent. These themes, the common threads that weave together the separate episodes of the *Works and Days*, are here replaced by a new thread, the rhythm of the seasons.

It is this ebb and flow that makes the farm, for Hesiod, a microcosm of the order of Zeus, and human life on the farm an image of the life we live within the larger whole. As we will see in following it through, the whole itself is simple, although the elements which have gone into its composition—the weather, the needs of the crops, the emotions of men, the lives of birds and beasts—are both numerous and complex. It is the creation of this simplicity that is the hallmark of Hesiod's art, and what has so often led scholars astray.

Hesiod's account of the farmer's year throws us *in medias res*, introducing us to the rhythm of the year with a description of what has just passed and of what is just beginning:[36]

> When the heat of the sharp sunbeams ceases its sweaty warmth,
> and the autumn rain has fallen from mighty Zeus
> and men's skins are turned lighter—for this is when the Dog Star
> hangs only briefly in daytime on the heads of men reared for doom,
> but shares most of its time with night—
> then is the timber you cut with the axe freest from the worm;
> it has dropped its leaves on the ground, and its branching has ceased;
> cut your wood then and remember the timeliness of your work.

> ἦμος δὴ λήγει μένος ὀξέος ἠελίοιο
> καύματος εἰδαλίμου, μετοπωρινὸν ὀμβρήσαντος
> Ζηνὸς ἐρισθενέος, μετὰ δὲ τρέπεται βρότεος χρώς
> πολλὸν ἐλαφρότερος· δὴ γὰρ τότε Σείριος ἀστήρ
> βαιὸν ὑπὲρ κεφαλῆς κηριτρέων ἀνθρώπων
> ἔρχεται ἠμάτιος, πλεῖον δέ τε νυκτὸς ἐπαυρεῖ·
> τῆμος ἀδηκτοτάτη πέλεται τμηθεῖσα σιδήρῳ
> ὕλη, φύλλα δ' ἔραζε χέει πτόρθοιό τε λήγει·
> τῆμος ἄρ' ὑλοτομεῖν μεμνημένος ὥρια ἔργα.   WD 414–22

Hesiod here establishes the pattern that will run throughout the section. His episodes are the seasons, not simply the seasons' tasks. But through his use of a sequence of temporal adjectives that will soon become habitual—"when . . . then . . . then is the time for . . ."—Hesiod subsumes his description of the season into his identification of the task. The impression he thus creates, that our interest is simply in the work to be done, is illusory. The three-sentence vignette, in fact, both creates a sense of a dynamic background and captures, in one frame, the star Sirius, the heat of summer, the relief of Zeus' rain, the trees shedding their leaves in the woods, and the farmer who needs to make a plow. The farmer is part of the scene. Moreover, the way he is introduced, with the pleasant relief of a cool autumn shower, invites us to feel his response to the world.[37] Hesiod is describing, primarily, neither the task, nor the season; he is describing how the task, and the season, feels.[38]

Hesiod's account of farming now moves from woodcutting into preparing tools, and from description into direct advice. This is the second model episode. It is explicitly didactic. Before we consider why this is, however, we should look at what the episode is contributing to the farmer's year. Its tone is expansive and leisurely, reflect-ing Hesiod's choice to begin the year at a time when there is nothing much to do. Hes-iod argues for the best kind of wood for the plowtree, the best age for the oxen and for the plowman, even what the plowman should be given for supper. In the tone of a man resolving an argument over which kind of plow is better, Hesiod advises us to keep two plows, one of each kind (WD 432–33).[39] This is the stuff of an evening's discussion beside the fire, long, leisurely, and theoretical. Hesiod hardly replaced either his oxen or his plowman annually, as they passed the respective ages of nine and forty.[40] I doubt that he personally superintended the dividing of his plowman's loaf into either four or eight parts. What Hesiod is really capturing here is the feeling of early autumn. The harvest has been threshed and stored for the winter. There is plenty of time before one needs to worry about sowing next year's crop. In order to reinforce this sense of leisure Hesiod ignores the fact that he himself, at this time of year, would be getting in the vintage.

Nor is the section as straightforward as it appears. Hesiod's advice is given casu-ally, but with a purpose. The apparently arbitrary list of tools gradually leads us away from woodcutting, theoretically the task of the season. A mortar and pestle lead to an axle, and so to a wagon, and finally to a plow. A discussion of the plow leads to a dis-cussion of the oxen who pull it, and to the man who follows it, and to the man who sows the seed. Here, suddenly, Hesiod points out the voice of the crane, the sign that it is time to start plowing and sowing (WD 448). We realize, belatedly, where the dis-cussion has been taking us.[41] This, the plowing and sowing of late fall, is the critical moment of Hesiod's year. It has come upon us unawares. Hesiod has shown us, along-side the relaxation of early fall, the dangers of becoming absorbed by it.

Of the two openings to the farmer's year, the first, Hesiod's vivid description of how the season feels, will prove to be typical of the section as a whole.[42] His second section, with its straightforward, detailed, and prosaic set of instructions—"Cut three foot for a mortar, and three cubits for a pestle, / and seven for an axle" (ὅλμον μὲν τριπόδην τάμνειν, ὕπερον δὲ τρίπηχυ, / ἄξονα δ' ἑπταπόδην WD 423–24)—has been taken as typical of the farming section. It contains, in fact, the only detailed instruc-tions in the entire section. Nonetheless, its placement and pointedly didactic tone are clearly meant to leave exactly the impression that they have left, that this is a man-ual for farmers.[43] If Hesiod is misread it is his own fault. We must interrupt our passage through the farmer's year to ask, briefly, why Hesiod wants to mislead us.

The primary reason lies in the "you" to whom the Works and Days is addressed. At the opening of the poem this "you" was established as Perses, and so it continued, until we reach the farming section. Here Perses drops out.[44] Hesiod's first description makes us feel the farmer's relief at the coming of the autumn rains. Having identified ourselves with the farmer, the imperatives which follow seem to be addressed to us. We are now the "you" to whom Hesiod speaks. Hesiod's tone of instruction is designed to serve exactly the same end. His didactic stance creates the impression that we are farmers, and as farmers observe the farm from inside. Hesiod has made us part of his description of farming in the simplest way possible. He has just assumed that we are part of it.

If Hesiod's first reason for creating a didactic illusion is to bring us into his descrip-tion; his second is to effect a description of a particular kind. Homer's kind of epic poetry described a world of long ago, sometimes even, as in Odysseus' wanderings, a world of fairytale. The *Theogony* also described a world of prehistory, a world occurring not in human time, but in the mythic time before the order of Zeus. These were the settings familiar to Hesiod's audience. The *Works and Days*, in contrast, is emphatically set in human time. It is about how the world is here and now. In this way it is more like the wisdom literature of the Near East, poetry designed to convey instruction rather than to tell a story, than it is like the Homeric poems. Hesiod may or may not have been familiar with this tradition of poetry.[45] In the farming section he uses something very much like it.

Depending on how we view Hesiod's sophistication, we may see him as resorting to the conventions of wisdom literature as the only way he can think of to describe the day-to-day world around him, or we may think of him as quite consciously employing these conventions for the sake of their implicit assumption that the world being described is the ordinary world. Which we choose is unimportant. What matters is that we understand why Hesiod deliberately creates the impression that he is teaching us to farm. On the one hand, the didactic stance makes us see the world from the farmer's point of view. On the other, it ensures that the world we see is the ordinary world that we, like Hesiod, encounter every day.

Having established his didactic stance and reaped the benefits thereof, Hesiod has no need to continue the lessons.[46] With the possible exception of the final description of the vintage there will be no more detailed instruction. Instead, Hesiod settles into the type of descriptive episode that began the year. But as he moves from woodcutting to the plowing and sowing of late fall, he slightly changes his technique. Overall, the farming section is composed of a series of vignettes, one for each season and its characteristic task. But for the fall sowing we are given not one vignette, but four, one describing the voice of the crane, one following the movement of the farmer and his men onto the field, one of the first moment of plowing, and one of the hopes and forebodings which accompany it. Hesiod is picking up the tempo.[47] In terms of concrete advice Hesiod's first vignette (*WD* 448–57) only repeats what he has already said in the course of the wood-cutting. What the section does contribute is a change of tone. We are no longer thinking of the best age for the oxen; we are worrying about having them at all (*WD* 453–55). Then we described building wagons. Only a fool would think about building wagons now (*WD* 455–57).

With the second vignette of sowing (*WD* 458–62), the rhythm of Hesiod's verse becomes even more urgent, and more personal. From his initial advice, "you and your slaves make haste," Hesiod moves to the farmer alone. The more urgent the task, the greater is the farmer's involvement. Hesiod employs the association in reverse, underlining the urgency by speaking as if only the farmer were involved. He will employ this device again in the harvest and, conversely, in the threshing, where the urgency of the task is downplayed by being left to the servants.[48] Here, in the fall plowing, Hesiod ends by committing the plowing entirely into the farmer's hands. Scholars have wondered what happened to the forty-year-old plowman.[49] He has, in the urgency of the task, given way to our sense that this is a job to do ourselves.

But first we run into a brick wall. As we, with ever-increasing haste, move into the field for the fall sowing, Hesiod suddenly tells us: "Plow in spring; if you plow again

in the summer / the land will not play you false" (ἔαρι ποιεῖν· θέρεος δὲ νεωμένη οὔ
σ' ἀπατήσει WD 462). It is irrational and unkind of Hesiod to tell us that we should
plow in the spring, when it is already fall.[50] An abrupt change in the rhythm of the
verse emphasizes the abruptness of the chronological jump. The line is meant to pull
us up short. It reflects the farmer's last-minute despair, that the land which he is about
to sow has not, after all, been sufficiently prepared. If it has not, it is now too late. The
chronological anomaly forces us to feel the farmer's momentary despair. It also reinforces the theme of due season: we must do our plowing in time; later is too late.

The next vignette describes the moment the entire year has been leading to:

> Pray to Zeus-Under-Earth and to Demeter the Holy
> that the sacred corn of Demeter be heavy when ready for harvest;
> pray as you first begin plowing, a hand on top of the top of the plowstilt
> and with your goad come down on the backs of the oxen straining
> at the peg at the plowpole's middle; and let a small boy behind you
> make work for the birds with his mattock, covering up the seeds.

> εὔχεσθαι δὲ Διὶ χθονίῳ Δημήτερί θ' ἁγνῇ
> ἐκτελέα βρίθειν Δημήτερος ἱερὸν ἀκτήν
> ἀρχόμενος τὰ πρῶτ' ἀρότου, ὅτ' ἂν ἄκρον ἐχέτλης
> χειρὶ λαβὼν ὄρπηκι βοῶν ἐπὶ νῶτον ἵκηαι
> ἔνδρυον ἑλκόντων μεσάβῳ· ὁ δὲ τυτθὸς ὄπισθεν
> δμῷος ἔχων μακέλην πόνον ὀρνίθεσσι τιθείη
> σπέρμα κατακρύπτων·   WD 465–71

A moment is captured here in which farmer, oxen, slave-boy and birds have come
together into a single picture. The picture resolves the increasing urgency of the previous paragraphs and recreates the farmer's feeling, as he begins once again a familiar,
and yet anxiously anticipated, task.[51] Hesiod's description demands that we visualize
the scene—the oxen struggling in harness, the small slave-boy with his mattock, the
birds he strives to frustrate. But we are asked not to see, but to feel, the plowstilt, the
stick as it comes down on the backs of the oxen, the response of the oxen as they struggle in their harness.[52] Hesiod shows us our place in the picture. It is, once more, the
farmer's place.

But perhaps the most memorable detail of the scene is the littlest one, the slave-
boy. It is, to say the least, surprising that Hesiod devotes so much attention to a
slave-boy, when he does not so much as mention the man central to the task, the one
scattering the seed (WD 445–46). The boy himself is surprising, and has, quite rea-
sonably, given rise to emendations. It is absurd to think that this job needs to be done
by a child, or to think that every farmer has just such a small slave-boy at his disposal.[53]
But then neither is it necessary to have Bibline wine at a summer picnic (WD 589).
The detail does much, in either case, to bring the picture to life. Hesiod's specification
of a small slave-boy would be absurd in general instruction. In a dramatic picture of
the fall sowing it is the detail that rivets the imagination.

As he moves ahead in the furrow, the work becoming ever more rhythmic and
familiar, the crucial first moment and its anxiety receding into the past, the farmer's

thoughts begin to turn from the task at hand to the prospect before him—the coming harvest. As the farmer's thoughts jump ahead to the spring so, out of all chronological order, does Hesiod's account of farming. Hesiod shows us the farmer's hopes and fears, and reinforces his own warning by giving us three contradictory pictures of the harvest, one of the good harvest which comes if we follow Hesiod's advice, one of the bad harvest which comes if we ignore it, and, finally, one of a harvest rescued from disaster, at the last moment, through the inscrutable will of Zeus.

The vivid detail of Hesiod's descriptions manipulates our feelings of identification. We share the reasonable and cheerful expectations of the early plowman, the first description; only to be crushed, in the second description, by the dismal prospects haunting the mind of the farmer late at his plow. As we experience the late plowman's despair, we also feel, with the gradual dawning of a remedy (*WD* 483–85), a sudden hope. With the slow unfolding of the remedy, detail by excruciating detail, the nearly impossible occurs. Despite our folly in plowing late, the harvest is saved. Hesiod's final warning—"Keep all this well in your mind—let the grayness of spring when it comes / not go unheeded by you, nor unheeded the rain in due season" (ἐν θυμῷ δ' εὖ πάντα φυλάσσεο, μηδέ σε λήθοι / μήτ' ἔαρ γιγνόμενον πολιὸν μήθ' ὥριος ὄμβρος *WD* 491–92)—depends upon this feeling of having been snatched from the brink of disaster. Literally, the line should mean that we must keep in mind the chance that we might be rescued. In fact, Hesiod is telling us to remember how close we came to disaster.[54]

Hesiod's next paragraph simply defies chronological understanding. He advises us to prepare for the helplessness of winter when, as he emphatically points out, it is winter already. His final words—"While it is still midsummer, tell your servants, 'It will not be so / always—make huts for yourselves'" (δείκνυε δὲ δμώεσσι θέρεος ἔτι μέσσου ἐόντος· / "οὐκ αἰεὶ θέρος ἐσσεῖται· ποιεῖσθε καλιάς" *WD* 502–3)—abandon even the pretense of chronology.[55] The theme of the vignette is, nonetheless, obvious; it is the story of the ant and the grasshopper, a warning against, as Hesiod says, "empty hope." Hesiod's description of sowing ended with the unexpected success of the harvest, a dramatic rendition of the farmer's feeling as, finishing the fall sowing, he views the harvest ahead. The first lines of *this* section—"In wintertime pass by the seats at the forge where men chatter in warmth, / when the cold keeps a man from his work" (πὰρ δ' ἴθι χαλκεῖον θῶκον καὶ ἐπαλέα λέσχην / ὥρη χειμερίη *WD* 493–94)—remind us abruptly, and firmly, that that harvest was only speculation. It is still winter. The grain is not yet in the barn.

Above all, what Hesiod's transitional paragraph does is to make us uncomfortable. We are told to work, but we are not told what we can do. We are warned of the "helplessness" (ἀμηχανίη *WD* 496) of winter, when it is already winter. We are told that we should have seen to these things last summer; it is too late now. This sense of frustration carries into Hesiod's long and detailed description of the month of January ("Lenaion"). The description stands out as exceptional among Hesiod's vignettes. It occupies nearly a fourth of the farming section, ranges over the whole extent of the farmer's world, and gives us nothing to do.[56] When the farmer is finally mentioned he is advised to dress warmly and to avoid the north wind (*WD* 505, 557). This *is* the helplessness of winter. When Hesiod turns from the north wind to winter clothing we are impressed not by the farmer's ingenuity, nor by the vulnerability he must protect. Our impression is a simple sense of relief from the cold.[57] This is winter, the other side of the balance, and the relief we feel now matches the relief we felt at first, from the heat of summer.

In contrast to the abrupt and despairing introduction of January—"The month Lenaion, dreadful days all, that would skin the hide from an ox—/beware that month" (μῆνα δὲ Ληναιῶνα, κάκ᾽ ἤματα, βουδόρα πάντα, / τοῦτον ἀλεύασθαι *WD* 504–5)— Hesiod's lengthy account of winter gives way only gradually to the opening of spring. But spring comes, finally, and with it an increase in the tempo of the year. Seven lines describing the signs of the season culminate in the arrival of the swallow, and all of the agricultural advice we are given: "before this, prune your vines" (τὴν φθάμενος οἴνας περιταμνέμεν *WD* 570).[58] It is a little perverse to give us as a sign of the season a bird who arrives only when the season is over. It is also a rather abrupt way to introduce the vineyard.

But we have barely been told about the vines, before, in the next line, Hesiod is scolding us for wasting too much time on them: "But when the House-Carrier climbs from the ground to the plant, avoiding / the Pleiades, then is no longer the season for digging round vines—" (ἀλλ᾽ ὁπότ᾽ ἂν φερέοικος ἀπὸ χθονὸς ἂμ φυτὰ βαίνῃ / Πληιάδας φεύγων, τότε δὴ σκάφος οὐκέτι οἰνέων *WD* 571–72). The hurry of Hesiod's advice also indicates why, here and at the end of the year, the vines are introduced at all. Like Edgar's battle with Edmund in *King Lear*, the vines serve to distract our attention from the hero of the piece. It is the grain that we should have been thinking about. The importance of the harvest is underlined by the attention we have, inadvertently, directed elsewhere. We reproach ourselves, as we hurry into the field.

In contrast to the sixty lines (*WD* 504–63) which described the single month of January, less than ten lines (*WD* 564–73) have moved us from early spring to harvest-time, a space of more than three months.[59] The long, frustrating wait of winter is thus contrasted with the bustle of spring. The two together also repeat, and balance, the gradual giving way of the woodcutting to the hurry of the sowing. Hesiod draws out the parallel of sowing and harvest in his description, a parallel already intimated in his opening proverbs (*WD* 383–92). Here vine-pruning, there woodcutting, is introduced to distract our attention from the crops. In both, Hesiod underlines the urgency of the task by moving from a farmer commanding his slaves, to farmer and slaves together, to the farmer himself. In the case of the harvest this urgency serves as content as well as form; Hesiod's only piece of advice is to get up early.

Then, just as suddenly as it began, the work is over. A summer picnic follows, with a return to the relaxed, extended, and predictable sequence of temporal adjectives which we last saw in Hesiod's description of woodcutting.[60] The scene serves as a vivid contrast to the rush of spring and fall, and as a direct counterpoise to Hesiod's description of winter. As the Persians said to Cyrus, then we had everything bad, now we have everything good.[61] Cold has given way to heat, sparing to abundance, anxious watching to the security of a harvest safely in. Hesiod reinforces our sense of leisure by postponing the threshing until after his summer picnic. When it comes, it comes almost as an afterthought, an impression Hesiod strengthens by inverting his usual sequence of season, then task: "For your servants—bid them thresh the holy grain of Demeter / when, at his first appearing, Orion has shown his strength" (δμωσὶ δ᾽

ἐποτρύνειν Δημήτερος ἱερὸν ἀκτήν / δινέμεν, εὖτ' ἂν πρῶτα φανῇ σθένος Ὠαρίωνος *WD* 597–98).

The grain, now safely indoors, can be left to the servants to thresh. With the results of his labor safe, the farmer recedes into the role of overseer, while Hesiod's vignette fades into a list of loose ends to be tied up, storing and measuring the grain, hiring and firing servants,[62] acquiring a guard dog, bringing in fodder and bedding for the winter. The paragraph ends: "Then, after that, your servants / may relieve their poor legs; and do you take the yoke from your oxen." (αὐτὰρ ἔπειτα / δμῶας ἀναψῦξαι φίλα γούνατα καὶ βόε λῦσαι *WD* 607–8). It has been a long year. Hesiod has carefully lent to its end the proper note of finality.

Except just for the vintage. It arrives unexpectedly, both because it was not mentioned in our account of the previous fall, and because we have not had occasion to think about the vines since spring. Hesiod's account of how many days and nights to set out and cover the grapes is detailed and unhurried, like his account of the wood-cutting. While our attention is so occupied, the Pleiades, just as at *WD* 572, where they signaled the unexpected arrival of the harvest, have moved back into their usual emphatic position (*WD* 615).[63] We are, in mid-line, back at the time for fall sowing. Hesiod has failed to prepare us for it. By neglecting the wood-cutting, and introducing instead the vintage, he has once more distracted our attention. The year has come full circle. Before we noticed, just when the year was complete, it begins again. Hesiod's little surprise serves to reinforce our sense of the cycle which is the farmer's year. There are no closures. The end of every season, and of every year, is the beginning of the next.

A simple description of farming does not need to masquerade as a manual. We can appreciate the simple joys of the countryside, the pastures and hills, the ripening corn and the lowing oxen, without any pretense that we are learning to farm. And so we do, in the bucolic poetry of nineteenth-century England. It is precisely this that Hesiod's didactic stance avoids. In the first place, instruction has no place for the fuzzy edges of bucolic poetry. By portraying itself as didactic, Hesiod's description of farming insists on its claim to hard reality. But more importantly, a farmer's manual is addressed to, not merely written about, farmers. We are to experience farming from inside. Only thus, to Hesiod's mind, can we see the inner truths that farming holds for human life. Only in this way can we come to understand what it means to "work at the tasks that the gods have set for men to do" (ἐργάζεο . . . ἔργα, τά τ' ἀνθρώποισι θεοὶ διετεκμήραντο *WD* 397–98).

Hesiod is not teaching us how to farm. He is teaching us what the cycle of the year, with its balance of summer and winter, of good and evil, of profit and risk, of anxiety and relaxation, implies about the will of Zeus.[64] Within1 the overarching framework of the farmer's year Hesiod has brought together, into one dramatic unity, the stars and winds, the heat and cold, drought and rain, the birds and beasts of the forest, the crops and the fields and the oxen who work them, the farmer and his workmen, the small slave-boy and the young girl "still unknowing in the works of golden Aphrodite" (*WD* 521), and a crane, a snail, and an octopus. They are united by the drama of Hesiod's seasons, a drama created by aberrations of description, allowed by the poet because he had no intention of teaching farming in his poem. His intention was rather to show us how the order of Zeus permeates nature and includes ourselves. This is a fact about farming as important to the gift-gobbling kings as it is to the farmers, and as important to us as it was to Hesiod.

2

THE MYTHIC
BACKGROUND

Hesiod's Outlook

Hesiod's prologue to the *Works and Days* closes unexpectedly. After eight lines describing the power of Zeus he suddenly declares: "Hear, see, give ear; straighten court judgments with justice. / This is your part. I would wish to speak very truth to Perses" (κλῦθι ἰδὼν ἀιών τε, δίκῃ δ' ἴθυνε θέμιστας / τύνη· ἐγὼ δέ κε Πέρσῃ ἐτήτυμα μυθησαίμην *WD* 9–10). Perses who? Who Perses is, or why Hesiod should address the poem to him, is not explained. Hesiod moves directly into his description of the two goddesses Strife, a bad goddess who causes war, thievery, and litigation, and a good goddess who encourages men to work and keep to straight justice.

But the topic of the poem to come is still unclear. Hesiod's opening appeal to Zeus has described the many changes of human life: "Lightly he makes a man strong and lightly maims one who is strong. / Lightly he lessens the famous and will exalt the obscure" (ῥητοί τ' ἄρρητοί τε Διὸς μεγάλοιο ἕκητι. / ῥέα μὲν γὰρ βριάει, ῥέα δὲ βριάοντα χαλέπτει *WD* 5–6). That Hesiod should open with Zeus and the fluctuations of human life is no surprise. To Hesiod, "Zeus" and "the gods" are interchangeable,[1] and the divine lies at the center of human experience. Nor does Hesiod, in turning from Zeus to Perses, cease to see Zeus as central to the poem. Within ten lines the superiority of the elder (that is, the good) Strife is demonstrated by Zeus' having placed her "in earth in its roots" (*WD* 19); within twenty more, Hesiod is urging Perses to follow straight justice (*WD* 36), the kind that Zeus favors; and within another ten we are launched on the story of Pandora (*WD* 47), a story that explains that human life is as it is because "there is no way / to escape from the purpose of Zeus" (οὗτος οὔ τί πῃ ἔστι Διὸς νόον ἐξαλέασθαι *WD* 105).

Nor has Perses been forgotten; he too has only gone before. As with Zeus, Hesiod introduces Perses and then, apparently, drops him. This is not merely carelessness. Hesiod's introduction of Perses also introduces, intertwined in his story, the opposition that will turn out to be central to the *Works and Days*. The theme is introduced only gradually, hidden within a complex example of one of Hesiod's favorite literary devices, chiasmi, or cross-parallels. We have seen the structure before, and emphatically, in lines like (translated word for word) "Alike unfamed and famed / Spoken and unspoken of, at the will of great Zeus" (ὁμῶς ἄφατοί τε φατοί τε / ῥητοί τ' ἄρρητοί τε Διὸς μεγάλοιο ἕκητι *WD* 3–4).[2] By establishing it as the foundation of his Proem Hesiod has fixed the A B / B A pattern in our minds before we encounter it in our introduction to Perses.

Hesiod shows us how to find the meaning underlying his initial vignette by showing us the pattern within which it can be found. This, as it turns out, is itself a model for the poem as a whole, which shows us that there is an underlying meaning to human life, but one we can only perceive through a sensitivity to the patterns life contains. Here, however, the pattern is a simple one: A B / B A, and so is the story, about the two kinds of Strife. The bad Strife fosters war. In contrast the good Strife fosters the opposite of war, peaceful competition.[3] Hesiod expands his declaration that Zeus has set the good Strife "in earth in its roots" (γαίης τ' ἐν ῥίζῃσι *WD* 19) with a five-line description of how she encourages farming. The good Strife is now farming. The bad Strife changes, in response, to the opposite of farming—hanging around in the marketplace, listening to court cases (as, we now discover, Perses has been doing), and trying (emphatically) to get hold of other men's goods (*WD* 33–34). In other words, the bad Strife now encourages thievery. In response, the good Strife, Hesiod's one, refrains from such attempts. The good Strife, which keeps men on the farm, is thus linked to straight justice. The bad Strife works through a justice which is crooked. For example (we finally learn), Perses bribed the judges in order to get his brother's share of the farm (*WD* 37–39).

Hesiod has used the two Strifes, presented as the patron goddesses of himself and Perses, to summarize his poem.[4] Both goddesses illustrate Hesiod's central truth, that one cannot gain wealth without work. Hesiod's Strife illustrates the point by succeeding; Perses' does so by failing. In the course of his series of oppositions, however, Hesiod has also turned Perses' Strife from an obvious evil, war, into a specious good, the gaining of wealth through crooked decisions. Similarly, the self-evident good of a well-filled barn has turned into the rather less obvious good of hard work and self-restraint.[5] The good Strife does not look quite as good as she did at first. We are also forced to reconsider the initial description of the other Strife: "The one increases vile war and enmity; she is cruel. / No mortal loves her! Only under Necessity / through designs of the Immortals do they honor her, this harsh Strife" (ἡ μὲν γὰρ πόλεμόν τε κακὸν καὶ δῆριν ὀφέλλει, / σχετλίη· οὔ τις τήν γε φιλεῖ βροτός, ἀλλ' ὑπ' ἀνάγκης / ἀθανάτων βουλῇσιν Ἔριν τιμῶσι βαρεῖαν *WD* 15–16). This no longer seems entirely accurate. Perses, at any rate, looks like he is following her with great enthusiasm. Hesiod has managed to introduce, along with the two kinds of Strife, both the essential opposition of the *Works and Days*, and the ambiguity of that opposition. Good and evil, in the *Works and Days*, are opposites, but not simply so. They are also twins.[6]

Nonetheless, Hesiod insists that his way is the best way, and that not only Perses, but also the "gift-gobbling kings," are fools to follow their particular Strife. The first major section of the *Works and Days*, which includes the myths of Pandora and of the Five Ages and the fable of the Hawk and the Nightingale, explains why. Zeus *wants* human life to be hard. Perses' and the kings' attempt to win an easy living is therefore doomed to failure. The section thus provides a mythological framework for Hesiod's exploration of justice and farming. But before we begin our consideration of Hesiod's myths, we must look briefly at an even larger framework, the views shared by Hesiod and his contemporaries, and assumed in Hesiod's poetry. The three questions that we need to address have already appeared, implicitly, with the goddesses Strife. How did Hesiod understand the gods, and myth, to operate in the world? Does he not distinguish between a practical necessity, like farming, and a moral necessity, like justice? And what does Hesiod mean by making good and evil into twins?

Hesiod, if he wrote, wrote in what we think of as capital letters. In other words, he no more distinguished in writing than any of us do in speech between Strife, the goddess, and strife as we encounter it every day in our ordinary lives. The Strife that is good for human beings, encouraging potter to strive with potter and singer with singer (*WD* 24–26), *is* the strife of potter and potter. This is to say that she, like all of Hesiod's gods, is immanent in a world which she informs, and in which she is manifested.[7] Hesiod does not see the divine as transcendent, transcending and acting upon a world separate from itself. We may think of the difference thus: Jehovah, as a transcendent God, acts upon the earth and the heavens; Zeus is born from them.[8] Jehovah creates nature; Zeus manifests it.

The difficulty with seeing Hesiod's gods as immanent occurs when we remember the myths. In the genealogical mode of the *Theogony*, Zeus is the final expression of a divine order which has appeared spontaneously. This is Hesiod's expression of his immanence. In the narrative mode of the poem, however, Zeus is transcendent, and with a vengeance. So far from being one with either "the gods" or his own divine order, Zeus, in the narrative of the *Theogony*, imposes his rule through a combination of force and deceit. In the *Theogony*, Hesiod alternates between these two ways of presenting Zeus. In the *Works and Days*, Zeus is presented as transcendent only in the myths of Pandora and the Five Ages. To understand the discrepancy we must look briefly at Hesiod's sense of myth.

A "myth," to Hesiod, is certainly not what we often mean by "myth"—simply a false story. Nor is it, although it is a story, simply "made up." It is not fictional, but traditional, something one has heard, rather than something one invents.[9] Nonetheless, the *Theogony* is filled with genealogies, and even gods, who seem to have originated with Hesiod. A clue to the problem is provided, again, by the goddesses Strife. In the *Theogony* a single god, Strife, is born to Night (*Th.* 225). The opening words of the *Works and Days* imply that Hesiod has changed his mind: "After all, there is no single breed of Strife, but on earth there are two of her" (Οὐκ ἄρα μοῦνον ἔην Ἐρίδων γένος, ἀλλ' ἐπὶ γαῖαν / εἰσι δύω *WD* 11–12).[10] The particle which Hesiod uses here (ἄρα), translated as "after all," indicates discovery.[11] Hesiod has created a new myth. But his myth, his new vision of the goddesses is to him a discovery, and not an invention.[12]

To the extent that Hesiod believes that he can "discover" a god, or the true account of a mythological event, he clearly feels that there is some sort of evidence, discoverable in his experience, by which he can judge. Myth is not simply arbitrary. On the other hand, Hesiod is perfectly comfortable returning to a single Strife at the end of the *Works and Days*, when she happens to suit his purposes better (*WD* 804). Discovering a second Strife is not like discovering America; Strife, unlike America, can be discovered and then undiscovered again. The appropriate answer to the question we tend to ask about the myths—did the Greeks believe in their myths? did they think they were true?—is not, therefore, either "yes" or "no." The question cannot be answered either positively or negatively, because it cannot be answered at all. The question, did Hesiod think that the myths were true? proposes a simple dichotomy between true or false, belief or disbelief, which myth by its very nature denies. Hesiod's statement that there is not one Strife, but two is, for him, "true," just as his account of the birth of Aphrodite is the true one.[13] This does not mean that he thinks that Night bore the Strifes in the same way that his mother bore himself and Perses, or that he sees Aphrodite's emergence from the foam surrounding Ouranos' severed penis as the same kind of thing as his, or Agamemnon's, trip to Aulis.

Perhaps the easiest way to talk about myth is to distinguish between human and mythic time. "Human time" is historical; its events have occurred within a framework of time and space continuous with our own experience. "Mythic time" is the time of prehistory, the time before the world of our experience arose.[14] It is therefore, by definition, not continuous with the time of our daily experience. It exists, rather, as a way to explore our world, by positing a prior world that is not ours, and from which our world came to be.[15] When we ask if a myth is "true" we should mean, does it reveal a truth about our world? What we often mean instead is, could it really have occurred in human time? The answer, by definition, is "no." To conclude from this that the myth is therefore false is essentially to conclude that there is no such thing as mythic time, and that an event either obeys the conditions of human time, or is not an event. This is not to find the myth false; it is to deny that there is any such thing as myth.

It is when Hesiod is working within mythic time that his gods appear as transcendent actors upon the world. This is not because Hesiod sees gods as transcendent, but because actors and sufferers is the mode that myth most frequently, although not always, uses to express its sort of truth. When Hesiod is discussing human time, that is, the world he and Perses and the gift-gobbling kings live in, he presents Zeus as immanent. This is Zeus manifested, primarily, in nature. There is a reason for this.

A "natural" event is not singular. It is rather one manifestation of a principle which holds true for all the individuals of nature, and so links them into an order. For Hesiod this "principle" is Zeus, and for this reason I use the phrase "the order of Zeus" for Hesiod's conception of the cosmos. In Exodus, or the Gospels, where God is understood to be transcendent, a miracle, an event contrary to the ordinary workings of nature, is paradigmatically divine. For Hesiod, who views Zeus and his order as immanent, the paradigmatically divine event is a natural one.[16] Given this, it is clear that our tendency to see an event as *either* natural *or* caused by God would be incomprehensible to Hesiod. Hesiod can say, interchangeably, "Zeus rains" (*WD* 415–16, 488), or that it rains because the north wind draws up and releases water from the rivers (*WD* 550–53), either that Zeus "accomplishes" the seasons (*WD* 564–65), or that the seasons pass. What happens according to nature, and what happens because of Zeus, are, for Hesiod, one and the same.

Justice, to a modern audience, is a moral question; farming is a practical one. The first tells us how to live, the second merely how to make a living. From a Christian, not to mention a Kantian, perspective the primary distinction between the practical and the moral is that the practical is done for the sake of gain, while the moral is done for its own sake. A truly just person is just not because justice pays, but because justice is right. It was not so to Hesiod.[17] As he says:

> I would not be just myself
> nor would I have my son so—for it is a bad thing
> to be just if the unjust should get more justice than the just man;
> but I do not believe that yet Zeus of Counsel will make such an ending.

> νῦν δὴ ἐγὼ μήτ' αὐτὸς ἐν ἀνθρώποισι δίκαιος
> εἴην μήτ' ἐμὸς υἱός, ἐπεὶ κακὸν ἄνδρα δίκαιον
> ἔμμεναι, εἰ μείζω γε δίκην ἀδικώτερος ἕξει·
> ἀλλὰ τά γ' οὔ πω ἔολπα τελεῖν Δία μητιόεντα.   WD 270–73

For Hesiod what is right is, quite simply, what is in accordance with the will of Zeus, and the will of Zeus is what makes one way succeed and another fail. The will of Zeus is as close as Hesiod comes to what we call "moral" action. But since Hesiod's gods are immanent rather than transcendent, the divine will is to be discovered not in a sacred or a philosophic text, but in the day-to-day world in which Hesiod lives. Our life manifests Zeus' will. What succeeds in the world is what Zeus has prescribed for us. Farming, which is the necessary way in which we procure food, is, therefore, necessarily also the will of Zeus. This is also how Hesiod knows that Zeus has placed Strife in the roots of the earth. Similarly, if it is true that only justice succeeds, this is sufficient proof that justice is Zeus' will. Morally right action is action in accordance with the will of god. Practically right action is action which succeeds in the world. The two are, and must be, for Hesiod, one and the same.[18]

The fact that Hesiod does not divorce moral and practical good sheds light, as well, on his feeling that good and evil are deceptive, and on his sense that what men require, above all, is understanding. Human beings may not desire *moral* goodness, and choose instead to pursue evil. But not to desire success, which is *practically* good, is simply a contradiction in terms.[19] No one wants to be a failure. If people choose what is practically evil it is not because their will is defective, but because their understanding is. People choose what is bad for them because they do not understand the consequences of what they are choosing. When Socrates made this claim, many hundreds of years after Hesiod, he attributed the fact to our own failure, or inability, to know what is best. When Hesiod made it, he attributed it to Zeus' deliberate intention to make the world deceptive. Human beings find it difficult to see which is the good and which the evil Strife. For Hesiod this is because Zeus has chosen this particular way of making human life hard.

Pandora and the Nature of Hardship

The two myths which open the *Works and Days* are inconsistent as narrative, but not inconsistent in theme.[20] The two operate as, for example, the two accounts of creation which open Genesis, as parallel ways of exploring the same problem. What Hesiod is exploring is the nature of human hardship. He does this, as a myth does, by showing us how the hardship of human life came about. The myth of Pandora is explicitly told for this reason. The myth of the Five Ages is another story to the same effect: "There is another story—if you like I will tell you its substance . . . / [about] how the gods and mortal men spring from the same beginnings" (εἰ δ' ἐθέλεις, ἑτερόν τοι ἐγὼ λόγον ἐκκορυφώσω . . . / ὡς ὁμόθεν γεγάασι θεοὶ θνητοί τ' ἄνθρωποι *WD* 106, 108). As the gods, or Zeus, are said in this myth to "make" each successive generation, Hesiod can only mean by "springing from the same beginnings" that gods and human beings once lived alike. This is precisely how Hesiod describes the golden age: "They lived like gods, their hearts undisturbed by cares, / without labour, without misery" (ὥστε θεοὶ δ' ἔζωον, ἀκηδέα θυμὸν ἔχοντες / νόσφιν ἄτερ τε πόνου καὶ ὀϊζύος *WD* 112–13).[21] What the myth goes on to describe is precisely what the Pandora myth describes, how human life, once free from care and hardship, became hard.

The Pandora myth of the *Works and Days* expands and adapts an episode out of the *Theogony*'s Prometheus myth, but to serve a very different end.[22] Hesiod, here, is not primarily interested in the rivalry of Prometheus and Zeus, nor even in the fact that human life has become hard. Any fool can see that. What he is interested in is *how* human life became hard. It became hard through concealment.[23] The hiding of man's livelihood introduces the myth, and connects its introduction to Zeus' hiding of fire from man. Prometheus steals fire back by hiding it in a fennel (or narthex) stalk. Zeus retaliates by hiding a bitch's mind and a thief's heart inside a beautiful woman. Epimetheus accepts the package without looking. Zeus wins. We lose.

There are two sorts of hiding involved here. The first is "hiding" in the way that Zeus originally "hid" fire. This is hiding in the way that seeds are "hidden" in the ground—so that it seems as if nothing were there. The second hiding is like Prometheus' bringing fire down to human beings hidden in the fennel stalk—it is clear that something is there, but what is there is not what it seems to be.[24] Hesiod has taken this kind of hiding from the sacrifice myth of the *Theogony*, where Prometheus tricked Zeus into choosing the worse portion of the sacrifice by hiding the bones inside a little meat and fat, making it look good, and the meat inside the stomach, making it look bad. This kind of hiding can make something appear to be different than it is. Even more, it can make something appear to be the opposite of what it is. This is the sort of hiding Hesiod associates with Pandora. As Zeus predicts:[25]

> "Son of Iapetus, whose cunning excels all others',
> you are glad now you have stolen fire and have cheated
> my mind; but it shall be to yourself
> great mischief and also to men of the days that are still to be.
> To them to match their gaining of fire I shall give

an evil in which they will all joy,
welcoming each in his heart his own ill."
So he spoke and laughed outright, the Father of gods and men . . .

" Ἰαπετιονίδη, πάντων πέρι μήδεα εἰδώς,
χαίρεις πῦρ κλέψας καὶ ἐμὰς φρένας ἠπεροπεύσας,
σοί τ' αὐτῷ μέγα πῆμα καὶ ἀνδράσιν ἐσσομένοισιν.
τοῖς δ' ἐγὼ ἀντὶ πυρὸς δώσω κακόν, ᾧ κεν ἅπαντες
τέρπωνται κατὰ θυμόν, ἑὸν κακὸν ἀμφαγαπῶντες."
ὣς ἔφατ', ἐκ δ' ἐγέλασσε πατὴρ ἀνδρῶν τε θεῶν τε   *WD* 54–59

Zeus' laugh should dispel any notion that Hesiod sees him as a beneficent deity. The point of Zeus' trick, and the part that particularly tickles him, is that men will deliberately choose their own destruction.[26] They will do so because of the particular nature of Pandora, an evil hidden inside of a good.

The "thievish way" which is Pandora's constant characteristic is, in light of her name, doubly ironic. Pandora is above all a gift, named All-Gift, "for all that live / in Olympus had given her as a gift, as a bane / to men that live by bread" (ὅτι πάντες Ὀλύμπια δώματ' ἔχοντες / δῶρον ἐδώρησαν, πῆμ' ἀνδράσιν ἀλφηστῇσιν *WD* 81–82).[27] It is because Pandora is a gift, a good that the unwary Epimetheus believes comes for nothing, that Epimetheus is tricked. But Pandora is even more deceptive; she is a gift which conceals a theft. Hesiod's startling juxtaposition: "Gave her as a gift, a bane to men" makes his point clear. There are no free gifts. There is, for human beings, no good without hardship. In apparently getting something for nothing we, rather, lost the goods we formerly had.[28]

Hesiod's description of the acceptance of Pandora also makes it clear why the role of accepting her belongs to Epimetheus, "Afterthought," in contrast to Prometheus, "Forethought:"

> and Afterthought never bethought him how Prometheus-Forethought
>   had said:
> "Never accept a gift, that comes from Olympian Zeus;
> send it back lest in some way some ill come about
> to mortal men." But Afterthought took it
> and—only when he had taken the evil thing—understood.

οὐδ' Ἐπιμηθεύς
ἐφράσαθ', ὥς οἱ ἔειπε Προμηθεὺς μή ποτε δῶρον
δέξασθαι πὰρ Ζηνὸς Ὀλυμπίου, ἀλλ' ἀποπέμπειν
ἐξοπίσω, μή πού τι κακὸν θνητοῖσι γένηται.
αὐτὰρ ὁ δεξάμενος ὅτε δὴ κακὸν εἶχ ἐνόησεν.   *WD* 85–89

The description closes off this episode of the myth in a ring pattern, and makes it clear that the moral of the story lies here, in the theme of evil hidden inside of good, and in Epimetheus' name. Like Hesiod's utterly useless man (*WD* 296–97), Epimetheus neither considered himself nor listened to one who did.[29] Zeus has given us hardship by hiding evil inside of good. We fall for the trick because we, like Epimetheus, don't see the need to look beyond the surface.

The first theme of the Pandora myth is that for human beings nothing is purely good; something that looks entirely good, like Pandora, or wealth won without work, always turns out to contain evil as well. The second theme complements the first: evil is inescapable. In the *Theogony*, woman herself is the evil that balances the good of fire (a "beautiful evil in exchange for good" καλὸν κακὸν ἀντ' ἀγαθοῖο *Th.* 585). In the *Works and Days*, Pandora appears to be this evil until, rather unexpectedly, she takes the lid off of the great jar of troubles. This second episode seems to have been introduced because even Hesiod could not blame *all* the ills of human life on the existence of women. Moreover, the jar enables Hesiod to bring us from a condition where we had only goods, and the jar kept all the evils hidden, to a condition where we have only evil, and good, in particular our livelihood, is hidden.[30] The end of the myth thus returns us to our condition at the myth's introduction, completing the ring pattern, and reminding us of the reason why the myth is being told:

> But other ten thousand evils have gone wandering among men;
> the earth is full of these ills, and the sea is full,
> And diseases by day and every night, too,
> come of themselves, and bring
> to mortal men trouble—in silence, for Zeus has stolen their voice.
> So true it is there is no way
> to escape from the purpose of Zeus.

> ἄλλα δὲ μυρία λυγρὰ κατ' ἀνθρώπους ἀλάληται·
> πλείη μὲν γὰρ γαῖα κακῶν, πλείη δὲ θάλασσα·
> νοῦσοι δ' ἀνθρώποισι ἐφ' ἡμέρῃ, αἱ δ' ἐπὶ νυκτὶ
> αὐτόμαται φοιτῶσι κακὰ θνητοῖσι φέρουσαι
> σιγῇ, ἐπεὶ φωνὴν ἐξείλετο μητίετα Ζεύς.
> οὕτως οὔ τί πῃ ἔστι Διὸς νόον ἐξαλέασθαι.   *WD* 100–4

"In silence" is the key, and most sinister note of the passage. We cannot avoid diseases because Zeus took away their voices, and we cannot hear them coming. Hesiod has here returned to the first idea of hiding, the hiding of something so that it cannot be perceived at all. Some evils, like Pandora, men may avoid or mitigate through foresight and understanding. But not all evils.[31]

Hope, however, remains.[32] Hesiod's image of hope, caught fluttering under the lip of the jar while the other, evil contents fly away, is an example of how an image may move us even when we do not know exactly what it means. Commentators tend to ask whether the image implies that hope is present or absent from human life, and as a good or an evil.[33] Unfortunately, if we take into consideration what Hesiod says elsewhere about hope, none of the possible combinations make sense:

A man who does no work, waiting on hope that is empty,
short of livelihood, has a power of bad things to say to his spirit.
Hope is no good companion for a needy man sitting inside
and no secure means to live.

πολλὰ δ' ἀεργὸς ἀνήρ, κενεὴν ἐπὶ ἐλπίδα μίμων
χρηίζων βιότοιο, κακὰ προσελέξατο θυμῷ.
ἐλπὶς δ' οὐκ ἀγαθὴ κεχρημένον ἄνδρα κομίζει
ἥμενον ἐν λέσχῃ, τῷ μὴ βίος ἄρκιος εἴη.   WD 498–501[34]

Since Hesiod sees hope as a fact of human life, its presence in Pandora's jar cannot signify either that it is the one good, or the one evil, denied us. Nor, since it at least can be an evil, is hope the one good we still have left. But the last possibility, that hope is just one more evil that afflicts us, renders meaningless the charming picture of hope trapped under the rim of the jar. If hope is just another evil in human life, there is no reason for it not to escape from the jar with the rest of them.[35] We seem to be on the wrong track.

Our mistake is to try and classify hope as *either* good *or* bad. Hesiod is not inclined to see the world that way. Hope, for Hesiod, is evil when we rely on hope rather than on our own efforts, as with the man "whose riches are all in his head," who takes his dreams for a real wagon, and fails to note that he will need a hundred planks as well (WD 455–56). This is the "hope that is empty."[36] But hope, like trust (WD 372), or shame (WD 317–19), or Strife, has two faces. It is, after all, exactly through the hope of having more that the good Strife spurs us on (WD 20–24). Hesiod's "hope" (ἐλπίς) has more a sense of "foresight" or "expectation" than does our "hope."[37] When it replaces effort, it is expectation that is ungrounded—mere idle dreaming. But when it encourages work, it is a reasonable expectation, one that steels us to choosing the evil of toil over the specious good of idleness or cheating.

The evils that escaped from Pandora's jar escaped also from human control; they wander the earth free, self-determined (αὐτόμαται WD 103), and inescapable. Sickness, toil, and old age afflict us whether we will or no. Hesiod's rather unexpected choice of disease as the paradigmatic evil reinforces his point. Diseases are entirely evil, and entirely outside of our control. This is not true of hope. The brothers Prometheus and Epimetheus bear a strong resemblance (at least in Hesiod's account) to another set of brothers, Hesiod and Perses.[38] As Epimetheus was deceived by the appearance of Pandora, Perses has been deceived by the appearance of the bad Strife. He has trusted in the hope of getting wealth without work. He has also, now that he has been reduced to begging from his brother (WD 393–97), learned his lesson. Like Epimetheus, "when he had taken the evil thing—he understood." Perses, however, can still listen to the brotherly warning that Epimetheus ignored at his peril. He can follow the good Strife, with its reasonable expectations, rather than the empty promises of the bad one. The image of hope fluttering under the rim of the jar remains with us as the one bright spot in an otherwise bleak picture. The bright spot may be that while most evils, like diseases, afflict us at their own pleasure, the choice between idle hope and reasonable expectation remains within our control.[39]

The Five Ages: The History of Hardship

Hesiod's myth of Pandora views Zeus as myths most commonly do, as simply an actor. The myth of the Five Ages belongs to a different genre. The pattern which Hesiod is following here, of a progression of ages from an original paradise to a future devastation, is a common one in Indo-European mythology.[40] Of the various ways of exploring how evil came into the world, of itself, through our fault, through an evil power, or through God himself, this pattern tends to view evil as simply the development of an element inherent in the cosmos.[41] Evil is not *done* so much as *happens*. The myth thus adopts a viewpoint similar to that of the genealogies of the *Theogony*. Both are, as it were, a mythic way of seeing god as immanent. In the Pandora myth Hesiod examined the coming of evil into the world as an event caused by Zeus. In the myth of the Five Ages he examines it as a progression worked out through time, in which Zeus' will is more manifested in the series of ages than imposed upon it.

It is simply because Pandora cannot be placed into any of Hesiod's Five Ages that the Pandora myth and the myth of the Five Ages are irreconcilable as narrative.[42] The Golden Age has no troubles, the Silver Age does not sacrifice, the Bronze Age has its evils already, and the Heroes already have women. This catalogue, however, conceals a far more important difference between the myths. There is no one of the Five Ages that suits Pandora because the transition from good to evil occurs *within* the Pandora myth, while the same transition occurs, without explanation, *between* the various ages. This is a result of the difference noted above: in the Pandora myth Hesiod does, and in the myth of the Five Ages he does not, attribute an anthropomorphic will to Zeus. The Zeus who so decisively acts in the Pandora myth now has his role largely confined to the formula which ushers in each successive generation.[43]

Which is not to say that Zeus does nothing; he destroys the Silver Age, and will destroy the future Iron Age, he settles the Heroes on the Blessed Isles, and he "makes" both the Bronze Age and the Age of the Heroes. But his action is, nonetheless, different in kind from his action in the Pandora myth. There Zeus' will was motivated by anger, revenge, and malice, and was the center of the piece. Here there is no motivation, and Zeus comes in largely as a matter of course. Zeus "makes" the Bronze and Heroic Ages, in his turn, just as "the gods," before his rise to power, made the Golden and Silver Ages. The complete colorlessness of this "making" becomes apparent if we set it against, for example, the myth of Epimetheus giving all the good things away to the animals, and leaving nothing for man, the myth of Pyrrha and Deucalion re-creating mankind from the "bones" of their mother, the Earth, or against the myth of man's creation, and hence sin, from the ashes of the Titans. Most strikingly we may set this "making" against a near neighbor, the elaborate fashioning of the first woman, Pandora. The colorlessness shows us that, this time, this is not where Hesiod's interest lies. Zeus' "making" the ages here is simply a way of saying "the ages came to be through the will of Zeus," just as "Zeus rains" is a way of saying "it rains through the will of Zeus," and "Zeus accomplishes the seasons" is another way to say "the seasons pass."

The people of each of Hesiod's five ages end in a way that is simply the natural outcome of who they are.[44] The Golden Race dies precisely as it has lived, without trouble, as if they were falling asleep (*WD* 116). As they lived as gods, with all good things in abundance, so after their death they become spirits, *daimones*, and givers of wealth to men (*WD* 126). The Bronze Age, created as warriors, perish in battle, "conquered by their own hands" (ὑπὸ σφετέρῃσι δαμέντες *WD* 152).[45] Since they are warriors their essential attribute is their mortality; they are the first race to simply descend into Hades (*WD* 154). The essential nature of the Heroes, in Hesiod's account, is that they are half-human and half-divine: "It was the breed divine, of the men who were heroes; / they are called demi-gods" (ἀνδρῶν ἡρώων θεῖον γένος, οἳ καλέονται / ἡμίθεοι *WD* 160–61). Their lives are characterized by distinctions: half of them make war on Thebes, half on Troy; half perish on land, half on sea. Hesiod contrives a particularly neat destiny for this race. Being half-human and half-divine, half of the generation perishes and goes down to Hades; the other half Zeus settles, to live like gods, on the Blessed Isles.[46]

Unlike the other ages, both the Silver Age and our own, the Iron Age, are ended by Zeus. In both cases Zeus "acts" much as he does in settling the Heroes on the Blessed Isles, in fulfillment of the natural destiny of the race. In the case of the Silver Age, this means acting directly. Hesiod uses Zeus' action here to mark the beginning of his reign, in the form, appropriately, of a small reminder of divine superiority. The Silver Age, who "lived but a little while, and through their folly had pains as well" (παυρίδιον ζώεσκον ἐπὶ χρόνον, ἄλγε᾽ ἔχοντες / ἀφραδίης *WD* 133–34), expressed this folly primarily in their failure to honor the gods. The natural outcome of impiety is divine vengeance. This Zeus accomplishes.[47] After their deaths the Silver Age, like the Golden, becomes *daimones*, but *daimones* halfway between the fully-fledged spirits of the Golden Age and the completely mortal human beings of the Bronze. Hesiod, in a rather odd characterization, describes them as mortal gods: "mortal Blessed-Ones-Under-the-Earth" (τοὶ μὲν ὑποχθόνιοι μάκαρες θνητοὶ καλέονται *WD* 141).[48] Not Zeus' anger, but the fact that they are between the Gold and the Bronze Ages, seems to have determined their ultimate fate. Hesiod's description reinforces rather than detracts from the supposition that it is who they are that has determined what they become.

We are, understandably, most concerned with our own case. Hesiod tells us, of our own age, that "Zeus will destroy these also, this race of mortal men" (Ζεὺς δ᾽ ὀλέσει καὶ τοῦτο γένος μερόπων ἀνθρώπων *WD* 180). This will happen when justice has completely broken down. Hesiod's description culminates in the departure of Shame and Indignation, the forces that keep us honest. Then "misery and pain / are left for mortal men; there shall be no cure for ill" (τὰ δὲ λείψεται ἄλγεα λυγρά / θνητοῖς ἀνθρώποισι, κακοῦ δ᾽ οὐκ ἔσσεται ἀλκή *WD* 200–1). Shame and Indignation, however, are not unlike Strife. They "leave the earth" not because they are arbitrarily summoned home by Zeus, but because human beings have ceased to feel them: "justice shall be in their hands only, / and shame shall be no more" (δίκη δ᾽ ἐν χερσί, καὶ αἰδὼς / οὐκ ἔσται *WD* 192–93).[49] Zeus' destruction of the Iron Age is not necessarily apocalyptic. Hesiod's horrifying description of the breakdown of justice and order is not only the cause, but also the working out, of the Iron Age's destruction. A generation which has no respect for the bonds of family, of companionship, or of justice, has gone, after all, a long way towards destroying itself.[50]

The Silver Race is destroyed by Zeus because it does not honor the gods. Our own age will be destroyed by him when, through violence and injustice, we have destroyed ourselves. This is not to say that Zeus does *not* cause the end of the Iron Age. He does, just as directly as he caused the end of the Silver Age. As the natural outcome of impiety is divine vengeance, the natural outcome of injustice is the end of life as we know it. As with the rain, the act of Zeus and the natural event are not, to Hesiod, different things. As Heraclitus was to put it much later: "for human beings *ethos* is destiny" (ἦθος ἀνθρώπῳ δαίμων frag. 247).[51] For Hesiod that "ethos" stems from Zeus.

As in the genealogies of the *Theogony*, the sequence of the Five Ages happens more than it is done. Unlike the genealogies, however, the "happening" here manifests Zeus' will, rather than bringing it into the world. Hesiod wanted us to note that this was so. One of the oddities of Hesiod's version of this myth is his creation anew of each of the successive races. One of the reasons for the addition is the continual reminder it provides of the will of Zeus lying in the background of each age. It is in the nature of a Golden Age myth to present the ages not as changing through the will of God, but as simply changing. Once we see this, Zeus' role in Hesiod's version of the myth becomes perfectly clear. Hesiod has not removed Zeus from the myth; he has added him. He has not taken away from Zeus an anthropomorphic reason for changing the ages; he has rather ensured that we notice that at the core of the Ages' spontaneous change is Zeus.

Each of Hesiod's successive ages finds the fate appropriate to it. This does not, however, answer the question central to the myth: why this particular succession? If this myth traces the development of human hardship, what stages does Hesiod mean us to notice in that development? Or are there no stages at all, but, as the discontinuity of the ages might suggest, merely five successive, unconnected, and arbitrarily placed descriptions of human possibilities?

Before we can consider what the pattern behind Hesiod's ages is, however, we must consider what it is not. Hesiod's myth ends with a horrifying image of a world in which justice has been completely perverted. The power of the image has led many commentators to read Hesiod's indignation back into the previous ages of the myth, and so to see the myth in its entirety as describing the moral degeneration of human beings. As each age becomes increasingly degenerate, Zeus' punishment of them becomes increasingly severe, until the pattern culminates in the complete inversion of justice and the resulting obliteration of the future Iron Age.[52] Attractive as this may be as an explanation of the emergence of evil, it does not seem to have been Hesiod's. In the first place, if Zeus' various punishments were intended to make us mend our ways, they seem to have failed miserably. Secondly, this "moral" interpretation is clearly not applicable to the myth parallel to this one. Whatever else is true of the Pandora myth, it certainly describes hardship as entering into human life through no fault of our own.[53] Finally, although Hesiod's overall scheme of metals deteriorating in quality, value, and purity guarantees that he saw the myth as one of degeneration,[54] the degeneration does not take place in the moral condition of life. It takes place rather in the *material* conditions of human life, and progresses irrespective of whether successive generations are more, or less, just than their predecessors.

In fact, there is no consistent moral degeneration in the Five Ages myth, and Hesiod seems to have gone out of his way to ensure that there is not.[55] He describes the Golden Race as living without hardship, not without sin.[56] Insolence, or *hubris*, is attributed to both the Silver and the Bronze Ages, but, by any traditional standards, the earlier Silver Age, which honors neither the right nor the gods, is far worse than the Bronze.[57] The members of the earlier race are destroyed for their impiety. The members of the later one, a race of fighters, direct their insolence not towards the gods but towards each other. There is, if anything, an unexpected note of pathos in their end:

> By their own hands were they conquered, and went to the
>   moldering
> home of chilly Death. They had no names;
> but for all their terribleness black Death laid hold of them,
> and they left the bright light of the sun.

> καὶ τοὶ μὲν χείρεσσιν ὑπὸ σφετέρῃσι δαμέντες
> βῆσαν ἐς εὐρώεντα δόμον κρυεροῦ Ἀΐδαο
> νώνυμνοι· θάνατος δὲ καὶ ἐκπάγλους περ ἐόντας
> εἷλε μέλας, λαμπρὸν δ' ἔλιπον φάος ἠελίοιο.   WD 152–55

This is more like pity than condemnation. Like them, and unlike the Golden or Silver Races, we too must go down, nameless, into Hades' cold house.

Most importantly, however, the theory of moral degeneration cannot explain why Hesiod inserts into the myth the Race of Heroes, whom he goes out of his way to describe as "better and more just" (δικαιότερον καὶ ἄρειον WD 158) than the race which preceded them.[58] Hesiod himself has, apparently, decided to include this race.[59] He has certainly chosen to point out that they do not conform to any pattern of moral degeneracy. This can only argue that Hesiod either did not see the myth as one of moral degeneration, or that, feeling that the myth carried these overtones, he wanted to counteract them.

The fact that the myth describes neither man's moral degeneration nor Zeus' consequent punishment of human injustice is important primarily because of the ideas that tend to sneak in alongside a "moral" interpretation of the myth. Prominent among these are the notions that human beings have hardship because they will not abide by justice, that if they would abide by justice, they could return to a time free from hardship, and, most importantly, that human beings, in this way, have control over their own destiny. It is here, most critically, that we must avoid attributing to Hesiod views that belong to the Jewish and Christian traditions. A sense that the divine permeates the cosmos may suggest to us the impossibility of avoiding the wrath of an angry God. Hesiod is far more pessimistic than that. He does see Zeus as inevitably punishing transgressions. He does not believe, however, that we can therefore shape our own destiny through our choice of either virtue or sin. "Transgressions" are not, for Hesiod, a matter of violating an established set of rules. Hesiod has no Commandments. He is playing a game in which human beings are never able, completely, to understand the rules, and where Zeus is always able to change them.

Scholars have universally agreed that Hesiod himself has introduced into an earlier myth the discordant element of the Heroic Age. In an oversight almost paradigmatic

of Hesiodic scholarship, they have not gone on to the conclusion that Hesiod introduced the Heroes because they suited his particular aim in telling the myth. This
seems rather unreasonable. Given that Hesiod has added a whole new age to the myth,
it seems only fair to examine it as a possible clue to his intention in telling the story.

Let us begin with the obvious. The Heroic Age, unlike the preceding three ages,
is an age very like the present. Traditionally, in fact, at least some human beings of the
present are directly descended from the Heroes. By including this age Hesiod has
heavily underlined a natural tendency of the myth to have the ages become progressively more and more like our own.[60]

The myth of the Golden Age is by nature a myth of prehistory. It describes the
preceding ages of human life as a way of examining the present. Hesiod has adopted
this method before, in the *Theogony*, where the prehistory of Zeus' order was described
as a way of exploring the present nature of that order. He adopts the same means here.
Towards this end he closes his account of the Heroic Age with a description of the
Blessed Isles which parallels his opening image of the Golden Age. The repetition is
not intended to suggest a possible return to the Golden Age; for that we would have
to become semi-divine.[61] It is, rather, a closure, grouping together the first four ages
as the past of human life, and setting off the Iron Age as their culmination. The closure is reinforced by Hesiod's abrupt, and suddenly unformulaic, introduction to the
Iron Age: "For now indeed is the race of iron" (νῦν γὰρ δὴ γένος ἐστι σιδήρεον *WD*
176). Our age is why Hesiod is telling the myth. He describes the past only to show
how the present has come to be. To that extent his races must inevitably tend to
become more and more like ourselves. The introduction of the Heroes strengthens the
movement.

Hesiod's additional age, however, not only reinforces this pattern, it also transforms it. The addition of the Heroes is a much stranger move than may at first appear.
There was, first of all, no necessity that the Heroes be included.[62] Hesiod is as happy
to ignore, for the purposes of this myth, Pyrrha and Deucalion, or the transfer of power
from Ouranos to Cronos, as he is to ignore Pandora. The Heroes no more had to be
included than they did. The myth of the Five Ages bears a striking resemblance to history. It is, nonetheless, a myth, and not history. *History* cannot cavalierly skip an age
as well-attested as that of the Heroes. Myth, unlike history (as evidenced by the incompatible myths of Pandora and the Five Ages), makes no claim to exclusivity, and therefore has no such need to be all-inclusive.

The first oddity of Hesiod's account is that he includes the Heroes at all. The second is that he includes them as a separate age. Hesiod was as familiar as we are with
the idea that the Heroes, the men of our historical "Bronze Age," were users of bronze
rather than of iron. He could, consequently, easily have included them in the Bronze
Age. Or, if he preferred, since the Heroes also traditionally knew of iron, he could have
placed them at the beginning of the Iron Age.[63] In either way he could have used the
Heroes to clinch the pattern of Gold, Silver, Bronze, and Iron. Instead, by including
them as a separate age, he ostentatiously breaks the metallic pattern established by the
myth. In order to do so, moreover, he has had to paper over the difficulty that the heroes
were *not* a separate race, but the ancestors of the people of the present.[64]

Hesiod's first four ages are, in the regular mythic pattern, the past of human life;
his last is its present and future. In the usual mythic pattern the first four would also

occur in mythic time, and only the last, as the focus and aim of the myth, in human time. Hesiod's Age of the Heroes introduces human time into the part of the myth that has been carefully closed off as prehistory, what should be the mythic past, as opposed to the human present. It is difficult to see why Hesiod would have done this, unless he meant, in part at least, to break down precisely this distinction. The Heroes enable the earlier, self-evidently mythic ages to blend smoothly into the human time of the present. By including them, Hesiod has, on the one hand, reinforced the pattern normal to the myth, of a movement from an ancient past to our own time. On the other hand, he has also, it seems deliberately, undercut the distinction between mythic and human time which would normally interrupt this progression. His desire to represent the emergence of hardship as in some way continuous, or even historical, has overcome even the natural tendency of the myth.[65]

Hesiod has placed together two traditions, the tradition of a Golden Age, and the tradition that the generations prior to ourselves, our ancestors, were greater and stronger than we are. Both traditions point towards degeneration, the second, in particular, towards a degeneration in human beings themselves. There is an even more basic tradition which Hesiod underlines by including the Heroes. The Heroes were supposed to have lived in an age greater than our own, but greater in a very particular way, greater, somehow, because it was simpler.

The only direct evidence we have as to Hesiod's conception of Heroic life is what Hesiod himself says in his description of the Heroic Age, and in references scattered, albeit rather sparsely, throughout the *Theogony*. All of these references are consistent with the picture of Heroic life found in the *Iliad* and *Odyssey*. As all of these poems have been composed in the same poetic dialect, and appear to share an oral tradition, this is as we would expect. We may therefore assume, provided that we realize that it is an assumption, that Hesiod viewed the Heroes much as they are portrayed in the Homeric poems. The Homeric Heroes live in a world that is both greater, and less complex, than the world of the poets. Hence Homer's rather confusing pictures of the Heroes' dwellingplaces, on the one hand larger, but on the other plainer, than the homes he knew. Hence also the society of the Heroes, that had no courts and no petty politics, where Agamemnon and Menelaus can give cities away, and Achilles can declare a truce simply by nodding his head. Even in the details of Heroic life, the fact that the Heroes ate no fish and did not ride on horses, that they roasted rather than boiled their meat, that their weapons were bronze and not iron, one senses a grandeur based as much on simplicity as on size. In the Heroic age one man was able to lift a stone such as it would take two men to lift now. It is not only the size, but also the image of a time when boulders were part of warfare, that creates the feeling of the Heroic Age.

Hesiod's picture agrees in detail with Homer's, and yet the life of the Heroes does not seem terribly simple. Unlike the previous ages they have ships and cities, and flocks and wives to fight over. It is a relatively complex life, compared, in particular, to that of the age that went before them, the Bronze Age, where men were simply warriors, and did not need to bother either with armies or with agriculture. In turn, however, this life of the Bronze Age seems a complex life, compared to that of the dwellers in the Silver Age, who spent a hundred years as children, and whose lives were complex only if compared to the age that preceded them, the Golden. The age of the Heroes is a greater and simpler age only when it is compared to our own, an age of diseases and bad harvests, squabbling in lawcourts and fighting over petty patrimonies. This is precisely what Hesiod wanted to achieve. By introducing the Age of the Heroes he has introduced an idea that the degeneration of the ages occurs in ourselves. He has also bridged human and mythic time, and so projected a movement which he saw as historical, from a better, simpler, Heroic Age to a harder and more complex present time, back through the mythic history of human life. And, finally, he has put the coping-stone on the pattern that runs through his ages, a pattern not so much of ever-decreasing goods, as of ever decreasing simplicity, due, as he sees it, to ever increasing needs.

In order to describe how hardship entered the world, Hesiod begins with a time free from care. Between this time and the present he places three vignettes. The first is of a people childish and without sacrifice; the second is of a race who are fighters only, who have no iron and eat no bread; the third is of the Heroes, warriors rather than mere fighters, with ships and armies, and with cities, flocks, and wives to defend or attack. These Heroes are men much like ourselves, but with one critical difference; they lived by war, not by labor, by force, not by justice. No assembly met in Ithaca for the twenty years that Odysseus was away (*Odyssey* 2.25–28). It is a situation inconceivable in Thespiae.[66]

What occurs over Hesiod's ages is the development of sacrifice, of weapons, of cities, armies and agriculture, and finally of the courts that, in the future of the Iron Age, will become completely corrupt. The story is both strange and familiar. It is familiar because it is a story we know well, the story of the history of human beings. It is strange because we are more accustomed to see it in another guise, not as a myth of human degeneration, but as the history of human civilization and progress.[67]

Once again Hesiod has taken over a motif from the traditional myth and made it serve his purpose. The Golden Age myth traditionally portrays the rise of civilization among human beings as a continual growth of needs. An Indian version of the myth, for example, runs thus:

> In the beginning, people lived in perfect happiness, without class distinctions or property; all their needs were supplied by magic wishing-trees. Then because of the great power of time and the changes it wrought upon them, they were overcome by passion and greed. It was from the influence of time, and no other cause, that their perfection vanished. Because of their greed, the wishing-trees disappeared; the people suffered from heat and cold, built houses, and wore clothes.[68]

Hardship enters the world, civilization arises, and life becomes increasingly complex, because human beings acquire more needs. One implication of this is that we do not share a common human nature with the people who went before us. It is an implication that Hesiod is perfectly comfortable with. In Hesiod's descriptions of the ages it is the men themselves, not merely their ways of life, that are different. The Silver Race is "neither in form nor in mind . . . like the Golden" (χρυσέῳ οὔτε φυὴν ἐναλίγκιον οὔτε νόημα WD 129). The Bronze "equaled the Silver in nothing" (οὐκ ἀργυρέῳ οὐδὲν ὁμοῖον WD 144). This difference is mirrored in their physical characteristics. The

Golden Race did not grow old, and died as if falling asleep. The Silver Race were children for a hundred years.[69] The Bronze Race were made from ash trees (*WD* 145). In the future babies will be born with gray hair.[70]

Hesiod makes no attempt to establish any continuity between the ages. His own reminder of the presence of Zeus, through the creation of the separate races, reinforces this discontinuity. The races are completely separate units, each completely destroyed before a new one is created. Where continuity is forced on him, the Heroes being the ancestors of the people of the present, Hesiod glosses over it. A "human nature" passed down from one generation to the next is emphatically no part of Hesiod's vision of human life.[71]

There are many echoes of Hesiod in the plays of Aeschylus. One such occurs in the *Prometheus Bound*, when Prometheus describes how he transformed human life by introducing, along with fire, sacrifice, agriculture, sailing, medicine, and the metals, bronze and iron, silver and gold (*PB* 500). In Aeschylus' version this is a story not of human degeneration, but of the rise of civilization.[72] He has made it so through one critical, and very informative, change in the story. Aeschylus, unlike Hesiod, attributes to human beings a nature independent of the conditions of his life.

When Aeschylus' Prometheus describes a time before medicine he describes people as perishing, helpless against the diseases which afflicted them (*PB* 478–83). When Hesiod pictures life before Prometheus' intervention he sees it not only as a time before medicine, but as a time before people *needed* medicine, a time before human beings had diseases. Aeschylus' Prometheus describes the time before humans had houses or agriculture, before oxen were domesticated, or people knew how to mine metals, as a time when people hauled loads themselves, and huddled in holes in the ground. When Hesiod pictures a time before agriculture he sees it is a time when the earth, unassisted, grew grain, or as a time when human beings did not need to eat bread. In Aeschylus' account Prometheus gave human beings agriculture in order to satisfy their needs. In Hesiod's version we farm because Zeus, when he hid our livelihood from us, gave us a new kind of need.

Hesiod's myth is one of degeneration because he sees no continuity of human nature, and so no continuity of needs. Human beings of the present do not have more resources to satisfy their needs; they simply have more needs.[73] Aeschylus' myth is one of progress because he pictures the human beings of the past as having a nature like our own, and the gifts of Prometheus as satisfying needs that had previously gone unfilled. But even this element of the myth is responding to something in Hesiod. By introducing the Age of the Heroes Hesiod moved the Golden Age myth away from mythic and towards human time, thereby introducing into it a curious continuity in the ages. It is to this continuity, a continuity that makes Hesiod's myth begin to resemble history, that Aeschylus has responded.

The end result is that Hesiod's ages, although they are different in nature, are not different in kind. We are not like the people of the past. But we are not utterly different either. Not our natures, but our dependence on the will of Zeus, links us to the former ages. Hesiod's γένη, literally "races," are also, and equally, "ages." They can be both because the two, the time and conditions under which human beings live, and the kind of beings they are, to Hesiod's eyes are the same.[74] We are not creatures with a nature to which Zeus must accommodate himself. We are as the conditions of Zeus' order make us.[75] Human beings do not determine the conditions of their life, either by their virtue or their sin. They are, rather, determined by those conditions, continually young when their life is without hardship, gray from birth when their life is one of labor and sorrow. This is as true of the present age as it was of any of the prior ages. It is this continuity that Hesiod seems to want to reinforce.

Hesiod's willingness to see the people of earlier times as simply different from ourselves is not what is unusual in his version of the myth. What is unusual is, first, his complete destruction of each age, making their progression occur, necessarily, through Zeus, and second, his inclusion of the Heroes, giving the myth its particularly historical cast. The myth thus reveals Hesiod's sense of the complete interpenetration of human nature, human life, and the order of Zeus. Hesiod has turned his version of the Golden Age myth into a myth of history. He has done so not in order to explore history, but in order to reveal how completely the will of Zeus informs human life.[76]

The focus of Hesiod's myth, both in number of lines and in tone, is on the future of the Iron Age. Unlike most Golden Age myths, however, Hesiod's focus is not on the destruction of the age, but on its particular nature. As each previous age has reached a culmination in which it perished of its own nature, it is not surprising that it is also in the final state of our own age, rather than in its present, that Hesiod sees the culmination of the myth as a whole. What may seem surprising is the particular culmination Hesiod envisions. It is not, as it appears at first, labor and disease (WD 176–79). The final hardship, it turns out, is justice.[77] As Hesiod's description develops, it becomes clear that the few goods mingled with our evils have to do not with work, but with the traces of straight justice that remain among us. As war was the characteristic evil of the Bronze Age, or as impiety was the particular evil of the Silver Race, the characteristic evil of the Iron Age turns out to be crooked justice.

To understand why, we must recall Hesiod's vision of human hardship. An evil, in Hesiod's myth of the Ages, and usually in Golden Age myths, is paramountly a need. The Golden Age had no evil because they had no needs. The "impiety" of the Silver Age was simply the fact that they ignored the necessity of sacrifice. The Bronze Age men perish because they have a new need, for society. The Heroes have society, but they do not have, because they do not need, the paramount necessity of the Iron Age, justice, in particular justice as it is manifested in the lawcourts. The Iron Age introduces the need for justice. As such it will be dealt with not here but in the fifth chapter, on the place of human beings.

Justice is not, for Hesiod, as it is for Plato's Protagoras (Protagoras 322b–d), a gift provided by the gods to cure our ill condition. It is, rather, itself the ill condition. Hesiod's vivid picture of the perversion of justice does not reveal the blessings of justice; it shows us that justice is inescapable. As it was with Perses' Strife—"No mortal loves her! Only under Necessity / through designs of the Immortals do they honor her" (οὔ τις τήν γε φιλεῖ βροτός, ἀλλ' ὑπ' ἀνάγκης / ἀθανάτων βουλῇσιν Ἔριν τιμῶσι βαρεῖαν WD 15–16)—hardship, for Hesiod, is necessity. Justice is the hallmark of our age, not as a gift we may accept or decline, but as a necessity decreed by the inescapable will of Zeus. It is the new need.

Hesiod's Fable and the Justice of Zeus

Hesiod ends his introductory section of the *Works and Days* with a fable. His myths have moved us from purely mythic, to semi-mythic, to human time. His fable, like all fables, occurs outside of time. It refers not to a mythic past, but to a universal present.[78]

The myths have demonstrated to Perses that hardship exists in the world through the will of Zeus. They conclude by showing him that our present need for justice is an intrinsic part of that will. Hesiod now turns from Perses to the kings who have charge of, but pervert, justice. He tells them that, as the nightingale cannot escape the hawk, so they cannot escape the will of Zeus. As the hawk says: "He is witless who seeks to contend with rivals stronger than he is; / he loses the fight and besides suffers pain and shame together" (ἄφρων δ' ὅς κ' ἐθέλῃ πρὸς κρείσσονας ἀντιφερίζειν· / νίκης τε στέρεται πρός τ' αἴσχεσιν ἄλγεα πάσχει *WD* 210–11). Such will be the fate of the kings if, through their crooked judgments, they persist in contending against Zeus.[79] The myths have shown us that it is Zeus who introduced hardship and the necessity of justice into the world. The fable shows us that his will is both present and inescapable.

This understanding of the fable is not, however, that of most commentators. With a few exceptions the nightingale of the fable, because it is described as a singer, has been taken to represent Hesiod, and the hawk, therefore, to represent the kings.[80] Under this interpretation, the hawk's words represent the claim of the gift-gobbling kings: Hesiod must submit to the king's unjust treatment because he is weaker and they are stronger. A qualification is required in order to restore the correct moral, that injustice of this sort cannot prosper: "So said the hawk" (but—we must add—he was wrong); "Perses, you listen to Justice." The qualification is found by interpreting Hesiod's later declaration that Zeus gave justice to human beings, but not to the animals, as a retraction of the fable.[81] The hawk, as an animal, can behave this way. The kings cannot.

There are a number of difficulties with this interpretation, most of which I will explore below. The primary problem, however, with the way scholars have read the fable applies equally to either interpretation. Scholars have universally read the fable as fixed: either nightingale = Hesiod and hawk = kings, or hawk = Zeus and nightingale = kings. As we have seen, both in Hesiod's description of the two kinds of Strife and in his use of the myths, Hesiod does not tend to work this way. Hesiod's explicit identification of the nightingale as a singer invites us to identify the weaker bird with himself. Hesiod's introduction of the bad Strife just as clearly identified her with the heroic world of war. But this identification finally served to show us not that the bad Strife belongs only in Homeric poems of battle, but to show us that things such as Strife, or petty cheating, are not always as they seem. Similarly in the fable. Hesiod begins by inviting us to see himself as the helpless victim of a greater power. He ends by showing us that not he, but the mighty kings, are in the clutch of a power far stronger than themselves.

The controversy is more important than it might at first seem. If the kings are seen as the hawk, the fable is relatively uninteresting—Hesiod is merely saying in an oblique fashion what he says directly, and even abusively, elsewhere: that he has been mistreated. But if Hesiod saw *Zeus* as the hawk of his fable then the fable is very interesting indeed. It tells us that Hesiod saw Zeus as completely dominating human life. And it tells us that Hesiod, the great champion of justice, did not believe that Zeus himself was just.

The moral of Hesiod's story is expressed, as is almost universal in fables, in a final speech by one of the characters.[82] Hesiod himself alerts us to this in his opening to the fable: "Here is a fable for the kings, although they are knowing themselves. / This is what the hawk said when he spoke to the dapplenecked songbird" (νῦν δ' αἶνον βασιλεῦσ' ἐρέω, φρονέουσι καὶ αὐτοῖς. / ὧδ' ἴρηξ προσέειπεν ἀηδόνα ποικιλόδειρον WD 202–3). The moral belong to the hawk. The problem is that the moral tells us that the nightingale is wrong to struggle. If this is the moral, our initial impression that Hesiod himself is the nightingale is simply not tenable. Scholars have reacted by denying that the hawk's words provide the moral. Hesiod, I believe, intended us to react by revising our understanding of whom the hawk and the nightingale represent.

It is not hard to see why Hesiod might want to lead his audience from one interpretation of the fable to the other. Read in this way, Hesiod's fable is uniquely suited to lead us, as it does, from the injustice of the Iron Age (WD 180–201), a situation which seems at first mirrored in the fable, to Zeus' punishment of such injustice (WD 213–83), the situation that the fable finally settles upon. Moreover, a fable achieves its force in part by leaving its audience to provide its parallel for itself. Hesiod's audience, tempted into seeing Hesiod as the nightingale, may have expected that the hawk would meet his match.[83] If so, they were disappointed. The fable shows us no power greater than the hawk. The need for a readjustment of vision thus created by Hesiod's abrupt ending brings home the message of the fable even more forcefully.

Here, however, Hesiod was not as clever as his interpreters. It probably never occurred to him that his later statement, that human beings have justice while animals do not, could be taken as a retraction of the fable. There are good reasons for his oversight. There is, for example, no reason why the poet could not have omitted or revised the fable itself if he had felt that it was unsatisfactory, nor is there any reason for him to wait sixty-five lines before "correcting" it.[84] More significantly, however, the "correction" denies the basic presupposition of a fable as such, that a parallel can be drawn between human and animal behavior.[85] Hesiod's "correcting" his fable by pointing out that animals and men behave differently is like correcting it by pointing out that birds do not in fact speak in Greek hexameter verse. Animals of fable can, and often do, have justice. It is real animals who do not, and it is, presumably, exactly because WD 276–80 is about real animals that Hesiod places the greatest possible distance between the two passages.

Having established the hawk's words as the moral of his fable, Hesiod points us towards an interpretation which sees not himself, but the kings, as the nightingale of the fable. If the hawk's final words were supposed to show us that Hesiod must submit to injustice, Hesiod's following line, "Perses, you listen to Justice," must be *contrasted* to this claim.[86] This sort of adversative Hesiod uses elsewhere, in the form "But you rather . . ." (ἀλλὰ σύ γ').[87] What Hesiod says here, however, is different:

So said the hawk, swift-flying, bird with long outstretched wings.
Perses, you listen to Justice; do not magnify your insolence.

For Insolence is bad in a man of insignificance;
not even a great man can carry her . . .

ὣς ἔφατ᾽ ὠκυπέτης ἴρηξ, τανυσίπτερος ὄρνις.
ὦ Πέρση, σὺ δ᾽ ἄκουε δίκης, μηδ᾽ ὕβριν ὄφελλε·
ὕβρις γάρ τε κακὴ δειλῷ βροτῷ· οὐδὲ μὲν ἐσθλός
ῥηιδίως φερέμεν δύναται   WD 212–15

The formula Hesiod uses here, "Perses, you listen . . ." (ὦ Πέρση, σὺ δε . . .), does not
serve as an adversative. It serves instead to bring home a point, originally addressed
to another, to a new addressee.[88] Hesiod uses the phrase again at *WD* 248 and 274, in
both cases telling Perses or the kings to take note of a lesson originally addressed to
the other, but applicable to them as well. This is also its meaning here. The final sense
of the hawk's words must be that not even the mighty kings can escape the power of
Zeus. Hesiod continues by pointing out that since this is so, a mere nothing like Perses
should not even dream of getting away with injustice.

Hesiod has prepared us for this reading. In accordance with his usual method of
composition through key words and concepts, the language of the fable is reflected in
other passages of the poem, particularly in those which immediately precede and follow it. These echoes associate "the stronger" hawk, not with the kings, but with the
very much stronger Zeus, and so with justice.[89] They also associate the "sufferings" of
the nightingale, not with Hesiod, who is not pictured in the poem as either suffering
or weak, but with the sufferings of those who pervert justice, vividly described just
above.[90] In particular, the hawk's power to do either a thing or its complete opposite,
as he himself wishes (*WD* 209), associates him, as the Proem makes abundantly clear,
with Zeus, while the hawk's description of one who would challenge the stronger as
"senseless" (ἄφρων *WD* 210) recalls Hesiod's favorite epithet for Perses, for the kings,
and for anyone who thinks he can get away with grabbing wealth: "foolish" (νήπιος).[91]

The nightingale, who is pictured as having deliberately challenged the hawk
("seek[ing] to contend with the stronger" ὅς κ᾽ ἐθέλῃ πρὸς κρείσσονας ἀντιφερίζειν *WD*
210), does not at all resemble Hesiod's position in regard to the kings. What it
resembles is rather the common scenario of a mortal challenging a god, and being duly,
and mercilessly, punished for the *hubris*. What it resembles, in short, is Hesiod's vision
of the kings' attempt to pervert justice.[92]

Having invited us to see himself as the nightingale Hesiod uses the abruptness of his
closing moral to show us that the victim here is in fact the kings. There are a number
of reasons why Hesiod's audience would have made this transition more easily than
we do. In the first place Hesiod's audience was quite alive to the fact that Hesiod
chose, not the particular birds that the fable describes, but the fable as a whole.[93] As
the usual way of referring to fables—"the fable of the fox and the sour grapes" or "the
fable of the hare and the tortoise"—implies, the actors of a fable are a given. They are
not altered to fit the situation, nor does one expect them to be so altered. As we would
not tell a fable of a beaver and sour grapes because we were applying it to a notably
industrious person, Hesiod would not be expected to choose or alter the bird to suit
the situation at hand.[94]

A fable applies a traditional story to a particular situation. Hesiod makes it clear that his fable is directed toward the kings and concerns the relation of power to help-lessness. He also implies, perhaps, that this is a story that the kings already know.[95] But most of all, in telling us that this is a fable (particularly if it is one that his audience already knows), Hesiod tells us that the birds involved were not chosen to represent either Hesiod or the kings. The nightingale, as a singer, could represent the poet. It could, just as easily, represent someone with no particular connection to song.

Nor does Hesiod's own identification of the nightingale as a "singer" clinch the matter. In fact, it is precisely this identification that makes it impossible to see the nightingale as representing Hesiod: "You fool, why have you screamed so? He that has you is far stronger / and you go where I shall bring you, even if you are a songster" (δαιμονίη, τί λέληκας; ἔχει νύ σε πολλὸν ἀρείων· / τῇ δ' εἶς ἦ σ' ἄν ἐγώ περ ἄγω καὶ ἀοιδὸν ἐοῦσαν WD 207–8). The hawk's point is that his singing is of no help to the nightingale. Hesiod can hardly mean us to conclude from this that his own words are ineffectual. We are moved, by precisely the lines that identify the nightingale as a "songster," to seek another referent.

A particular kind of relation, as of the country and the city mouse, or of the hare and the tortoise, is the usual focus of a fable. The usual relation of hawks and nightingales in fable is, as it is here, power in contrast to helplessness.[96] The particular contrast of power to helplessness that Hesiod describes by emphasizing the nightingale's role as a singer, is the impotence of mere words against force. We, as a postmodern audience, may feel drawn to the idea that a suddenly despairing Hesiod has abandoned his belief in the power of poetry. There is no evidence for this despair in the Works and Days. Hesiod was not a postmodernist. If he is declaring that words are of no avail against force he must mean the words of the kings. If so, the force can only be that of Zeus.

To a modern imagination a "king" is associated largely with power, hereditary, political, or military, while a "song" is primarily distinguished by its music. Hesiod, however, associates "song" not with melody, but with words, in particular, with persuasive words, and "kings" not with war, but with judgments.[97] A king, like a singer, causes men to forget their grievances, and, like a singer, he uses honey-sweet words to do so (Th. 96–103).[98] In the Theogony, Hesiod describes how the Muses favor a good king: "Upon his tongue they pour sweet dew, / And the words from his mouth run like honey" (τῷ μὲν ἐπὶ γλώσσῃ γλυκερὴν χείουσιν ἐέρσην, / τοῦ δ' ἔπε' ἐκ στόματος ῥεῖ μείλιχα Th. 83–84). The result is that he persuades with soft words (Th. 90) and "speaks without failing / And swiftly and knowingly resolves even a great quarrel" (ὁ δ' ἀσφαλέως ἀγορεύων / αἶψά τε καὶ μέγα νεῖκος ἐπισταμένως κατέπαυσε Th. 86–87). Similarly, in the Works and Days, Hesiod advises the bad kings, who "[pervert] the course of justice in suits, by crooked speeches" (ἄλλη παρκλίνωσι δίκας σκολιῶς ἐνέποντες WD 262), "Watch these things, you kings, and straighten your speeches" (ταῦτα φυλασσόμενοι βασιλῆς ἰθύνετε μύθους WD 263).[99]

Hesiod's kings are judges. Their tools are not swords, but words. Their power lies in their decisions. When these are straight they are backed by Zeus, and are powerful. When they are crooked they are like the lies the Muses, the kings' patrons, know how to tell. They do not, as true songs do, reflect the mind of Zeus (WD 661–62). They are merely words.[100]

Hesiod's fable, under the prevailing interpretation, describes as inevitable precisely what Hesiod is declaring to be impossible, that the kings can succeed in perverting justice. Nonetheless, scholars have been unwilling to see the hawk as Zeus. This is, I believe, for a largely unstated reason. Hesiod makes no attempt to soften the clutch of the hawk's talons.[101] The moral the hawk delivers is, quite simply, that might makes right. If this is Zeus then Zeus operates in the human world, not through justice, but through force. Is it not a contradiction that Hesiod, for whom Zeus is the ultimate champion of justice, should picture Zeus himself as the persecutor of the nightingale?

"The justice of Zeus" is not a phrase that would be meaningless to Hesiod. But it would not mean to him what it means to us. "The justice of Zeus," for Hesiod, means precisely what he says it means, that Zeus does not allow men to transgress the bounds of justice. Zeus punishes the guilty. It does not mean what it might suggest to a Christian, that Zeus either rewards the just or spares the innocent.[102] The *Works and Days* provides ample evidence that Hesiod is not uncomfortable with the idea that Zeus causes the innocent to perish. In Hesiod's myth we were forced out of Eden not because we sinned, but because Prometheus challenged Zeus, and had a foolish brother.[103] The descendants punished for their ancestor's injustice are themselves innocent (*WD* 280–85, 325–26).[104] The citizens involved when a city is destroyed for the crimes of corrupt judges (*WD* 240–41, 260–61) are not only guiltless; they are the victims of that injustice. Sailing, Hesiod declares, can be, at the right season, safe, "unless with his fullest intent Poseidon the Earth-Shaker / or Zeus, King of the Immortals, will your destruction outright" (εἰ δὴ μὴ πρόφρων γε Ποσειδάων ἐνοσίχθων / ἢ Ζεὺς ἀθανάτων βασιλεὺς ἐθέλησιν ὀλέσσαι *WD* 667–68). The argument of the *Works and Days* is that justice is necessary for success in life; it is not that it is sufficient. The most just man in creation, if he will not, or cannot, farm his piece of land, will not escape hunger.

Justice, in Hesiod's eyes, is a condition of human life determined by the will of Zeus. The goddess Justice derives her authority from Zeus. So do the kings, who are also "from Zeus" (ἐκ δὲ Διὸς βασιλῆες *Th.* 96). She does not control Zeus' actions any more than they do. The fact that Zeus ensures that men cannot transgress against justice does not mean that he himself is bound by this obligation. Zeus also ensures that men cannot live without farming. This does not make him a farmer.

Hesiod does not specify that Zeus' actions need not be just in the way that men's actions must be just, that Zeus can destroy the innocent as well as the guilty, or that Zeus rules through force rather than through righteousness. He does not because it has never occurred to him that it might be otherwise. Hesiod's understanding of justice is, to his mind, the ordinary one. He does not see any need to explain it. It is not Hesiod's understanding, but our own, that makes us unwilling to see Zeus as the arbitrary hawk of the fable. Justice, for Hesiod, is not a positive good that the gods too must possess. It is the condition of human life that ensures the balance of good and evil that is our lot.[105] The concept is not applicable to the gods, who have only goods. Zeus holds the balance; his share is not measured by it.

3

THE COMPOSITION
OF THE GEORGICS:
VERGIL'S FARM

Farming, and a sense that farming provides us with a clue to our place in the cosmos, is what the *Georgics* and the *Works and Days* have in common. It is nearly the only thing. The poet of the *Works and Days* presents himself as stern and uncompromising, a pessimist and a realist. The poet of the *Georgics* writes as an idealist, a lover of peace and beauty, and a man deeply sympathetic with all that suffers. There is a passionate intensity to the expressions, descriptions, and almost violent juxtapositions of the *Works and Days*; the *Georgics* is so carefully crafted that the poet's own views appear only in the nearly imperceptible modulations of his tone. Hesiod's "country" is centered in his local town, a town united only by language to even the rest of Greece. Vergil's "country" is centered, whether he likes it or not, in Rome, the focal point of the civilized world. During the century in which Hesiod lived Greece emerged, gradually, from a dark age into the beginnings of Classical civilization. Vergil lived to see an end to the civil war that had torn the Roman Republic apart for centuries, achieved at the price of the Republic. Even the farms they knew were different—Hesiod's the small, self-sufficient farms of a poor rural society, Vergil's the huge slave-run estates or *latifundia* which were consuming Roman farming.

And yet, surprisingly, Vergil adopts not the *latifundia* of his own time as the farm of the *Georgics*, but the small family-run farm of the *Works and Days*. He thus does precisely what he claims to do, he sings "the song of Ascra through Roman towns" (*Ascraeumque cano Romana per oppida carmen* 2.173–76).[1] Exactly because of this, the *Georgics* is a poem very unlike the *Works and Days*. There is no better way to point out differences than to juxtapose them. Aeneas expresses the radical differences between the Roman and the Greek visions of life nowhere more clearly than when he is, unwittingly, acting out the roles of Odysseus and Achilles. The *Georgics* is not the *Works and Days* dressed up in a toga. Vergil shows us Hesiod's Ascran farm in a Roman setting in order to show us not the similarities, but the differences between them. The *Georgics*, like the *Works and Days*, finds in farming a clue to the universe. It is a very different clue. This is not because the farm is different, but because it is a very different universe.

What Hesiod sees in the cosmos, as on the farm, is a unity and order, not simple but profound. What Vergil sees is ambiguity and ambivalence. His is a vision deeply split and multifaceted, and more than multifaceted, since in Vergil the facets contradict one another. The poems mirror the visions. The *Works and Days* is a conglomerate that only gradually reveals the common threads that are its unity. So, also, Hesiod's description of farming is a casual sequence of tasks and seasons that gradually reveals the balance and rhythm of a profound order. The *Georgics* at first appears seamless. It is only when we start placing passages together that we see the poem's discrepancies. It is only when we place these discrepancies side by side that we see that the poem is claiming contraries to be both, and equally, true.[2]

The first 350 lines of the *Georgics* will both show us Vergil's farm and provide an example of how the poem operates. As we are introduced to Vergil's farmer the season, the wind, the oxen, the farmer, and the gleaming plow all work to the same end, forming a single, unified, and Hesiodic, picture:

> At first spring, when cold streams run from white mountains,
> And the clods, with Zephyrus, break themselves into crumbling,
> Then would I have the bull groan over the deep-driven plow,
> And the plowshare begin to gleam as it is rubbed by the furrow.

> Vere novo, gelidus canis cum montibus umor
> liquitur et Zephyro putris se glaeba resolvit,
> depresso incipiat iam tum mihi taurus aratro
> ingemere et sulco attritus splendescere vomer.   1.43–46

Within fifty lines, however, Vergil's view of nature begins to shift. The "crumbling" clods become "sluggish"; the farmer's role as plowman becomes not cooperative but military, and Vergil's verse becomes more violent, both in rhythm and in connotation:

> Much does he too, who breaks the sluggish clods with mattocks,
> And helps his fields by dragging wicker hurdles. Golden
> Ceres sees him, not in vain, from high Olympus.
> And he who, going crosswise with turned plow,
> Breaks through the backs raised when he cut the plain,
> And, ever exercising his land, commands the fields.

> multum adeo, rastris glaebas qui frangit inertis
> vimineasque trahit cratis, iuvat arva, neque illum
> flava Ceres alto nequiquam spectat Olympo;
> et qui, prociso quae suscitat aequore terga,
> rursus in obliquum verso perrumpit aratro
> exercetque frequens tellurem atque imperat arvis.   1.94–99

The need for discipline and control, which here arises from the ground's unwillingness, takes on a more urgent look as Vergil describes how farming first came to be:

> Soon came labor to the corn, so that the baneful
> Mildew ate the stalks, and there bristled in the fields
> The lazy thistle. Crops die; a prickly forest succeeds,
> Burrs and caltrops, and, amid the smiling corn
> Unhappy darnel and barren oats hold sway.

> mox et frumentis labor additus, ut mala culmos
> esset robigo segnisque horreret in arvis
> carduus; intereunt segetes, subit aspera silva
> lappaeque tribolique, interque nitentia culta
> infelix lolium et steriles dominantur avenae.   1.150–54[3]

The farmer's initial cooperation with nature has now become a struggle against her; if man does not dominate, nature will. This is not Vergil's darkest vision. In his description of a spring storm, nature has turned from persistent encroachment to all-out war:

> Often have I seen, as the farmer was bringing the reaper
> Into his golden fields and already stripping the barley
> From the brittle stalk, all the winds join battle, everywhere
> Rushing together to tear up the heavy crop from its roots,
> And, uprooted, hurl it high. So, with a black whirlwind,
> The storm would bear off the light stalks and with them the flying stubble.

> saepe ego, cum flavis messorem induceret arvis
> agricola et fragili iam stringeret hordea culmo,
> omnia ventorum concurrere proelia vidi,
> quae gravidam late segetem ab radicibus imis
> sublimem expulsam eruerent: ita turbine nigro
> ferret hiems culmumque levem stipulasque volantis.   1.316–21[4]

But, lest we feel that Vergil has revealed within a comfortable Hesiodic picture, the farmer's true, and violent, relationship to nature, Vergil presents us immediately with a very different vision:

> Above all, worship the gods, and pay to great Ceres
> Her yearly rites, sacrificing on the joyful grass
> At the setting of winter's last days, now that it is clear spring.
> Then are lambs fat, and then the wine is most mellow,
> Then sleep is sweet, and thick are the shadows on the hills.

> in primis venerare deos, atque annua magnae
> sacra refer Cereri laetis operatus in herbis
> extremae sub casum hiemis, iam vere sereno.
> tum pingues agni et tum mollissima vina,
> tum somni dulces densaeque in montibus umbrae.   1.337–42

The communion of man and nature in this picture reflects that of Hesiod's summer picnic. To mark the association, Vergil's line 341 is almost a direct translation of Hesiod's "then are goats fattest, then is the wine at its best" (τῆμος πιόταταί τ' αἶγες καὶ οἶνος ἄριστος *WD* 585).[5] Vergil has come full circle. From the "new spring" (*vere novo*) of 1.43 through the spring storm, to the "bright spring" (*vere sereno*) of 1.339 Vergil has shown us not a vision of farming, but a series of incompatible visions. Fall, and the moment of sowing, is the paradigmatic season of the *Works and Days*. Spring, the season which gives life, and which breeds the storms which destroy it, is the paradigmatic season of the *Georgics*.[6]

Vergil often uses allusions to other works as an element of his own.[7] The *Georgics* is studded with references both to the *Works and Days* and to many other works, both poetry and prose. Some of these are quite detailed, as the one cited above; some are much more general, as Vergil's farm, or his didactic persona, which will be examined below. This book does not pretend to be a study of Vergil's art of allusion. It is concerned with a far more general question, Vergil's vision of farming, as set against the background of the *Works and Days*. Still, it is hard to resist the occasional parallel passage. To satisfy the urge we may look briefly at Vergil's version of the Golden and Iron Ages.

For Hesiod the Golden Age was a time before men had the need to farm; Zeus had not yet hidden our livelihood; the earth produced grain on its own. The Iron Age, in contrast, is characterized by work and by the necessity of justice. For Vergil, too, farming can characterize the Iron Age. This theme appears early in the first Georgic, when Vergil explains how Jupiter ended the Golden Age by introducing farming into human life. He did so by introducing violence, hostility, and hatred into the world. He turned nature against man, and so man against nature:

> Before Jove no farmers subdued the fields;
> Even to mark or divide the country with boundaries
> Was wrong. Men sought in common; the earth herself
> Bore all things freely, no man needing to ask.
> [Jupiter] it was put the venom in black serpents,
> And ordered the wolves to prey, the sea to swell,
> Shook honey from the leaves, hid fire away,
> And stopped the wine which ran everywhere in streams

> ante Iovem nulli subigebant arva coloni;
> ne signare quidem aut partiri limite campum
> fas erat: in medium quaerebant, ipsaque tellus
> omnia liberius, nullo poscente, ferebat.
> ille malum virus serpentibus addidit atris,
> praedarique lupos iussit pontumque moveri
> mellaque decussit foliis, ignemque removit,
> et passim rivis currentia vina repressit   1.125–32

> Then men found how to capture game in toils, and how to cheat
> With bird-lime, how to cast with hounds around great coverts
> And now one lashes a broad stream with casting-net,
> Seeking its depths; another in the sea drags dripping lines;

Then came the rigor of iron, the shrill saw-blade
(For first with wedges they split the fissile wood),
Then came the various arts. Labor conquered all,
Remorseless labor, and need, pushing in hard times.

tum laqueis captare feras et fallere visco
inventum et magnos canibus circumdare saltus;
atque alius latum funda iam verberat amnem
alta petens, pelagoque alius trahit umida lina.
tum ferri rigor atque argutae lammina serrae
(nam primi cuneis scindebant fissile lignum),
tum variae venere artes. labor omnia vicit
improbus et duris urgens in rebus egestas.

1.139–45[8]

In the first Georgic farming is the life of hostility and violence that put an end to the Golden Age. Vergil reinforces the point with his next topic: the farmer's "weapons" (*arma* 1.160). But Vergil can also see farming as the opposite, a Golden Age life of peace and harmony. At the conclusion of Book 2 farming *is* the life of the Golden Age, a feature not of Jupiter's world, but of Saturn's:[9]

Oh only too happy, if they knew their own blessings,
Farmers! For whom, far from discordant arms, the most just earth
Herself pours from her soil an easy livelihood.

O fortunatos nimium, sua si bona norint,
agricolas! quibus ipsa, procul discordibus armis,
fundit humo facilem victum iustissima tellus.

2.458–60

Before even the rule of Dictaean Jove, and before
An unholy age feasted on slaughtered oxen,
This was the life golden Saturn lived on the earth;
Not yet had men heard the war trumpet blare, not yet
The clang of the sword, laid on the hard anvil.

ante etiam sceptrum Dictaei regis et ante
impia quam caesis gens est epulata iuvencis,
aureus hanc vitam in terris Saturnus agebat;
necdum etiam audierant inflari classica, necdum
impositos duris crepitare incudibus ensis.

2.538–40

Hesiod's Golden Age was a time before men had to work; Vergil's is a time before men had to fight, either nature or each other. By focusing not on the need to work, but on the existence of violence and disunity as the feature that distinguishes the Iron from the Golden Age, Vergil changes the Golden Age from an irretrievably lost paradise into an ever-present ideal. By removing the intervening ages he also turns Hesiod's gradual movement from a long-distant past to a (hopefully) far-off future into an opposition of extremes. In so doing he gives the *Works and Days* a characteristically

Vergilian twist. Hesiod's farm is a paradigm of life now, in the Iron Age. It is at the fur-
thest remove from a Golden Age life. For Vergil, too, farming can be the opposite of
the idyllic life of the Golden Age, but it can also be our closest connection to it.[10]

This contrast between an Iron and a Golden Age runs through the *Georgics* just
as the opposition of Hesiod and Perses runs through the *Works and Days* . Around the
two concepts Vergil gathers a series of oppositions, of war and peace, division and unity,
violence and sympathy, force and understanding, Jupiter and Saturn, empire and
poetry, Octavian and Vergil, and finally, of Aristaeus and Orpheus. The opposition also
appears in the structure of the poem. Each of the four books of the poem sees farming
in its own way. They occur in opposed pairs, of farming as war and as peace, and of farming as division and as unity. The farmer of the first Georgic is, overall, at war with
nature.[11] His task is to create an ordered haven, protected from the constant invasions
of weeds, birds and pests, at the mercy of the ever-present threat of storm and drought,
and continually resisted by the grudging unwillingness of soil and climate. He is like
a man laboring to row upstream:

> So all things, through fate,
> Rush to the worst, and slipping away, fall back,
> Just as with one whose oars hardly force his craft
> Against the stream. Let his arms just once slacken—
> Headlong down the current the channel sweeps him away.

> sic omnia fatis
> in peius ruere ac retro sublapsa referri,
> non aliter quam qui adverso vix flumine lembum
> remigiis subigit, si bracchia forte remisit,
> atque illum in praeceps prono rapit alveus amni.   1.199–203[12]

This is one view of farming. In the second Georgic another view is considered.
Here the dominant image of the first Georgic, of the farmer battling a grudging earth
to create a place for his vulnerable crops, gives way to a new image, of the cooperation
of man and nature in the grafting of domestic trees onto wild. Here nature furthers the
farmer's efforts by lending her innate strength to man's direction, producing an order
both fertile and useful. At its most extreme, the second book of the *Georgics* pictures
a farmer who "plucks the fruit which the boughs, which the country, itself, / Willingly
bears" (*quos rami fructus, quos ipsa volentia rura / sponte tulere sua, carpsit* 2.500–1). We
have moved a long way from the rower swept downstream.

The pattern of the first two Georgics, of a pessimistic or dark view of farming followed by an optimistic or light one is continued in the third and fourth Georgics.[13]
The third Georgic views the farm with despair, the fourth Georgic with hope. But our
view of the farmer has shifted. In Books 1 and 2 the farmer is viewed as essentially separate from nature, whether nature is seen as the domestic nature inside the farm,
which the farmer tends, or as the wild nature outside of the farm. In Books 3 and 4,
the farmer is part of nature.[14] Vergil's farmer is here an individual who, like any creature, is subject to joy and suffering, and who may either be divided from or in harmony
with his world. In Book 3, Vergil describes the destructive, irrational, and divisive

forces of sex and death, which refuse to allow the farm, or the cosmos, unity. In Book 4, with his description of the bees, Vergil considers the possibility of a natural order and community which gives meaning to the deaths, as it does to the lives, of all individuals.

Vergil is not picturing different farms with these oppositions; he is picturing different ways in which farming exists. When the rain falls at the right time, when the spring sun brings indulgence and strength to the farm's creatures, when all things thrive, the farmer lives in cooperation and sympathy with nature. When lumps of soil resist the plow, when weeds and birds attack the crops and disease the animals, when a storm destroys the harvest, the farmer is divided from nature and at war with her. These are Vergil's conflicting visions of farming.[15] They are not resolved.[16] The final myth of Orpheus and Aristeaus provides a conclusion to the *Georgics* by summing up, and polarizing, the poem's contradictions. Vergil has transformed Hesiod's image of farming not by finding in it a different meaning, but by finding that there is no such meaning. For Hesiod the farm's contradictions reflect the complex and deceptive balance of an overarching whole. For Vergil, the contradictions are all there is.

Roman Farming

Vergil was born in 70 BC near Mantua in the north of Italy, a district populated largely by small farmers. In 37 BC, at the age of 33, he published the *Eclogues*. In 29 BC, having spent seven years on its composition, Vergil published the *Georgics*, and began the work he was to spend the rest of life on, the *Aeneid*. In the year that Vergil was born, Crassus and Pompey were consuls and a young man named Cicero was making a name for himself by prosecuting Verres. In the year that the *Georgics* was published, Octavian, soon to be Augustus, controlled the Roman world, and consuls existed in name only. The years in between had moved, as in a row of toppling dominoes, from one civil war to another: Pharsalus, Philippi, Actium. Vergil was 40 when he first saw the peaceloving land of Saturn experience peace. The seven years during which he had composed the *Georgics* had seen the culmination of what looked like Rome's nightmarish need to destroy itself. When those years ended, the Republic was gone forever, and with it the civil war which had been the subtext of Roman history *ab urbe condita*—since the foundation of the city.

Vergil was a man of peace. As such, he was intensely aware of war. The *Georgics* is not a pastoral escape from contemporary history. Rather, it holds that history just under its surface, only occasionally allowing it to break through, but always aware of its latent presence. This is only natural. Farming had a long and paradoxical relation to the Roman ideal, a relationship which Vergil fully exploits in the *Georgics* and which was a major reason for his choice of farming as the poem's subject, and of the *Works and Days* as its model. By choosing farming as the subject of his poem, Vergil had already made an implicit and complex reference to the history of Rome, both contemporary and traditional. This reference, not immediately apparent to us, had a long history for Rome in both fact and legend. In writing a poem about farming Vergil was, *ipso facto*, writing a political poem.

As the names Cincinnatus and Cato suggest, the virtue of a Roman was the virtue of a farmer.[17] The Greeks might savor stories about Themistocles, whose cleverness secured both his country's wellbeing and his own—without specifying which came first. The Romans' stories of themselves had to do with simplicity, honesty, and self-sacrifice. Odysseus, the quintessential Greek, is master of the sea, a treacherous and ever-changing element, to be conquered not by force but by craft. Cato, the quintessential Roman, is master of the land, an element ruled by neither craft nor brute force, but by the watchful, persistent labor of the farmer, who can change nothing at once, and everything over time.[18]

The farmer was also the ideal Roman because farming, which demands strength, endurance, patience, and discipline, creates, as Cato tells us, the best soldiers:

> It is from farmers that both the bravest men and the sturdiest soldiers come; their calling is most proper and stable and least liable to envy, and those engaged in that pursuit are least inclined to be disaffected.

> At ex agricolis et viri fortissimi et milites strenuissimi giguntur, maximeque pius quaestus stabilissimusque consequitur minimeque invidiosus, minimeque male cogitantes sunt qui in eo studio occupati sunt.   *De Agricultura* 1.1

It was with an army of such small farmers that the little Latin settlement on the Tiber defended itself from attackers. It succeeded so well that it found itself, eventually, staring across Sicily at Carthage, across the Alps at Gaul, and across Illyria at Macedon. Suddenly the farmer-soldier, whose aim had been to defend the peace a farmer must have, was an instrument of war. The price was the farms they defended. Soldiers spent more and more time farther and farther from their farms. Their farms, desolate from want of care, abandoned, or widowed, were bought by wealthy patricians debarred from investing their money in trade. The traditional Roman farm, small, self-supporting, and family-run, was replaced by huge, slave-run estates. Farming was paradigmatic of Rome. The small farmers whose endurance and sense of duty conquered the world were destroyed, not by their failure, but by their own success.[19]

Farming is an ideal topic for Vergil because it calls up images of both Roman virtue and Roman self-destruction. The Roman farmer-soldier is both the victor of the Roman empire and its victim. As Rome's wars became civil wars this became only more true. On the one hand, Vergil recalls for us farming as the life that made Rome great: "This life once the old Sabines lived, / and Remus and his brother; thus grew Etruria strong, / And surely thus Rome became, of all things, the fairest" (*hanc olim veteres vitam coluere Sabini / hanc Remus et frater, sic fortis Etruria crevit / scilicet et rerum facta est pulcherrima Roma* 2.533–34). On the other, he shows us the farmer-turned-soldier both destroying and being destroyed in civil war:

> The plow has not a scrap of honor
> Worthy it; the farmers gone, the fields grow squalid
> And the curved scythe is beaten into a rigid sword.

non ullus aratro
dignus honos, squalent abductis arva colonis
et curvae rigidum falces conflantur in ensem.   1.506–8

Farming implied many things to a Roman. Out of these many things Vergil creates the ambivalence of his poetry. Farming is the opposite of war, requiring and fostering peace, destroyed by violence. But the "farmers who are gone" are gone to become soldiers. The farmer who is opposed to the soldier also *is* the soldier. This is no academic paradox for Vergil. It is the question of how human life, which can flourish only in peace, comes so inevitably to be dedicated to war. It is in particular the question of why this had, so inevitably, to happen to Rome.

The farmer of the *Georgics* is metaphorically, as well as literally, both a soldier and the opposite of a soldier. The farmer lives with nature, as the city dweller cannot, but also fights her, as the city dweller need not. This complexity is, once more, intensified by the particular situation of Rome. Roman roads were built straight. Whatever natural obstacle lay in the way of that straightness was removed. It is a small detail, but it is indicative of an attitude that adapts nature to human ends, and not human ends to nature.

This desire to force nature into a human mold is familiar to us. What lay behind it, for a Roman, is less so. The Roman vision tends to see nature not as kind and nurturing, but as hostile and destructive, not as the innocent deer hunted down, but as the wolf doing the hunting, not as the pure mountain stream watering the ferns, but as the tornado heedlessly destroying them. A farm, within this vision, is a tiny niche, tamed by human beings, and protected by them against nature's self-consuming violence. To borrow Joyce's phrase, nature is a sow that consumes her own farrow.

The problem with this analysis is that there were, of course, no "Romans." There was only an infinitely various collection of individuals living in extremely varied times and circumstances. The vision described above is one possibility. Another is Vergil's own. Roman as he is, Vergil's sympathy for nature, both wild and domestic, is unmatched in Western literature. Nor was it unique to Vergil. Vergil uses the strain of Roman feeling which saw nature as hostile, and sets it against an idyllic Golden Age vision of the lion lying down with the lamb. Romans, particularly the Romans of an urban and sophisticated age, were as likely as we are to see the farm as a return to nature. They too could see farming as a union of human beings and nature, and one devoutly to be wished. If farming is, traditionally, our war against nature, it is equally, as Rome experienced urban sprawl, our peace with her.

The major difficulty we have in understanding why Vergil, or Hesiod, would write a poem about farming comes from our tendency to see farming as one job among many. Hesiod and Vergil saw farming not as a factor in the economy but as the way human beings live within nature. Hesiod did so because he was a peasant farmer. Vergil did so because he was a Roman.[20] As a Roman, Vergil saw the moral and social significance of farming, but he also saw a division between the economic and the moral sides of farming that had not existed for Hesiod. Farming had been the life and livelihood of Rome. Both one's land and one's servants had been beings to whom one had a personal, social, and religious commitment. In Vergil's time, both were simply for sale. This type of farming was, or at least could be, an expression of the willingness of a new generation of Romans to exploit both land and men, ruthlessly, in the pursuit of wealth. And it was, or could be, an expression of a new generation's extravagance and ostentation.[21] Farming embodied the virtues of the past, and the vices of the present; the qualities which had made Rome great, and the qualities which threatened to destroy her; a vision of life that valued only what could not be bought, and a vision of life that cared for nothing else. It was, for Vergil, a natural subject.

Vergil's *Works and Days*

The farm of the *Georgics* is often treated as, at best, a symbol, at worst, a mask, for the political and philosophic speculations which are seen as the poem's true subject. With this assumption, Vergil's relation to Hesiod necessarily disappears. It is hard to know which loss is more serious. Farming was, for Hesiod, the most literal level of reality: the fact that human beings cannot get food out of the ground without work. In this fact Hesiod saw also the deepest metaphysical implications about the nature of human life. When Vergil chose the *Works and Days* as his model he made the same claim, that the philosophical speculations which modern critics find, quite correctly, in the *Georgics*, are implicit in the dirt of the earth. It is from the real facts of farming that Vergil's sense of our place in the universe grows, and in which it remains rooted.[22] Vergil's farm is no more an abstract symbol for our place within nature than Aeneas is an abstract symbol for the place of the individual in history. As it is from the deeply individual reality of Aeneas that the complexities of the *Aeneid* grow, it is from the basic facts of farming that the deepest concerns of the *Georgics* arise. To treat the *Georgics* as if farming were merely its symbolic subject is to deny the poem precisely the roots Vergil sought in choosing the song of Ascra to sing through Roman towns.

It is also because these *are* the real facts of farming that they are, for Vergil, so deeply troubling. If farming is a life of ambivalence, it is not an ambivalence that we can take or leave. When the farmer of the *Georgics* is pictured in his most hostile relation to nature, imposing suffering on wild creatures who are both innocent and uncomprehending, it is nonetheless clear that his alternative is not to renounce violence and return to the Golden Age. It is, rather, to renounce control and starve. The evils of the *Georgics* are not like the evils of war, evils that can be preached against, however dubious the effect. They are like the evils of old age. The world Vergil pictures in the *Georgics* is one from which there is no escape. Whether farming is seen as a joyful sympathy with nature, or as an unrelenting war against her, human beings, if they wish to live, must farm.[23]

The *Georgics* is thus set against the background of the *Works and Days* just as the *Eclogues* is set against Theocritus and the *Aeneid* against Homer.[24] And here, as there, Vergil uses not only the general tone of the work, but also its particular features, to set off his particular aims. The first we have already mentioned: the farm. It is the same farm, but in its new setting it looks very different. Vergil's farm is Hesiod's farm, but it is no longer representative. The *latifundia* of Augustan times were enormous estates, worked by sometimes thousands of slaves, managed by overseers, often slaves themselves, and owned by wealthy men as a profitable sideline or as a luxurious country estate.[25] These farms did not produce grain, the food that sustained life for ordinary people; this was supplied from abroad. They produced instead the more profitable luxury goods, meat, honey, even flowers, that were demanded by the enormous urban market of Rome.

The farm of the *Georgics* is, in contrast, a farm like Hesiod's. The growing of grain is the farmer's main concern. The farmer makes, rather than buys, his tools, and looks to the stars, rather than to the (newly revised) calendar, to note the seasons. This is a farm where the farmer and his family plow and harvest and care for the animals.[26] Buying and selling, either of produce or supplies, is a topic that scarcely arises. The farm, not the marketplace, is the center of the farmer's life: "Hence his year's labor, hence his fatherland and small grandchildren / He sustains, from hence his herds of cattle and his deserving oxen." (*hinc anni labor, hinc patriam parvosque nepotes / sustinet, hinc armenta boum meritosque iuvencos* 2.514–15). Vergil's farmer sees farming neither as a relaxation from the tensions of city living nor as a business for profit. Vergil's farmer sees farming as Hesiod did, as a way of life.

The kind of farm which Vergil describes is not a contemporary farm. It is not therefore unreal. It is the kind of farm that Vergil, like ourselves, would have seen as traditional and paradigmatic. It is probably the kind of farm Vergil grew up with. It is also the kind of farm from which Rome grew, both in tradition and in fact. But by adopting a farm like Hesiod's, Vergil complicates rather than acquires the stable and self-evident reality of Hesiod's farm.[27] Vergil portrays the traditional Roman farm. It is a farm that is paradigmatic of farming. It is not, however, a representative of contemporary Roman farming. A contemporary Roman farm, on the other hand, may provide a life within nature far better than the life of the city. It is not, however, what farming paradigmatically is.

The farm is only the first of the features that Vergil takes, and transforms, from the *Works and Days*. Vergil borrows, along with the subject of the poem, the tone of the poet. The poet of the *Georgics* is, like the poet of the *Works and Days*, pointedly didactic, concerned with a commonplace subject, and personally involved in his poem.[28] In all of these ways Vergil out-Hesiods Hesiod. The commonplace, even vulgar, nature of his subject is explicitly pointed out: "I can repeat for you many old precepts, / Unless you would avoid the vexation of knowing such minute occasions of care" (*Possum multa tibi veterum praecepta referre, / ni refugis tenuisque piget cognoscere curas* 1.176–77). His subject matter makes the poem a great challenge: "And well I know how great a task it is / To conquer these with words, and bring honor to narrow matters" (*nec sum animi dubius, verbis ea vincere magnum / quam sit et angustis hunc addere rebus honorem* 3.289–90). And finally, the most elevated verse and the most commonplace subjects are deliberately juxtaposed: "Now, worshipful Pales, now must there be song in lofty strain. / First I decree that the sheep in soft pens / eat their grass" (*nunc, veneranda Pales, magno nunc ore sonanda / Incipiens stabulis edico in mollibus herbam / carpere ovis* 3.294–6). Vergil's didactic treatment of a commonplace subject distinguishes the *Georgics* from both the *Eclogues* and the *Aeneid*. It also makes what is straightforward in the *Works and Days* ambiguous in the *Georgics*. Lucretius smeared the honey of poetry around the rim of his cup. Vergil deliberately puts his small beer into a crystal goblet.

The result is a feeling of discrepancy, between the subject and the poetry, and between the subject and the poet. Vergil, unlike Hesiod, is never quite part of his poem. Hesiod implicitly vouches for the truth of what he describes by involving himself. Vergil does the same, explicitly: "I would dare entrust vines to even a shallow ditch" (*Ausim vel tenui vitem commitere sulco* 2.289); "nor do I dislike [a cow] marked with spots of white" (*nec mihi displiceat maculis insignis et albo* 3.56). The poem's most dramatic scenes—the spring storm of Book 1, the degeneration of seeds, the old Corycian gardener—are introduced as things the poet himself has seen.[29] But Vergil never did see fullgrown trees transplanted, as he claims in the last passage, nor does he expect us to believe that he did. The explicit personal testimony is explicitly a poetic device. Vergil's use of himself in his poem thus accomplishes, finally, the opposite of what Hesiod accomplishes; he does not overcome, but only confirms, the distance between reader and poet.

The *Georgics*, like the *Works and Days*, and unlike the rest of Vergil's poetry, introduces the poet into the poem.[30] But Vergil, unlike Hesiod, does not portray himself as a farmer. In the *Works and Days* Hesiod boasts about his poetic victory at Aulis. But we also hear about how Hesiod and his brother divided the farm, how their father came to have it, what kind of place it is. In the *Georgics*, Vergil refers to the *Eclogues*, to a future poem about Caesar, and to his present task, a poem about farming, written at Maecenas' request. This is all that Vergil has to say about himself. As Hesiod "signed" the *Theogony*, Vergil signs the *Georgics*, the only time he ever uses his name in his poetry. Again he adopts the Hesiodic device only to transform it. Hesiod identifies himself as poet and shepherd; Vergil identifies himself as the writer of a poem *about* shepherds. Hesiod's role in the *Works and Days* is as farmer and poet. Vergil's, in the *Georgics*, is as the poet of farming.[31]

Like the *Works and Days*, the *Georgics* is a poem, not an autobiography. The fact that Vergil presents himself to us as a poet rather than as a farmer means neither that he is not writing about farming nor that he does not understand it. Vergil's poetry can be as expressive of the spirit of a rather cynical small farmer as Hesiod's. His witty paraphrase of Hesiod's "Give your praise to a small boat, but put your freight in a big one" (νῆ᾽ ὀλίγην αἰνεῖν, μεγάλη δ᾽ ἐνὶ φορτία θέσθαι *WD* 643), "A large estate is for praising, / A small one's for farming" (*laudato ingentia rura, / exiguum colito* 2.412–13);[32] his injunction to order the vines "not *only* that the view may feed an idle fancy" (*non animum modo uti pascat prospectus inanem* 2.285); and his exposition of the virtues of the old Corycian's meal, "returning home late at night / He would load his table with food, *unbought*" (*seraque revertens / nocte domum dapibus mensas onerabat* inemptis 4.132–33), are comments made by a man who knows farming, and a farmer's foibles, as a farmer does.[33] Nonetheless, Vergil presents himself, quite deliberately, not as a farmer but as a poet. In order to understand why we must look at how the identification affects the poem.

Vergil's address to Caesar, the lines which open the *Georgics* proper, separates Vergil the poet from the farmers he is concerned with: "And pitying with me the farmers, ignorant of the way, / Begin, and even now learn to be called with prayers" (*ignarosque viae mecum miseratus agrestis / ingredere et votis iam nunc adsuesce vocari* 1.41–42). His later celebration of farming—"Oh, only too happy, if they knew their own blessings, / Farmers!" (*O fortunatos nimium, sua si bona norint, / agricolas!* 2.458–59)—is again spoken with the voice of an outsider. The impression is reinforced by Vergil's sudden reference to himself, not among the farmers whose happiness he has just been describing, but in contrast to them:

> But for me, first above all may the sweet Muses,
> Whose sacred emblems I, greatly enamored, bear
> Accept me, showing me the ways of skies and stars
> . . . .
>
> But if I cannot reach these realms of nature
> Because the blood about my heart is cold,
> Then let the country please me, and the streams
> Watering her valleys; may I love the woods
> And the rivers, and live without fame.

> Me vero primum dulces ante omnia Musae,
> quarum sacra fero ingenti percussus amore,
> accipiant caelique vias et sidera monstrent
> . . . .
>
> sin has ne possim naturae accedere partis
> frigidus obstiterit circum praecordia sanguis,
> rura mihi et rigui placeant in vallibus amnes,
> flumina amem silvasque inglorius.   2.475–77,[34] 483–86

In a similar scene—"then is the moment / for the shade of the rock and the Bibline wine, / for the milk-baked cake, and the milk, when the goats are drying off" (ἀλλὰ τότ' ἤδη / εἴη πετραίη τε σκιὴ καὶ Βίβλινος οἶνος / μᾶζά τ' ἀμολγαίη γάλα τ' αἰγῶν σβεννυμενάων WD 588–90)—Hesiod wishes for summer shade and wine. He does not wish for his own contentment with them. Hesiod presents himself as part of the countryside he is describing. Vergil presents himself as one who would like to be.

The importance of Vergil's presentation of himself as a poet rather than as a farmer lies in the perspective it creates within the poem. As a farmer, Hesiod saw the farm from inside. As a poet, Vergil watches it from outside.[35] He sees, as Hesiod saw, harmony and order on the farm. But because he looks from different points of view, he also sees diversity and conflict. He sees peace on the farm, but he also sees war. In identifying himself as a farmer, Hesiod creates a single and unifying point of view from which to see farming. By identifying himself as a poet, Vergil leaves his own point of view undetermined. In so doing he gives us the culmination of his transformation of Hesiod—in not a single, but in a multiplicity of visions.

Vergil and the Animals

One peculiarity of the *Georgics*, as compared, in particular to the *Works and Days*, stands out immediately. Vergil's animals are all but human.[36] His oxen are ready for the yoke "when their free necks / Are accustomed to servitude" (*ubi libera colla / servitio adsuerint* 3.167–168). His colts are trained "weak and still tremulous, still ignorant in years" (*invalidus etiamque tremens, etiam inscius aevi* 3.189). His goats are "mindful" (G 3.316), his stricken sheep "listless" (G 3.465), his ox "mournful" (G 3.518), his defeated bull "humiliated" (G 3.226). Wild nature is no less personal. Vergil's ant is "fearful for a destitute old age" (*inopi metuens formica senectae* 1.186); his frogs "croak their ancient complaint" (*et veterem in limo ranae cecinere querellam* 1.378); and even the viper, lurking in the stables, flees the light in terror (*caelumque exterrita fugit* 3.417), as fearful as it is feared.

Vergil adopts many points of view during the course of the *Georgics*. One is the point of view of the farmer. Another is the point of view of nature, both wild and domestic. Vergil's sense of nature is real and immediate. It is expressed directly, not as it appears to the farmer, but as their individual joys or sorrows appear to the birds, beasts, or plants that constitute nature.[37] By attributing to the plants and animals of the *Georgics* human emotions and human motives, Vergil gives them an individual and completely personal life. This personalization may create a sense that Vergil's birds, beasts, plants, and (most especially) bees, are merely symbols for human beings, and his "nature" no more than an extended allegory.[38] The impression is natural, but wrong. The animals of the *Georgics* are not symbols; they are themselves. To see them otherwise is to deprive the poem of its essential theme. The *Georgics* does not use nature as a tool in considering its true topic; its true topic is nature itself.[39]

Hesiod, in general, does not view nature in a human light. This, like any good rule, has its exception—the octopus. Hesiod's octopus, or "boneless one" (ἀνόστεος), "gnaws / his own foot in his fireless home, and his miserable haunts. / The sun shows him no pasture to hasten to" (ὃν πόδα τένδει / ἔν τ' ἀπύρῳ οἴκῳ καὶ ἤθεσι λευγαλέοισιν· / οὐ γάρ οἱ ἠέλιος δείκνυ νομὸν ὁρμηθῆναι *WD* 524–25). The description sheds light on Vergil. The octopus' "fireless" underwater home, and its lamentable lack of pasturage, are not details added to make the octopus serve as a trope for man. They are added to bring home to us, in terms that we immediately understand, the miserable life of an octopus. Vergil's personalization of nature serves the same end. Vergil's plants and animals do not *act* as human beings do; they act as themselves.[40] They are *described* in human terms, because these are the terms to which we respond. Vergil's "pathetic fallacy" thus serves to lend nature an individuality and immediacy that brings it to life for the reader, as it is alive in fact.[41]

Vergil's description of a nature made personal reveals his profound sympathy for the world that is not human. It also lends to nature a point of view.[42] In so doing, it allows us to view the farm of the *Works and Days* from an entirely new perspective, the perspective of the birds who lose their nests to newly cleared plowland, of the young vines whose vigorous growth is trimmed back, of the colt who feels the bit for the first time, the stallion who must be discarded, the bees protecting their hive. When Hesiod describes the crane, we see the crane from the farmer's point of view:

> Take heed when you hear the voice of the crane, as she cries her yearly cry,
> from high up in the clouds;
> she gives you the signal for plowing, and shows the season in winter
> when the rain comes; and she bites the heart of the oxless man

φράζεσθαι δ᾽ εὖτ᾽ ἂν γεράνου φωνὴν ἐπακούσεις
ὑψόθεν ἐκ νεφέων ἐνιαύσια κεκληγυίης,
ἥ τ᾽ ἀρότοιό τε σῆμα φέρει καὶ χείματος ὥρην
δεικνύει ὀμβρηροῦ· κραδίην δ᾽ ἔδακ᾽ ἀνδρὸς ἀβούτεω·   WD 448–51

When Vergil describes birds, the case is different:

> You may see them pouring great showers over their shoulders,
> Now dunking their heads in the waves, now dashing into the water,
> And zealously, in vain, exulting in their contest of bathing.

> certatim largos umeris infundere rores,
> nunc caput obiectare fretis, nunc currere in undas
> et studio incassum videas gestire lavandi.   1.385–87

> Then the rooks, with narrowed throats, repeat, three
> Or four times their soft cries, and often in their high nests
> Joyful with some strange, some unwonted delight,
> Amid the leaves they chatter to one another

> tum liquidas corvi presso ter gutture voces
> aut quater ingeminant, et saepe cubilibus altis
> nescio qua praeter solitum dulcedine laeti
> inter se in foliis strepitant   1.411–13

These birds are not revealing to us our point of view; they are shown us as creatures independent of ourselves.

Vergil personalizes nature not in order to show us ourselves, but to the opposite end, to show us that nature's viewpoint is *not* our own. Side by side with the viewpoint of nature, Vergil gives us a very different viewpoint, that of the farmer. This contrast, which runs throughout the Georgics, appears most vividly in Vergil's description of fertile land:

> From no other plain will you see
> More wagons, behind slow oxen, wend homeward;
> Or from where an indignant plowman has taken the wood
> And overturned groves idle through many years,
> And ripped up the ancient homes of the birds, down to the
> Roots; they seek the sky, nests abandoned behind them,
> But the rough plain glistens under the driven plowshare.

> non ullo ex aequore cernes
> plura domum tardis decedere plaustra iuvencis;
> aut unde iratus silvam devexit arator
> et nemora evertit multos ignava per annos,
> antiquasque domos avium cum stirpibus imis

eruit; illae altum nidis petiere relictis,
at rudis enituit impulso vomere campus.   2.205–11

Against the dispossession of the birds is placed the farmer's glad appreciation of slow wagons and gleaming fields, an appreciation that comes alive in the beauty of Vergil's verse.[43] This appreciation the birds cannot share. This is partially because of their loss, but more importantly because plowed fields are no part of their world, and have for them no beauty. These birds are not symbols for human beings. They are beings on their own, whose vision is different from, and at times irreconcilable with, that of the farmer.

By portraying himself as a poet, Vergil has given himself access to a multiplicity of perspectives. By suddenly switching his perspective, as he does in describing the newly deforested fields, he is able to create, from one scene, two very different visions of farming. This is, in small, the critical difference between Hesiod's description of farming and Vergil's. Hesiod's farm is a whole. His aim is to show us both the unity and the complexity of that whole. Vergil's farm speaks with many voices.[44] His aim is to make us hear them all.

4

GOD

The Divine Order

At the paradigmatic moment of his year Hesiod's farmer prays:

> Pray to Zeus-Under-Earth and to Demeter the Holy
> that the sacred corn of Demeter be heavy when ready for harvest;
> pray as you first begin plowing . . .

> εὔχεσθαι δὲ Διὶ χθονίῳ Δημήτερί θ' ἁγνῇ
> ἐκτελέα βρίθειν Δημήτερος ἱερὸν ἀκτήν
> ἀρχόμενος τὰ πρῶτ' ἀρότου . . .
>
> WD 465–67

The prayer reflects the advice Hesiod gave earlier to Perses: "work, you stupid Perses, / work at the tasks that the gods have set for men to do" (ἐργάζεο νήπιε Πέρση, / ἔργα, τά τ' ἀνθρώποισι θεοὶ διετεκμήραντο WD 397–8). Farming, for Hesiod, is indissolubly linked to God. Why this must be the case is clear from Hesiod's overall point of view. Hesiod does not feel a need to distinguish the natural from the divine. In fact, Hesiod never uses a word for "nature" at all. This does not mean, of course, that he had no sense of what we call "natural." Hesiod was, as anyone interested in farming must be, vividly aware of the most important implication of our word "nature," that it works regularly. Spring follows winter; summer follows spring. The crane flies by at the time for plowing; at the time for harvesting the Pleiades, after forty days of being hidden, reemerge from the ocean (WD 383–6). Nature is an order. For Hesiod it is the order of Zeus. This is the order Hesiod lives within in the *Works and Days*, and the order whose development he describes in the *Theogony*.

98

Traditionally, Zeus conquered his father Cronos and the earlier generation of gods, the Titans, in the battle called the Titanomachia, or War of the Titans. Hesiod, in the *Theogony*, brings together four myths—the chaining of Prometheus, the War of the Titans, the challenge of Typhoeus, and the swallowing of Wisdom—in order to create a victory in four parts. The two middle conquests are accomplished through force, as traditionally.[1] The first and last are, unusually, victories of cunning. As such they provide a clue to Hesiod's aim in expanding the victory; by so expanding the myth, he is able to attribute Zeus' success not to force alone, but to force combined with cunning. In so doing Hesiod draws from the myths of tradition the thread that he sees as their underlying meaning, that the order of Zeus came about, and is permanent in the cosmos, through the uniting of force and intelligence in Zeus.[2]

Hesiod's aim peeks out again through the inconsistencies that he is willing to tolerate in order to achieve it. As Aeschylus saw, the myth of Prometheus naturally tends to pit Prometheus' craft against Zeus' power, an aspect dramatized in the opening of *Prometheus Bound*, where Force and Power, Zeus' allies, nail Prometheus to his rock (PB 1–85; Th. 385–405).[3] Even in Hesiod's account, Prometheus' *actual* punishment is clearly accomplished by force: "And he bound in inescapable fetters Prometheus of the shifting counsels, / With painful chains, and through his middle he drove a pillar" (δῆσε δ' ἀλυκτοπέδῃσι Προμηθέα ποικιλόβουλον, / δεσμοῖς ἀργαλέοισι, μέσον διὰ κίον' ἐλάσσας Th. 521–22).[4] The event in which the *Theogony*'s account climaxes, Zeus' outwitting of Prometheus through the creation of woman, does Prometheus no harm at all. Nonetheless, the creation of woman is Hesiod's focus.

As human beings are, at best, incidental to this part of the *Theogony*, the reason for Hesiod's focus must be that he wants Zeus' victory to be one of intelligence, even against the natural bent of the story.[5] Prometheus' tricking Zeus, first into choosing the wrong sacrificial portion, and then by the theft of fire, is designed to lead into and culminate in Zeus' retaliation, the "sheer deception, impossible for men" (δόλον αἰπύν, ἀμήχανον ἀνθρώποισιν Th. 589) that ends the myth. Having told the myth as a story of cunning, Hesiod can draw from it the lesson he sought: "Thus there is no way to deceive the mind of Zeus, or to pass beyond it" (ὣς οὐκ ἔστι Διὸς κλέψαι νόον οὐδὲ παρελθεῖν Th. 613).[6]

A certain development of the theme of intelligence also runs through the victories by force. At the opening of Hesiod's account of the War of the Titans, it is clear that force alone is not going to be enough:[7]

> They, at that time, with piercing war in their hearts,
> Had fought, straining with each other, ten years together.
> Nor, from the harsh quarrel, was there end or release,
> For either side, but equally stretched was the war's culmination.

> οἵ ῥα τότ' ἀλλήλοισι μάχην θυμαλγέ' ἔχοντες
> συνεχέως ἐμάχοντο δέκα πλείους ἐνιαυτούς·
> οὐδέ τις ἦν ἔριδος χαλεπῆς λύσις οὐδὲ τελευτὴ
> οὐδετέροις, ἴσον δὲ τέλος τέτατο πτολέμοιο.   Th. 635–38

Earth breaks the deadlock by advising the recall of her primal sons, the Hundred-

Handers. Here, however, there is a critical shift in the game plan. The Hundred-Handers attribute their recall, this plan, and intelligence altogether, not to Earth, but to Zeus: "But we ourselves know / That you are exceeding in wisdom, and in understanding exceeding" (ἀλλὰ καὶ αὐτοὶ / ἴδμεν ὅ τοι περὶ μὲν πραπίδες, περὶ δ' ἐστὶ νόημα *Th.* 655–56).[8]

Zeus' next victory is again primarily a victory of force. It is now over the last child of Earth, Typhoeus:

> And then might have been a deed undoable on that day,
> And [Typhoeus] have been the ruler of gods and of men,
> Had the father of men and of gods not used his sharp mind.
> But harshly he thundered and strong, and, Earth, round about,
> With terrible sound resounded, and wide Heaven above,
> And Sea, and streams of Ocean, and Tartarus, under the Earth.

> καί νύ κεν ἔπλετο ἔργον ἀμήχανον ἤματι κείνῳ,
> καί κεν ὅ γε θνητοῖσι καὶ ἀθανάτοισι ἄναξεν,
> εἰ μὴ ἄρ' ὀξὺ νόησε πατὴρ ἀνδρῶν τε θεῶν τε·
> σκληρὸν δ' ἐβρόντησε καὶ ὄβριμον, ἀμφὶ δὲ γαῖα
> σμερδαλέον κονάβησε καὶ οὐρανὸς εὐρὺς ὕπερθε
> πόντός τ' Ὠκεανοῦ τε ῥοαὶ καὶ τάρταρα Γαίης   *Th.* 836–41

Completing the development which started with the previous episode, both the force and the intelligence of the victory now belong entirely to Zeus. Neither the Hundred-Handers nor Earth is needed. As we see by disregarding modern distinctions between lower-case and capital letters, the reaction of Earth/earth to this victory is identical to her earlier reaction. When her former children, the Titans, were suppressed by their father Ouranos, and hidden in her secret places, Earth/earth groaned. In the only other use that Hesiod makes of the verb, when Typhoeus is suppressed, she groans again.[9] Earth, the fountainhead of female cunning, has been bested, along with her son, by Zeus.[10]

The incongruity that we saw in the Prometheus myth appears again, in a rather more striking form, in Zeus' conquest of Wisdom. Zeus must prevent his first wife, Wisdom, from bearing the child that will supplant him. He does this by swallowing her. One might imagine Zeus seizing and swallowing Wisdom by virtue of his superior strength. It is difficult to imagine what arguments, however crafty, convinced her to allow herself to be swallowed. Nonetheless, this is Hesiod's presentation:

> Zeus, king of the gods, first made Wisdom his wife,
> Who among gods was most knowing, and among mortal men.
> But just when the goddess, gray-eyed Athene, was about
> To be born, just then, with a trick, deceiving her wits
> With slippery words, he stowed her away in his stomach,
> Through the counsels of Earth and of the starry Heaven.

> Ζεὺς δὲ θεῶν βασιλεὺς πρώτην ἄλοχον θέτο Μῆτιν,
> πλεῖστα θεῶν εἰδυῖαν ἰδὲ θνητῶν ἀνθρώπων.

ἀλλ' ὅτε δὴ ἄρ' ἔμελλε θεὰν γλαυκῶπιν Ἀθήνην
τέξεσθαι, τότ' ἔπειτα δόλῳ φρένας ἐξαπατήσας
αἱμυλίοισι λόγοισιν ἑὴν ἐσκάθετο νηδύν,
Γαίης φραδμοσύνῃσι καὶ Οὐρανοῦ ἀστερόεντος·

Th. 886–91

This is the final episode of Zeus' rise to power. In it Zeus, by swallowing "Wisdom," literally unites force and intelligence within himself.[11] By so doing he establishes not only his order, but also its permanence. Practically, he has done so because he can no longer be overthrown by either force or craft, and there is no third alternative.[12] Mythically, he has done so because Athene's brother, the son destined to supplant Zeus as he supplanted his father, Cronos, and as Cronos supplanted his father, Ouranos, can now not be conceived.[13] Even more importantly, however, he cannot be conceived because Zeus has accomplished the union of himself and Wisdom which should have occurred in the child (*Th.* 894–98), in himself.

Ouranos hid his children in their mother, Earth. Cronos, by swallowing them, hid his children in himself. In both cases the mother remained to plot, successfully, against the father who suppressed her children. Zeus finds the correct solution to the problem. He swallows the mother.[14] Hesiod thus resolves a theme that has run throughout the succession myths of the *Theogony*. Craft, in the *Theogony*, is predominantly a female characteristic, above all of Earth, the primeval female. Force is the attribute of the male gods.[15] In the usual pattern of overthrow, as, for example, the castration of Ouranos, Earth, the cunning female, joins her wise counsel to the strength of one of her powerful, but mostly brainless, sons.[16] In his defeat of Typhoeus, the last and most violent son of Earth, Zeus broke this combination.[17] In swallowing Wisdom he has, by listening to the counsel of Earth for one last time, combined the female and the male, force and craft, within himself.

This combination of force and intelligence which is explicit in the narrative of the *Theogony* is implicit in the poem's genealogical development. The distinction we feel between the primeval gods, the nature gods, and the Monsters, on the one hand, and the anthropomorphic Olympian gods, on the other, is essentially the contrast between sheer power in the former, and directed power, that is force combined with intelligence (νόος), in the latter. The contrast between Typhoeus and Zeus exists on both the narrative and the genealogical levels. On the genealogical level Typhoeus is a throwback to the Giants and the Monsters. He is, like them, the child of primal deities, here Earth and Tartarus, and he is a composite, with hands and feet, and a hundred snake-like heads which glance fire from their eyes. Each of his heads has a voice, and each voice is different; now he speaks as a god, now as a bull, now a lion, a whelp, or a snake (*Th.* 823–35). Of all of Zeus' challengers, Typhoeus is the hardest to draw.

Typhoeus' similarity to the Giants and Monsters also provides a clue to his role in the narrative of the *Theogony*. The Monsters are destroyed by the civilizing, ordering force of Zeus' children; Typhoeus must be destroyed by Zeus himself. This is because Typhoeus, as pure force, completely divorced from intelligence, is also the embodiment of disorder.[18] As such, he is the source, even after his defeat, of the erratic and irregular winds which wreak havoc on the sea and in farmers' fields (*Th.* 871–85). Opposed to these are Boreas, Notus, and Zephyr, the north, south, and west winds which are "from the gods," and so have their origin, ultimately, in Zeus. These, the winds of

Hesiod's description of farming and "a great boon to mortals," (*Th.* 871) are the orderly winds, each playing, in its season, its particular role within the order of Zeus.[19]

As the embodiment of force alone Typhoeus is the champion of disorder. He thus reveals, by what he is not, what the union of force and intelligence means to Hesiod. It means the creation of order. Craft without force, like that of Earth, can move nothing. Force without intelligence, like Typhoeus', can only destroy. When they are only combined, as in the combination of Earth and Typhoeus, or of Earth and Cronos, they can also be separated, and so defeated. But as copper and tin can be fused together into bronze, force and intelligence may also be united into a new element, order. This is a fusion that cannot be reversed, and so cannot be overcome. Traditionally in Indo-European mythology, the victory of the weather god over the snake monster occurs after the weather god has established his reign, a dominance which he then loses, temporarily, to the challenger. Accordingly, in Greek mythology, we find traces of a tradition that sees Zeus as having to *regain* his throne from Typhoeus.[20] It is not so for Hesiod. Hesiod emphatically sets the victory over Typhoeus *before* the beginning of Zeus' reign. He does so because Zeus, for Hesiod, is the source of an order which entered into the cosmos simultaneously, and permanently, with himself.[21] Once it has been created it cannot be dissolved.

With the ascension of Zeus, the universe becomes a cosmos. Hesiod's central image for the establishment of this order is Zeus' distribution of "honors" (τιμαί) to the gods. It is with this image that Hesiod frames the narrative of the *Theogony*, forming a ring pattern which matches the opening Hymn to the Muses, set in human time, against the final birth of the children of Zeus' new order.[22] The image is first used when the Muses first see their father:

> In heaven he was reigning,
> Himself holding the lightning and the bright thunderbolt,
> In strength having conquered Cronos, his father. And well in each thing
> He had ordered the immortals' ways and assigned them their honors.

> ὁ δ' οὐρανῷ ἐμβασιλεύει,
> αὐτὸς ἔχων βροντὴν ἠδ' αἰθαλόεντα κεραυνόν,
> κάρτει νικήσας πατέρα Κρόνον· εὖ δὲ ἕκαστα
> ἀθανάτοις διέταξε νόμους καὶ ἐπέφραδε τιμάς.   *Th.* 70–74

It then reappears as Zeus, after his conquest of Typhoeus, is made king:

> And when the blessed gods had accomplished their labor
> And with the Titans decided their honors by force,
> Then it was that, through the counsels of Earth, they urged
> Zeus to be king and to rule, far-seeing Olympian Zeus,
> Over the immortals. And he divided amongst them their honors.

> αὐτὰρ ἐπεί ῥα πόνον μάκαρες θεοὶ ἐξετέλεσσαν
> Τιτήνεσσι δὲ τιμάων κρίναντο βίηφι,
> δή ῥα τότ' ὤτρυνον βασιλευέμεν ἠδὲ ἀνάσσειν

Γαίης φραδμοσύνῃσιν Ὀλύμπιον εὐρύοπα Ζῆν
ἀθανάτων· ὁ δὲ τοῖσιν ἐὺ διεδάσσατο τιμάς.   Th. 881–85

Zeus' "distribution of honors" to the gods is, primarily, his granting each of them
a place within his new reign. As such the distribution both frames the narrative and
is responsible for a good deal of the story.[23] Zeus' success is achieved largely through
his extensive co-optation of the old gods (*Th.* 392–6).[24] Thus the Cyclopes, who give
Zeus the thunderbolt; Styx and her significantly named children, Victory, Power,
Force, and Striving; the Hundred-Handers; Leto, Memory, and Right, who are to be
Zeus' consorts; and Hecate, who is most honored by Zeus, all become part of Zeus' new
order. Given that Prometheus, Atlas, and Menoetius, the children of Iapetos, have
already been conquered, we see why Hesiod never names the "Titans" that Zeus must
defeat. There are very few of them left.[25]

It is of critical importance to Hesiod that Zeus should be the source of honors even
for the gods who predate him. In order that there should be no confusion on this
point, Hesiod takes the radical step of ignoring the tradition that the gods decided their
places by lot, in particular, that Zeus, Poseidon, and Hades drew lots to determine their
provinces.[26] That Hesiod is perfectly conversant with the tradition is clear from his
description of Hecate, whose honors "from the first division" are now hers through Zeus
(*Th.* 421–28). But he never describes it. For him, this drawing of lots, which traditionally determined the constitution of the cosmos, was merely the *old* distribution, a
no doubt necessary makeshift prior to the coming of Zeus.[27]

The source of the distribution of honors is an important issue for Hesiod because
what this distribution constitutes is no less than the divine order itself. In his description of Hecate, Hesiod equates the goddess's "honors" with her "prerogative" (γέρας),
her "share" (αἶσα), and her "portion" (μοῖρα) (*Th.* 411–15; 424–28). Either of the last
two Greek words could also be translated as "fate," that is, the "portion" or "share" one
is allotted altogether.[28] For Hesiod, each god has his (or her) share in the cosmos. That
share is at once their portion, their prerogative, their particular sphere of influence,
and their honor. Taken together, all the divine "honors," as all the divine "portions,"
comprise the cosmos itself.[29] This is why Hesiod refuses to believe that the source of
the divine honors was a lottery. Not chance, but the combination of intelligence and
force in Zeus are, for Hesiod, the sole source of divine order.[30]

Hesiod's interest in the "portions" of the gods appears once more in his somewhat curious treatment of what are, to us, "abstract" gods. On the one hand, Hesiod seems
indifferent to the difference between "kinds" of gods, grouping gods together regardless of whether they are, from our point of view, abstract, primal, natural, or anthropomorphic. On the other hand, however, the abstract gods, as such, seem somehow
to be favored. For one thing, there is their longevity. The older generation of Titans
are, as a group (if not individually), imprisoned in Tartarus (*Th.* 715–20). The monstrous progeny that descend from Sea through Ceto are slain by the heroic sons of Zeus.
But the abstract descendants of Night are not eliminated in Zeus' new order; they are
supplemented and so transformed by their good twins, Zeus' abstract children. Moreover, Zeus' children, together with much of the last generation of gods, *are* overwhelmingly abstractions. This same phenomenon appears in the *Works and Days*.

Here the Olympians are largely notable for their absence. Zeus occupies center stage, with a fairly colorless Demeter on one side of him, and arguably the most alive and anthropomorphic goddess of the poem, Justice, on the other.

In fact, Hesiod groups the gods not according to kind but according to their "portion."[31] Thus Gap (the basic meaning of the Greek word "Chaos"), Earth, Tartarus, and Sexual Love (Eros) are Hesiod's primal gods; the river Styx, the force by which the gods themselves swear, is mother to Power and Force; Demeter, goddess of farming, is the mother of Wealth; Ares is father to Panic and Fear; and the Graces, Muses, and Seasons are the sisters of the lovely and harmonious twins, Apollo and Artemis. Similarly, in Hesiod's description of Aphrodite:

> With her went Love, and lovely Desire followed,
> At her birth, when first she came to the gathering of the gods.
> This from the beginning was her honor, and her allotted
> Portion among men and among the immortal gods:
> The whisperings of maidens, smiles and deceits
> And sweet pleasure and friendship and graciousness.

> τῇ δ' Ἔρος ὡμάρτησε καὶ Ἵμερος ἕσπετο καλὸς
> γεινομένῃ τὰ πρῶτα θεῶν τ' ἐς φῦλον ἰούσῃ·
> ταύτην δ' ἐξ ἀρχῆς τιμὴν ἔχει ἠδὲ λέλογχε
> μοῖραν ἐν ἀνθρώποισι καὶ ἀθανάτοισι θεοῖσι,
> παρθενίους τ' ὀάρους μειδήματά τ' ἐξαπάτας τε
> τέρψίν τε γλυκερὴν φιλότητά τε μειλιχίην τε.   *Th.* 201–6

Love (Eros) and Desire, a primal god and an abstraction, follow Aphrodite not because they are similar in kind, but because her portion, smiles, deceits, and pleasure, is also theirs.

From another point of view Hesiod could easily have included Love and Desire in the concluding list of Aphrodite's areas of influence, her "honors." In fact, just below, two of her "portions," Deceit and Friendship, *are* born as goddesses in their own right (*Th.* 223–24). Portion and divinity seem to be interchangeable for Hesiod. This is not really surprising. Hesiod did not distinguish Justice and justice, Wisdom and wisdom, Strife and strife. A fact of the human world is, for Hesiod, simultaneously the portion of a god within the order of Zeus. When Hesiod discovers the power and place of Gossip among human beings he draws the necessary conclusion: "it is itself a kind of god" (θεός νύ τίς ἐστι καὶ αὐτή *WD* 764). In essence divinity *is*, for Hesiod, a portion of Zeus' order. The "abstract" gods continue to enjoy their portions in Zeus' order simply because, in a sense, they are portions.[32] If Hesiod favors the abstract gods it is because they embody the idea of portion which is at the heart of his idea of divinity.

Zeus and His Children

Zeus is, for Hesiod, the center of the divine order.[33] This is true to such an extent that Hesiod can refer to "Zeus" or to "the gods" interchangeably. In the narrative of the

Theogony, where Zeus' will is most often opposed to that of the other gods, such an identification was clearly impossible; it is made only after Zeus' distribution of honors.[34] The identification does not imply that Zeus controls the action of the other gods—Hecate, for example, acts like Zeus himself, if and for whom she will (*Th.* 429–46). Zeus and "the gods" are the same not because "the gods" do not have free will, but because Zeus has given the gods their portions, and their portions are their identities.[35] In determining the gods' portions and ways (νόμοι) Zeus has determined their natures as surely as he determined ours when he gave us justice and farming to be our "ways" (*WD* 276–80, 388–93).[36]

Zeus has incorporated the old gods into his order by assigning to them their portions. With the new gods he takes an entirely different tack. He begets them. Fatherhood, more in a biological than in a social sense, is Hesiod's model for Zeus' relation to his order. Zeus' sexual activity is, consequently, delayed until after his succession. At that point it becomes understandably intense. It is nonetheless remarkable that Zeus, and only Zeus, is ever described as having more than one "wife." Even more significantly, he is virtually the only Olympian to have divine children. The notorious immorality of the Olympian gods may, inadvertently, have been created by Hesiod's sense of how profound the implications of paternity could be.

Hesiod ends the *Theogony* with first Zeus' descendants, and then the descendants of the other Olympians, progressively divine, heroic, and human.[37] As he does so Hesiod returns us to the Zeus of human time encountered in the Proem, immanent rather than transcendent, acting through his order rather than upon it, and as he appears in the genealogical mode of the *Theogony* rather than as he is in the narrative mode.[38] It is within this order that the significance of Zeus' paternal role becomes clear. Zeus acts through his children, not imposing his order, but begetting it.[39] He has, in essence, become the genealogical mode. Zeus, as father, is a moving cause which develops order from the inside. This image of begetting order rather than imposing it carries within itself, wonderfully, all the implications of an immanent rather than a transcendent God. As such it also carries us from the *Theogony* to the *Works and Days*.

The order which is begotten by Zeus can reflect his nature and express his will without his active interference.[40] Thus the Muses of the Proem inspire the kings who are "Zeus-born" and "from Zeus" (διοτρεφέων and ἐκ Διὸς, *Th.* 82, 96), as in the *Works and Days* "it is through Zeus that mortal men / become famous or fail of fame. / It is through mighty Zeus / they are spoken of or left in silence" (ὁμῶς ἄφατοί τε φατοί τε / ῥητοί τ' ἄρρητοί τε Διὸς μεγάλοιο ἕκητι *WD* 3–4)—but not without the Muses.[41] In human time, Hesiod can indiscriminately ascribe the ills that fall upon the unjust to Zeus, to Zeus acting upon the complaints of his daughter Justice, or simply to Justice (*WD* 238–39, 258–62, 220–24). He can declare either that the eye of Zeus sees all, or that Zeus has 30,000 guardians who watch for him (*WD* 252–55, 267), that Zeus causes his daughters, the Seasons, to change, or that they change on their own (*WD* 564–65, 663–64). As Zeus' action is not distinguished from nature, neither is it differentiated from the action of his children. This is how "Zeus" and "the gods" have come to be the same.

Zeus' children are not a threat to his order, but, as their nature reveals, an expression of it. His order has been established through the union of intelligence and force. His children, the Seasons (Peace, Justice, and Good Order), the Portioners (or Fates), the Graces, Persephone, the Muses, Apollo and Artemis, and Hebe ("Youth"), are characterized, overwhelmingly, by beauty. Theirs is not the sexual allure of Aphrodite, but the loveliness that comes with order and harmony.[42] It thus comes as a surprise that the list should end with Ares and, finally, with Athene:

> But himself, from his head, he gave birth to gray-eyed Athene,
> Terrible, strife-stirring, host-leading, unwearied Lady,
> To whom war-cries are pleasure, and warfare and battles.

> αὐτὸς δ' ἐκ κεφαλῆς γλαυκώπιδα γείνατ' Ἀθήνην,
> δεινὴν ἐγρεκύδοιμον ἀγέστρατον ἀτρυτώνην,
> πότνιαν, ἧ κέλαδοί τε ἅδον πόλεμοί τε μάχαι τε·   *Th. 924–26*

Of all of Zeus' children Athene is most emphatically Zeus' child: "equally possessing with her father strength and intelligent counsel" (ἴσον ἔχουσαν πατρὶ μένος καὶ ἐπίφρονα βουλήν *Th.* 896). She is born from Zeus' own head, the child of Zeus and the swallowed Wisdom, the sister of the son that would have overthrown Zeus. She is also a reminder that the intelligence to which force has been united in the new order has nothing to do with compassion. The beauty of Zeus' children characterizes the harmony of his order. The birth of Athene reminds us of the grimmer side of the force, and the intelligence, that constitute that beauty.

Another group of Zeus' children, those to whom he "gave the greatest honor," also have a good claim to be considered the most characteristic of his order. As Zeus has established new portions for the gods, he has also begotten a new set of Portioners, or Moirai (a word also translated as "Fates"). Their birth is somewhat anomalous, in that it occurs twice.[43] The first set of Portioners, the children of Night, are born at the opening of the *Theogony*. The second set are born to Zeus and Right (Themis) at the poem's close. Hesiod appears to have found that the old Portioners, goddesses without whom a theogony could not exist, could not fit into Zeus' new order.[44] He solved the difficulty not by twinning them, as with the other abstract children of Night, but by replacing them with a similar, but significantly different, version of themselves.

Hesiod's two sets of Portioners bear a striking resemblance to the Furies of Aeschylus' *Oresteia*, transformed, at the conclusion of the trilogy, into Eumenides, or "Well-Minded Ones." For Aeschylus, the transformation signified a change in the cosmic order, from the old way of automatic vengeance to the new rule of justice and courts. "Thus," for Aeschylus, "all-seeing Zeus and Fate have come together" (Ζεὺς παντόπας / οὕτω Μοῖρά τε συγκατέβα *Eumenides* 1045–46). Hesiod has, in many ways, a similar conception. He describes the old Portioners, the children of Night, as pursuing "the transgressions of men and of gods, / Nor ever leave off the goddesses from their terrible anger / Until they pay back with dread vengeance one who has erred" (αἵ τ' ἀνδρῶν τε θεῶν παραιβασίας ἐφέπουσιν, / οὐδέ ποτε λήγουσι θεαὶ δεινοῖο χόλοιο, / πρίν γ' ἀπὸ τῷ δώωσι κακὴν ὄπιν, ὅστις ἁμάρτῃ *Th.* 220–22).[45] In contrast, the birth of the new Portioners is significantly preceded by their elder sisters Peace, Good Order, and, most importantly, Justice. It is odd, to say the least, that Good Order should be born before the goddesses who represent order altogether, and it is completely anomalous for Right to bear *two* sets of children to Zeus. The anomalies seem to have been necessary because the Portioners could not be born until after the birth of Justice, who is now to dictate the portions.

The original Portioners are the traditional Fates, the three ancient sisters who appear at the birth of children and allot them their destiny. They are therefore described as those who "to mortals / At their birth give the having of good and of evil" (italics mine) (αἵ τε βροτοῖσι / γεινομένοισι διδοῦσι ἔχειν ἀγαθόν τε κακόν τε *Th.* 219).[46] The second Portioners give, more generally, "to men who are mortal the having of good and of evil" (αἵ τε διδοῦσι / θνητοῖς ἀνθρώποισιν ἔχειν ἀγαθόν τε κακόν τε *Th.* 906).[47] The human portion, under the order of Zeus, is a balance of good and evil. The Portioners, now expressing not their own, self-determined, order, but the order of their father, give us that evil and good. They, the Portioners, "to whom Zeus the Counselor gave the greatest honor" (ἧς πλείστην τιμὴν πόρε μητίετα Ζεύς *Th.* 904), owe their own honor, or portion, to Zeus. It is important to Hesiod that the new order be apportioned according to justice rather than following an automatic vengeance. It is probably more important to him that the goddesses who represent order altogether be expressions of their father, Zeus.

The Theology of Farming

Zeus' most significant children, from a theological point of view, should be the Portioners. Hesiod gives that role to the Seasons, making them the first children, and so the hallmark, of Zeus' new order.[48] The position is quite deliberately contrived. To manage it the Seasons have had to supplant not only the Portioners, but also Athene, the child of Zeus' first marriage. This Hesiod manages by postponing his description of Athene's birth, a device that also allows him to frame the birth of Zeus' children with first the predicted, and finally the actual, birth of Athene.[49] But for all this, not she, and not the Portioners, but the Seasons, have the honor of being Zeus' eldest children.

This presents us with not one problem but two. Hesiod apparently originally identifies the Seasons as Peace, Justice, and Good Order. This tells us that Hesiod felt that there was a connection between the natural seasons, which are the harmony and balance of nature, and peace, justice, and order, the forces which provide harmony and balance in human life. It does not tell us what Hesiod thought that connection was, nor does it tell us whether Hesiod had in mind Justice, or Spring, when he made the Seasons the eldest children of Zeus. We will consider the role of justice in the next chapter. Here we will look only at the role of the "natural" seasons, spring, summer, fall, and winter. This returns us to farming.

The *Theogony* portrays the divine order as an order composed of many and disparate gods, whose center, unity, and permanence lies in the union of force and intelligence in Zeus himself. This same sense of the divine lies at the basis of the *Works and Days*, and with it the same difficulty. Hesiod's religious sense is overwhelmingly, even monotheistically, focused on Zeus.[50] It is also completely polytheistic.[51] Both the *Theogony* and the *Works and Days* give us a vivid sense of Hesiod's focus on Zeus, and an equally vivid sense of his vision of a world informed by a multiplicity of gods. Both aspects of Hesiod's religious sense are nowhere more apparent than in his description of farming. It is in farming, as well, that we may see how Hesiod reconciles the two.

The opening of the farming section—"At the rising of the Pleiades, the daughters of Atlas, begin / your harvest, and your plowing at their setting" (Πληιάδων ᾽Ατλα-γενέων ἐπιτελλομενάων / ἄρχεσθ᾽ ἀμήτου, ἀρότοιο δὲ δυσομενάων WD 383–84)—sets the work of the farmer in a context which is both cosmic and divine.[52] The Pleiades are, simultaneously, stars and the daughters of Atlas, brother to Prometheus, and among the first of Zeus' defeated challengers (Th. 517–20). This sense of the divinity inherent in nature runs throughout Hesiod's description of farming.[53] For Hesiod the malevolent influence of the star Sirius (WD 416–19) and the relief which comes with Zeus' rains (WD 415–16) are equally divine. Boreas, the north wind, whose portion is the winter, and Zephyr, the west wind, whose portion is the summer, are gods, as is Orion, whose rising marks the time for threshing, and Arcturus, who tells us when to prune the vines. Even, or especially, the earth which Hesiod tills is a goddess, the mother and wife of Ouranos, Zeus' grandmother, and the mother of all (Γη πάντων μήτηρ WD 563).

Hesiod's sense of the divine is all-pervasive, extending throughout his poetry, as it does throughout his sense of farming. The formulae which Hesiod uses to express the divinity of nature are not just poetic decoration. Hesiod's description of fire as "the strength of Hephaestus" (Th. 866), sex as "the works of Aphrodite, the golden" (WD 521), wine as "the gifts of Dionysus, the joyful" (WD 614), and the crops, throughout, as "the sacred grain of Demeter" (Δημήτερος ἱερὸν ἀκτήν)[54] are as deeply meant as his injunction to pray to Zeus and Demeter before plowing. This same sense also informs the next sections of the Works and Days, on taboos and on lucky and unlucky days. Divinity is inherent in the sun, the night, rivers, springs, the crow that perches on the roof-top, the birds which bring signs from heaven.[55] Even particular days of the month are "from Zeus the Counselor" (Διὸς πάρα μητιόεντος WD 769). For Hesiod all the forces of nature are forces because each has its portion within the order of Zeus. To secular minds, Hesiod's description of farming may mean no more than a careful working with nature. To Hesiod, advice on how to be a successful farmer is also, necessarily, advice on honoring and obeying the gods.[56]

The gods of Hesiod's description of farming are immediate, omnipresent, and, above all, part of a divine order, the order which creates the dramatic arrangement of the farmer's year.[57] It is just this sense of the whole that lends Hesiod's vignettes their pictorial quality. The interconnections also appear more subtly. At WD 385–87, for example, Hesiod describes how the Pleiades appear at just the time that the scythes are being sharpened. Not only does no element act in isolation, but Hesiod refuses even to subordinate one event to the other, to say, as we would expect, that one should sharpen the scythes when the Pleiades appear. The refusal leaves us with the impression of an all-encompassing order, within which the farmer, the stars, and the scythes, at this particular moment, each have their allotted task.

This sense of the whole is as present in the succession of Hesiod's vignettes, the drama of the year as a whole, as it is within the vignettes themselves. Hesiod's swallow, the daughter of Pandion, accompanies Arcturus as he deserts the holy stream of Ocean at dusk (*WD* 564–69). The snail moves from the earth to the plants, fleeing the Pleiades (*WD* 571–72), who are themselves playing hide and seek with the harvest (*WD* 383–87). Rosy-fingered Dawn meets Arcturus, once more, as he rises in early fall (*WD* 610). The Pleiades and Orion conduct a year-long drama of flight and pursuit;[58] Boreas gives way to Zephyr in season; the oxen and the plowing fade into and emerge from the background of Hesiod's description, and the farmer's consciousness, in a yearly pattern. This is the unity captured by Hesiod's dramatic account of farming, the whole which exists not in any given moment or season, but in the rhythm that emerges over the course of the year.

Only the role of Zeus is unspecified. He is everywhere and nowhere. He fixes the good Strife in the roots of the earth, and thus ensures that human beings must work. Alongside his daughter Justice, he sees to it that people do not prosper by insolence (*hubris*) . With Demeter, he determines the final outcome of the crops. With Poseidon, he accomplishes good and evil at sea. The lucky and unlucky days which end the poem are his. On the farm, he sends the autumn rains (*WD* 415–16), determines the outcome of the crops (*WD* 474), brings the spring solstice (*WD* 564–65), inflicts poverty (*WD* 638), threatens shipwreck (*WD* 667–69), and, most unexpectedly, is somehow responsible for Hesiod's knowledge of "the measures of the sea" (*WD* 647–48, 661–62). Zeus has a share in everything, and yet seems to have no portion of his own.

The most unexpected is also the most informative. What Hesiod describes in his sailing section is not how to sail, but when the sea is passable. As this is all that he describes this, presumably, is the "measures of the sea" that he knows by knowing the mind of Zeus.[59] It is not sailing *per se* which is Zeus' concern. That is, of course, the sphere of Poseidon. It is the fact that there is a time when sailing is seasonable (ὡραῖος), a time when it has its own particular place in the whole that is the year.[60] Both in any given season, and in the dynamic force which creates their cycle, Hesiod is intensely aware of the honors of each of many gods. It is, nonetheless, the entirety of the order which captures his imagination, the fact of "seasonableness," whether in the lucky and unlucky days or in the whole cycle of the year.[61] This is the role of Zeus.

Within Hesiod's sense of the divine, Zeus himself has no particular sphere. Nor can he, since it is he who is responsible for the order and permanence of the whole.[62] This is why the seasons are so important. The seasons of the *Theogony* are Zeus' first children. The seasons of the *Works and Days* are the dynamic force which informs the farmer's year. Within the world of nature, they *are* the order of Zeus.[63]

Hesiod's particular association of Zeus with the seasons illuminates Hesiod's ability to see simultaneously a multiplicity of gods, and a single divinity, Zeus, whose will informs the whole. Unlike even a river or a constellation, a season is not a thing, but a conjunction of events. Fall is the time of Zeus' rains, the time when the heat abates, when Sirius travels largely by night, when the trees cease to sprout and begin to shed their leaves. Summer is when the crickets sing, the golden thistle flowers, Zephyr has his place, and Sirius his strongest influence over men and (particularly) women. And so on, through each of Hesiod's vignettes. If we see nature as a multiplicity of powers, it is the seasons which are the dynamic and ordering element which makes of this multiplicity a whole. There is no contradiction between this multiplicity and the whole which it composes. Like Zeus and the many gods who make up his order, the two are the same.

Hesiod is a poet of peace and peasant farming. Homer, his more or less close contemporary, is a poet of war and of the aristocratic values of the warrior. Homer's sense of the divine order is based upon a sense of the honors and privileges which comprise each god's share within the order of Zeus. So is Hesiod's. There is, however, a difference. Homer is describing a world within which such relations make sense. Hesiod is not.[64]

The Homeric warrior understands that he must award honor to the gods, as his inferiors must award honor to him. It is this system which holds society together, and which unites humans and gods in a larger sort of "society." As the Homeric warrior feels a violent resentment towards any affront to his honor, so, naturally, do the gods. As he punishes such an affront, so do they.[65] None of this applies to Hesiod.[66] Hesiod has no use for the values of a heroic culture. War, for him, is not the stage of heroism, but a curse of god (WD 228–29, 245–47). Ships and sailing are anathema to him. When Hesiod declares that the gods have placed sweat before excellence (ἀρετή), he means it literally. The only way to success is work. Status in society is as important to Hesiod as it is to Homer.[67] The difference is that Hesiod seeks it by working in his fields, not by quarrelling over matters of honor in the marketplace.

"Honor," for Hesiod, is no longer defined by human relations.[68] It is therefore no longer (primarily at any rate) the "honor" of a particular god, an honor which cannot be ignored without incurring that god's anger. Hesiod's gods, in this respect strikingly unlike Homer's, do not tend to have a personal and jealous concern with honor. In fact, considering the deeply religious nature of the Works and Days, the poem contains astonishingly few references to libations, sacrifice, prayer, or the need to propitiate, or even avoid offending, any particular god.[69] A god's "honor" has become, for Hesiod, the place that that god holds within Zeus' order. A recognition of that honor continues to be our direct obligation to the god.[70] But that recognition is now not so much an acknowledgment of the god's particular eminence, as it is of the god's particular place within the order of Zeus.[71]

Hesiod has moved the concept of "honor" from the battlefield to the farm. Like Homer, he sees our relation to the gods as based on our need to acknowledge and respect divine honor. But Homer understood this obligation under the aspect of the honor a person must recognize in and accord to a superior. Hesiod understood it as he saw it in farming. He models the human relation to the gods not on the need to acknowledge a potentially violent king, but on the need to understand and work with a potentially disastrous climate. The honors of particular gods are, within Hesiod's vision, like the places held in the farmer's world by the soil, the stars, the sun, the North wind, or the rainfall. Each has its own particular sphere and influence, which must be known, acknowledged, and dealt with. But that sphere and influence stems ultimately from its place in the larger order. Our task is partially to placate all the disparate elements of the world. It is, even more critically, to acquire the understanding necessary to adapt ourselves to the whole. Hesiod's Zeus is the center of that whole. As its center he is not in conflict with its multiplicity; he is rather what gives that multiplicity meaning.

The Gods of the *Georgics*

Hesiod begins his poem with Zeus. Varro too, the model for the invocation of the *Georgics*, invokes

> First Jupiter and Tellus, who, with sky and earth, embrace all the fruits of agriculture; and thus, because they are said to be the universal parents, Jupiter is called "Father," and Tellus "Mother Earth."

> Primum, qui omnis fructos agri culturae caelo et terra continent, Iovem et Tellurem; itaque, quod ii parentes magni dicuntur, Iuppiter pater apellatur, Tellus terra mater.
>
> *Rust.* 1.1.5

But in the invocation of the *Georgics*, Jupiter is missing. Vergil's first set of deities are Ceres and Bacchus, Varro's second pair. The *Georgics* envisions no all-encompassing pairing of divine Earth and Sky.[72] Where there should be a center to the divine order there is a blank, or, perhaps worse, only the center that human beings themselves may create. At any rate, if we must find a figure to replace Jupiter, it must be the one who ends the invocation, and who is given precisely as many lines as all the other gods put together, Octavian.[73]

As we see in the *Georgics'* initial invocation of twelve deities, ranging from Ceres and Bacchus, to the Fauns and Dryads, to the purely Italian Silvanus and Aristaeus, the *Georgics* is well supplied with gods. What the poem lacks is not gods, but a center that could make out of these many gods an ordered whole. Zeus provided such a center for the *Theogony*; Zeus together with Demeter and Justice provide the same for the *Works and Days*. When Jupiter does finally appear, in the theodicy of *Georgics* 1.125–59, there is a hope that he may provide the same central and organizing meaning for that work. His presence, however, soon becomes worse than his absence.

Vergil's introduction of Jupiter does indeed appear to be a "theodicy," a vindication of divine justice.[74] It reads, in fact, like a positive version of the myths of the *Works and Days*. Vergil's Jupiter, like Hesiod's Zeus, puts an end to the Golden Age because he wants human life to be hard.[75] But Vergil, unlike Hesiod, offers an explanation. Hesiod's Zeus gave human beings hardship because he was angry at Prometheus. Vergil's Jupiter made life hard because he saw that the ease of the Golden Age would lead to sloth, and that hardship, by sharpening our wits, would in the end prove better for us (1.121–24).[76]

Jupiter made farming difficult in order to awaken human intelligence. This intention appears, at first, entirely comprehensible in human terms. But as Vergil's myth expands, it denies its own purpose. Jupiter awakens human intelligence by introducing violence, envy, and hatred into the world. The end result is the world of the Iron Age. As Vergil's final, unsettling image of the present age warns us, a race who once "sought food in common" (*in medium quaerebant* 1.127): "You will eye in vain the huge store of another / And with an oak, shaken in the woods, solace your hunger" (*heu magnum alterius frustra spectabis acervum / concussaque famem in silvis solabere quercu* 1.158–59). Potential violence has come, finally, to underlie human relations, just as it has come to underlie the human relation to nature.[77]

What has gone wrong with Vergil's theodicy is precisely his attempt to explain Jupiter's action in terms of good and evil, the terms that matter most to human beings. The life that Jupiter gave us in order to "sharpen our wits" is a life of violence, hostility, and suffering. The evil of the means entirely out-balances the good proposed as their end. It is exactly the sense of right and wrong which the myth itself proposes that makes the suffering which results from Jupiter's act incomprehensible. Vergil, like Hesiod, has attempted to discover in farming the meaning of our relation to the cosmos. He has only added that this meaning should satisfy our natural sense of what is right. The addition has baffled the attempt. Hesiod, who had no notion of judging Zeus' acts by such a standard, encountered no such difficulty.

As we see in looking at Athene, "intelligence," for Hesiod, is linked to "craft;" it is not linked to compassion, or to the "understanding" that implies sympathy. It is precisely this "understanding," linked to compassion, peace, and harmony, the characteristics of the Golden Age, that Vergil seeks. Opposed to it, for Vergil, as for Hesiod, is force. For Vergil, however, this "force" is the opposite not simply of intelligence, but of understanding as well. The vision of divinity that expresses this, a world haunted by a malevolent demon is best expressed in the third Georgic:[78]

> Ghastly Tisiphone rages, and sent forth into the light
> From the gloom of Hell, she drives before her Disease
> And Dread, and day by day raising her greedy head, emerges.
>
> saevit et in lucem Stygiis emissa tenebris
> pallida Tisiphone Morbos agit ante Metumque
> inque dies avidum surgens caput altius effert.   3.551–53

Within one vision of god, a vision expressed in the fourth Georgic, divinity forms the cosmos into a meaningful whole, where (some say) suffering and isolation are only apparent, and death has no place at all.[79] This is the other extreme. Here Tisiphone, the demon of the plague, has taken Vergil's image of Juno tormenting the innocent Io with her gadfly (3.152–3) to its extreme. Divinity itself has become the force of unreason, unleashing a violence which is worse than blind, because it is not unaware of what it destroys, only uncaring.[80]

The force characteristic of the *Georgics* is destructive force, or "violence," the characteristic feature of the Iron Age. What Vergil's theodicy has attempted, and failed, to discover is a explanation of violence that is satisfactory not merely to reason, but also to "understanding." In terms of achieving its goal, of sharpening man's wits, Jupiter's action is thoroughly rational. It is only when we add the assumption that Jupiter did this because it was better for human beings, that the means come to contradict the ends proposed. Violence has gotten in the way. Force, and even violence, may be entirely compatible with intelligence or craft. They are difficult to reconcile with harmony and understanding.

Vergil's Jupiter governs the divine world, and as such has established the order of the weather signs (1.353) and given the bees their particularly orderly, harmonious, and law-abiding nature (4.149–52). But he attained this position by supplanting his father,

Saturn, who is far more deeply linked to a Golden Age, and a particularly Italian Golden Age, than his Greek counterpart, Cronos.[81] In this role, Jupiter is the enemy of order, first destroying our harmony with nature by instituting farming and the arts, and then, in Vergil's vivid description of the spring storm, destroying the very arts which he has just instituted:

> The lofty heaven falls
> And, with its deluge, the glad crops and labors of the oxen
> Wash away
> ·
> The Father himself, in the midnight of storm clouds wields,
> With flashing hand, his thunderbolt. And at that shock
> The great earth trembles, wild beasts flee, and mortal hearts
> Are everywhere laid low by crouching terror.

>   ruit arduus aether,
> et pluvia ingenti sata laeta boumque labores
> diluit
> ·
> ipse pater media nimborum in nocte corusca
> fulmina molitur dextra, quo maxima motu
> terra tremit, fugere ferae et mortalia corda
> per gentes humilis stravit pavor   1.324–26; 328–31

Perhaps ironically, but certainly underlining the contradiction, Jupiter is described both when he institutes farming and when he destroys it as "the father himself" (*ipse pater* 1.121, 328). Jupiter is both order and violence, both king and usurper, both the god of rain, who nourishes the earth, and the god of storm, who destroys what has been nourished. Vergil did not create these contradictory aspects of Jupiter's personality. They came about as the attributes of gods often do, through a combination of local deities, an association of Roman with Greek gods, and, to some extent, from a natural human tendency to see the divine as paradoxical. But Vergil seized upon them. In a sense Jupiter does play, for Vergil, the role that Zeus plays for Hesiod. As Zeus' order informs the cosmos of the *Works and Days*, Jupiter embodies the contradictions which are themselves the cosmos of the *Georgics*.

The Georgic of Force

The Georgic most directly modeled on the *Works and Days* is the first.[82] With this book Vergil begins to accustom us to the relation between his and Hesiod's visions of the world. The relation is that what Hesiod has brought together, Vergil, literally, puts asunder. The farmer's tasks and their seasons, the "Works" and "Days" which Hesiod forged into one, are divided by Vergil into two separate sections, concluded by a third section, adopted from Aratus, on weather signs. Each of Hesiod's vignettes, which had united weather, season, and task, are thus divided into three separate and separated injunctions. Vergil treats Hesiod's chronological organization in much the same manner. He moves, in the central section of the book, not from season to season, but from seasons to holidays, to days of the month, to day and night, and then suddenly outward, to hot and cold, summer and winter, fall and spring.[83] Hesiod gave us an illusively regular cycle for the farmer's year. Vergil's version makes it impossible to predict what topic, even what season, will be treated next.[84] The reader of the first Georgic, like the farmer of the first Georgic, encounters, at every turn, new and unexpected dangers. If we are bewildered it is not because Vergil has nodded, but because he is dismantling, before our eyes, the natural harmonies of the Hesiodic farm.

Vergil opens the *Georgics* with a Hesiodic picture of plowing and with a Hesiodic program, proposing to discuss how the farmer must learn nature's laws and adapt himself to her order. The topics here proposed, nature's order, nature's rich variety, and the natural suitability of crop to climate, will, in fact, be addressed in the second Georgic. Here nature's presumed order stands in stark contrast to what Vergil does discuss, not nature's laws, but nature's extremes, and human beings' consequent need to carve for themselves a small but ordered refuge. Vergil moves from excessive fertility to barrenness, from land left idle to crops which burn the land, from too great heat to too much cold, and from irrigation to counteract drought to drainage to deal with flooding.[85] The ordering comes not from nature, but from ourselves. Vergil's advice to pray for wet summers and dry winters leads directly to a discussion of the necessity of irrigation and drainage (1.100–10).

The farmer of the first Georgic lives a life poised between extremes, either of which threatens to destroy him. The gradual development of Hesiod's Five Ages have become, in the *Georgics* overall, the two extremes of the Golden and Iron Ages. In the first Georgic Vergil pictures as well five zones in the cosmos, converting Hesiod's temporal image into a spatial one:[86]

> Five zones hold the skies: of them one always glows
> With a flashing sun, scorched always by fire;
> Around this, to right and to left, at the extremes
> Are stretched dark regions, frozen in ice and black storms;
> Between these and the middle, two zones are conceded,
> By the gift of the gods, to wretched mortals.

> quinque tenent caelum zonae: quarum una corusco
> semper sole rubens et torrida semper ab igni;
> quam circum extremae dextra laevaque trahuntur
> caeruleae, glacie concretae atque imbribus atris;
> has inter mediamque duae mortalibus aegris
> munere concessae divom   1.233–38

Arable nature, for Hesiod the rule and paradigm of Zeus' order, has become for Vergil two precarious zones, balanced between the extremes of a greater cosmos, and grudgingly conceded to human beings.[87] As we saw in the chapter 3, Vergil begins the *Geor-*

gics with a Hesiodic image of farming that he then moves into its extremes. Here he uses another favorite technique; he adopts the Hesiodic point of view only to pull back from it, revealing the larger context within which it exists. In so doing he transforms the initial picture.[88] It is as if a movie camera had pulled back from a pleasant dinner party, to reveal that it is taking place on the Titanic.

Vergil's first Georgic ends with what is perhaps the most terrifying description of uncontrolled violence ever written. It comes directly out of his description of farming. If human beings are violent, it is nature who has taught us to be so. The violence emerges gradually and almost imperceptibly, as the snake of irrational violence will later creep into the heart of Amata (*Aeneid* 7.341 ff.). It underlies the theodicy, and is implicit in Vergil's description of the farmer's "weapons" (*arma* 1.160–75) and the countless "monsters" (*monstra* 1.181–6) which the farmer's battles.[89] It appears in the image of the oarsman struggling against the current, and in the reminder that the fifth is a bad day because then Typhoeus and/or the Giants attempted to tear down heaven (1.277–83).[90] It creeps into the heart of the book with the increasing focus on the extremes within which farming exists. Finally, like the fire in the orchard of the second Georgic that creeps under the bark of the trees, and, gradually moving through the leaves and branches, reaches the tree-tops to burst out suddenly with a fury that can no longer be opposed (2.303–14), the violence of the first Georgic breaks out. The first outbreak is the spring storm. Vergil models the storm upon a simile from the *Iliad*, where Patroclus' onslaught is compared to a storm sent by Zeus "when, angered, he is hard upon men / who with force, in the *agora*, crookedly judge the *themistes* / and drive out justice, not fearing the wrath of the gods" (ὅτε δή ῥ᾽ ἄνδρεσσι κοτεσσάμενος χαλεπήνῃ, / οἳ βίῃ εἰν ἀγορῇ σκολιὰς κρίνωσι θέμιστας, / ἐκ δὲ δίκην ἐλάσωσι, θεῶν ὄπιν οὐκ ἀλέγοντες *Iliad* 16.386–88). The reason for the storm is the one detail that Vergil leaves out. There is no reason offered for his storm, or for the destruction it wreaks.[91] Jupiter here is not sending destruction upon the unjust. Rather, the sheer irrationality of the storm's violence is underlined by Vergil's image of Jupiter, "the father himself," destroying the arts that he himself just established.

The spring storm introduces the weather signs that will finally culminate in Vergil's description of civil war. Following a pattern that has already appeared several times in the book, Vergil here promises us order and harmony, only to lead us into a series of increasingly violent extremes. Thus Vergil's first promise to show us the laws of nature (1.50–70) led into drought and flood; his promise to explain the divisions and seasons marked off by the sun led into the five zones (1.231–59); his promise to show us the order of the days into the Typhoean attack on heaven (1.276–83). Here the final section of the first Georgic begins hopefully:

> And, so that we should be able, by sure signs, to learn these things,
> The heat and rains and winds driving the cold,
> The Father himself established what the monthly moon should warn ...

> Atque haec ut certis possumus discere signis,
> aestusque pluviasque et agentis frigora ventos,
> ipse pater statuit quid menstrua luna moneret ...   1.351–53

There is, unfortunately, a catch. The farmer can learn to predict the violence of nature, but, as in the simile of the *Aeneid*, he can do nothing about it:[92]

> The hearts of farmers shudder,
> Foreseeing [the storm] far off; it will bring downfall
> To the trees, ruin to the crops, and overthrow all far and wide.

> miseris, heu, praescia longe
> horrescunt corda agricolis; dabit ille ruinas
> arboribus stragemque satis, ruet omnia late.   *Aeneid* 12.451–55

The outbreak of irrational violence we encountered in the spring storm can be anticipated, but it cannot be controlled.

The impossibility of preventing violence becomes more sinister as Vergil moves from nature to human beings. There is a likeness between ourselves and nature throughout the *Georgics*. In the second Georgic it lies in peace and sympathy. In the first it lies in irrational violence.[93] Vergil blends the signs of storm into the portents of the civil war so gradually that it is difficult to know when the violence of nature yields to human violence We are thus forced to see that the "warnings" which alerted Rome to the coming civil war (1.464–65) were as powerless to prevent it as the warnings of coming storms are to prevent them. Human violence, and the destruction which it causes, turns out to be neither more preventable, nor more rational, nor any more touched by compassion, than that of nature:

> Here Euphrates, and there Germany wakes war,
> Neighboring cities, the laws that bound them broken,
> Bear arms; unholy Mars rages through all the world:
> As when the chariots from the barriers pour forth
> Gathering speed, increasing over the course, the driver vainly
> Pulls them back, is borne along; the car hears not the reins.

> hinc movet Euphrates, illinc Germania bellum;
> vicinae ruptis inter se legibus urbes
> arma ferunt; saevit toto Mars impius orbe,
> ut cum carceribus sese effudere quadrigae,
> addunt in spatia, et frustra retinacula tendens
> fertur equis auriga neque audit currus habenas.   1.509–14

There is no attempt in Vergil's lines to explain, justify, or even condemn the civil war. It is described rather as the spring storm of Book 1, as the fire in the orchard of Book 2, or as sex and the plague in Book 3. It is sheer, irrational, and terrifying violence, and it sweeps all before it.[94] When order is lost men, like the bees of Book 4 (4.212–14), destroy themselves. The fact can be neither explained nor comprehended. It is, in its very essence, irrational.

The farmer of the *Works and Days* could, through understanding, accommodate his efforts to nature. He could do so because the features of nature with which Hesiod was concerned were the regular seasons. Vergil alters everything by discussing not the ordered cycle of the seasons, but nature's spontaneous and erratic eruptions of violence. The one is comprehensible and can be managed and the other is not, and cannot, for precisely the reason that they were chosen as paradigms. The violence of a spring storm is not rational. It is, like the winds that stem from Typhoeus, and unlike the orderly winds that accompany the seasons, disordered and destructive. It is force divorced from intelligence.[95] The order of the seasons, being regular, is rational and can be comprehended. It is force informed by intelligence. For Hesiod this is the rule. For Vergil it is a possibility.

The Georgic of Understanding

The movement from the end of the first Georgic to the opening of the second has been described as like waking up from a nightmare on a fine spring day.[96] Vergil opens the second Georgic with a program that carefully follows that of the first (1.1–5) and that simply ignores the civil wars that we have just been through: "Thus far the cultivation of fields and the stars of the sky: Now, Bacchus, I will sing of thee" (*Hactenus arvorum cultus et sidera caeli: nunc te, Bacche, canam* 2.12). The world of the second Georgic is first established through purely agricultural advice:

> [Trees] that of their own will lift themselves to the light,
> Unfruitful indeed, but joyful and strongly spring up,
> For, see, nature is in the soil. Yet these too, if someone
> Graft them, or transplanting, commit them to well-worked trenches,
> Will shed their wild spirit, and with constant care
> Into whatever arts you wish, will readily follow.

> Sponte sua quae se tollunt in luminis oras,
> infecunda quidem, sed laeta et fortia surgunt;
> quippe solo natura subest. tamen haec quoque, si quis
> inserat aut scrobibus mandet mutata subactis,
> exuerint silvestrem animum, cultuque frequenti
> in quascumque voles artis haud tarda sequentur.   2.47–52 [97]

The advice lives in a world where man and nature are in harmony. Nature gives to man variety and richness, strength and indulgence. Man gives to nature direction. This theme proceeds, with varied modulations, throughout the book, culminating in Vergil's famous celebration of rural life. The harmony first manifested in the human relation to nature is now reflected throughout the farmer's life:

> Autumn gives forth its varied fruits; high up
> The mellow vintage warms on sun-baked rocks.
> Meanwhile his children hang about his kisses
> His pure home guards its modesty, the udders on his cows
> Hang down with milk, and fat in the joyful grass,
> The young goats wrestle, horn against budding horn.

et varios ponit fetus autumnus, et alte
mitis in apricis coquitur videmia saxis.
interea dulces pendent circum oscula nati,
casta pudicitiam servat domus, ubera vaccae
lactea demittunt, pinguesque in gramine laeto
inter se adversis luctantur cornibus haedi.

2.523–6

Within the vision of the second Georgic Vergil is able to eliminate even Hesiod's
sense of the hardship of labor. Man's "labor" here is simply the gathering in of nature's
bounty:

> No rest, but the year teems with fruit
> Or with the herds' increase or sheaves of Ceres' corn,
> And burdens the furrows with yield or bursts the barns.
>
> nec requies, quin aut pomis exuberet annus
> aut fetu pecorum aut Cerealis mergite culmi,
> proventuque onerat sulcos atque horrea vincat.

2.516–19

The "holidays" of the first Georgic were a time when one could still squeeze in a little
work (1.266–75).[98] The festivals of the second reintroduce the harmony seen briefly
in Vergil's celebration of Ceres, the mirror of Hesiod's summer picnic (1.335–50). In
the two festivals of the second Georgic, both dedicated, as the book is as a whole, to
Bacchus (2.1–8, 380–89, 527–31), Vergil illustrates his famous line: *fortunatus et ille,
deos qui novit agrestis* ("Happy too the man who knows the country's gods" 2.493). The
communion of farmer and nature has spread to a communion with the divine. The divisions instituted by Jupiter, between human beings, and between human beings and
nature, have disappeared. With them violence has disappeared as well. The "violence" of the second Georgic occurs in the javelin contests and the rustic wrestling
matches that are our version of the play of the young goats. It is the play violence of
festivals. Like work, it has become the joyful shadow of itself.

Vergil's image of the farmer in harmony with nature ends in his explicit vision of farming as the life of the Golden Age. To illustrate the point Vergil contrasts this world to
that of the first Georgic: "Others trouble the blind seas with oars and rush onto the /
Sword, push themselves over the thresholds, into the courts of kings" (*sollicitant alii
remis freta caeca, ruuntque / in ferrum, penetrant aulas et limina regum* 2.503–6). But as
Vergil's image of what "others" do becomes increasingly elaborate it begins to run
away with the poem. It is with something of a shock that we are returned, abruptly, to
our starting point:

> Soaked in their brother's blood they rejoice,
> Change their homes and sweet thresholds for exile,
> And seek for a fatherland under an alien sun.
> The farmer furrows his land with his curving plow,

From here is his year's labor, from here he supports his country
And his infant grandchildren, from here his herds and good oxen.

> gaudent perfusi sanguine fratrum,
> exsilioque domos et dulcia limina mutant
> atque alio patriam quaerunt sub sole iacentem.
> agricola incurvo terram dimovit aratro:
> hinc anni labor, hinc patriam parvosque nepotes
> sustinet, hinc armenta boum meritosque iuvencos.   2.511–15

The farmer at his plow is as oblivious to the violence of Rome as if he were, literally, in a different picture. Vergil has not allowed us, his readers, to share the farmer's point of view.[99]

The conclusion of the second Georgic tends to be remembered for its idyllic image of farming, and rightly so. But that ideal is brought out through the violence that sets it off. The farm of the first Georgic was, in the rush of the book's last lines, absorbed into the irrational violence surrounding it. The farm of the second Georgic, "far from discordant arms" (*procul discordibus armis* 2.459), is simply removed from that violence. The juxtaposition of Golden and Iron Age visions of life that ends the second Georgic mirrors the abruptness of Vergil's transition from the first to the second book. Both reveal what it is that has allowed the harmony of the second Georgic to appear, the disappearance of the violence that came to dominate the first.

The first Georgic falls roughly into three sections, on tasks, seasons, and weather signs, the last leading into the vision of civil war. The second, similarly, falls roughly into a section on grafting trees and suiting one's product to the farm, a section on vines, and a section on trees that do not need tending, the last leading into the final description of rural life. The central section of the first Georgic is the most optimistic of the book. If it does not approach the Golden Age vision of the second Georgic, it at least allows some hope for a harmony with nature, as marked by Vergil's version of Hesiod's cardinal rule: "Naked plow, naked sow; winter is the farmer's lazy time" (*nudus ara, sere nudus; hiems ignava coloni* 1.299). Similarly, the central section of the second Georgic, although far from the terrifying vision which ends the first, is the book's most pessimistic, marked again by an adapted Hesiodic reflection: "A large estate is for praising, / A small one's for farming" (*laudato ingentia rura, / exiguum colito* 2.412–13). The central sections of the first and second Georgics are the most Hesiodic because they are, in the context of either Georgic, the least extreme. In both cases they reveal a world like the momentary present of Hesiod's Five Ages, where there are still some goods mixed with our evils.

The section on vines develops only gradually out of the need to suit soil and conditions to one's crop. Once established, however, it begins to move into the extremes with which we are familiar. The first is the irrational and all-conquering destruction of a fire in the orchard, a reminder of the violence of nature strongly reminiscent of the spring storm of the first Georgic. It differs from the storm in having its origin in human carelessness, in the insidious and unseen way in which it spreads, and in the complete devastation which follows.[100] In all these ways it recalls Vergil's images of civil war. It is also, as an image, a recapitulation of the first Georgic.

The fire in the orchard is not, however, the last word. From an image of complete devastation:

> Where this happens the trees have no strength in their stock and,
> cut down,
> Cannot revive and from the earth's depth grow green as before;
> But the luckless wild olive with its bitter leaves survives.

> hoc ubi, non a stirpe valent caesaque reverti
> possunt atque ima similes revirescere terra;
> infelix superat foliis oleaster amaris.   2.312–14

Vergil moves into his gentlest image, of the indulgence, and rebirth, of spring:

> Nor could tender things last through this hardship
> If such rest came not between the heat and cold
> And heaven's indulgence so receive the earth.

> nec res hunc tenerae possent perferre laborem,
> si non tanta quies iret frigusque caloremque
> inter et exciperet caeli indulgentia terras.   2.343–45

The fire has recalled the underlying threat of irrational violence that must be eliminated before we can be in harmony with nature. The image of spring recalls the other extreme, of understanding and harmony. But now the extremes, instead of moving apart, begin to blend together.[101] It is the farmer who accomplishes this. Vergil warns us that to flourish the young vines must be guarded from heat and cold, wet and dry (G 2.346–53), and the hostile incursions of animals (2.371–79). The festival which brings men together to "call on thee, Bacchus, in joyful songs" (et te, Bacche, vocant per carmina laeta 2.388) appears now not spontaneously, but as a symbol of the farmer's need to protect nature from itself, by killing the goat who has killed the vines (2.376–96). It is the farmer who must provides spring's glad indulgence for the vines: "And while their early youth buds with new leaves, / Spare what is tender" (Ac dum prima novis adolescit frondibus aetas, / parcendum teneris 2.362–63), but the indulgence is set against the stern discipline he must impose later:

> then strip their locks and clip their arms
> (Earlier they dread the knife), then finally impose
> Your harsh commands, and check the flowing branches.

> tum stringe comas, tum bracchia tonde
> (ante reformidant ferrum), tum denique dura
> exerce imperia et ramos compesce fluentis.   2.362–70

With Vergil's "impose your harsh commands" (or "exercise your despotic military power") we are back in the world of Georgics 1.99 ("And, ever exercising his land, [the farmer] commands the fields": *exercetque frequens tellurem atque imperat arvis*). The military metaphor was prepared at the opening of the section, when the carefully ordered vines were described as soldiers deployed in their ranks along the field of battle (2.276–84). The metaphor will reappear. Here, having seen the division Vergil has made between force and intelligence, we can appreciate its significance. It is an image of force, but of force like that of the horse still under the control of the driver, a force ordered, and subject to reason.

Vergil finally moves the extremes of the Golden and Iron Age visions back together by restoring labor. The labor that the vines require is neither the play labor of the end of the second Georgic, nor the endless battle of the first, but Hesiodic labor, careful, continuous, and backbreaking, but for the benefit of vines, rather than simply against their enemies, constructive, rather than destructive. It is order rather than violence, but a laboriously created order, rather than a natural harmony. It is Hesiodic not only in situating itself between extremes, but also in the way in which it does so, by returning to a focus on the regular cycle of nature: "The farmer's work returns, moved in a circle, / And over its own footsteps, to itself, the year again revolves" (*redit agricolis labor actus in orbem, / atque in se sua per vestigia volvitur annus* 2.401–2). It is just this cycle that has created the sense of labor:

> Now the vines are bound, now the vineyard lays down the pruning knife,
> Now the last vine-dresser sings his finished rows; nonetheless
> The soil must be worried, the dust must be stirred
> And now Jupiter's rain must be feared for the now ripened grapes.

> iam vinctae vites, iam falcem arbusta reponunt,
> iam canit effectos extremus vinitor antes:
> sollicitanda tamen tellus pulvisque movendus,
> et iam maturis metuendus Iuppiter uvis.   2.416–19

This is the *Works and Days*. In the contrast between the fire in the orchard and the labor that the vines require we see the difference between Hesiod's sense of hardship, brutal and inescapable, but ordered and comprehensible, and the Vergilian nightmare of completely unbridled violence. We also have, in the vine itself, an exquisite image of the interplay of the cycle of the year and the Hesiodic sense of labor.

The plants that Vergil selects as paradigmatic for the second Georgic are the olive, the trees of the forest, and the vine (2.2–3). Vergil's short description of the olive follows his section on vines and leads into his description of the forest trees that need no tending (2.420–25). The olive is the fruit of peace. When young it must be indulged; once it has grown strong it will maintain itself. It thus matches the opening image of grafting as an image of the cooperation of man and nature. In contrast, the vine requires constant care and attention to the seasons. It is, in this sense, "Hesiodic." It is also, in its contradictions, Vergilian. The vine, like the olive, brings men gladness and rejoicing, but with a much more equivocal fruit. It brings men to the peace and harmony of Vergil's festivals, and also to the violence which dissolves festivals. Having shown us the one Vergil ends the agricultural advice of the second Georgic with the other, the battle of the Centaurs and Lapiths that destroys the union and harmony of a wedding and ends Vergil's account of forest trees (2.454–6).[102] Bacchus, like

Jupiter, has a double nature. He is the god of joy and peace, but he is also the god of sudden and irrational violence. When set against the irrational violence of the fire, the vines are an image of the order of civilization. When set against the trees of the forest, who owe none of their beauty or utility to man (2.426–28, 438–39), they recall civilization's irrational violence. It is deeply appropriate that it is of Bacchus that the second Georgic sings (2.1–8).

To move from the end of the first Georgic into the opening of the second is like waking from a nightmare to a fine spring day. There is one difference; the nightmare the Roman civil wars was real. So also, however, is the spring morning to which we awaken. Modern scholars have rightly reacted against a traditional reading that portrayed Vergil as a cheerful imperialist. Empire, in Vergil's poems, is no uncomplicated blessing. No matter how deeply he may have longed for a more simplistic vision, Vergil's poetic imagination was too profound, too complex, and too compelling, to allow him to be an apologist for Augustan policy. But as one leaps from the frying pan it is wise to watch out for the fire. If Vergil was no jolly John Bull, neither was he a subversive revolutionary disguising his despair in ambiguities and cynical double meanings. Vergil *is* ambiguous, but this is not because he is unwilling to say what he means. It is rather because what he means is by its nature ambiguous. The nightmare of the civil wars was real. So was Vergil's hope for a spring morning.

The second Georgic depicts a world where nature and the farmer exist in a perfect and unforced harmony. It is a real world. It is necessary to point this out because revisionism can be as hard on the *Georgics* as on the *Aeneid*. Traditionally the *Georgics* was seen as a celebration of the simple life, of life as it may be lived in harmony with nature. This reading ignored the dark side of Vergil's vision. More recent scholars have seen the poem as a condemnation of man's brutal exploitation both of nature and of other men. The joyful side of the poem has been dismissed as composed of falsehoods designed to call attention to themselves as falsehoods. The dismissal is as unfair and as one-sided as the earlier, optimistic, reading. More importantly, it cripples the poem.

There is no doubt that Vergil employs "falsehoods." They are not, however, confined to the positive side of his vision. It is true that Italy has never enjoyed an eternal spring (2.149). Nor was there ever a plague which destroyed all forms of life indiscriminately (3.474–566). As Vergil's praise of spring ignores the dangers of spring storms (2.323–45), so does his vision of the destructive fury of sex ignore the usually related themes of consummation, conception, and birth (3.242–83). Pears cannot be grafted onto elm trees (2.71–72), nor do stallions become any less useful when they are old (3.95–100). Bees, when the queen is dead, die of lethargy; they do not, as in Vergil's terrifying image, tear apart their own hives (4.212–14). Vergil's deeply moving description of an apian war ended with a handful of dust is in fact taken from a passage in Varro, in which the bees are engaged not in warfare, but in forming a new hive (4.67–87; Varro, *Rust.* 3.16.29–31). Finally, the impossibility of *bougonia*, of generating life from the carcass of a bullock, is balanced by Vergil himself against the macabre image of Orpheus' severed head unable to find rest from its grief even in death (4.295–314, 523–27). Both sides of Vergil's vision are real, and that reality can be expressed, on both sides, through exaggeration.[103] It is not adequate to read *labor omnia vicit* ("labor conquers all") without the following *improbus* ("ruthless labor" 1.145–46). Nor is it adequate to dismiss Vergil's praise of Italy and of farming, of the joy of spring and of the old Corycian gardener, as deliberate falsehoods. To do so reduces the rich paradoxes of the *Georgics* to cheap cynicism, and the deeply divided, and as deeply felt, contradictions of the poem to mere lies.

The second Georgic creates an ideal vision of order. Unlike the Hesiodic view, which sees order as the union of force and intelligence, Vergil here pictures harmony as the product of understanding only, entirely removed from the opposite and equally "ideal" extreme, a world of pure violence.[104] We must not misunderstand what an "ideal vision" is. Vergil did not believe that the world he lived in was a world informed entirely by either understanding or violence. He saw in the world around him an order such as Hesiod's, where force and understanding, in various combinations, coexist. He, unlike Hesiod, sought within that order the unadulterated elements of which it is composed.

Vergil, in this respect, might be compared to Newton, who also attempted to understand the world through an understanding of the pure laws which compose it. These laws are discovered through experience of the world; they can never be experienced in it. Newton looked at a world where objects put in motion stop of their own accord, and found the first law of motion, that moving objects stop only when opposed by an outside force. Vergil looked at a world where force and understanding coexist, and saw, on the one hand, a Golden Age life of peace and harmony and, on the other, an Iron Age world of irrational violence. Within the struggles of a farmer's life there is both peace and war, both the principle of understanding and the law of violence. Vergil, no more than Newton, believed that such concepts could ever be experienced in their pure states. There is always friction. That does not make the pure vision any less real, or any less informative.

Jupiter's introduction of violence into the world separated human beings from nature. Vergil undoes this separation in the second Georgic by removing that violence. We see more clearly how the harmony of the rural festival came about when we glance back to its opposite, the violence of nature which lies in the background of the first Georgic's section on weather signs. All of Vergil's interest in, affection for, and whimsically vivid portrayal of wild nature emerges in his weather signs.[105] It could not appear in a context more opposed to the feelings of the farmer. The heavenly bodies, birds, and animals that came together in the *Works and Days* to make up the great cycle of the year, here foreshadow the irrational and aberrant violence of nature.[106] They are themselves, from the thirsty rainbow, to the blushing moon, to the garrulous frogs, vividly personal, and utterly unconcerned with the farmer's forebodings.

Nature does not feel as the farmer does, nor does nature understand man's feelings. Vergil's "explanation" of how animals can understand the weather denies that they have understanding (*ingenium* or *prudentia* 1.415–23), claiming instead that their emotions mirror the condensation and rarefaction of the air. In other words, the deeply personal creatures that Vergil has presented us with are in tune with impersonal nature, and not with ourselves. They are able, as we are, to anticipate the coming of storms. They do not fear them. It is not that the creatures of nature do not know that the storms are coming, or even, perhaps, that they do not know that storms are violent; it is that, as in the theodicy, they have no sense that violence is bad.

The final image of the first Georgic, of the chariot out of control, recreates the situation of the weather signs. The horse is no more able to understand its driver's terror than the complaining frogs can understand the farmer's fear of rain. This image does, however, allow for another possibility, the parallel image with which Vergil closes the second Georgic: "But we, in our course, have traversed a mighty plain, / And now it is time to release the steaming necks of the horses" (*Sed nos immensum spatiis confecimus aequor, / et iam tempus equum fumantia solvere colla* 2.541–42). Here horse and driver can work together, as in the second Georgic nature and human beings can work together.[107] What must be removed is what has separated them, the irrational violence that is simply a part of nature, and that we can neither comprehend nor accept

Vergil has not eliminated violence from the world of the second Georgic. He has distilled it out, leaving us with two extremes, the peace and harmony of the Golden Age, and the insane, irrational, and self-consuming violence of the Iron Age. As we will see more explicitly in the next chapter, Vergil, like Hesiod, saw himself as living in a world that was a blend of force and understanding. But Vergil, unlike Hesiod, saw it not as a union, but as a partnership. Force and intelligence, like the horse and the charioteer, can work together. It is a combination necessary for human life. It is also one terribly liable to come apart.

5

THE HUMAN CONTEXT

Justice, Perception, and Farming

Hesiod's *Theogony* describes the development of the cosmos from its first beginnings to the final establishment of the order of Zeus. It does not mention us. This is unusual. As cosmogonies are human explanations told by and to human beings, our creation and the reason for our creation is generally a central point.[1] In the *Theogony* we are merely presupposed.[2] Human beings exist, but do nothing.[3]

Hesiod does not imagine a time before human beings He imagines rather a time when our presence was relegated to the background of the cosmos. Even the *Works and Days'* myth of the Five Ages, whose theme is the development of human beings, is completely uninterested in the question of how, or why, we were created. There are, of course, Greek accounts of the creation of human beings, by Prometheus, or from the ashes of the Titans. Hesiod did not use them.[4] Human beings, in the *Theogony*, are simply a factor in the cosmos, no more created *for* something than Earth or Zeus himself. We are, however, a factor that took some time to come into our own.

We are told, in Aeschylus' *Prometheus Bound*, that Zeus, having come to power and distributed the gods' honors, intended to blot out the human race and replace it with something more useful.[5] When Prometheus gave human beings fire Zeus abandoned the plan, apparently because human beings, now part of the order of the universe, could no longer be destroyed. As is so often the case, Aeschylus' thought mirrors Hesiod's. What Prometheus gives us, essentially, is intelligence (νόος): "I found them as infants before / And placed in them intelligence and wits that give counsel" (σφας νηπίους ὄντας τὸ πρὶν / ἔννους ἔθηκα καὶ φρενῶν ἐπηβόλους *PB* 443–44). Along with the arts, Prometheus teaches human beings about the seasons, the rising and setting of the stars, numbering, omens, and divination (*PB* 454–506). He makes them a part of the cosmos by showing them the signs whereby they can perceive and comprehend the order that exists around them.

For Hesiod, the order of Zeus has come about through the union of force and intelligence. In relation to this order we have no share in force. We can change nothing. What we do have is intelligence. We cannot affect Zeus' order, but, because we can perceive it, we can work within it. It is this ability which gives us our peculiar place in the cosmos. As Hesiod says: "That man is best who himself perceives all, / taking notice of what is better afterwards and in the end" (οὖτος μὲν πανάριστος, ὃς αὐτὸς πάντα νοήσει, / φρασσάμενος τά κ' ἔπειτα καὶ ἐς τέλος ᾖσιν *WD* 293–94). Like Aeschylus, Hesiod understood human beings to participate in the cosmos through their ability to comprehend it.[6] Unlike Aeschylus, Hesiod does not picture human beings as ever having been without this ability.[7] Instead he pictures a cosmos which was once without an order for us to perceive. Until such an order emerges human beings must remain a shadowy presence, latent in the background of the *Theogony*.

The importance of human perception appears in Hesiod's standard word of abuse, which is not "scoundrel" but "fool." A νήπιος, originally one "without words" or a "child," is a "fool" in the particular sense of not comprehending the world around him. Thus Prometheus (above at *PB* 443) describes the helpless humans he found as νήπιοι, and hence, in the Homeric poems, the formula "Fool, nor did he know . . ." is used to describe a person's ignorance of the plans of Zeus.[8] Hesiod is barely forty lines into the *Works and Days* when he first uses the formula. He is telling Perses why kings who render crooked judgments are fools. In so doing he connects justice and farming:

> Fools they are—not to know how much better the half than the whole is
> and what great blessing there is in mallow and asphodel.
>   For the gods have steadfastly hidden his livelihood from mankind.
> You could easily work a day's space and so for a year have a living
> with never a hand's turn of work.
> At once you could hang up your steering oar over the smoking hearth,
> and the work of oxen and drudging mules would be ended.

> νήπιοι, οὐδὲ ἴσασιν ὅσῳ πλέον ἥμισυ παντός,
> οὐδ' ὅσον ἐν μαλάχῃ τε καὶ ἀσφοδέλῳ μέγ' ὄνειαρ.
> κρύψαντες γὰρ ἔχουσι θεοὶ βίον ἀνθρώποισιν·
> ῥηιδίως γὰρ κεν καὶ ἐπ' ἤματι ἐργάσσαιο
> ὥστέ σε κεἰς ἐνιαυτὸν ἔχειν καὶ ἀεργὸν ἐόντα·
> αἶψά κε πηδάλιον μὲν ὑπὲρ καπνοῦ καταθεῖο,
> ἔργα βοῶν δ' ἀπόλοιτο καὶ ἡμιόνων ταλαεργῶν.   *WD* 40–46

What the kings have failed to perceive is that the fact that grain is difficult to grow means that they cannot get away with rendering crooked judgements. The connection may not be immediately apparent to us.[9] The kings do not need to follow the plow and will not, even if they resort to honest dealing.

The connection is obscure, however, only if we regard farming as just another way to earn a living. If, instead, we see it as Hesiod did, as the way of life determined for human beings by Zeus, we see that the fact that grain can be produced only with hard work has a much more than technical significance. It is direct evidence that Zeus *wants* human life to be hard, that he has deliberately made it impossible for us to get something for nothing.[10] This fact is as relevant to the kings as it is to the humblest plowman. It is a clue to the nature of the cosmos.

It is also a clue to Hesiod's sense of justice. Hesiod elaborates on the ignorance of the judges with two parallel, apparently proverbial, and equally paradoxical statements, that the half is more than the whole, and that there is some great benefit to mallow and asphodel. The inclination of commentators has been to add a proviso: "Better is the little [which the righteous has] than the great wealth [of the wicked]" (Proverbs 15.16).[11] There is no such proviso in the Greek, nor was there meant to be. The "half," to Hesiod's mind, is more not because it is righteous, but simply because it is half. That the gods are jealous and allow us, at best, only a modest share of goods is perhaps the single most basic tenet of Greek religious thought. This is why the half is preferable, because one who strives for the whole is most likely to end up with nothing.[12] The proverb on mallow and asphodel reinforces the point. Mallow and asphodel, probably the most miserable fare a human being could find, do not need to be farmed.[13] They are so miserable that the earth produces them, as she will not produce grain, of her own accord (αὐτομάτη). In other words, they are so miserable that the gods do not grudge them us. The blessing of the simple life, from this point of view, is not that it is humble and therefore holy. It is that it is humble and therefore safe.

By adding the proviso we have robbed Hesiod of his particular insight. Taken by themselves, Hesiod's proverbs do not imply any particular connection between poverty and righteousness, nor is it likely that Hesiod, who was no Christian, would have associated the two. Hesiod's proverbs say simply what Solon told Croesus and Amasis told Polycrates, that too much good is dangerous (Herodotus 1.32; 3.40). Nonetheless, in context, Hesiod's meaning clearly is that a small but honest living is better than great wealth unjustly gained. The conclusion is Hesiod's own. In order to see how justice fits into human life, Hesiod has adopted a new way of seeing injustice. Instead of looking from the victim's point of view, to whom the wickedness of the injustice stands out, Hesiod looks from the point of view of the doer of injustice. What he sees is an easy profit. But it is just this easy profit that the gods do not allow. Zeus' punishment of injustice is thus revealed as simply another case of the gods not allowing us goods unmixed with evil.[14] Justice, accordingly, is the necessity of accepting the hardship that the gods have determined shall be our lot.

Clearly, if the gods do not allow injustice, if we cannot simply take what we need, we must work for our living.[15] What Hesiod has shown is the converse: the fact that we must work for our living tells us that the gods do not allow injustice. The very fact of farming reveals that the gods do not allow human beings a good, such as a livelihood, without a concomitant evil, such as work. So does the nature of farming. The sense of what the Greeks called the jealousy (φθόνος) of the gods is a daily fact of any farmer's existence. If all went well, if the rain fell at the right time and in the right amount, if it was neither too hot nor too cold, too windy nor too calm, if the animals did not fall sick, and if the growth of the crops was not interrupted, farming would be easy. But the gods, who have placed sweat before success (WD 289–90), do not grant these ifs. Human goods, in small things as well as great, are always accompanied by evils. In the case of goods we work for this is the evil of labor. In the case of goods that are "snatched" it is the evil of punishment. This is, for human beings, the order of the cosmos.

As Hesiod says: "Justice in the end comes out over Insolence. He is a fool who only / understands when he suffers." (δίκη δ' ὑπὲρ ὕβριος ἴσχει / ἐς τέλος ἐξελθοῦσα· παθὼν δέ τε νήπιος ἔγνω WD 217–18). People like Perses and the kings who fail to see that Zeus allows no free lunches learn their lesson, just as a farmer who tries to sow without having sufficiently prepared the land learns his, by suffering the consequences. That is why they are fools. It is the intermediate step that connects Hesiod's sense of justice to his sense of the importance of human perception, and that adds the very significant wrinkle to Hesiod's sense of justice. Justice wins over insolence *in the end*.[16] As with the good Strife who is always praised, when one has come to know her (WD 12), as with Epimetheus, who found out, when he had the evil, what it was he had chosen, and as with the rough road to success and the easy road to failure that only appear in their true colors at the end of the journey (WD 286–92), what it is critical to perceive is (translated literally) "what is better afterwards in the end" (WD 294).

From one point of view this is reassuring—eventually the unjust are always punished. From another point of view, however, it is the lynchpin in the deceptive nature of the world around us. Human beings judge badly because the consequences of our actions are hidden from us.[17] And (perhaps most significantly, for the *Works and Days* at any rate), when the "eventually" of Zeus' punishment comes can never be known. Hesiod knows that Perses and the kings are fools. He can only hope that that fact will become apparent to them during their own lifetimes.

Hesiod sees all human good as necessarily balanced by a proportionate share of evil. This, the balance that Perses and the kings have sought to avoid, is for Hesiod the foundation of justice. His claim is not that justice is rewarded, nor that it is good in itself. It is simply that injustice, eventually, meets with disaster.[18] This is what Perses and the kings are going to find out—the hard way. Such a view sees justice as a condition of human life rather than as a positive benefit. It implies, as well, that the "rewards" of justice are entirely negative: in acting "justly" a person accepts the evils inherent in life and so avoids the punishments consequent upon injustice.

In one instance, however, the *Works and Days* does seem to ascribe rewards to justice, and so to view justice as a positive good. This occurs at the conclusion of the section on justice, where Hesiod declares that a perjurer's descendants become obscure, while to someone who swears truly Zeus gives wealth, and his descendants prosper (WD 280–84). The first part of this statement recurs fairly soon, under a new rubric: "Riches are not for grabbing; when God gives them they are far better" (χρήματα δ' οὐχ ἁρπακτά· θεόσδοτα πολλὸν ἀμείνω WD 320)—which also contrasts injustice and divine gifts. Here Hesiod explains: "such a man [a thief or perjurer] the gods easily maim, and make meager his household, / and only for a moment in time does prosperity attend him" (ῥεῖα δέ μιν μαυροῦσι θεοί, μινύθουσι δὲ οἶκον / ἀνέρι τῷ, παῦρον δέ τ᾽ ἐπὶ χρόνον ὄλβος ὀπηδεῖ *WD* 325–26).

The addition explains the exception. What Hesiod has done is to combine two traditions, that Zeus may punish someone's posterity for their injustice, and that wealth won by injustice is inherently unstable.[19] The combination serves to rationalize the tradition: since wealth won by injustice does not last, it cannot further a person's household or posterity. In contrast, wealth that is acquired justly does last, and so prospers the household and further generations. To a farmer, whose "investment" in the land, whether of work or of wealth, may find its return only generations later, the thought is a natural one.[20] How your grandparents farmed the land may determine your own success or failure. How you farm yourself will have repercussions for your grandchildren. For Hesiod, future generations are punished for their progenitors' injustice by the diminution of the common stock, and benefit from their justice through the strengthening of the household. This is "god-given" prosperity. Where it comes from we see in the topic introduced between our parallel passages: "But, Perses, do you remember all that I urge—and work" (ἀλλὰ σύ γ᾽ ἡμετέρης μεμνημένος αἰὲν ἐφετμῆς / ἐργάζεο Πέρση *WD* 298–99).

The "god-given" wealth which is opposed to wealth snatched from others is wealth won by work. It is "god-given" because it is wealth won under the conditions that Zeus has intended for human beings, justice and toil.[21] Such wealth Zeus allows men to keep. This connection between justice and work is presented in its most positive aspect in Hesiod's description of the just city, where justice allows for a communion of human beings and nature that gives the passage a peaceful, even joyful, quality unusual in Hesiod. The communion itself comes from farming. Hesiod seems to take pains to point out that these people do not live in a new Golden Age. In the Golden Age "The grain-growing earth bore them crops, full, ungrudgingly / of its own accord" (καρπὸν δ᾽ ἔφερε ζείδωρος ἄρουρα / αὐτομάτη πολλόν τε καὶ ἄφθονον *WD* 117–18). Hesiod uses precisely the same description for the just city, but stops just short of αὐτομάτη ("of its own accord"): "the grain-growing earth yields them its fruits" (καρπὸν δὲ φέρει ζείδωρος ἄρουρα *WD* 237), hardly a miraculous occurrence.[22] Nature is generous here, but the fields of the just city bear fruit because the farmers work them. The citizens enjoy the blessings of peace and plenty; they do so because they keep their hands off each other's goods, and tend to their farms instead.

The blessings enjoyed by the people of the just city are the absence of war, famine, and plague and the ability to live with the earth in the way that Zeus ordained for human beings.[23] These are the true rewards of justice. They come not from justice itself, but from hard work. The cosmos, for Hesiod, is an interrelated order. So too is human life. There are no rewards for justice *per se* within Hesiod's vision. But for Hesiod justice is not *per se*—it is one element of the complex which makes up human life and which gives it its meaning.

The Balance of Justice

The Greek word δίκη, which I translate as "justice," means both decent human behavior in general, and the judicial system. In the former sense the word can be so universal as to indicate not merely the proper way for human beings, but even the ultimate balance which is the fundamental way of the cosmos.[24] In the latter sense the word has a purely concrete and pragmatic meaning. The "justices" (δίκαι) or "judgments" are the decisions given by the kings; "justice" (δίκη) is the system under which these decisions are rendered, our "judicial system."[25] Hesiod introduces justice into the *Works and Days* in a way that seems to blend these two meanings and to bring out their interrelation. His topic is a very specific "justice" indeed, his own court case against Perses. But what the mythic section of his poem reveals is that even this case is rooted, finally, in Zeus' determination of the proper way for human beings. With such universal beginnings the section of the *Works and Days* that follows the fable, in which Hesiod turns specifically to justice, seems to promise great things.

It does not deliver them. Hesiod's section on justice is entirely concerned with justice as a concrete particular, that is, justice as it is seen in court.[26] Even more specifically, it continues to center around "this justice here" (τήνδε δίκην WD 38–39, 268–69), the case between Hesiod and Perses that provides the dramatic setting for the poem. Correspondingly, Hesiod's section on justice makes two points and two points only: Zeus punishes perjury (read Perses') and crooked decisions (read in Thespiae).[27] They are made in completely traditional terms.[28] This is not surprising. If Hesiod's aim is to show Perses and the kings that Zeus punishes injustice the traditional wisdom that supports his claim is the best evidence. Evidence which he had himself invented would hardly have been convincing.

Hesiod uses the word "justice" exclusively of the courts. Of twenty-five uses of the word in the *Works and Days*, twenty-one occur in this section, which is specifically about the courts. Of *all* the uses of "justice" in the poem, only one occurs outside of any judicial context whatsoever.[29] This is not because Hesiod was unaware of the wider range of the word. That he was is evident, first, from the end of the Iron Age, which links perjury and crooked judgements (WD 190–94) with offenses against guest friends, brothers, and parents, the paradigmatically traditional offenses against justice, and secondly from a passage that describes the punishment Zeus wreaks not on courts, but on individuals.[30] A thief, Hesiod tells us, is punished just as surely as a man who wrongs a suppliant, a guest-friend, or a parent (WD 327–34).[31] With such a one, "Zeus himself is angry and for his deeds of injustice / in the end requires bitter requital" (τῷ δ' ἤτοι Ζεὺς αὐτὸς ἀγαίεται, ἐς δε τελευτήν / ἔργων ἀντ' ἀδίκων χαλεπὴν ἐπέθηκεν ἀμοιβήν WD 333–34). Hesiod's claim here is that the offense he is concerned with, the snatching of wealth, is precisely the same as the offenses that everyone, himself included, knows are unjust, in the most general sense of the word.[32]

One reason for Hesiod's focus on the judicial sense of justice and on his own dispute with Perses is his tendency, which is also the tendency of epic in general, to focus on particulars rather than on abstractions. Thus the *Works and Days* is introduced not as an inquiry into the nature of justice, but as a warning to Perses. Having established a particular case as his focus Hesiod centers his more general claims around it. "Just-ice" and "just" are words of strong moral approbation. The foolhardiness of abusing a suppliant, a traditional violation of justice, is simply a given of Greek thought.[33] In using "justice" and "just" insistently of the judicial system, and in insistently coupling the noun and the adjective, Hesiod makes evident the linguistically inherent con-nection between the courts and proper behavior.[34] Those who "give straight decisions to strangers and citizens" are, it is implied, precisely the same as those who "in no way transgress the limits of Justice" (οἵ δὲ δίκας ξείνοισι καὶ ἐνδήμοισι διδοῦσιν / ἰθείας καὶ μή τι παρεκβαίνουσι δικαίου *WD* 225–26). The double sense of the word itself indi-cates that crooked judgments are as dangerous as injuring a guest-friend.

In the one instance where Hesiod moves from the courts to an individual's injus-tice it is specifically theft that is regarded as equivalent to injuring a suppliant or a guest-friend. This is also our clue to Hesiod's main reason for limiting justice to the courts. Offenses against the broader, more traditional senses of justice are always punished by Zeus. They do not necessarily come under the jurisdiction of the courts. Offenses against property do. The court in Thespiae probably spent a good deal more time on property disputes than on cases brought by suppliants or guest-friends. By focusing on the courts, Hesiod has moved the paradigmatic concern of justice from hospitality, offenses against suppliants and guest-friends, to property. He has done so because his sense of justice, like Aristotle's, is primarily economic.[35]

Hesiod focuses on the courts because "justice," for Hesiod, is the justice which plays a crucial role in his own life, the impossibility of snatching wealth. This is also the place where the connection of justice to the overall life that Zeus has intended for human beings is clearest. Hesiod feels the connection between βίος "life" and βίος "livelihood" very deeply. "Possessions," he tells us, "are the life of unhappy mortal men" (χρήματα γὰρ ψυχὴ πέλεται δειλοῖσι βροτοῖσιν *WD* 686). This is the significance of Hesiod's "economic" concept of justice. Economics, as our livelihood, is our life. By keeping justice in the courts, Hesiod, finally, extended rather than restricted its range.

Hesiod's section on justice is extremely limited. This is because it is not meant to be taken on its own. Zeus, in this account, influences human life only on the level of the *polis*. He punishes not cutthroats and thieves but corrupt judges and false witnesses.[36] Hesiod does not describe the punishment which follows the injustices of private men until the next section, the section on honest hard work. This section is the comple-ment to the section on justice in the courts, as we see in noting an important fact. Hes-iod's section on justice is not, in fact, about justice. It is about injustice; not what we should do in order to be just, but what we should avoid in order to avoid punishment. This is not unusual. In the case of virtues like courage or wisdom it is not difficult to identify a wise or courageous act. In the case of justice it is hard to say anything except that a just act is one that is not unjust.

What is unusual about Hesiod's section on justice is not that it is about injustice, but that it is followed by a section which *is* about justice. This section, together with the section that follows farming and sailing, has been regarded as mere "freewheeling" and largely neglected.[37] It is not difficult to see why. If the section on justice is too single-minded, these sections are dazzling in their multiplicity. They cover relations with wives and children, brothers and hired men, friends and neighbors, when to open a jar, when to lend or borrow, trust and shame, work and idleness, understanding and ignorance, gossip, parties, and when to pare one's fingernails. Scholars may well be excused for not having seen what the sections are about, since what they are about covers all of human life. They are about the way human beings ought to behave. That is to say, they are about justice.

The principle of the sections is simple: do as you are done by. The reason is that this, reciprocity, is the way of the world:

> Invite your friend to supper, but let your enemy be;
> most of all invite him who is your nearest neighbor.
> For if anything untoward happens on your estate,
> your neighbor comes ungirdled, but your kin only after they are girdled.

> τὸν φιλέοντ' ἐπὶ δαῖτα καλεῖν, τὸν δ' ἐχθρὸν ἐᾶσθαι·
> τὸν δὲ μάλιστα καλεῖν, ὅστις σέθεν ἐγγύθι ναίει·
> εἰ γάρ τοι καὶ χρῆμ' ἐγχώριον ἄλλο γένηται,
> γείτονες ἄζωστοι ἔκιον, ζώσαντο δὲ πηοί.   WD 342–45

> Take good measure from your neighbor, and give him again good measure
> with just the same measure—or better, if you can do so;
> that when you need him again you can rely on finding him.

> εὖ μὲν μετρεῖσθαι παρὰ γείτονος, εὖ δ' ἀποδοῦναι,
> αὐτῷ τῷ μέτρῳ, καὶ λώιον, αἴ κε δύνηαι,
> ὡς ἄν χρηίζων καὶ ἐς ὕστερον ἄρκιον εὕρῃς.   WD 349–51

> Love one that loves you, meet him that is ready to meet you.
> Give to the one who gives; do not give to the ungiver.
> One gives to the giver of gifts, but he that gives no gifts gets none.

> τὸν φιλέοντα φιλεῖν καὶ τῷ προσιόντα προσεῖναι,
> καὶ δόμεν ὅς κεν δῷ, καὶ μὴ δόμεν ὅς κεν μὴ δῷ·
> δώτῃ μέν τις ἔδωκεν, ἀδώτῃ δ' οὔ τις ἔδωκεν·   WD 353–55

> Do not make a friend the equal of a brother, or if you do,
> let you not be the first to do injury to him;
> do not lie to him to please him, but if he is the first to say
> the word or do the act that vexes your heart, remember
> and pay him back twice over; but if he again would lead you
> back into friendship, and is willing to give compensation,
> accept him.

> μηδὲ κασιγνήτῳ ἶσον ποιεῖσθαι ἑταῖρον·
> εἰ δέ κε ποιήσῃ, μή μιν πρότερος κακὸν ἔρξεις,
> μηδὲ ψεύδεσθαι γλώσσης χάριν· εἰ δὲ σέ γ' ἄρχῃ
> ἤ τι ἔπος εἰπὼν ἀποθύμιον ἠὲ καὶ ἔρξας,

δὶς τόσα τείνυσθαι μεμνημένος· εἰ δέ κεν αὖτις
ἡγῆτ᾽ ἐς φιλότητα, δίκην δ᾽ ἐθέλησι παρασχεῖν
δέξασθαι·   *WD* 707–13·

This last "compensation" is, in the Greek, "justice," but not justice as determined by a judge in court.[38] It is rather the amends which make up for an injury, and so restore friendship. It is also the one non-judicial use of the word in the *Works and Days*. People give good for good and evil for evil—this is reciprocity.[39] They may also, and in just the same way, give "justice," the measure that restores reciprocity and so reestablishes the balance of human relations.

Hesiod has already made the point that if one gives evil, evil is what one will get: "A man working ill to another works ill to himself, / and wicked counsel is wickedest to the wicked giver" (οἷ τ᾽ αὐτῷ κακὰ τεύχει ἀνὴρ ἄλλῳ κακὰ τεύχων, / ἡ δὲ κακὴ βουλὴ τῷ βουλεύσαντι κακίστη *WD* 265–67). These lines occur not in the section on social relations, but in the section on justice in the courts. There they appeared to refer simply to the punishment that results from violating justice. Here it is apparent that they, and with them Hesiod's certainty that there *is* such a punishment, are a necessary part of Hesiod's sense of reciprocity. Viewed *sub specie aeternitatis* justice is another case of the gods refusing to allow us goods unaccompanied by evil. Viewed from a strictly human perspective, the punishment that follows injustice is simply another case of what you give is also what you get.

This connection between justice and reciprocity is inherent in a basic image of Greek literature, the balance or scales. In the *Iliad* the fates or "portions" of dueling warriors are determined by Zeus' weighing them in his balance. In the *Hymn to Hermes* Apollo brings Hermes before Zeus to answer the charge of stealing his cattle: "For there the scales of justice were set for them both" (κεῖθι γὰρ ἀμφοτέροισι δίκης κατέκειτο τάλαντα *Hymn. Hom. Merc.* 324). The idea of justice as a pair of scales is as familiar to us as to Hesiod. The difference is that for Hesiod the balance had a far more mundane use as well. When Hesiod figured out what he owed he used neither a cash register, nor pencil and paper. He used a balance. Scales determined what made a fair exchange, in fact as well as in metaphor, in trade as well as in justice.[40]

Justice and reciprocity both manifest the fact of balance which, to Hesiod's mind, underlies and connects all of human life. This balance is embedded in the world. It is also embedded in our own emotional response to the world, in our good will (χάρις) towards those who do good to us, and in our indignation at those who do evil. The first is, as Aristotle points out, the basis of reciprocity.[41] The second is nemesis, the indignation that we naturally feel against people who take without giving (*WD* 303–6). This is the force, together with shame (αἰδώς) that keeps justice straight.[42] In the proverb attributed to Hesiod—"If a man sows evil, he will reap an evil profit; / If he suffers as he has done, justice will be straight" (εἰ κακά τις σπείραι, κακὰ κέρδεά κ᾽ ἀμήσειεν· / εἰ κε πάθοι τά τ᾽ ἔρεξε, δίκη κ᾽ ἰθεῖα γένοιτο Fragment 286)—justice is seen as a balance of acting against suffering.[43] Another case of suffering as one has done, "One gives to the giver of gifts, but he that gives no gifts gets none" (*WD* 355), explains how this justice operates in the word. When we discover, with indignation, that Perses, having stolen Hesiod's share of the farm, is now begging from him (*WD* 394–97) we see how pervasive the force which balances acting against suffering is.[44] Hesiod's response, "I shall give you no more, / nor measure out more to you" (ἐγὼ δέ τοι οὐκ ἐπιδώσω / οὐδ' ἐπιμετρήσω WD 396–97), is also our own.

Hesiod, like any small farmer, understands men to live together through a mutual and grudging cooperation.[45] If you give to others they will give to you; if you help out a neighbor in need you will get help when you need it. If you do not, others will be glad enough to neglect you: "It is so easy to say, 'Lend me a team and a wagon,' / but the answer is easy, too, 'The oxen have work to do.'" (ῥηίδιον γὰρ ἔπος εἰπεῖν· "βόε δὸς καὶ ἄμαξαν·" / ῥηίδιον δ' ἀπανήνασθαι· "πάρα δ' ἔργα βόεσσιν" WD 453–54). Reciprocity is an essential, underlying fact of human life, crucial to a small farmer and to society as a whole. There is, nonetheless, a tension. Reciprocity is a basic fact of human life, but so also, as the first lines of the Works and Days have told us, is strife (WD 11–26).

Hesiod sees both the farm, and the world within which the farm exists, as an ordered whole. As he sees farming as informed by the order of the seasons, so he sees human relations as informed by a basic principle of balance. To us, who tend to see a vision of a natural human congruity with nature and with other human beings as a lost Eden, Hesiod's vision may seem idyllic. It is not. As Hesiod sees hardship and suffering as an element inherent in farming, so he sees conflict and injustice as inherent in human relations. Human relations may be a balance, but it is not a balance that finds an easy equilibrium. Hesiod's sense of reciprocity exists against the background of what we might call zero-sum economics. The economic understanding of Classical Greece happens, in this respect, to agree with a basic peasant view of the world; both assume that what one person acquires another must simultaneously lose.[46] Within such a vision reciprocity is clearly critical, and conflict is just as clearly inevitable.

Hesiod's sense is that the world is ordered, but not that it is therefore easy. The gods compel human beings to acknowledge the bad strife that leads to injustice and to the misery that comes in its wake (WD 15–16). The good strife is not carefree either. Objectively reciprocity is a balance of good done against good received. To the individual, however, it is a balance of the advantage of receiving help later against the disadvantage of giving help now. People give only to a giver. On the other hand, "It is best that [things] be at home; what is abroad is endangered" (οἴκοι βέλτερον εἶναι, ἐπεὶ βλαβερὸν τὸ θύρηφιν WD 365). The difficulty is not limited to lending.

The two sections of the Works and Days that show us that reciprocity and balance are basic to human life are also the sections that reveal most vividly the deceptive nature of the world within which we live. Every good turns out to have an evil double. A good wife is the best thing a man can have; a bad wife is the worst. (WD 202–5). The same is true of neighbors (WD 346). It is a bad thing to have too many friends, but you should not have none either (WD 715). A sense of shame (αἰδώς) keeps people on the path of justice; when it leaves the earth in the Iron Age it heralds destruction. But it is not always good (WD 317–19). Even sparing, the great secret of any peasant farmer's success, can be overdone: "When the barrel is at its beginning, and at its end too, drink your fill; / spare when you are in the middle; sparing is base in the dregs" (ἀρχομένου δὲ πίθου καὶ λήγοντος κορέσασθαι, / μεσσόθι φείδεσθαι· δειλὴ δ' ἐν πυθμένι φειδώ WD 368–69). Trust, too, is ambiguous: "Trust and distrust alike . . . have been men's destruction" (πίστεις δ' ἄρ' ὁμῶς καὶ ἀπιστίαι ὤλεσαν ἄνδρας WD 372).[47] Even straight and crooked justice are not as easily distinguished as Hesiod would have Perses believe. The good and wise kings of the *Theogony*, the ones favored by the Muses, are able to find the right balance (*Th.* 84–90). Hesiod's emphasis on the ease with which *these* kings settle disputes seems to indicate that it is not always so easy.[48]

Along with the doubleness of things comes, therefore, the necessity of measure and seasonableness: "let it be dear to you to arrange your work in due measure, / that your granaries may be filled with seasonable grain" (σοὶ δ' ἔργα φίλ' ἔστω μέτρια κοσμεῖν, / ὥς κέ τοι ὡραίου βιότου πλήθωσι καλιαί WD 306–7). "Take good measure from your neighbor, and give him again good measure/ with just the same measure—or better, if you can do so" (εὖ μὲν μετρεῖσθαι παρὰ γείτονος, εὖ δ' ἀποδοῦναι, / αὐτῷ τῷ μέτρῳ, καὶ λώιον, αἴ κε δύνηαι WD 349–50). "[I]f you wish to do all of the tasks / of Demeter at proper season—and so in *their* proper season / shall your crops increase" (εἴ χ' ὥρια παντ' ἐθέλησθα / ἔργα κομίζεσθαι Δημήτερος, ὥς τοι ἕκαστα / ὥρι' ἀέξηται WD 392–4). "At the right time of your life bring home a wife to your house" (Ὡραῖος δὲ γυναῖκα τεὸν ποτὶ οἶκον ἄγεσθαι WD 695). "The best treasure of the tongue among mortals is its sparing, / and when it runs in measure that is its greatest grace. / If you use a bad word to someone you will soon hear a worse yourself" (γλώσσης τοι θησαυρὸς ἐν ἀνθρώποισιν ἄριστος / φειδωλῆς, πλείστη δὲ χάρις κατὰ μέτρον ἰούσης· / εἰ δὲ κακὸν εἴπῃς, τάχα κ' αὐτὸς μεῖζων ἀκούσαις WD 719–21). As this last indicates, the idea of measure is intrinsically connected, in Hesiod's mind, with the idea of reciprocity. It is also connected with the doubleness of things.

The balance of human relations is by no means an automatic balance. On the contrary, noticing what is better "afterwards and in the end" (WD 294) can be an almost infinitely complicated task. The only solution lies in "measure" (μέτρα), "proportion" (καιρός), and "due season" (ὡραῖος), key words used throughout the *Works and Days* to indicate just this underlying theme.[49] The words are automatically associated with justice, reciprocity, and balance. They apply throughout human life. Hesiod's definitive statement, "Keep watch on measure; in all things best is the when and how much" (μέτρα φυλάσσεσθαι· καιρὸς δ' ἐπὶ πᾶσιν ἄριστος WD 694), is directly about not overloading a boat or a wagon. In farming one must always watch for the right time and the right amount.[50] So, also, in general, one must also know how much to give and how much to spare, and when. Similarly with trust, hope, children, wives, neighbors, friends, and shame: one must know the right time, the right way, and the right amount. To choose the good side of the double qualities that permeate human life you must perceive the right measure.[51] To choose the evil side is precisely not to discern it.

The Place of Justice

That human beings insist that acts of injustice be punished, and feel anger when they are not, that in cities where injustice is not punished the social fabric frays and finally is torn apart, that war, famine, and disease follow the disruption of such a society, are, to us, natural consequences. They are, to Hesiod, part of the divine order and the punishments sent by Zeus against injustice.[52] Like Hesiod's sense of the "rewards" earned by justice—as the result of hard work—his sense of the punishment which follows injustice is, in our terms, completely natural.[53] There is an unexpected consequence. When society breaks down under the burden of unjust decisions this is not, for Hesiod, the end of justice, but only another manifestation of it.

Hesiod's description of the end of the Iron Age begins with the violation of justice in its traditional garb: the undoing of the relations of parents and children, guests and hosts, comrades and brothers.[54] He then describes the breakdown of the courts: "nor shall oath-keeping have any grace among them, nor yet justice nor good . . . The evil man / shall injure the better, speaking / with crooked lies and swear with an oath to top them" (οὐδέ τις εὐόρκου χάρις ἔσσεται οὐδὲ δικαίου . . . βλάψει δ' ὁ κακὸς τὸν ἀρείονα φῶτα / μύθοισι σκολιοῖς ἐνέπων, ἐπὶ δ' ὅρκον ὀμεῖται WD 190, 193–94). Then "justice shall be in their hands only, / and shame shall be no more" (δίκη δ' ἐν χερσὶ, καὶ αἰδώς / οὐκ ἔσται WD 192). When human beings cease to feel shame and indignation (αἰδώς and νέμεσις), the goddesses leave the earth (WD 199–201). With them goes all human appreciation of the balance which makes human life livable. There will then be no remedy for evil (WD 201).

When Shame and Indignation leave the earth, however, Justice does not go with them. Justice remains, distorted by human corruption and perjury, not maintaining society, but undermining it. This is the Justice that follows behind those who abuse her, weeping, and bringing evil upon them (WD 223–25). She is now the scourge that destroys cities that do not respect her, and in so doing restores the balance that human beings have upset.

In describing a time when "justice is in men's hands" Hesiod is not imagining a return to the Bronze or Silver Ages when there were no courts, no oaths, and no law, but only force.[55] His vision of the Iron Age rather pictures a time when justice has become the *equivalent* of violence, a time when people use the courts, rather than clubs, as their weapons. In so doing the age is to discover that their manhandling of justice has produced, as with each of the previous ages, a self-destruction peculiar to themselves. Justice is a permanent condition of human life, determined not by human beings, but by the order of Zeus. It exists whether we abide by it or not. When people follow the ways of insolence Justice does not abandon them. The destruction that follows when justice is subverted is itself justice.[56]

Hesiod's sense that the end of the Iron Age will be a time of corruption, rather than of brute force, reflects the view of the poem as a whole.[57] Violence as such is not a major concern of the *Works and Days*. It comes up only as a possible alternative to perjury, another kind of "unjust deed" that brings a harsh exchange from Zeus (WD 320–34).[58] Debt, perjury, and theft, hidden rather than open assaults, are what Hesiod fears.[59] In a particularly vivid case of what happened to the old, evil abstractions when their good twins, the children of Zeus, were born, violence was irrevocably transformed when justice entered the world. In primitive times, as in Hesiod's picture of the Silver or Bronze Ages, violence was the distinguishing feature of life, as it still is among the animals. After the entrance of justice into our world violence became, as it is in the *Works and Days*, just another kind of injustice.

For Hesiod, courts that deal out straight justice, and the destruction that comes upon cities where the justice is crooked, are equally manifestations of the justice of Zeus. For an individual as well, Zeus' punishment may be meted out by indignant neighbors, by the courts or, where both fail, by Zeus himself. This last and critical resort is also, from Job's day to our own, the most problematic. Hesiod is not unaware of the problem. Beginning with a passing reminder of the difficulty of understanding Zeus' will—"The eye of Zeus sees all, takes note of all, / and, *if he please*, he watches this too unerringly" (πάντα ἰδὼν Διὸς ὀφθαλμὸς καὶ πάντα νοήσας / καί νυ τάδ' αἴ κ' ἐθέλησ' ἐπιδέρκεται WD 267–69; my emphasis)—Hesiod gradually moves into a statement that questions the entire foundation of his belief: what if wealth *could* be won by injustice? What if men *could* get wealth simply by taking it? In that case, Hesiod is forced to admit, justice clearly would not be a part of Zeus' will, and a man would be a fool to be just. Hesiod does not believe this will happen.[60] But, as he has just reminded us, the mind of Zeus cannot be completely fathomed.[61] Hesiod cannot know with certainty that Zeus will not bring it to pass that injustice, rather than justice, will profit a man.

Hesiod's implicit question is answered by the passage that follows:

> Perses, do you lay up these things in your mind;
> and listen to Justice, forgetting entirely violence.
> For this is the Rule for men that the son of Cronos has given —
> for the fish and the beasts and the winged birds,
> that they should devour one another, for they have no Justice
>   among them—
> but to man he has given Justice and she proves to be far the best

> ὦ Πέρση, σὺ δὲ ταῦτα μετὰ φρεσὶ βάλλεο σῆσιν,
> καί νυ δίκης ἐπάκουε, βίης δ' ἐπιλήθεο πάμπαν.
> τόνδε γὰρ ἀνθρώποισι νόμον διέταξε Κρονίων,
> ἰχθύσι μὲν καὶ θηρσὶ καὶ οἰωνοῖς πετεηνοῖς
> ἔσθειν ἀλλήλους, ἐπεὶ οὐ δίκη ἐστὶ μετ' αὐτοῖς·
> ἀνθρώποισι δ' ἔδωκε δίκην, ἣ πολλὸν ἀρίστη
> γίνεται·   WD 274–80

At first glance this looks like simply the old injunction followed by the old reason: listen to justice because this is Zeus' will.[62] But there is a difference. The word "*nomos*" or "Rule" also means "way" and even "way of life." With "For this is the Rule for men that the son of Cronos has given" Hesiod has moved from "follow justice because this is Zeus' will" to "follow justice because this, and not violence, is the way of life that is human."[63] This is not to say that Hesiod has forgotten Zeus. Far from it. The fact that justice *is* the rule, or way of life which is human, is Hesiod's ultimate argument that it is, and will continue to be, Zeus' will for human beings.

Hesiod's implicit objection to his advocacy of justice is that no one can know the mind of Zeus. He answers the objection by declaring that justice is the "way" for us, just as eating one another is the "way" for animals. If the adequacy of the answer is not immediately apparent it is because we do not share Hesiod's sense of a "way" or *nomos*.

The other human *nomos* that Hesiod mentions in the *Works and Days* is farming (*WD* 388). As the animals' eating of one another defines the place that they hold within the cosmos, and as Zeus' determination of the "honors" and *nomoi* of the gods determined their places within his order (*Th.* 73–74), so farming and justice define our place in the cosmos. For Hesiod, a being's *nomos* is also its place within the order of Zeus. This, as we saw in the Myth of the Five Ages, is the closest Hesiod comes to our concept of a being's "nature."[64]

Work and justice are not, for Hesiod, arbitrary ordinances which Zeus has enacted and which he might repeal. They are the conditions of Zeus' order which, by determining our place in the cosmos, makes human nature what it is. When Zeus gave us justice he gave us courts. But more importantly he gave us courts by giving us the *need* for courts, by determining that we would no longer be able to live as the animals do, singly, and by force. The fact of justice implies that human beings, as they cannot take what they need, must work, must be dependent upon others, and must live in society. Conversely, the fact that we must live in society means also that we must have justice. Justice determines not only that we must live together, but also how we must live together, through the exchange of good for good which is the other side of our returning evil for evil. Justice, for Hesiod, is thus interwoven, inextricably, throughout human life. It is what makes us who we are. For Zeus to make justice *not* the rule for human beings would be to obliterate the distinction between us and the animals. It would be to make human beings not human. This is what Hesiod thinks that Zeus will not yet do.

Force and Order: Vergil and Caesar

Hesiod saw, as Vergil did, that peace and justice on the one hand, and violence and the dissolution of society on the other, are inseparable. These alternatives are, for him, two sides of one coin. Injustice, a doomed attempt to find goods not tied to evils, and justice, a recognition of the necessity of hardship, both point to the ultimate fact of Zeus' order. Shame and Indignation may flee the world; Justice remains behind.

Vergil adopts another tradition.[65] For him, it is Justice herself who has fled: "[Farmers] for whom the most just earth herself, far from discordant arms / Pours from the ground an easy livelihood . . . amongst these / Justice, fleeing the earth, left her last traces" (*quibus ipsa, procul discordibus armis, / fundit humo facilem victum iustissima tellus . . . extrema per illos / Iustitia excedens terris vestigia fecit* 2.459–60, 473–74). Even among farmers, and even at their most ideal, only the half-seen traces of justice remain, suggesting what justice was, and showing us that it is gone.

As is appropriate, not the abstract noun *iustitia*, "justice," but the concrete *ius*, "right" or "law," is the Vergilian equivalent of Hesiod's δίκη or "justice." But where Hesiod identified the concrete and the abstract senses of "justice," Vergil separates them. For Hesiod violence, as it exists among men, is only another kind of injustice. For Vergil violence is a real and independent entity, capable of existing without reference to either justice or reason. *Iustitia*, the opposite of this vision of violence, is a Golden Age ideal of unforced cooperation.[66] Between the two lie *ius*, the *ferrea iura* ("iron laws"

2.501) of our own Iron Age world. The phrase occurs at the end of the second Georgic, in contrast to the ideal cooperation of the countryside:

> [The farmer] plucks the fruits that the boughs themselves,
> That the willing country bears of its own will, nor iron laws
> Nor the Forum's madness, nor the people's tables sees.

> quos rami fructus, quos ipsa volentia rura
> sponte tulere sua, carpsit, nec ferrea iura
> insanumque forum aut populi tabularia vidit. 2.500–2

"Justice" is no longer to be found in human life. The closest we can come is law.

The difference between *ius* and *iustitia* is enforcement. For Vergil *iustitia* is unforced cooperation and spontaneous harmony. The *iura*, the laws, promote the same end, cooperation and order. They, however, are effective only when force lies behind them:

> Thus I was singing the care of the fields, and about cattle,
> And trees, while great Caesar, beside deep Euphrates
> Thundered in war, and, as victor, gave willing peoples
> Law, and essayed the path to Olympus.

> Haec super arvorum cultu pecorumque canebam
> et super arboribus, Caesar dum magnus ad altum
> fulminat Euphraten bello victorque volentis
> per populos dat iura viamque adfectat Olympo. 4.559–62

The world of law is the world where the charioteer controls the horse, the world where force, under the control of reason, creates order. It is a world identified in the *Georgics* with Caesar. It is thus that Book 3 of the *Georgics* begins, promising us a new beginning, one which will unite force and poetry into a single ordered whole: "In the middle will I set Caesar; he shall keep the temple" (*in medio mihi Caesar erit templumque tenebit* 3.16).[67] As Vergil expands on the temple he will build for Caesar, the images that have united force and reason in the first two Georgics, the horse and chariot (3.17–18) and the mock violence of games (3.19–20), reappear, now culminating in battles refigured by the ordering power of art (3.26–33). They are accompanied by an unexpected figure, Vergil himself.

Again Vergil has borrowed from Hesiod. As Hesiod opposes farming to injustice he opposes himself, the farmer-poet, to Perses, the cheat. A similar opposition runs throughout the *Georgics*, between a still minor and relatively unknown poet, Vergil, and the sole ruler of the known world, the man who is soon to be Augustus Caesar.[68] The comparison is audacious enough to explain Vergil's opening and closing references to his own boldness (1.40; 4.565). It is also too marked to be accidental. At all of the crucial junctures of the *Georgics*, at the close of the poem's invocation, at the conclusion of the praise of Italy in Book 2, in the proem to the poem's second half which opens Book 3, and in the poem's final lines, Vergil and Caesar appear together; Vergil as a poet, living in peace and sympathy with nature, Caesar as a warrior, creating order through force. Caesar appears without Vergil only once, at the end of Book 1, as the hope for an end to the civil wars. As a balance, Vergil appears without Caesar at the end of Book 2, craving, if knowledge is not possible for him, the peace, sympathy, and contentment of the countryside. While Caesar thundered in war, giving law to willing peoples,

> In those days I, Vergil, was nursed by sweet
> Naples and flowered in the works of inglorious leisure,
> I, who had dallied with shepherds' songs, and, bold in youth,
> Tityrus, sang of you, in the shade of a spreading beech.

> illo Vergilium me tempore dulcis alebat
> Parthenope, studiis florentem ignobilis oti,
> carmina qui lusi pastorum audaxque iuventa,
> Tityre, te patulae cecini sub tegmine fagi.   4.559–66

So the *Georgics* ends.

The opposition of Vergil and Caesar has moved us one step away from the pure opposition of violence and understanding. As Vergil discreetly reminds us at the opening of the third Georgic, the fame of the warrior depends upon the work of the poet. It is the other side of the coin, however, that Vergil is more interested in. In a brilliant stroke of self-reference Vergil uses the first line of the *Eclogues*: "Tityrus, reclining in the shade of a spreading beech . . ." (*Tityre, tu patulae recumbans sub tegmine fagi . . .*: *Eclogues* 1.1) as the last line of the *Georgics*. The reference contrasts the *Georgics* with the poetic world of peace and sympathy which Vergil created in his youth. It also recalls the dependence of even that world.[69] Tityrus' response to Meliboeus' opening address, "Meliboeus, a god has created for us this leisure" (*O Meliboee, deus nobis haec otia fecit: Eclogues* 1.6), is Vergil's earliest reference to Caesar. The warrior's fame is dependent upon the poet, but so is the poet's world of sympathy and peace dependent upon the order, and so the force, of Caesar.

Caesar, the warrior, enables peace to exist through violence; Vergil, the poet, depends upon that peace. Vergil represents a life of peace and harmony, but one dependent upon force. Caesar represents a life of force, but a force which may create and guard order, rather than destroy it. His is a life of violence, but it is a violence which may, possibly, end civil war, rather than continuing to feed its fury.[70] At the opening and the closing of the *Georgics* Caesar, invoked in prayer and thundering in war, appears to replace Jupiter. At its bleakest, the replacement seemed to suggest that there is no divine order which unites the cosmos, only whatever fleeting order human beings, in the person of Caesar, may manage to sustain. After the vision of civil war which ended the first and second Georgic, the possibility is not quite so bleak. There may be only a manmade order to the universe, but there is, at least, that.

The Third Georgic: The Problem
of the Individual

In the first two Georgics Vergil looks at the farm from outside. In the third he moves into the farm itself. As he does so, he also adopts a new model for the farm. The farm is now associated with neither the ideal natural harmony of the second Georgic, nor with the purely irrational violence of the first; it is now associated with order, but with an order created through force. Image becomes reality. The reigning image of force under the command of reason, the horse broken to the bit, is also the initial subject of the book. The horse, the ox broken to the yoke, and the sheep and goats led through their seasonal pasturage, all show us the farm as a place where reason, in the person of the farmer, is able to order and direct the recalcitrant force of nature.

It is here, on the farm, rather than in an explicit treatment of human relations, that Vergil examines human society. Having replaced the natural harmony of justice with the enforced order of law, Vergil has been left with a question that would hardly be comprehensible to Hesiod. What the third and fourth Georgics examine is not the basis of society, but whether society is anything more than a facade, a label attached to a collection of isolated individuals. Hesiod felt that justice, like society, was unique to ourselves, that neither animals nor gods require it. Far from making him doubt its validity, the fact demonstrated to him that it is justice that makes us human. Vergil seeks something more universal, something that transcends humanity. His question is not what unites human beings, but whether anything can unite individuals, human or not.

In the first two Georgics, the farm was an element of the world, either removed from, or absorbed by, the violence that surrounded it. In the second two, the farm is a microcosm. Having abandoned his image of a natural harmony, Vergil now looks to force ordered by reason for the unity which Hesiod captured in his image of farmer, oxen, slave-boy, and birds, united at the moment of plowing. To a certain extent he finds it. The third and fourth Georgics contain moments of sympathy and shared experience between farmer and animals that are the more exquisite for being the less ideal. The *iuvenis* ("young one") utterly absorbed in the hope and excitement of the chariot race, is both horse and charioteer (3.103–12).[71] The joyful summer which beckons the flocks to pasture is joyful to both sheep and shepherd (3.322–26). The bees' "love of flowers, and pride in producing honey" (*amor florum et generandi gloria mellis* 4.205) is felt just as strongly by the old Corycian gardener who tends them.[72] The sympathy which comes from these shared experiences is real. But it cannot always direct the farmer's actions.

The first difficulty arises with a topic which, up until now, has been notably absent from the *Georgics*. The topic is profit. The first two Georgics examined how the farmer raises crops, vines, and trees. They did not mention why he does so. In contrast, Vergil introduces each of the subjects of the third and fourth Georgics with reference to their use, and so to their profit (both English words translating the Latin *usus*): "Whether coveting the prize of Olympian palm / A man raises horses, or whether strong oxen for the plow . . ." (*seu quis Olympiacae miratus praemia palmae / pascit equos, seu quis fortis ad aratra iuvencos . . .* 3.49–51); "[Goats] too must we watch over, with no lighter care, / And for no less profit" (*hae quoque non cura nobis leviore tuendae, / nec minor usus erit* 3.305–6); "Next, the celestial gift of honey from the skies / I will pursue" (*protinus aërii mellis caelestia dona / exsequar* 4.1–2).[73] The advice which follows focuses on the end towards which the farmer works, the plow, the chariot race or war, milk or wool, and finally a good crop of honey. By restoring the profit to the farm Vergil reassociates it with the society that it serves. He also gives the farmer an interest separate from the interests of the farm's creatures.

Profit does not necessarily divide the farmer from his charges. Vergil's description of raising a young ox ends with the need to feed him well:

> Nor will your newly calved cows,
> In the way of our fathers, fill milk pails snow-white,
> But spend their whole udder on their sweet young.

> nec tibi fetae
> more patrum nivea implebunt mulctraria vaccae,
> sed tota in dulcis consument ubera natos.   3.176–78

The conclusion to the colt's training strikes a slightly different note:

> Then finally let their bodies grow great with a fattening
> Mash, now they are broken; for, before breaking,
> They would raise their spirits too high, and, caught, refuse
> To endure the pliant lash, or obey the harsh curb.

> tum demum crassa magnum farragine corpus
> crescere iam domitis sinito; namque ante domandum
> ingentis tollent animos, prensique negabunt
> verbera lenta pati et duris parere lupatis.   3.205–8

The slight discord that underlies these lines is forced upon our attention when the farmer's interests are directly in competition with the young: "Many even bar newborn kids from their mothers / And fix iron muzzles onto the tips of their noses" (*multi etiam excretos prohibent a matribus haedos, / primaque ferratis praefingunt ora capistris* 3.398–99).[74] The addition of the iron halters explains how, in Vergil's first description of the goats, the goats managed to have both kids beside them and full udders for milking: "Of their own accord they return to their shelter, leading / Their young, heavy udders scarcely clearing the threshold" (*ipsae memores redeunt in tecta suosque / ducunt et gravido superant vix ubere limen* 3.316–17). It also transforms it.

Profit is simply a given of Hesiod's farm. On Vergil's it has driven a wedge between the farmer and his farm. This is not because profit is wicked, but because Vergil has given the creatures of nature a voice. They use that voice to make us see their own, individual, point of view.[75] In so doing they disrupt the unity of the farm. The creatures of the farm do not see that the farmer represents force under the control of reason. To them the farmer is just another impersonal force of nature. Nor do they feel gratitude for the farmer's care and orderly direction of their world. They feel, when they are fed, content, and when they are not, hungry.

Death, one of the two great themes of the third Georgic, is common to man and beast. Vergil points this out in lines whose pathos is almost overwhelming:

> The best days of life for pitiful mortals
> Are first to flee; diseases and sad old age take their place
> And suffering, and the merciless harshness of death snatches all.

> optima quaeque dies miseris mortalibus aevi
> prima fugit; subeunt morbi tristisque senectus
> et labor, et durae rapit inclementia mortis.   3.66–68

The lines that immediately follow abruptly shift both tone and perspective:

> There will always be some whose form you will want to change,
> So always replace them, and, lest later you miss your losses,
> Anticipate, choose stock for the herd every year.

> semper erunt, quarum mutari corpora malis:
> semper enim refice ac, ne post amissa requiras,
> ante veni et subolem armento sortire quotannis.   3.69–71

Vergil is no longer indulging in poetic reflections on the shared fate of farmer and animals. He is speaking to farmers, and farmers have no time for such things.[76] The shift is a positive one. The farmer cannot keep old age and death from individual animals, as he cannot keep them from himself. He can, however, ward them off from the herd as a whole. Although the individuals must die, the herd can continue.[77] If farming does not imply a natural harmony between man and nature, it may at least imply an actual harmony, possible because of man's wider vision.

But our sense of the farmer's care for his herd takes on a new coloring when Vergil describes *how* the farmer must look to the whole, for example, by the elimination of a stallion too old for service:

> This one too, when he fails, heavy with disease or sluggish
> With years, shut him up inside; do not pity his disgraceful old age.
> He is cold in the works of Venus when old; his labor is futile
> And thankless. And, should he come ever to battle,
> As when a great fire rages, without strength, in the stubble,
> He rages in vain.

> Hunc quoque, ubi aut morbo gravis aut iam segnior annis
> deficit, abde domo, nec turpi ignosce senectae.
> frigidus in Venerem senior, frustraque laborem
> ingratum trahit, et, si quando ad proelia ventum est,
> ut quondam in stipulis magnus sine viribus ignis,
> incassum furit.   3.95–100

Vergil has not changed the situation; the elimination of the old stallion is just as critical as the need to renew the herd, and as necessary as the elimination of degenerate seeds in Book 1 (1.194–203). He has, however, introduced a new and incompatible factor, the personality of the stallion.[78] Vergil's injunction not to pity the stallion's old age is self-contradictory.[79] We cannot help pitying the stallion for precisely the same reason that we know we must not pity him, because the effects of old age upon him are no different than they are upon us.

Vergil's description of the old stallion juxtaposes the necessity of sacrificing the individual with the perspective of the individual himself. In explaining why the stallion must be sacrificed, Vergil makes us feel the effort, the frustration, and even the shame of an old man, as he vainly attempts what once came easily. The farmer can save the herd as a whole. He can do so only by refusing to acknowledge what Vergil has made us feel so deeply, the similarity between the farmer and the animals he tends.

This theme, of the sacrifice of the individual, closes as well as opens the advice of the third Georgic. It has now become a question of life or death:

> [A sheep] that you see inclined often to seek the soft shade,
> Listlessly cropping at only the tops of the grass
> Or following far behind, or lying down in the field
> While grazing, one who returns late at night and alone—
> Check the culprit straight off with the knife, before
> The dire contagion spreads throughout the oblivious flock.

> quam procul aut molli succedere saepius umbrae
> videris aut summas carpentem ignavius herbas
> extremamque sequi, aut medio procumbere campo
> pascentem, et serae solam decedere nocti—
> continuo culpam ferro compesce, priusquam
> dira per incautum serpant contagia vulgus.   3.464–69

The one use of animals not present in the *Georgics* is for meat.[80] Vergil's cattle are raised for the plow, his sheep and goats for milk and wool. Pigs and poultry are never mentioned. Even in describing the now useless stallion, Vergil's advice is to shut him inside, not to have him killed. In other words, Vergil has set the *Georgics* up in such a way that here, when the farmer is finally forced to kill, the situation is one in which there is no escape. To resolve the situation by condemning the farmer's cruelty is simply not to understand the situation. Not to kill is to condemn the rest of the flock to death.[81] And yet the picture of the individual, whose helpless solitude is the focal point of the picture, and who is, as Servius comments, hardly "guilty" (*culpam* 3.468) for falling sick, will not allow us to see simply the good of the flock.[82] The innocence of the individual is irrelevant here. The farmer's care for the whole does explain, and fully, why the individual's death is necessary. The difficulty is that it cannot explain this to the individual. The stricken sheep does not see the consequences for the farm as a whole. It sees that, for no reason, it suffers, and, for no reason, must die.

Vergil has created a double vision, which sees, simultaneously, the demands of the whole and the claim of the individual. They are incompatible. On the farm this occurs under a use of force rationally directed. The "digressions" on sex and the Noric plague which occupy the center and the conclusion of the third Georgic reintroduce the unrestrained and irrational violence of nature.[83] The farmer whose care is for the whole cannot allow himself to be moved by the individual suffering that he is inflict-ing. This vision is a cheerful one in comparison with Vergil's vision of the plague. This is impersonal nature. It does not need to ignore the individuality of those who suffer. It is what the farmer must pretend to be. Like the "eyeless rage" of the storm which batters Lear, impersonal nature is not aware of the suffering it is imposing upon indi-viduals; it can neither see individuals, nor understand suffering.

From the farmer's careful direction of the sexual drive for the good of the herd Vergil moves into a description of uncontrolled and violent sexual passion. From the use of violence to prevent plague he moves into the irrational destruction of the plague itself. The moves reverse the separation of the farmer from the animals he tends, and return the farmer to his role as simply another mortal creature:

> Every single race on earth, both man and beast,
> The fish in the sea, the cattle, the colorful birds,
> Race into fires of passion; love is the same for all.

> omne adeo genus in terris hominumque ferarumque,
> et genus aequoreum, pecudes pictaeque volucres,
> in furias ignemque ruunt: amor omnibus idem.   3.242–44

Sex and death are universal. They are also divisive. As sexual passion strikes, the ties that connect individuals are undone. The lioness forgets her cubs, the horse his rider, the young man his parents. There is no coming together in Vergil's picture of sex, no love, and no suggestion of birth.[84] There is only the violence which overmasters each individual separately. The same is true of the victims of the Noric plague; all die of the same cause; all die alone. The ghastly community established—"The wolf no longer sets his ambush around the sheep-pen / Nor prowls by night against the flocks; a sharper care / Has tamed him" (*non lupus insidias explorat ovilia circum / nec gregibus nocturnus obambulat; acrior illum / cura domat* 3.537–39)—is created by the all-consuming absorption of each individual, man and beast, in his own suffering.[85] The fact that sex and death, the central themes of the third Georgic, are common to all of nature establishes neither harmony nor community. What all of nature shares turns out to be each individual's exclusive sense of its own suffering.

The *Georgics* has introduced two new factors into the world of the *Works and Days*, irrational and uncontrolled violence, and the absolute claim of the individual. The two are connected. Both are negative. The positive images of the *Georgics* are of union and community, of the Golden Age, of the harmony of human beings and nature, of the sharing of experience and emotion within which individual barriers are forgot-ten.[86] The intense sense of the individual found in the *Georgics* is expressed in Vergil's feeling for the pain and isolation of suffering. Individuality, for Vergil, is not a gift to be cherished. It is the terrible recognition that comes, most intensely with suffering, that one is alone. It is this growing understanding that makes Vergil's vision of the

Noric plague so devastating. Vergil's picture of an ox dying of the plague (4.525–30) articulates the tension which underlies the third Georgic. It does so by expressing the only reaction that individuals can have to their own suffering, the simple question, why?[87] The only possible answer—that there is no reason—is no answer. The individuals of Vergil's world demand a reason why they, as the individuals they are, should suffer. As the innocent victims of a violence they cannot understand individuals, sheep, ox, or human beings, one by one register a claim against the universe. It is a claim that the universe will not, and cannot, answer.

The Fourth Georgic: The Promise
of the Whole

The transition between the third and the fourth Georgics is like that between the first and second, abrupt.[88] From a world dissolved by violence and suffering we emerge suddenly into a world of community, and into the gentle and elusive humor of Vergil's first view of the bees.[89] Here Vergil describes a protected and ordered world which enables the bees to pursue the goal that they and the farmer genuinely have in common. The description is detailed, loving, and amused, concluding with the bees' own joy (4.55) and willingness: "They themselves will settle on the fragrant seats, themselves / In their own way, inhabit, deep within, the cradling chambers" (*ipsae consident medicatis sedibus, ipsae / intima more suo sese in cunabula condent* 4.65–66). Vergil has found, in his combination of bees and streams, winds and sun, flowers and herbs, the natural unity of Hesiod's farm, a unity that reflects the joyful natural order we were promised in the *Georgics*' first lines. The farmer is part of this world, a watchful guardian, protecting his bit of nature against its natural enemies.

The unity of the beekeeper and his bees, expressed in their joint care for the hive, is expressed on a deeper level by the humor of Vergil's description. This humor is the final expression, and the resolution, of a discrepancy which has been building up throughout the *Georgics*. The subjects of the *Georgics*, crops, trees, vines, cattle and horses, sheep and goats, and finally bees, have become, as they grow progressively smaller and more vulnerable, also more social and so more like ourselves.[90] Both lines culminate in the bees. The farmer who must protect the bees can also understand them. He can do so because they are like him, and because they are like him, he gains through them a new insight into himself:

> The monarchs, with conspicuous wings, amid the ranks,
> With mighty spirits working in small breasts
> Are steadfast not to yield, until the weight of victory
> Forces these or those to turn their backs in flight.
> The swellings of such spirits, these great contests
> Will, suppressed with a handful of dust, grow quiet.
>
> ipsi per medias acies insignibus alis
> ingentis animos angusto in pectore versant,

usque adeo obnixi non cedere dum gravis aut hos
aut hos versa fuga victor dare terga subegit.
hi motus animorum atque haec certamina tanta
pulveris exigui iactu compressa quiescent.   4.82–87 [91]

With that handful of dust, which ends both the bees' battles and the last scene of human life, Vergil unites all mortal nature in an exquisite balance of humor, sorrow, and acceptance. It is precisely the reconciliation of light and dark which Vergil so often refuses to make.[92] It is a vision which expresses the deepest unity of human beings and nature.

This first vision of the unity and harmony of the farmer's relation to the bees is seen from the farmer's point of view. Vergil's second description of the bees is taken from their own point of view.[93] Here the unity is in the hive itself. The ominous phrasing of Book 3's "love is the same for all" (*amor omnibus idem* 3.244) has become, at least while order remains, fruitful rather than destructive: "For all one rest from work; for all one labor" (*omnibus una quies operum, labor omnibus unus* 4.184); "while the king is unharmed, for all a single will" (*rege incolumi mens omnibus una est* 4.212). Labor is here combined with an inherent and spontaneous order.[94] Each bee fulfills his role in a world united and interdependent, and it is that role, that place within the whole, that gives each apian life its meaning.[95] Moreover, to the bees, the suffering or even death of the individual is not an obstacle to an all-encompassing vision of the whole. They willingly sacrifice the individuals who are harmful to the hive (4.165–68), just as they willingly sacrifice themselves (4.203–4). The good of the hive *is* their individual good:

> And so, however narrow the limit of life that awaits them
> (For it never stretches further than seven summers),
> The race remains immortal, and through many years stands
> The fortune of the house, and grandfathers' grandfathers are told.

> ergo ipsas quamvis angusti terminus aevi
> excipiat (neque enim plus septima ducitur aestas),
> at genus immortale manet, multosque per annos
> stat fortuna domus, et avi numerantur avorum.   4.206–9

From here Vergil is able to move towards the purest vision of unity that the *Georgics* achieves. The unity of the hive is (some say) a mark of the divine:

> for God, they say, moves through all lands,
> All expanses of sea, and the depth of the sky;
> And hence are the flocks and the herds, men, all kinds of beasts,
> And whatever at birth draws into itself scant life.
> And surely thither at last all things return, and, dissolved,
> Are restored; death has no place, but, living, all flies
> To the star's ranks and reaches the heights of heaven.

> deum namque ire per omnis
> terrasque tractusque maris caelumque profundum;
> hinc pecudes, armenta, viros, genus omne ferarum,
> quemque sibi tenuis nascentem arcessere vitas:
> scilicet huc reddi deinde ac resoluta referri
> omnia, nec morti esse locum, sed viva volare
> sideris in numerum atque alto succedere caelo.   4.219–27

The suffering of the individual is an illusion inevitable within our own partial visions. The truth is a unity of the whole that we may never, while we are trapped in our individual selves, be able to see.[96]

Vergil has found one indication of the unity of nature in the relation of beekeeper and bees, another in the bees' own society. These two accounts of the bees are divided by his description of an old Corycian gardener, a character who seems ideally suited to bring the two images together. The Corycian gardener's trees, and his satisfaction with his few possessions, recalls the farmer of the second Georgic, while his industry and his love of flowers recalls the bees who are his main concern.[97] The promise of the Corycian gardener goes even farther. In his retirement and self-sufficiency he lives, unselfconsciously, the Epicurean ideal, reconciling the philosopher and the lover of nature whose opposition closed Book 2.[98] And so both nature and bees cooperate with his efforts:

> Thus would he be first with breeding bees
> And a plentiful swarm, and, with honeycombs pressed,
> First to gather the foaming honey. His limes and laurels flourished,
> And as many fruits as his tree donned in its early bloom
> So much, in the ripeness of autumn, the bounteous blossoms bore.

> ergo apibus fetis idem atque examine multo
> primus abundare et spumantia cogere pressis
> mella favis; illi tiliae atque uberrima tinus,
> quotque in flore novo pomis se fertilis arbos
> induerat, totidem autumno matura tenebat.   4.139–43

The separate points of view of the farmer and of the bees meet in the Corycian gardener. But the meeting serves, finally, only to reveal the differences between them. The farmer sees and governs the bees' world with the profound humor of self-recognition. To the bees there is no humor, no governor, and no self-recognition. Vergil's second account of the bees continues the implicit comparison of bees and men that was begun with the gentle humor of the first. But the bees, who "willingly give their lives under their burdens" (*ultroque animam sub fasce dedere* 4.204), more dependent on their king than the Egyptians, the Parthians, or the Medes (4.210–14), are deadly serious.[99]

Moreover, for the bees, there is no beekeeper. The bees run their own world in their own way. Contrary to the Corycian gardener's view, there are no breeding bees and no need for a breeder—the bees themselves gather their own young from the fields (4.197–207). They also protect themselves, and themselves see to the hive's production. Vergil's bees are, in fact, farmers, which is why the farmer sees his connection to them so clearly.[100] The bees do not see it that way. From their point of view the work is theirs. The beekeeper who enters into the picture after the work is done, is not, to them, "gathering foaming honey from pressed combs" (4.140–41). He is raping the hive. The bees respond accordingly:

> Their rage is measureless; when hurt they breathe poison
> Into their bites, and, having fixed in the veins, they leave
> Unseen stings behind, laying their lives down in the wound.

> illis ira modum supra est, laesaeque venenum
> morsibus inspirant, et spicula caeca relinquunt
> adfixae venis, animasque in vulnere ponunt.   4.236–38

We have been prepared for the violence. Vergil's farmer did not, in fact, maintain his humorous distance throughout the first description of the bees. In the last few scenes the beekeeper gradually lost his sense of distance. As he entered further and further into the world of the bees he became more and more brutal. From their protector, to their ally, to their governor, he turned, finally, into their tyrant.[101] The old Corycian is different. He holds out the promise of a harmony between human beings and nature that is based on similarity rather than on control. It is nature, in the person of the bees, that refuses the harmony.

The bees are no Epicureans: "an inborn love of gain spurs them on" (*innatus amor urget habendi* 4.177).[102] The unity of bees and beekeeper, which we have seen from the beekeeper's point of view, and the unity of the hive, which we have seen from the point of view of the bees, almost meet in Vergil's description of the old Corycian gardener. As so often with Vergil, the narrowness of the division serves only to point out its depth.

Vergil's description of the bees' fury at the theft of their honey occurs as a throwback. After his digression on the divine unity that the hive implies, Vergil has, overall, resumed the point of view of the beekeeper.[103] Now incorporating the fact that the bees and the farmer have irreconcilable points of view, Vergil attempts, once again, to see what farming implies about our relation to the cosmos.

After honey gathering Vergil advises fumigation and cutting out excess wax from the hive. This is done to ward off the attacks of nature, the beetles and birds, hornets and spiders, that ravage the hive for its honey. Vergil gives us a particularly vivid and sympathetic description of these enemies and the threat that they pose. His conclusion comes unexpectedly:

> The more they [the bees] are drained, the more eagerly all
> Set on to restore the remains of their fallen state,
> Filling their cells and weaving their flowery granaries.

> quo magis exhaustae fuerint, hoc acrius omnes
> incumbent generis lapsi sarcire ruinas
> complebuntque foros et floribus horrea texent.   4.248–50

Adversity, it turns out, helps the bees.[104] With a greater understanding than is available to the bees, the beekeeper, by removing excess honey, both helps the bees against their enemies and encourages their production. The rape of the hive has turned into the theodicy of Book 1, but now in a positive form. Instead of telling us first about the plan to encourage industry, and then about the violence which implements it, Vergil has followed a despairing description of violence with the hope created by industry. The bees are as ourselves; the farmer is as Jove, "sharpening mortal hearts with care" (curis acuens mortalia cura 1.123). The interests of the bees and of the beekeeper are reconciled. And they are truly reconciled, because bees, unlike human beings, do not seek leisure and peace. Their glory consists solely in the creation of honey (4.205).

Vergil has found the point of view from which the bees' sufferings are only apparent. To the bees, whose vision is inevitably limited, the farmer's efforts seem to destroy their own. In fact, they further them. The farmer, whom the bees see as their enemy, is in fact their ally. The two are joined in a single goal. There is a vision of the whole which the beekeeper understands but which cannot be shared by the bees. So also there may be a vision of the cosmos, apparent to God, but not to us.

There is, however, a difficulty. Vergil's bees are, uniquely, not individuals. They have no interests particular to themselves; they are afflicted by neither the passion of sex nor the terror of death. When Vergil personalizes the bees he does so only as a community. We are not shown any bee's individual joy or suffering, only the hope or despair of the hive. There is no bee equivalent of the old stallion, the stricken sheep, or the ox dying of the plague. Vergil has found an image of order and meaning in the world, but only in a place where the individual, whose suffering has throughout prevented such a vision, has disappeared. Community is possible within the hive, and between the hive and the farmer, even though the bees may not see it. It may not prove possible in a farm, or a cosmos, populated by individuals.

In the first Georgic Vergil rejects a metaphysical explanation that claims that animals foresee the weather "because an understanding is given them from on high" (quia sit divinitus illis / ingenium 1.415–16). He proposes instead a "scientific" explanation. The explanation fails because, although rarefaction and condensation can explain the mechanics of the animals' behavior, it cannot explain what is expressed in Vergil's personalization.[105] The joy of the rooks—"often in their high nests / Joyful with some strange, unwonted delight, / They chatter to one another amid the leaves" (saepe cubilibus altis / nescio qua praeter solitum dulcedine laeti / inter se in foliis strepitant 1. 411–13), the solitude of the owl—"And from a high peak watching the setting sun / The night-owl plies her evening songs in vain" (solis et occasum servans de culmine summo / nequiquam seros exercet noctua cantus 1.402–3), and the terrible frozen nightmare of Nisus and Scylla, the sea-hawk and the ciris, cannot be explained mechanistically.

Vergil's "metaphysical" explanation, rejected in Book 1, has appeared again in Book 4, uniting the separate elements of the cosmos into a single, divinely informed, whole (4.219–27). A divine intelligence, pervading and unifying all things, may, more than they know themselves, explain the particular nature of the bees. But as Vergil moves from his theodicy to his final topic, diseases, and finally the total destruction of the swarm, the metaphysical claim that "death has no place" confronts the impersonal, inevitable, and ultimate fact. Death, the most isolating and individual of experiences, does not exist in a cosmos informed by God, as it does not in a mechanistic, Lucretian cosmos, and as it does not to the bees.[106] But if not to the individual bee, still to the swarm, and to the beekeeper, death remains the individual's ultimate encounter with the blank face of impersonal nature.[107] As his account of the bees fades into the myth of Orpheus and Aristaeus, Vergil reveals that there is a way to undo the effects even of death. If it is so, then the ultimate isolation of the individual may prove as illusory as the rape of the hive.

6

THE PLACE OF NATURE

The City, the Farm, and Nature

We are cultural beings, which is to say, it is our "nature" to live in society. Outside of and opposed to that society is also "nature," as wild nature, untouched by human beings and aloof from human concerns. But there is also domesticated nature, nature as it exists on the farm, somewhere between its wild ancestors and the "culture" to which its own cultivation gave a name. To discuss our relation to "nature" is to discuss the interconnection of society, wild nature, and domestic nature. It is, in other words, to discuss farming, since farming is where nature and culture meet.

As an artist might see the forest as a tangle of bright birch and dark pine, while a sugar maker sees in the same woods only a scattering of maple trees, what Hesiod and Vergil tend to notice reflects their visions of the world. Vergil is intensely aware of wild nature *as* wild nature, unconnected and unconcerned with human cares, sometimes a threat to the farm, sometimes its victim. In Hesiod's survey of those who feel the chill of the north wind: the beasts in the woods, horned and unhorned, the oxen, the goats, the old man with his stick, and the octopus, but not the young girl warm in her chamber and not the woolly sheep, what is notable is his lack of distinction between wild and domestic nature, or between nature and human beings.[1] Hesiod only once mentions the threat which the creatures of wild nature pose to the farm. Even here, in the little slave-boy's covering over of the seeds "in order to make work for the birds" (*WD* 469–71), the birds seem more part of the scene, simply pursuing their lawful business, than the enemy. The crane who gives the signal for plowing, the ox who stands ready in his stall, and the farmer who attends to both, are part of one and the same picture.

As Hesiod does not separate wild and domestic nature, he does not separate country and city. There is no visible transition in the *Works and Days* from the farm to the town, or from the town to the city, no particular movement from lawcourt to farm, or back again. Historical probability, not Hesiod, tells us that he and Perses must have gone to Thespiae, rather than to Ascra, for their court date. And as one cannot say where Thespiae ends and Ascra begins, one cannot say where the farm ends and the town begins. Hesiod tells us that we should pass by the blacksmith's shop, but does not identify that shop with either country or town (*WD* 493–4). It is true that Hesiod divides life between hanging about the marketplace and attending to the plow. To this extent the distinction between country and city is significant. But a young farmhand, too, will spend his time gaping after his friends, even in the midst of the sowing (*WD* 444, 447). It is not places, but dispositions in men, that Hesiod distinguishes in opposing the plow to the marketplace. These dispositions exist, indifferently, in country and city.

Hesiod's farmer lives on and by his land, within the world of the farm, but converging on the world of the town. He sees trade, which is dependent upon society, as as natural a part of farming as the seasons and the creatures that are wild nature. There is no sense of distance, either literal or metaphorical, between society, farm, and nature.[2] For Vergil, in contrast, "society" is exemplified not by towns like Ascra or Thespiae, but by Rome. The distance between Rome and the farm is enormous. Vergil emphasizes it by neglecting the existence of the "town" (*oppidum*) which lies between them.

Only twice does Vergil's farmer do any trading. His first trip, in Book 1, is perversely into "the city," a word which, in Latin, refers naturally to Rome. Few farmers visited it.[3] It is a long trip. Particularly on a donkey. Vergil's slow, driven, donkey, his millstone, his black pitch, and his spondaic conclusion make these three of the most laborious lines in Latin literature:

> Often the driver loads his slow donkey's back with oil
> Or cheap fruits, and returning carries back from the city
> An indented millstone or a mass of black pitch.

> saepe oleo tardi costas agitator aselli
> vilibus aut onerat pomis, lapidemque revertens
> incusum aut atrae massam picis urbe reportat.   1.273–5

Their slowness makes the space between the city and the farm seem both palpable and all but unbridgeable.

In contrast, in Vergil's other account of trading, the trip to town is made as a matter of course:

> [milk drawn] at dark, with the setting sun
> At dawn they carry out in baskets (when the shepherd goes to town);
> Or else they sprinkle it with salt, storing it for winter.

> quod [m1ere] iam tenebris et sole cadente,
> sub lucem exportant calathis (adit oppida pastor)
> aut parco sale contingunt hiemique reponunt   3.401–3

The tone of the lines belies the fact that this is the only trip to town in the *Georgics*, and the only time Vergil uses the word "town" in a strictly agricultural context. The trip occurs in the third Georgic. Here it shows us the natural interrelation of farm and town that Hesiod assumed, and that the *Georgics* as a whole denies. In context it helps to draw out the tension inherent in a book that treats the farm not as part of a larger world, but as a microcosm, and yet insists on the topic of profit.

In the *Georgics*, wild nature and society are separate worlds. Domestic nature is the pawn that lies between them. In the first Georgic, nature is the farmer's enemy and the farm, thereby linked to society, may be saved or destroyed politically, saved by Caesar, as suggested in Vergil's invocation (1.40–43), or destroyed by the civil war, as at the end of the book. In the second Georgic the farmer and nature are allies, and the city has become the enemy. The end of the second Georgic thus emphasizes the distance between farm and city, both in space, "far off from discordant arms" (2.459), and in time, as the life once lived by "Remus and his [not yet fratricidal] brother" (2.532–5).[4] But even here, in the midst of the second Georgic, Vergil's praise of Italy reminds us that the countryside has a political as well as a natural identity. As in the third Georgic, Vergil removes the farm from the city, only to remind us that they are also indissolubly connected. The *Georgics* refuses to unite city, farm, and nature. It also refuses to separate them.

Different visions of farming imply different visions of our relation to God and to other human beings. They also, of course, imply different visions of our relation to nature. In the case of Hesiod and Vergil the difference is apparent even in their use of the word. Hesiod never uses a word for "nature," presumably because he sees nothing from which "nature" needs to be distinguished. Human beings and human arts are as "natural," for Hesiod, as a mountain stream. Vergil, on the other hand, uses the word "nature" with all the equivocation of a modern. We are part of the "nature" Vergil attempts to explore (2.483), but we also, like the bees, have our own particular "nature" (4.149). The task of the farmer, we learn early on, is to learn nature's laws (1.61). But at the opening of the second Georgic, the ways of "nature" first include, and then are opposed to, the ways of cultivation (2.9, 20, 49). The relation of human beings to nature is thus like the relation of society, the farm, and nature. As human beings we both are, and are not, part of nature.

Vergil proposes two visions, one in which we are divided from, and one in which we are part of, the natural world. Where we are divided from nature (where the farmer is linked to the city) the farm, domesticated nature, is nature made "unnatural." Where we are one with nature (where the city is the enemy) the farm is our natural place, and it is the city that is unnatural. In other words, within the vision of the *Georgics* we may have nature, or culture, but not both. For Hesiod, there is no such split. Hesiod can, of course, see that human society, domesticated nature, and wild nature are different. To him, each of these has its "way" and its relation, hostile or cooperative, to the other two. As Hesiod, in the *Theogony*, saw force and intelligence as united into a new, third factor in the world, he sees society, the farm, and nature, as composing a whole. Vergil sees conflicting worlds. Hesiod sees necessarily different components of the single order of Zeus.

Orpheus and Aristaeus

Bacchus is, perhaps, the most representative god of the *Georgics*.[5] He unites human beings and divides them, is the god of joy and peace, and of sudden irrational violence. He is also a god both of the farm and of wild nature. As wine appears only late in human society, Bacchus symbolizes civilization. But in his association with ecstasy, madness, and violence, his are also the forces that tear down the distinctions of civilization (4.520–22). Bacchus is the partner of Ceres (1.7) and a god of culture. But he is also, as the Bacchants of the Orpheus myth remind us (4.520–22), the god of the *Bacchae*, lord of the untamed and untamable power of nature. For Hesiod there is no contradiction between tamed and untamed nature. Dionysus, in the *Works and Days*, is purely the god of the vineyard.[6]

Bacchus has another set of associations as well. As in the fifth Eclogue, he is a god associated with pastoral poetry (*Eclogues* 5.30, 69, 79). Farming, for Vergil, is both a sympathetic understanding of nature, and a violent control of her. His images for these extremes are war and poetry. When the farmer is seen as creating order within a hostile and threatening world he becomes a warrior, governing, as he must, with a harsh discipline: "and, ever drilling the land, he commands the fields" *exercetque frequens tellurem atque imperat arvis* 1.99).[7] But the farmer is also like the poet. Both enjoy the peace and sympathy of nature. Both prefer the simplicity of the farm to the violent sophistication of the city. In a book which begins "Now, Bacchus, I sing of thee" (*nunc te, Bacche, canam* 2.2), the farmer does just that: "And thou, Bacchus, they call on in joyful song" (*et te, Bacche, vocant per carmina laeta* 2.388).[8] This side of farming is at one with nature. Not force, but understanding, and the appreciation of beauty which comes with understanding, is its hallmark.

Vergil's deepest exploration of our relation to nature, the myth of Aristaeus and Orpheus, is also the one section of the *Georgics* which is not explicitly about farming.[9] Here, in particular, Vergil turns his model on its head. Hesiod began the *Works and Days* with two essentially incompatible myths, presented as alternatives, that in fact tell the same story. Vergil ends the *Georgics* with what looks like a single story, but proves instead to be two deeply incompatible myths, the myth of Orpheus and Eurydice and the myth of Aristaeus. In another sense, however, Vergil's concluding myths serve precisely the function of Hesiod's introductory ones. They point to the basic truths of the world which determine both the nature of farming, and our own place in the cosmos.

The single meaning expressed in both of Hesiod's technically incompatible myths expressed as well his sense of a single truth underlying the variety of human experience. It is exactly the duality of Vergil's (technically) single myth that makes it uniquely suited to point out the underlying truths of the *Georgics*. Aristaeus and Orpheus encompass all the oppositions of the poem, between the Iron and the Golden Ages, between violence and understanding, between Caesar and Vergil, between the farmer as warrior and the farmer as poet. The question central to both myths is the possibility of the recovery of life, and meaning, from the fact of suffering and death.[10] In the Aristaeus myth we see this in Aristaeus' attempt to recover his devastated swarm, lost when his attack on Eurydice caused her death. In the Orpheus myth we see it in Orpheus' attempt to bring Eurydice back from Hades. Implicit in this question are all the concerns of the *Georgics*, the relation of violence and understanding, of the individual and the whole, and of man and nature. The two myths, which are completely reconcilable as narrative, provide completely different answers to these questions.

Aristaeus is first introduced into the *Georgics*, unnamed, as one of the twelve agricultural deities invoked at the poem's opening, the *cultor nemorum* ("tender of groves") "for whom three hundred white cattle crop Cea's thickets" (*cui pinguia Ceae / ter centum nivei tondent dumeta iuvenci* 1.14–15). The title is ambiguous. As *cultor nemorum* Aristaeus may be a pastoral figure, a dweller in groves, but he may also be a cultivator of groves, that is, one who overturns them.[11] In the myth that ends the *Georgics*, Aristaeus appears first in the first sense, as *pastor Aristaeus*, "Aristaeus the shepherd" (4.317). But it is in the second sense that he encounters Orpheus. Late in the myth, as Orpheus mourns the loss of Eurydice, he is compared to a nightingale mourning the loss of her young "whom a harsh plowman / Has seen and torn, unfledged, from their nest" (*quos durus arator / observans nido implumis detraxit* 4.512–13). That "harsh plowman," the cause of Orpheus' loss, is Aristaeus.[12] Aristaeus' relation to nature turns out, after all, to be a straightforward one. He does not live with nature; he imposes his will upon her.

Aristaeus, the archetypal farmer of the *Georgics*, is part of the Iron Age world of the theodicy, the world of *labor omnia vicit / improbus* ("labor conquered all, / Remorseless labor" 1.145–46).[13] His initial address to his mother reminds us of the violence of this world:

> Nay then, come, uproot my fruitful woods with your own hands,
> Set fire to my stables, murder my crops,
> Burn my seedlings, swing the stout ax against my vines,
> If such a loathing of my fame has seized you.

> quin age et ipsa manu felicis erue silvas,
> fer stabulis inimicum ignem atque interfice messis,
> ure sata et validam in vitis molire bipennem,
> tanta meae si te ceperunt taedia laudis.   4.329–32

This suggestion of violence is carried out in the story. In the *Odyssey*, Vergil's model here, Proteus is ever-changing and ungraspable, an ideal representative of the power of untrustworthy nature. The Proteus that Aristaeus must control before he can regain his bees is different. He is a weary and helpless old man:

> Aristaeus, as soon as the chance was offered,
> Hardly allowing the old man to settle his weary limbs,
> Sprang, with a great cry, upon him, there as he lies,
> Surprising him with fetters.

> cuius Aristaeo quoniam est oblata facultas,
> vix defessa senem passus componere membra

cum clamore ruit magno, manicisque iacentem
occupat.   4.437–40

Aristaeus' conquest of Proteus suggests not man's victory over the hostile and terrifying powers of nature, but man's violent exploitation of a world unable to defend itself.[14]

For reasons that Vergil leaves somewhat vague, Aristaeus' conquest of Proteus
leads, ultimately, to the recovery of his swarm. The sense seems to be that by con-
quering nature Aristaeus has overcome even the power of death. But in describing
Aristaeus' victory, Vergil makes us wonder whether the success may not lose more than
it wins. The technique that recovers Aristaeus' bees, *bougonia*, brings life out of death
by producing bees from the carcass of a slaughtered bullock. There is only one flaw in
the suggestion; it would be madness to sacrifice a bullock for a far less valuable swarm
of bees. Aristaeus is the victor of the *Georgics*. It may well be a Pyrrhic victory.

In his relation to nature, a relation based not on violence but on poetry, Orpheus is
Aristaeus' doppelgänger. Both before and after Orpheus' venture into Hades, Vergil
locates the poet, singing, within a vast sweep of sympathetic nature (4.460–66,
507–20). Aristaeus, it is suggested, may impose his will upon nature; Orpheus is part
of it.

And yet Orpheus appears to exercise a control even more miraculous than Aristaeus', a control that can move nature spontaneously (4.509–10) and that extends even
beyond nature, to Hell. It is a control accomplished entirely without force, stemming
simply from wonder at the beauty of his song.[15] Orpheus is able to move Hell because
he can undo, through his song, Hell's blank incomprehension:

> He came to the Shades and to their terrible king,
> To hearts that know not how to soften at human prayers.
> But, moved by the song, from the deepest seats of Erebus
> Came the slight shadows and the images longing for light
>
> Manisque adiit regemque tremendum
> nesciaque humanis precibus mansuescere corda.
> at cantu commotae Erebi de sedibus imis
> umbrae ibant tenues simulacraque luce carentum   4.469–70

Orpheus' song can sound a chord even in the Underworld because all nature is akin.
In Vergil's haunting description of "mothers and men, and the bodies of great-souled
heroes, / Now deprived of life" (*matres atque viri defunctaque corpora vita / magnanimum
heroum* 4.475–76) we see the shadows of our own life, locked into their Underworld
existence, still able to respond to human cares. Because of the wholeness of nature there
is sympathy. Because of the possibility of sympathy Orpheus can act. This is a unity
which can conquer even death.

The conquest is only apparent. For a moment, Orpheus moves Hell. But the
moment is only that, a frozen instant, here made most vivid, and temporary, in the sudden stillness of Ixion's ever-turning wheel (4.481–85).[16] As Vergil shifts, abruptly, to
Orpheus and Eurydice's ascent, the impossibility of Hell's ever understanding human

suffering reasserts itself. If Orpheus' fault is "madness" (4.488), it is a madness "to be pardoned indeed, if the Shades knew how to forgive" (*ignoscenda quidem, scirent si ignoscere Manes* 4.489).[17] Orpheus' sudden panic, his need to reassure himself that the lost Eurydice has truly been regained, is, by any human standard, to be pitied, not condemned. But the world with which Orpheus must deal does not operate by human standards. Orpheus' momentary glance backward loses Eurydice forever.

Orpheus cannot move Hell with sympathy. He can, however, still move nature: "making tigers gentle and the oak to move with his song" (*mulcentem tigris et agentem carmine quercus* 4.510).[18] Orpheus' wife, Eurydice, was a nymph, a part of nature.[19] As she was when she died, wandering in the world of nature, so is Orpheus after her death. Both before and after his attempt to bring Eurydice back from Hell Orpheus seeks not human companionship, but the companionship of nature. Nature responds with understanding and sympathy:

> The Dryad band, her comrades, with their cries
> Filled the mountain-tops; the towers of Rhodope wept
> And high Pangea and Rhesus' martial land.
> The Getae wept, and Hebrus, and Acte's Orithyia.
> But he, with a hollow tortoise shell, solaced love's bitterness,
> Singing you, sweet wife, you, to himself alone on the beach,
> You, as the day came up, you, as it set, he sang.

> at chorus aequalis Dryadum clamore supremos
> implevit montis; flerunt Rhodopeiae arces
> altaque Pangaea et Rhesi Mavortia tellus
> atque Getae atque Hebrus et Actias Orithyia.
> ipse cava solans aegrum testudine amorem
> te, dulcis coniunx, te solo in litore secum,
> te veniente die; te decedente canebat.   4.460–66

There is, however, despite nature's sympathy, a solitude underlying this description. It is a tone that sounds even more strongly as Orpheus' story ends. Orpheus mourns even in death:

> "Eurydice," called the voice and the cold tongue
> "Ah poor Eurydice," as the spirit fled, it called;
> "Eurydice" echoed back the banks, down the whole stream.

> Eurydicen vox ipsa et frigida lingua,
> a miseram Eurydicen! anima fugiente vocabat:
> Eurydicen toto referebant flumine ripae.   4.525–27

The complicated pathos of the last line stems from its imitation of the fading echo of Orpheus' voice, as he takes his last voyage, singing his last song. The pathos comes from the fact that it is only an echo.[20] The understanding and sympathy which Orpheus appeared to find in nature, and the power his songs had over her, is in the end only the reflection of his own voice. As he was before his descent to the Underworld, so he is after it. Orpheus, amid the universal mourning of nature, is alone.

Orpheus, who seems at first to be at one with nature, and powerful through the sympathy created by his song, ultimately fails both to recover Eurydice and to find understanding in nature. Death cannot comprehend pity. But neither can the personal, individual, creatures of nature feel Orpheus' pain. Orpheus' isolation becomes most apparent in the simile which compares him to a nightingale lamenting the loss of its brood. The nightingale is, like the tigers and oaks that Orpheus moves, one of the individuals of nature. Unlike the Shades in the impersonal world of Hell, she can understand and feel loss. Orpheus weeps:

> As under a poplar's shade a nightingale mourns
> Weeping the loss of her brood, whom a harsh plowman
> Has seen and torn, unfledged, from their nest; she
> Weeps all night, and perched on a branch renews
> Her pitiful song, and fills all the land round with laments.
> No love, no wedding-song could move his heart.
>
> qualis populea maerens philomela sub umbra
> amissos queritur fetus, quos durus arator
> observans nido implumis detraxit; at illa
> flet noctem, ramoque sedens miserabile carmen
> integrat, et maestis late loca questibus implet.
> nulla Venus, non ulli animum flexere hymenaei: 4.511–16

Vergil has here achieved his most brilliant double reflection of human being and nature. The nightingale, who appears here in simile, is of the real world of the *Georgics*. Orpheus, the reality that the simile describes, exists within Vergil's account of the ancient story's account of Proteus' account of Orpheus. It is hard to tell which of the juxtaposed images is prior. All we know is that the nightingale cannot hear Orpheus, and he cannot hear her. The abruptness of Vergil's shifts, from Orpheus back to the world of the *Georgics*, and then from the simile suddenly back to Orpheus, creates the impression of two unrelated mourners caught in a single frame. Each mourns their own loss. Neither can hear the other.[21]

   It is probable that Vergil himself invented the link between the myths of Orpheus and of Aristaeus, the identification of Aristaeus' pursuit of Eurydice as the cause of her death. Commentators tend to assume that Aristaeus' motive was rape.[22] Vergil mentions no motive at all. The suddenness of Aristaeus' violence, and Vergil's failure to explain it, is not accidental. It is the last appearance in the *Georgics* of completely irrational, and utterly destructive violence. With it Vergil allows the ideal of sympathy, as expressed in the myth of Orpheus, to collide with the brutal fact of meaningless violence. Under the force of that violence the unity of human beings and nature that we glimpse in Eurydice, in the Nymphs and Dryads, and in Orpheus himself, dissolves, once again, into the pain and separation of individuals.

The relation to nature which Orpheus represents in the *Georgics*, a relation based on understanding, proves futile. It is lovely, but it is powerless. It moves us, but it cannot move nature. As Cyrene warned Aristaeus: "Without force he will give you no counsel, nor will you bend him / With entreaties" (*sine vi non ulla dabit praecepta, neque illum / orando flectes* 4.398). Nature yields to force, not to song.

Vergil's reader cannot but sympathize with Orpheus. Nature sympathizes with Aristaeus. Aristaeus finds sympathy and concern in his mother and her companions, who show no more concern for Orpheus than Aristaeus does.[23] Those who do sympathize with Orpheus, Proteus, the Nymphs, and finally Orpheus himself, are forced to give way. Vergil frames his myth, which is itself arranged in the ring pattern Aristaeus—Orpheus—Aristaeus, with a description of *bougonia*. His first detailed, and horrifying, description of the bullock's death, smothered and then beaten to death, so that the flesh is pounded into a pulp while the skin remains intact (4.300–2), is followed by a gentle image of the rebirth of spring:

> This is done when first a west wind ruffles the waves,
> Before the meadows blush with new colors, before
> The chattering swallow hangs her nest from the rafters.

> hoc geritur Zephyris primum impellentibus undas,
> ante novis rubeant quam prata coloribus, ante
> garrula quam tignis nidum suspendat hirundo.   4.305–7

The expectation of spring foreshadows the regeneration of the bees.[24] Nature, and nature in her most gentle mood, is in sympathy not with Orpheus, but with Aristaeus and the brutal killing of the bullock.

This is perhaps natural, since Aristaeus is himself a child of nature. Orpheus may be married to a nymph, but Aristaeus is born from one. Aristaeus' initial plea to his mother, her continual reference to him as *natus*, "son," or "child," and Vergil's description of the Nymphs' society all emphasize Aristaeus' kinship with nature.[25] Through his mother Aristaeus has access to the very roots of nature, the rivers that stem from Ocean, the great source of life, and which give fertility to the land. His father is Thymbraean Apollo, god of the sun, the other great element of growth. As Cyrene says: "He has the right to touch the threshold of the gods." (*fas illi limina divum / tangere* 4.358–59).[26]

As Proteus' address—"most presumptuous youth" (*iuvenum confidentissime* 4.445)—implies, Aristaeus takes his place within nature for granted. Orpheus, like the nightingale, can neither understand his loss nor accept his inability to understand it. Aristaeus also complains and questions the fate he was born to. *His* questions, however, are rhetorical. He no more truly wonders about his father, or his ultimate place in heaven, than he genuinely expects his mother to take an ax to his vineyard (4.321–31). Orpheus "lamenting the empty gifts of Hell" (*inrita Ditis / dona querens* 4.519–20) repeats our initial picture of Aristaeus "greatly lamenting" (*multa querens* 4.320).[27] In the case of Aristaeus it is the complaints, not the gifts, which are "empty" (*inanis fletus* 4.375). Aristaeus never actually asks why his bees have been lost. He simply demands them back.

Orpheus, who expresses all that one human being can feel for another, is a deeply sympathetic character. Aristaeus is not.[28] In Vergil's interplay of levels, Aristaeus is the harsh plowman who destroys the nightingale's brood. On the level of his own story, Aristaeus fares no better. His immediate accusation of his mother for the loss of his bees is distasteful. Once we have learned the reason for his loss it is revolting. The death of Eurydice appears never to have crossed Aristaeus' mind. The only response Proteus' account of Orpheus' suffering calls forth in Aristaeus is fear (4.530). Nor is this surprising, since Aristaeus nowhere shows any concern for anything except his own profit or loss.[29] Proteus' indignation, the suffering and death of Orpheus, even the wonder of rebirth, Aristaeus simply takes in stride. Only for a brief moment, as he enters his mother's underwater realm, does the beauty and wonder of the world strike him. It is a brief moment. Aristaeus soon comes to himself, responding to his mother's sympathy with his "empty complaints."

There is, however, another perspective from which we may view Aristaeus. To gain it we must move outside of his story, which is colored for us by our sympathy for Orpheus. We have seen the quality that characterizes Aristaeus before, in the bees that are his prime concern. Like Aristaeus, the bees live within a world of beauty and wonder. Like Aristaeus, this beauty means to them only another day's work:[30]

> But weary, late at night, the young take themselves home,
> Their legs laden with thyme; far and wide they pasture
> On arbute, on gray-green willows, on cassia, on gold-gleaming saffron,
> And on the rich linden and the rust-red hyacinths.
> For all one rest from working, for all one labor . . .

> at fessae multa referunt se nocte minores,
> crura thymo plenae; pascuntur et arbuta passim
> et glaucas salices casiamque crocumque rubentem
> et pinguem tiliam et ferrugineos hyacinthos.
> omnibus una quies operum, labor omnibus unus . . .   4.180–84

The contrast between the poet's and the bees' point of view is made vivid by Vergil's loving description of the colors that the bees do not appear to see. The bees, like Aristaeus, do not observe their world. They cannot, because they are part of it.[31]

From one perspective, Aristaeus is oblivious to the world around him. From another, however, he is not oblivious, but unselfconscious. Like the bees, he is intensely aware of the world within which he acts; he is oblivious only to his own separation from it. As with Vergil's characterization of himself in the *Georgics*, the distance necessary in order to see beauty also divides us from it. Those who see beauty are able to do so because they are separate from it. The failure to observe beauty may indicate only that there is no such distance. The qualities that make Aristaeus distasteful to us, his disregard of individuals, his failure to feel remorse, and his willingness to employ force and to see others suffer in pursuit of his own ends, are traits he shares with nature. Nature too is unselfconscious. For this reason Aristaeus, like his bees, has the place within nature that he assumes is his. Aristaeus can move nature because what he demands is precisely what nature is willing and able to give.

Unlike Aristaeus' self-confident use of force, Orpheus' yearning for Eurydice is no part of nature. Orpheus responds to his loss by isolating himself in a frozen solitude. Neither love nor marriage can move him. He dies at the hands of Bacchants, who, angered by his devotion to the dead Eurydice, strew his body over the fields like so much seed corn. Bacchus has taken his revenge. He has done so because Orpheus' refusal to forget is also a refusal to submit to the generative power of nature.[32] This generative power is the power that Aristaeus has been able to tap. He can do so because he, unlike Orpheus, is able to observe the one condition that nature has set. Aristaeus never looks back. For him the gaining of one swarm completely makes up for the loss of the other. For him death yields to life.

Death yields to life in Aristaeus' myth in exactly the way that death yields to life in fact. It is true that the death of one creature leads, ultimately, to the birth of others. We *are* part of a great cycle in which there is, ultimately, no place for death. This is what nature grants. What nature will not grant is what Orpheus demands, a thing that it would never occur to Aristaeus to want, not rebirth within nature as a whole, but the rebirth of an individual.

Vergil's final myth asks if life and meaning can emerge out of suffering and death. It gives us two answers. The story of Aristaeus is a story of distress pitied and relieved, of guilt redeemed, and of loss recovered. The story of Orpheus and Eurydice is a story of suffering unheeded, of innocence destroyed, and of complete, meaningless, and irredeemable loss. In the myth of Aristaeus life emerges from death. In the myth of Orpheus and Eurydice we encounter only death's blank finality. The difference hinges, once more, on the individual. In Aristaeus we are shown the farmer who, being part of the whole, deals with the whole, regardless of the consequences for individuals. Aristaeus recovers from loss. In Orpheus we are shown the dependence of one individual upon another. There is here no recovery. It does not matter to Aristaeus, or even to his bees, that the swarm that Aristaeus recovers is not the one he lost.[33] For Orpheus, Eurydice, and only Eurydice, matters. There is no place for this feeling within nature.

It is finally not the poet, but the warrior, who is akin to nature. Vergil has shown us what we gain by being part of nature. He has also shown us what we lose. Vergil's myth thus reverses Hesiod's in yet another respect. Where Hesiod saw human perception as giving us our place within nature, Vergil sees human self-consciousness as the factor that isolates us. We can be one with nature, losing our self-awareness in our sense of and participation in the world around us. We cannot entirely be so, because we are also individuals. Unlike Aristaeus, we cannot simply forget Orpheus and Eurydice.

Hesiod and the Balance of Nature

Vergil's vision of nature is reflected in a perhaps unlikely source:

> We behold the face of nature bright with gladness, we often see superabundance of food; we do not see or we forget, that the birds which are idly singing around us mostly live on

insects or seeds, and are thus constantly destroying life; or we forget how largely these song-sters, or their eggs, or their nestlings, are destroyed by birds and beasts of prey; we do not always bear in mind that, though food may now be superabundant, it is not so at all seasons of each recurring year. . . .

All that we can do is to keep steadily in mind that each organic being is striving to increase in a geometric ratio; that each at some period of its life, during some season of the year, during each generation or at intervals, has to struggle for life and to suffer great destruction. When we reflect on this struggle, we may console ourselves with the full belief, that the war of nature is not incessant, that no fear is felt, that death is generally prompt, and that the vigorous, the healthy, and the happy survive and multiply.

Darwin, *The Origin of Species*, ch. 3 (pp. 52 and 62)

Human beings can look at nature only through human eyes. Darwin, like Vergil, saw a unity in nature, and saw that we, as human beings, are part of that unity. He also saw that that unity consists in an unending struggle in which there is neither pity, remorse, nor guilt. As his offer of consolation implies, he could not abandon a sense that such a struggle implies a denial of what is essentially human. Deep down he could not, as Vergil could not, believe that it is natural for us to be a part of nature.

Hesiod saw no such difficulty. This does not mean that he saw no difficulty at all. Vergil speaks deeply to a world which has come to take a division in human consciousness for granted. The *Georgics* from the perspective of the *Works and Days* can seem over-sophisticated. Similarly, the *Works and Days* from the perspective of the *Georgics* can seem simplistic. Neither, of course, is true. The cosmos, for Hesiod, is informed by the will of Zeus, and so by a single meaning which makes of it a whole. If it were a meaning which could be easily comprehended, the one absolute necessity in human life would not be intelligence.

Hesiod's sections on farming and sailing are located between two more general sections on social and religious concerns, the latter of which leads into the lucky and unlucky days. In these sections not only the ambiguities of Hesiod's world, but also its absolutes, become most apparent. One may not injure a suppliant or a guest friend, one may not cross a river without washing one's hands, one had best not begin to sow on the thirteenth day of the month.[34] These are the absolute boundaries which limit human action. Within these boundaries operates the balance of good and evil that permeates human life.

Hesiod's placement of the farming section between these two sections on the overall right and wrong in human life invites us to see the farm in its larger context. When we look at the farming section on its own, the farm appears to be a world unto itself. When we examine it in context, we are reminded that the farm is only one aspect of a larger world, the human world of neighbors, family, friends, servants, the gods, reciprocity, and justice.[35] More importantly, we are reminded that what is true of farming, in both its ambiguities and its absolutes, is true of all of human life.

What is true of farming is, quite simply, the importance of due season.[36] Hesiod's introduction to the farming section gives us the theme in three-part harmony. Our first introduction, with the Pleiades (*WD* 383–87), allots farming its particular place in the cosmos. Here Hesiod stresses the universality of the rule:

This is the rule of the land, both for those who live near the sea,
and those that live in the rich land, far from the foamy sea,
in the wooded glens.

Naked, sow the seed, plow with your oxen, naked,
and, naked, harvest the crop if you wish to do all of the tasks
of Demeter at proper season—and so in their proper season,
shall your crops increase.

οὗτος τοι πεδίων πέλεται νόμος, οἵ τε θαλάσσης
ἐγγύθι ναιετάουσ' οἵ τ' ἄγκεα βησσήεντα
πόντου κυμαίνοντος ἀπόπροθι, πίονα χῶρον,
ναίουσιν· γυμνὸν σπείρειν, γυμνὸν δὲ βοωτεῖν
γυμνὸν δ' ἀμάειν, εἴ χ' ὥρια πάντ' ἐθέλησθα
ἔργα κομίζεσθαι Δημήτερος, ὥς τοι ἕκαστα
ὥρι' ἀέξηται.   WD 388–94 [37]

From the universal Hesiod glides back to the particular, to Perses, now revealed
as ruined by his idleness, and the need to work. Hesiod's reintroduction of Perses connects the section of the poem inaugurated, rather suddenly, with the Pleiades, to what
has gone before. It also gives an old injunction a new form. Hesiod's command—
"work, you stupid Perses, / work at the tasks that the gods have set for men to do"
(ἐργάζεο νήπιε Πέρση, / ἔργα, τά τ' ἀνθρώποισι θεοὶ διετεκμήραντο WD 397–
98)—implies not only that the gods mean men to work, but also that they have allotted for each work a particular time.[38] The addition gives a new coloring to the lines
which led into this section: "So if the spirit within you yearns for wealth, do thus, /
and work, piling work on work" (σοὶ δ' εἰ πλούτου θυμὸς ἐέλδεται ἐν φρεσὶν ᾖσιν, /
ὧδ' ἔρδειν, καὶ ἔργον ἐπ' ἔργῳ ἐργάζεσθαι WD 381–82). "Work upon (or "after") work"
appeared there to indicate simply the amount of work required. Here its secondary
meaning moves into the foreground; it is not simply work in the right amount, but work
in the right order, which is necessary.[39]

Finally Hesiod moves from Perses back to the basic essentials of farming.[40] Once
again we are led to the need to observe due season:

First of all get you a woman and an ox for the plow; the woman
not wedded but bought, one that can follow the cattle.
And in your house make all your gear ready
that you not ask another, to be denied and left without,
and the season goes by and so much the less work done.

οἶκον μὲν πρώτιστα γυναῖκά τε βοῦν τ' ἀροτῆρα,
κτητήν, οὐ γαμετήν, ἥτις καὶ βουσὶν ἔποιτο.
χρήματα δ' εἰν οἴκῳ πάντ' ἄρμενα ποιήσασθαι
μὴ σὺ μὲν αἰτῇς ἄλλον, ὁ δ' ἀρνῆται, σὺ δὲ τητᾷ,
ἡ δ' ὥρη παραμείβηται, μινύθῃ δέ τοι ἔργον.   WD 405–9

This is the third of Hesiod's three beginnings. Each has come to the same conclusion. The universal vision of the Pleiades, the particular situation of Perses, and the first beginnings of the farm, all lead us, finally, to the importance of acting in due season. In order to work the works that the gods have marked out for men, Perses must know what they are. What he requires is perception. What he needs to perceive is due season.[41]

The importance of due season is the central theme and the organizing principle of the farming section. In the section on sailing it becomes the only topic under discussion. It is also the section's *raison d'être*. Hesiod's description of farming drew us in, making us feel, rather than observe, the importance and complexity of adapting our works to the season. His description of sailing distances us, showing us the same truth from the outside. Perses is vividly reintroduced (with the account of his and Hesiod's father) to replace us as the person Hesiod is addressing; Hesiod emphasizes that sailing is a subject he dislikes; and, most directly in contrast to his description of farming, Hesiod refuses to show us what it would *feel* like to be at sea, making it clear that he could not, even if he were so inclined. Hesiod's description of sailing positions both himself and his audience safely on dry land. We are observers, not participants. What we are to observe is that the lesson to be learned from sailing is precisely the one we have just experienced in farming: "And you Perses, remember seasonableness, in all kinds of work and always / and most of all in seafaring" (τύνη δ' ὦ Πέρση ἔργων μεμνημένος εἶναι / ὡραίων πάντων, περὶ ναυτιλίης δὲ μάλιστα WD 641–42).[42]

Perhaps the oddest feature of Hesiod's manual on sailing is his determination to show us that he himself despises and fears sailing, and that he is right, because the sea is unpredictable, untrustworthy, and dangerous.[43] Hesiod's previous mentions of sailing have prepared us. Perhaps most memorable is his description of the blessings of the just city: "With all good things, utterly, they prosper, nor do they voyage on ships" (θάλλουσι δ' ἀγαθοῖσι διαμπερές· οὐδ' ἐπὶ νηῶν / νίσονται WD 236–37). The first line of the sailing section—"But if a desire possess you for a rough stormy voyage . . ." (εἰ δέ σε ναυτιλίης δυσπεμφέλου ἵμερος αἱρεῖ WD 618)—revives the impression. The section continues with a vivid description of the best part of sailing—when *not* to.[44] Hesiod's initial advice about sailing is that if you must, for God's sake don't do it at plowing time. His only detailed account of what a sailor does explains how to put the boat away for the winter.

Nor do Hesiod's personal digressions provide the budding sailor with much encouragement. Hesiod's father found sailing so unprofitable that even a miserable farm in Ascra was preferable. In contrast Hesiod himself, a successful poet, has hardly ever had occasion to step off the dry land.[45] But all this autobiography serves only to postpone the inevitable. Hesiod finally admits that there *is* a time when sailing is seasonable (WD 663–65). The fact that it has taken him forty-five lines to get from "But if you wish to sail" to "do it in fall" might leave the impression that the advice is given somewhat reluctantly.[46]

The recommendation that follows—"then you will not / break your ship upon rocks, nor the sea kill the men in it " (οὔτέ κε νῆα / καυάξαις οὔτ' ἄνδρας ἀποφθείσειε θάλασσα WD 665–66)—does not do much to alleviate the impression of reluctance. Nor does his reminder that you still can, of course, be shipwrecked even in the fall (WD 667–69). Three lines describing the safe time to sail (WD 670–72) lead into five more describing the dangerous one that treads on its heels (WD 673–77). Spring sailing, however, is even more dangerous. As Hesiod casually remarks, twice, it is a terrible thing to die at sea. All in all, in less than a hundred lines, Hesiod has mentioned the possibility of shipwreck six times. As an advocate of sailing he is somewhat less than encouraging.

Hesiod himself would certainly prefer a dry death. This is not, however, his only reason for harping on the terrors of the sea. Hesiod's dislike of sailing lends to his description a background of danger. Why he wants this appears in his first use of it:

> And you Perses, remember seasonableness, in all kinds of work
>   and always
> and most of all in seafaring.
> Give your praise to a small boat, but put your freight in a big one.
> The bigger the freight, the bigger will be gain added to gain,
> if only, of course, the winds refrain their cruel blasts.

> τύνη δ' ὦ Πέρση ἔργων μεμνημένος εἶναι
> ὡραίων πάντων, περὶ ναυτιλίης δὲ μάλιστα.
> νῆ' ὀλίγην αἰνεῖν, μεγάλῃ δ' ἐνὶ φορτία θέσθαι·
> μείζων μὲν φόρτος, μεῖζον δ' ἐπὶ κέρδεϊ κέρδος
> ἔσσεται, εἴ κ' ἄνεμοί γε κακὰς ἀπέχωσιν ἀήτας.   WD 641–45

The last clause, with its casually sinister γε ("of course"), links Hesiod's two apparently unrelated pieces of advice, to sail at the right time, and with the right amount of cargo.[47] The reminder of the possibility of storms, that is, the reminder of the danger involved, reminds us as well that the right amount of cargo depends on the season. More is better—when the seas are calm.[48] In general, as Hesiod declares later, it is best to leave most of one's produce at home (WD 689–90). It depends on the season.

Hesiod's discussion of sailing fills in, unexpectedly, the two empty slots of the farmer's year, the early autumn, before plowing, and the early spring, before the harvest.[49] In so doing it reinforces our sense of a task for each season. The two times of the year when the sea is passable are, it turns out, precisely the times when there is no pressing work on the farm. Our natural task in accordance with the seasons is farming. There is also a natural place for sailing, and so for the trading of what one has produced. Hesiod discovers the will of Zeus by looking at the world around him. Whether he likes it or not, Zeus seems to have left room for sailing.[50]

But the fact that Zeus has set out seasons for sailing does not necessarily mean that one should sail. There is profit in sailing, but there is also risk. In describing fall sailing, Hesiod warns us not to linger until the time that the new wine is ready. The reason for lingering, presumably, is the extra profit promised by returning with a cargo of new wine rather than returning empty. This is a natural congruence of task and season that might seem to indicate Zeus' will. But along with the new wine comes also the time of fall storms, and, as we should recall both from the description of our own vintage

(*WD* 609–17), and from the opening of this section, the time for fall plowing is at hand. The other season for sailing is in the spring. Hesiod advises against it. It is, he says, "snatched" (ἁρπακτός *WD* 684).[51] The reason for the adjective, and for its emphatic position, becomes clear when we recall the urgency with which Hesiod described the spring harvest. There are seasons naturally suited to sailing, but it may still be a tight-run thing.

Hesiod's section on sailing serves, essentially, as an appendix to the section on farming. As such it contributes to our sense of the farmer's year in much the same way as the unexpected return of the fall plowing and sowing. Once more our sense of completion is broken in upon. Just when we thought we had learned the cycle of the year there turn out to be additional possibilities. One can sail in both the fall and the spring, only in the fall, or at neither time. To trade in both seasons is most profitable— and most dangerous. To trade in neither is safest—and least profitable. Hesiod recommends (at most) the middle course.

He does so because trade, it turns out, is the final twist in Zeus' great game of slides and ladders. Trade can provide the final completion of both the seasons and the profit of the farm. But trading may also mean, if one is delayed, that one sows or harvests too late. Or it could mean the loss of one's goods, or one's life, at sea. Trade can complete the seasonableness and the profit of farming. It can just as easily destroy them.[52]

Hesiod's emphasis on the risk of sailing illustrates, once more, Zeus' basic will for human beings. If it is true anywhere in human life that we are not allowed goods without hardship, it is true in sailing. It is inconceivable to Hesiod that Zeus would hold out, with one hand, the chance of immense profits by trading, and not hold out, with the other, the equally likely chance of disaster. And so he does. The profit of trading is, in Hesiod's account, precisely balanced by the risk. The greater the cargo, and the longer the time at sea, the more profitable is one's trading. And the more dangerous.

Hesiod's description of sailing reinforces our sense of the necessity of due season and measure. It does so through the use of the simplest of devices—fear. Hesiod's epigraph to the section, "Keep watch on measure; in all things best is the when and how much" (μέτρα φυλάσσεσθαι· καιρὸς δ' ἐπὶ πᾶσιν ἄριστος *WD* 694), is introduced by the danger of overloading your wagon, breaking the axle, and spoiling the goods (*WD* 692–93). This is bad. But not so bad as to die in a shipwreck (*WD* 687–91). The danger of an empty barn, the price of unseasonableness on land, pales before the price you must pay for unseasonableness at sea. The essential human knowledge is a knowledge of due season. It is our only resource in a world that we cannot hope to control, and that threatens, continually, to destroy us. Hesiod can find no better paradigm for this condition than sailing.

Sailing is dangerous because one can know when sailing is seasonable only in general terms. Zeus can destroy someone who sails at what should have been the right season (*WD* 667–68), just as he can snatch someone else from the jaws of certain disaster. This truth is not limited to the sea. Due season and right measure can never be reduced to a formula. This is because, although the order of Zeus *is* an order, and hence comprehensible, it is one which is, to us, always uncertain. We perceive the order of Zeus, but only through a glass, darkly. Hesiod's description of sailing expresses this fact at its most dramatic. His description of farming expresses it not so luridly, but at greater depth.

The beginning of sowing is the paradigmatic moment of Hesiod's year.[53] It is charged with tension, a tension expressed in the farmer's grasp on the plow-stilt, in the stick coming down on the back of the oxen, in the oxen struggling in harness, and in the prayer, and the need for the prayer, which opens the description. In some ways, however, it is the final detail which is most interesting: "and let a small boy behind you / make work for the birds with his mattock, covering up the seeds" (ὁ δὲ τυτθὸς ὄπισθεν / δμῶὸς ἔχων μακέλην πόνον ὀρνίθεσσι τιθείη / σπέρμα κατακρύπτων WD 469–71). This hiding of the seed recalls Zeus' "hiding" of man's livelihood (WD 42, 47), the "hiding" of the Pandora myth, and the related theme of good appearing as evil, and evil as good, which has run throughout the Works and Days.[54] It is not difficult to see why the theme is relevant here. What the farmer can do to prosper the harvest he does before the seeds are sown. Once the seed is in the ground the success of the harvest depends on the vicissitudes of Zeus' weather. The outcome implicit in the hiding of the seed is known only to Zeus. As our long, cold, journey through Hesiod's winter should remind us, the farmer, now, can only wait. The moment of sowing is a moment of prayer and the paradigmatic moment of Hesiod's year for the same reason—because it hides an unknowable outcome.[55]

The essential ambiguity of the moment of sowing is emphasized in Hesiod's account by his description of three contradictory outcomes, the good harvest, the bad harvest, and the harvest rescued at the last moment. Hesiod at first only hints at the contingency of the harvest: "That is the way your ears, in their ripeness, will droop to earth, / if the Olympian himself shall later give a good end to the harvest" (ὧδέ κεν ἁδροσύνῃ στάχυες νεύοιεν ἔραζε / εἰ τέλος αὐτὸς ὄπισθεν Ὀλύμπιος ἐσθλὸν ὀπάζοι WD 473–74). It is made explicit with our unlooked-for rescue: "But sometimes the mind of Zeus, aegis-bearing, is one way / and sometimes another; for mortal men it is hard to fathom" (ἄλλοτε δ' ἀλλοῖος Ζηνὸς νόος αἰγιόχοιο, / ἀργαλέος δ' ἄνδρεσσι καταθνητοῖσι νοῆσαι WD 483–84). The ambiguity of Zeus' order, which will appear negatively in the account of sailing, here appears in its positive light. There Hesiod shows us the impossibility of being sure of safety. Here he shows us the impossibility of being certain of disaster.[56]

The drama which underlies Hesiod's description of the farmer's year should be impossible. The events of this drama are the seasons, coming and going in their regular and predictable cycle. But by causing us to identify with the farmer, Hesiod has added to this regularity an irrational element of surprise.[57] We do not take it simply as a matter of course that spring follows winter, and the harvest the sowing. We live the tension of waiting for spring and anticipating the harvest. Hesiod occasionally brings the ambiguity of farming directly into his account, as in his account of the fall sowing. Far more often our sense of it lies under the surface, in the dramatic tension that Hesiod's description creates. The structure of the section reveals the order of Zeus inherent in the seasons and in farming, as it is inherent in the cosmos. Its drama reveals the ambiguity that is also inherent in the farmer's year, as it is inherent throughout man's experience of the order of Zeus.

The Works and Days contains at its core a contradiction, the contradiction which saves it from being merely a handbook on how to succeed in life. Hesiod's most basic belief is that the order of Zeus is an order, and one whose basic conditions human beings can and must understand. But he also believes that life is deceptive, and that every human good has its evil twin. The contradiction is reflected in Hesiod's understanding of his own task. The *Works and Days* explains the will of Zeus to Perses and the kings. But it is impossible for a mortal like Hesiod ever to comprehend that will.

It is in Hesiod's sense of the seasons that we see how both can be true. Zeus is responsible for the regularity of the order of nature. He is also responsible for its aberrations.[58] Farming is possible because the seasons follow a regular cycle. It prospers or fails depending on the unpredictable variations that occur within that regularity. Hesiod can know, for example, that it will rain in the winter. He cannot know when, how much, and for how long.[59] But these are the details that are critical; it is through them that Zeus may, beyond all calculation, save a farmer who plowed too late, or destroy one who sailed when sailing is, in general, seasonable.

Hesiod understands the overall pattern of Zeus' will, as he understands the cycle of the seasons. What he cannot know is the individual quirks within that pattern. He knows that the order of Zeus demands that one sow early. The outcome of any particular sowing he cannot know. He knows the mind of Zeus in regard to the measures of the sea. The fate of any particular sailor, on any particular day, he cannot know. Similarly, he knows, and can show us, that Zeus has determined that human life should be hard, that good is balanced by evil, that human beings must live by justice and farming. What he cannot know, what no human being can know, is the vicissitudes that determine the happiness or misery of a day, of a person's life, or of history.

It is the general pattern of Zeus' will that we can know. The detail, which may make or destroy us, is inscrutable.[60] A farmer must live this truth. No farmer can succeed by following a set rule, that he should sow, for example, on the fifteenth of November, or harvest on the fifteenth of May.[61] The farmer must know a good deal more than can be learned by rule. He must know intimately the rhythm of the year, and understand from within the interaction of all the elements that make up that rhythm. This is an understanding that Hesiod can present only dramatically, an understanding that comes not from rule, but from a deep and fine-tuned response to conditions outside of oneself, and outside of one's control.[62] This is the understanding of due season. It is what allows the farmer to live, work, and succeed within an order both regular and ambiguous. The world of the farmer is, for Hesiod, a microcosm of the greater order of Zeus. The farmer's understanding of due season is Hesiod's most powerful image for the way we, as human beings, must live within Zeus' order.[63]

The vision of the cosmos expressed in the *Works and Days* is perhaps most like the archaic smile of the *kouroi* and *kourai*, the statues of Hesiod's own time, whose depth appears precisely in their surface simplicity. If we were to seek a similar model for Vergil it would be found, not surprisingly, in the twentieth century, in the designs of M. C. Escher. Escher's work, like the *Georgics*, is a composition not of objects, but of perspectives. Each perspective, each individual part of the whole, is uncomplicated. The whole, however, can be grasped only momentarily, before it dissolves again into its mutually exclusive parts. Hesiod shows us a world that is immediately comprehensible, and that, nonetheless, we cannot hope to fathom. Vergil shows us a world where we can choose either to remain outside, and so glimpse the unity of the cosmos, or to move inside, and in experiencing the depth of one perspective lose our understanding of the whole. There is an Irish proverb that runs; "Live as if to die tomorrow; farm as if to live forever." Hesiod would have seen in "farm as if to live forever" our always imperfect approach to the single and universal meaning of Zeus' order. Vergil would have seen in it the inherent contradiction that separates human life from the cosmos.

NOTES

PREFACE

1. This is just as true of the Latin *natura* or the Greek φύσις. For an exhaustive list of possible meanings of "nature" see the 148 listed in George Boas and Arthur O. Lovejoy, *Primitivism and Related Ideas in Antiquity*, vol. 1 of George Boas, Arthur O. Lovejoy, and Ronald S. Crane, eds., *A Documentary History of Primitivism and Related Ideas* (Baltimore: Johns Hopkins University Press, 1935).

2. M. L. West, *Hesiod: "Works and Days"*(Oxford: Clarendon Press, 1978), 41. On this point see also Bernard Knox, "Work and Justice in Archaic Greece: Hesiod's *Works and Days*," in *Essays: Ancient and Modern* (Baltimore: Johns Hopkins University Press, 1989), 5–7 "There is no doubt . . . that as a poem it is lacking in that architectonic quality which strikes every reader of the Homeric epics" (5). Although, as will be apparent, I disagree in large part with West's approach to Hesiod, the scholarship and inclusiveness of his commentaries on both the *Works and Days* and the *Theogony* (M. L. West, *Hesiod: "Theogony"* [Oxford: Clarendon Press, 1966]) have been invaluable to this work, as they must to any serious scholarly work on Hesiod. A reference to both commentaries should be understood throughout. Unless otherwise specified, text cited is from these editions. "West" in following notes refers to West's commentary on the *Works and Days*; "West Th." to his commentary on the *Theogony*.

3. For example, W. J. Verdenius, *A Commentary on Hesiod: "Works and Days,"* vv. 1–382, Mnemosyne Supplement 86 (Leiden: E. J. Brill, 1985), and C. J. Rowe, *Essential Hesiod: "Theogony" 1–232, 453–733, "Works and Days" 1–307* (Bristol: Bristol Classical Press, 1978), limit their commentaries to the first half of the poem. See also Richard Hamilton, *The Architecture of Hesiodic Poetry*, AJP Monographs in Classical Philology, ed. Diskin Clay (Baltimore: Johns Hopkins University Press, 1989), 47.

4. E. K. L. Francis, "The Personality Type of the Peasant According to Hesiod's *Works and Days*," *Rural Sociology* 10 (1945): 275–95, and Robert Redfield, *Peasant Society and Culture, An Anthropological Approach to Civilization* (Chicago: University of Chicago Press, 1956), 27, inau-

gurated this approach, but as their main interests lay elsewhere, they did little more than suggest the direction that it might take. Peter Walcot, *Greek Peasants Ancient and Modern: A Comparison of Social and Moral Values* (Manchester: Manchester University Press, 1970), who made the next significant contribution, limited himself to pointing out significant similarities, without undertaking a systematic reevaluation of Hesiod. The best modern studies I have found are Marcel Detienne, *Crise agraire et attitude religieuse chez Hésiode*, Collection Latomus, Revue des Études Latines, no. 68 (Brussels: Berchem, 1963), and Paul Millet, "Hesiod and his World," *Cambridge Philological Society Proceedings* 209 (1983): 89–90, who, like Francis and Redfield, has limited his study to anthropological concerns. As David Grene, "Hesiod: Religion and Poetry in the *Works and Days*," in Werner G. Jeanrond and Jennifer L. Rike, eds., *Radical Pluralism and Truth: David Tracy and the Hermeneutics of Religion* (New York: Crossroads, 1991), 146–47, puts it, it is "the total *picture* of the farmer's work" (italics original) that Hesiod is interested in. "He is inducting this pupil—or perhaps a hypothetical pupil as well as Perses—into farming as itself the imaginative clue to the universe."

5. One of the rare exceptions is M. Owen Lee, *Virgil as Orpheus: A Study of the "Georgics"* (Albany: State University of New York Press, 1996), 39: "It is not as if we were presented with an allegory, in which every object of vision corresponds to some other object; it is a case of another reality hovering over the poem, co-existing with the reality the poem presents." The tendency to disregard the importance of farming in the *Georgics* has been encouraged by the fact, noted by every commentator since Seneca (*Epistles* 86.15), that the *Georgics* is clearly not meant to teach farming. See Erich Burck, "Die Komposition von Virgils Georgica," *Hermes* 64 (1929): 279–321; L. P. Wilkinson, *The "Georgics" of Vergil: A Critical Survey* (Cambridge: Cambridge University Press, 1969), 3–15; A. J. Boyle, "Introduction," *Ramus* 8 (1979), 2–4; and Brooks Otis, "A New Study of the *Georgics*," *Phoenix* 26 (1972): 41–43.

For the farm as pretext see David Slavitt, *Virgil* (New Haven: Yale University Press, 1991), 46–49, 65; as trope see Michael C. J. Putnam, *Virgil's Poem of the Earth: Studies in the "Georgics"* (Princeton: Princeton University Press, 1979), 14; as metaphor, A. J. Boyle, *The Chaonian Dove: Studies in the "Eclogues," "Georgics," and "Aeneid" of Virgil*, Mnemosyne Supplement, no. 94 (Leiden: E. J. Brill, 1986), 37; as vehicle, Adam Parry, "The Idea of Art in Virgil's *Georgics*," *Arethusa* 5 (1972): 35; and as framework, Charles Segal, "Orpheus and the Fourth Georgic: Vergil on Nature and Civilization," *American Journal of Philology* 87 (1966): 307. Michael C. J. Putnam in "The Virgilian Achievement," *Arethusa* 5 (1972): 55 goes further: "Nature is unceasingly symbolized as human and made to reveal paradigms of flowering and decay, youth and old age, spontaneity and resistance, which offer formal comment on the world of man." For commentators who see the farm as specifically a symbol of Rome, or the farmer as political man, Joseph Farrell, *Vergil's "Georgics" and the Traditions of Ancient Epic: The Art of Allusion in Literary History* (Oxford: Oxford University Press, 1991), 328; Brooks Otis, *Virgil: A Study in Civilized Poetry* (Oxford: Oxford University Press, 1964), 144 ff., 384; A. Michel, "Virgile et la politique impériale: un courtesan ou un philosophe?" in Henry Bardon and Raoul Verdière, eds., *Vergiliana: Recherches sur Virgile* (Leiden: E. J. Brill, 1971), 228; Gary B. Miles, *Virgil's "Georgics": A New Interpretation* (Berkeley: University of California Press, 1980), xii; Christine G. Perkell, *The Poet's Truth: A Study of the Poet in Virgil's "Georgics"* (Berkeley: University of California Press, 1989), 8. Vergil *is* concerned with Rome, society, and mankind, but not with these rather than with farming, for which see David Ross, *Virgil's Elements: Physics and Poetry in the "Georgics"* (Princeton: Princeton University Press, 1987), 13.

6. For the "old," "optimistic" or "light" view of the *Georgics* see Edward Kennard Rand, *The Magical Art of Virgil* (Cambridge, Mass.: Harvard University Press, 1931; reprint, Hamsden, Conn.: Archon Books, 1966); Wilkinson, *"Georgics,"* passim; Friedrich Klingner, "Über das Lob des Landlebens in Virgils Georgica," *Hermes* 66 (1931): 159–89; Jacques Perret, *"The Georgics,"* in Steele Commager, ed., *Virgil: A Collection of Critical Essays* (Englewood Cliffs, N.J.:

Prentice-Hall, 1966), 37; W. E. Heitland, *Agricola* (Cambridge: Cambridge University Press, 1921), 213 ff.

For the now more common "pessimistic" or "dark" view see Ross, *Elements*, 25; Stella Revard, "Vergil's *Georgics* and *Paradise Lost*: Nature and Human Nature in a Landscape," in J. D. Bernard, ed., *Virgil at 2000: Commemorative Essays on the Poet and his Influence* (New York: Ams Press, 1986), 260; D. L. Drew, "The Structure of Vergil's *Georgics*," *American Journal of Philology* 50 (1929): 254; and the commentators above, on Vergil's farm.

The similarity of these two schools of thought to the two schools of thought on the *Aeneid* is immediately apparent. See Philip R. Hardie, *Virgil's Aeneid: Cosmos and Imperium* (Oxford: Clarendon Press, 1986); Michael Putnam, *Virgil's "Aeneid": Interpretation and Influence* (Chapel Hill: University of North Carolina Press, 1995), 150–58; and W. R. Johnson, *Darkness Visible: A Study of Vergil's "Aeneid"* (Berkeley: University of California Press, 1976), 8–16 for discussions of the *Aeneid* criticism, and Perkell, *Truth*, 4 ff. for a discussion of *Georgics* criticism. For a more promising approach, that sees itself not as "pessimistic" (or as "Harvard") but as "ambivalent see Richard F. Thomas, "Ideology, Influence, and Future Studies in the *Georgics*," *Vergilius* 36 (1990): 65–66.

7. For Vergilian allusions see also Richard F. Thomas, "Virgil's Georgics and the Art of Reference," *Harvard Studies in Classical Philology* 90 (1986) and *Virgil: "Georgics"* (Cambridge: Cambridge University Press, 1988); Gian Biagio Conte, *The Rhetoric of Imitation: Genre and Poetic Memory in Virgil and Other Latin Poets*, ed. Charles Segal (Ithaca: Cornell University Press 1986).

TRANSLATION: HESIOD'S WORKS AND DAYS

1. Lines 124 and 125, identical with lines 254 and 255, appear to be an interpolation. West, accordingly, brackets these lines.

2. θνητοῖς, "by mortal men," is an emendation by Peppmüller for θνητοί, which would give the translation: "they are called Mortal-Blessed-Ones-Under-the-Earth."

3. Line 189, "Justice in their hands, one will sack the city of another," appears to be an interpolation.

4. I follow the order of West here. In comparison with the text of Rzach, West places 757 after 736, and then after 759, 737 ff.

5. I.e., do not cut your fingernails.

6. Hesiod reckons the days of the month both as we do, from the first day to the thirtieth, and also as three sets of ten days, the ten days of the waxing of the moon, the ten days of the mid-month, and the ten days of the waning of the moon.

7. I.e., castrate them.

INTRODUCTION

1. Orpheus and Musaeus, the other two traditional founders, are a more complicated question. By the time of Herodotus they are beginning to lose their authority as real people (Herodotus. 2.53).

2. For a good account of the problem, and the course of Hesiodic scholarship, see Apostolos N. Athenassakis, "Introduction," *Ramus* 21 (1992): 1–10. As Athenassakis puts it (8): "Hesiod is barely beginning to be recognized as someone other than Homer." At the moment

the two primary schools of interest are the oral and the Near-Eastern influences, here on Hesiod in particular. On the oral tradition see James A. Notopoulos "Homer, Hesiod, and the Achaean Heritage of Oral Poetry," *Hesperia* 29 (1960): 177–97; Thomas G. Rosenmeyer, "The Formula in Early Greek Poetry," *Arion* 4 (1965): 295–311; Minna Skafte Jensen "Tradition and Individuality in Hesiod's *Works and Days*," *Classica et Mediaevalia* 27 (1966): 1–27; A. Hoekstra, "Hésiode et la tradition orale," *Mnemosyne*, 4th ser., 10 (1967): 193–225; Peter Walcot "The Composition of the *Works and Days*," *Revue des Études Grecques* 74 (1961): 1–19; and G. P. Edwards, *The Language of Hesiod in its Traditional Context* (Oxford: Oxford University Press, 1971). On Near Eastern influences, Peter Walcot, *Hesiod and the Near East* (Cardiff: 1966) and West, 3–25, are the primary proponents and, for a recent study, Charles Penglase, *Greek Myths and Mesopotamia: Parallels and Influences in the Homeric Hymns and Hesiod* (London: Routledge, 1994). See also G. S. Kirk, *Myth: Its Meaning and Function in Ancient and Other Cultures*, Sather Classical Lectures (Berkeley: University of California Press, 1970), and Mark Griffith, "Personality in Hesiod," *Classical Antiquity* 2 (1983): 37–63. For the effect on Hesiod see Mark Northrup, "Where did the *Theogony* End?," *Symbolae Osloenses* 58 (1983): 7; Millet, "Hesiod," 84.

3. Much of our "biographical" information about Hesiod stems from this poem which appears to date from the reign of Hadrian, but to be based on an earlier work, perhaps c. 400 B.C.

4. See Walcot, *Peasants*, 51 and Irwin T. Sanders, *Rainbow in the Rock: The People of Rural Greece* (Cambridge: Harvard University Press, 1972), 97–123. See West, 30–33 for a more detailed reconstruction, particularly of Hesiod's young life.

5. Friedrich Solmsen, review of *Hesiod: "Works and Days"* by M. L. West, in *Gnomon* 52 (1980): 212–13. Peter Walcot "Hesiod and the Law," *Symbolae Osloenses* 38 (1963): 21, refers to the quarrel as "a profound and formative interest which influenced Hesiod both as a personality and as a poet." However Bruno Snell's claim (*The Discovery of the Mind*, trans. T. G. Rosenmeyer [New York: Harper and Row, 1960], 255) that much of Hesiod's verse is "simply a tool for purposes of litigation" clearly goes too far. See also B. A. van Groningen, *Hésiode et Persès* (Amsterdam: Verhandelingen der Konnklijke Nederlandse Akademie van Wetenschappen, 1957), 153–66; Wade-Gery, "Hesiod,", *Phoenix* 3 (1949): 9 ff.; P. B. R. Forbes, "Hesiod vs. Perses," *Classical Review* 64 (1970): 82–87).

6. Herodotus 2.53. In 2.145 Herodotus places the Trojan War about 800 years before his time, or about 1250 BC, much the same date as modern scholars assign. For a good general account of Hesiod's age, done from the perspective of a social scientist, see the Introduction to David W. Tandy and Walter C. Neale, *Hesiod's Works and Days: A Translation and Commentary for the Social Sciences* (Berkeley: University of California Press, 1996), 1–48.

7. For the Lelantine War see West, *Th.* 43–4, and 40–48 for West's overall and very thorough discussion of Hesiod's date. West puts Hesiod's *floruit* somewhere around 700, arguing the less favored position, that he is earlier than Homer.

8. See below, chapter 1, for a discussion of oral poetry and writing in Hesiod's time.

9. In Hesiod's vision, the θέμιστες are basically an archaic, version of what he knows as the δίκαι, the decisions handed down by the kings more or less directly backed by Zeus. See Hatvig Frisch, *Might and Right in Antiquity*, trans. C. C. Martindale (Copenhagen: Gyldendale, 1949), 46–48, 91–96, 250–54; Ulrich von Wilamowitz-Moellendorff, *Hesiodos' "Erga"* (Berlin: Weidmannsche Buchhandlung, 1928), 65–68; J. Walter Jones, *The Law and Legal Theory of the Greeks: An Introduction* (Oxford: Clarendon Press, 1956), 32; Freidrich Solmsen, *Hesiod and Aeschylus*, Cornell Studies in CLassical Philology (Ithaca: Cornell University Press, 1949), 35. More generally see Rudolf Hirzel, *Themis, Dike und Verwandtes* (Leipzig: Verlag von S. Hirzel, 1907); Werner Jaeger, *Paideia: The Ideals of Greek Culture*, 2d ed. (New York: Oxford University Press, 1945), 1.102; John Ferguson, *Moral Values in the Ancient World* (London: Methien,

1958), 16–18; and Robert Bonner and Gertrude Smith, *The Administration of Justice from Homer to Aristotle* (Chicago: University of Chicago Press, 1930), 9–10.

10. The controversy over whether Hesiod was or was not a "peasant" seems to depend largely on how the term "peasant' is understood. If a "peasant" is seen as primitive, poor, ignorant, downtrodden or dependent Hesiod is not a peasant. If, as in Robert Redfield's commonly used definition, a peasant is someone to whom "agriculture is a livelihood and a way of life, not a business for profit" (*Peasant*, 27), Hesiod is a peasant. For different views of the controversy see Victor Davis Hanson, *The Other Greeks* (New York: Free Press, 1995), 107–8, 466–68; Alison Burford, *Land and Labor in the Greek World* (Baltimore: Johns Hopkins University Press), 85–86. A "peasant" in this second sense need not be poor, and may well, as Hanson argues Hesiod does, see farming as profitable as well as as a way of life, for which see Millet, "Hesiod," 89–90. Millet's work should be consulted overall for an excellent, and groundbreaking, study of Hesiod as a peasant. J. P. Barron and P. E. Easterling, "Hesiod," in *The Cambridge History of Classical Literature* (Cambridge: Cambridge University Press, 1985), 92–105, avoiding the word "peasant" because of its derogatory sense, describe Hesiod as a "yeoman." Rowe, *Essential Hesiod*, 3, comments: "to be surprised that a 'peasant' should compose real poetry merely reveals our own class assumptions." For Hesiod as a fallen ἀγαθός, or nobleman, see Arthur W. H. Adkins, *Moral Values and Political Behavior in Ancient Greece: From Homer to the End of the Fifth Century* (New York: Norton, 1972), 23–30; Chester Starr, *The Economic and Social Growth of Greece 800–500 B.C.* (Oxford: Oxford University Press, 1977), 123–28 and "Hesiod," in *The Cambridge Ancient History*, 3d ed. (Cambridge: Cambridge University Press, 1982); B. Bravo, "Remarques sur les assises sociales, les formes d'organisation et le terminologie du commerce maritime grec à l'époque archaïque," *Dialogues d'Histoire Ancienne* 3 (1977): 10–13; Verdenius, *Commentary*, 153–59 passim, and Millet, 86–89 for a summary of these views, and a refutation. See also K. D. White, *Roman Farming* (Ithaca: Cornell University Press, 1970), 273, on the farm required to support a team of oxen and G. Nussbaum, "Labor and Status in the *Works and Days*," *Classical Quarterly*, n.s., 10 (1960): 215. Here, since the word "peasant" in colloquial American usage has connotations false for Hesiod, his status will be referred to as that of a "small farmer".

11. And it is a pair, as opposed to the single ox of a man just starting out (*WD* 405) or of a poor farmer. See Archilochus, fr. 35; West, 260; Burford, *Land and Labor*, 148–51; and, for Hesiod's prosperity, Hanson, *The Other Greeks*, 98, 107–8.

12. It is worth recalling that, for all the reputed backwardness of Boeotia, Thebes was a major center of commerce, and no part of Boeotia was very far from Athens. On the economic activity of the time see Alison Burford-Cooper, "The Family Farm in Greece," *Classical Journal* 73 (1977): 167; Max Weber, *The Agrarian Sociology of Ancient Civilizations*, trans. R. I. Frank (London: NLB, 1909; repr. Atlantic Highlands, N.J.: Humanities Press, 1976), 163; Starr, *Growth*, 81; M. M. Austin and P. Vidal-Naquet, *Economic and Social History of Ancient Greece*, trans. M. M. Austin (Berkeley: University of California Press, 1977), 54. On the acquisition and ownership of land see Burford, *Land and Labor*, 15–55. For the importance of commerce, which Hesiod treats only as an adjunct to farming, Jules Toutain, *The Economic Life of the Ancient World*, trans. M. R. Dobie (New York: Knopf, 1930), 51; Starr, *Growth*, 49 ff.; Austin and Videl-Naquet, *Economic and Social History*, 54 ff. Although farming was difficult (a hundred years later the farmers of Attica were hopelessly in debt), Hanson, *The Other Greeks*, 108–26, argues for the rise of a new class of independent yeoman farmers during this period, who were to become definitive in Greek political culture.

13. Signe Isager and Jens Erik Skydsgaard, *Ancient Greek Agriculture* (London: Routledge, 1992), 71; Robin Osborne, *Classical Landscape with Figures: The Ancient Greek City and its Countryside* (London: Sheridan House, 1987), 56–58; White, *Roman Farming*, 385–88.

14. Grene, "Religion," 144: "[The *Works and Days*] is a personal poem full of the personal touches that color Hesiod's mind as he moves back through the remembered sequence of the

farming scene. The poetry springs from the depth of his vision and excitement in doing the work and responding to his joy in it." As a farmer , as well as a Classicist, Grene's testimony is doubly valid. Walcot, *Peasants*, 9: "Those who work on the *Works and Days* are scholars, far removed from the kind of rural background which will alone set Hesiod's poem in the correct perspective. To understand Hesiod's outlook on life, first the mind must be stripped of the debris of academic debate; secondly, and this I would stress is absolutely crucial, we must leave far behind the values of a sophisticated and complex culture to which the morality and motives of the peasant, a term I use of Hesiod in the sense that for him 'agriculture is a livelihood and a way of life, not a business for profit' . . . appear contradictory and even perverse." See also A. Hoekstra, "Review," *Mnemosyne*, 4th ser., 19 (1960): 407: "In my youth I heard our Calvinistic Dutch farmers on winter-nights quarrelling about matters of inheritance, blaming laziness, jesting, theologizing, preaching penitence, ('personal invective' of course included) and discussing details of farming. This is the way of the poet of the *Erga*. The 'problems' some scholars find in his sequence of thoughts and the solutions they propose have as much to do with his mentality as a lecture-room with a cow shed." Knox, "Work and Justice," 9, 14, points out that Hesiod's attitudes toward women and insolence, for example, are typical peasant attitudes; Hanson, *The Other Greeks*, 91–178 passim, points out the similarities between Hesiod's sentiments and those of modern farmers; White, *Roman Farming*, 26, notes that farmers are, in general, notorious jeremiahs. See Detienne, *Crise*, 33 and passim for a good study of Hesiod as a peasant, with peasant views on both justice and work.

15. Robert Lamberton, *Hesiod* (New Haven: Yale University Press, 1988), 23 argues that Hesiod is "collective expression rather than individual talent" and reads the poems with a "unitarianism" which "implies nothing about the origin and history of this material, least of all that it is in any sense the creation of a single imagination, and regards as futile the attempt to isolate the thought of a single individual in what is clearly a complex body of traditional material" (36) See also Gregory Nagy, "Hesiod," in T. J. Luce, ed., *Ancient Writers: Greece and Rome* (New York: Scribner's, 1982), 43–73; "Authorization and Authorship in the Hesiodic *Theogony*," *Ramus* 21 (1990): 119–30; and *Greek Mythology and Poetics* (Ithaca: Cornell University Press, 1990); and for the same argument regarding Theognis, "Theognis and Megara: A Poet's Vision of His City." In Thomas J. Figueira and Gregory Nagy, eds., *Theognis of Megara: Poetry and the Polis* (Baltimore: The Johns Hopkins University Press, 1985), 32–34. See Lamberton for an extensive bibliography. For a Hesiod who "found smug satisfaction in the life of a bard, honored, heeded, and well rewarded, who was welcome both in the market-place and in the halls of the nobles and certainly never had to turn his hand to physical toil," see C. Bradford Welles, "Hesiod's Attitude toward Labor," *Greek, Roman and Byzantine Studies* 8 (1967): 6. Against the etymological significance of Hesiod's name ("he who emits the Voice": Nagy, *Mythology*, 47–48) has, of course, to be set the fact that nearly all Greek names meant something. Demosthenes ("The strength of the people") bore a name no less appropriate to his role in history.

16. Griffith, "Personality," 47–62, argues for two distinct "personalities" in the two poems. Richard P. Martin, "Hesiod's Metanastic Poetics," *Ramus* 21 (1992): 11–33, argues that Hesiod establishes himself as an "outsider" in order to facilitate this. Welles, "Attitude," 8, confines himself to the statement: "I think that the picture which the author of the Works presents of himself and his family is too important to his plot to be accidental." It could, of course, be argued that the "plot" was created out of the life, rather than the "life" to suit the plot.

17. B. A. van Groningen, *La Composition littéraire archaïque grecque* (Amsterdam: Verhandelingen der Konnklijke Nederlandse Akademie van Wetenschappen, 1958), 257.

18. For work as a positive good see Detienne, *Crise*, 34; Erik Vandvik, *The Prometheus of Hesiod and Aeschylus*, Skrifter utgitt av det Norske Videnskaps-Akademi i Oslo, II. Hist.-Filos. Klasse, no. 2 (Oslo: Jacob Dybwad, 1942), 11; Paul Mazon, "Hésiode: La composition des *Travaux et des Jours*," *Revue des Études Anciennes* 14 (1912): 329–56; Svein Østerud, "The Indi-

viduality of Hesiod," *Hermes* 104 (1976): 23; Hanson, *The Other Greeks*, 99; and Joseph Fontenrose, "Work, Justice, and Hesiod's Five Ages," *Classical Philology* 69 (1974): 1–16. Welles, "Attitude," 9, is flippant but more accurate: "when Hesiod winds up his introduction with the order to his brother to tuck up his tunic and start digging, he was proposing something which no Greek (I would almost say, no human being) ever did if he could help it, ever looked on as anything but an unmitigated evil." As he points out, "Self-sacrificing toil for others is a Christian notion" (9, n. 3). See Verdenius, *Commentary*, 150, 156–57, Nussbaum, "Labour," 217, and Austin and Vidal-Naquet, *Economic and Social History*, 14 ff. for the Greek feeling against manual labor in general and farm work in particular. See Walcot, *Peasants*, 6 and R. Redfield, *Peasant*, 120–21 on Mediterranean peasants: "it is thought good in the nature of things not to work but to be free from work." The modern Greek for "work" is δουλεια, the Classical word for "slavery."

19. Xenophon also saw farming as a gentleman's occupation, but did not envisage actual plowing as part of it. See Heitland, *Agricola*, 66, 77 and, for a contrary view, Hanson, *The Other Greeks*, 99–107. Odysseus (*Odyssey* 18.365–80) is here, as so often , the exception to the rule. Julio Caro Baroja in "The City and the Country: Reflections on Some Ancient Commonplaces," in Julian Pitt-Rivers, ed., *Mediterranean Countrymen: Essays in the Social Anthropology of the Mediterranean* (Paris: Mouton and Co.,1963), 27–38, is somewhat misleading in attributing the late (and primarily Aristophanic) commonplace of virtuous country vs. vicious city life to ancient Athens. For a more popular view see Theophrastus' "Agroikos."

20. Lamberton, *Hesiod*, 104. See also Griffith, "Personality," 60, and, for the contrary view, Rowe, *Essential Hesiod*, 3–4. Nor does the supposition of a Near Eastern model explain the Hesiodic persona. Even assuming such a model, Hesiod's deviations from the usual pattern are best explained, as West himself points out, as his adaptation of the model to his own actual circumstances: West, 34–35; Walcot, *Near East*, 105; Knox, "Work and Justice," 7; Barron and Easterling, "Hesiod," 101. Griffith, "Personality," 57 ff., disagrees.

21. The difficulties with Perses are dramatically set out by West, 33–40, following Wilamowitz, *Hesiodos' "Erga,"* 133–35. Griffith, "Personality," 57, also feels that "the character and behavior of Perses vary according to the rhetorical point that Hesiod wishes to make." Arguments that the *Works and Days* was written for the lawsuit itself obviously contradict this view. If we do not assume that the aim of the poem's farming section is technical, the need to see Perses as "jerked back from the edge of the grave, back through his life as an established farmer, to be instructed in the first principles of farming" (West, 51–52) disappears and, with it, most of the inconsistency felt in Hesiod's picture of Perses. See Malcolm Heath, "Hesiod's Didactic Poetry," *Classical Quarterly*, n.s., 35 (1985): 245, for Perses' consistency.

22. This in contrast to scholars who assume that farming is, for Hesiod, just another kind of work. See, for example, Lionel Pearson, *Popular Ethics in Ancient Greece* (Stanford: Stanford University Press, 1962), 76; Walcot, "Composition," 8; and, in contrast, Adkins, *Moral Values*, 54; Detienne, *Crise*, 33.

23. West, 313; Pierre Waltz, *Hésiode et son poème moral*, Bibliòtheque des Universités du Midi, fasc. no. 12 (Bordeaux: Feret, 1906), 67; Hamilton, *Architecture*, 65. Mazon, "Composition," 351, and Walcot "Composition," 11, fail to notice that Hesiod's seasons for sailing are precisely the times when the farmer can afford to be away from the farm. Hesiod's sailor spends his winter plowing (*WD* 623).

24. Millet, "Hesiod," 93, and see R. Redfield, *Peasant*, 114–17, 124 and Eric R. Wolf, "Types of Latin American Peasantry," in George Dalton, ed., *Tribal and Peasant Economies: Readings in Economic Anthropology* (Garden City, N.Y.: National History Press, Doubleday, 1967), 510 for these same attitudes in other peasant societies.

25. No other Greek author, including, in the *Theogony*, Hesiod himself, allots a predominate position to farming, although agriculture remained the basic livelihood of Greece through-

out the Classical period, as Austin and Vidal-Naquet, *Economic and Social History*, 96; James M. Redfield, "The Women of Sparta," *Classical Journal* 73 (1977): 150; Heitland, *Agricola*, 3; Paul Halstead, "Traditional and Ancient Rural Economy," *Journal of Hellenic Studies* 107 (1987), 86.

CHAPTER 1

1. For Hesiod as an oral poet see Knox, "Work and Justice," 4–6; Hoekstra, "Tradition," 193–225; Walcot, "Composition," 1–19; G. Nagy, "Hesiod," 43–73; G. S. Kirk, "The Structure and Aim of the *Theogony*," in *Hésiode et son influence*, Entretiens sur l'antiquité classique, 7 (Geneva: Fondation Hardt, 1962), 64–67; Pietro Pucci, *Hesiod and the Language of Poetry* (Baltimore: Johns Hopkins University Press, 1977), 138–42. For Hesiod's formulaic diction see Edwards, *Langauge*, overall and, for a thought-provoking study of the implications of orality see G. Nagy, *Mythology*, 18–35 and *Poetry as Performance: Homer and Beyond* (Cambridge: Cambridge University Press, 1996).

2. For Hesiod's use of traditional material in the *Works and Days* see Charles Rowan Beye, "The Rhythm of Hesiod's *Works and Days*," *Harvard Studies in Classical Philology* 76 (1972): 23–43 and *Ancient Greek Literature* (Garden City, N.Y.:Doubleday, 1975), 100–6; A. Hoekstra, "Hésiode, *Les Travaux et les Jours*, 405–407, 317–319, 21–24: L'Élément proverbial et son adaptation," *Mnemosyne*, 4th ser., 3 (1950): 89–114. For the use of traditional material in general see G. Nagy's account of the "rhapsode" as one who "stitches together", *Poetry*, 60–66.

3. See Walcot, "Composition," and Kasimierz Kumaniecki, "The Structure of Hesiod's *Works and Days*," *London University Institute of Classical Studies Bulletin* 10 (1963): 79–96 for Hesiod's use of ring composition.

4. See West's synopsis, *Th.*, 16–18 and Peter Walcot, "The Problem of the *Prooemium* of Hesiod's *Theogony*," *Symbolae Osloenses* 33 (1957): 44–45.

5. Solmsen, *Aeschylus*, 21, sees the *Theogony* as a history that "brings out the evolution from a world of cosmic and physical forces to a world order of moral, social, and 'artistic' deities." Bruno Snell, *The Discovery of the Mind*, trans. T. G. Rosenmeyer (New York: Harper and Row, 1960), 35: "[Cronos and the Titans] are undisciplined and rude: mere brawn and little else. The Olympians brought about the rule of order, justice, and beauty." See also Lamberton, *Hesiod*, 75 and Kirk, "Structure," 93 ff.

6. Martin P. Nilsson, *A History of Greek Religion*, 2d ed., trans. F. J. Fielden (Oxford: Oxford University Press, 1949), 74 says of the *Theogony*: "The creation is a development of the cosmic material existing from the beginning and proceeds of itself, a development in the only form in which it could yet be imagined - that of procreation and conception." See also Francis MacDonald Cornford, *Principium Sapientiae* (Cambridge: Cambridge University Press, 1952), 192–93 and, in contrast, Jean-Pierre Vernant, *The Origins of Greek Thought* (Ithaca: Cornell University Press, 1982), 117.

7. This development is illustrated in the chart found on pp. 2–3.

8. Hamilton, *Architecture*, 29–32 sees Zeus as working through his children to accomplish a result parallel to his own conquest of the monster Typhoeus.

9. See M. Northrup, "Hesiodic Personification in Parmenides A37," *Transactions of the American Philological Association* 110 (1980): 223–32 , Northrup, "Theogony," 11 n. 4, and below, chapter 4.

10. See Solmsen, *Aeschylus*, 21 ff; Jaeger, *Paideia*, 65 ff.; Walcot, *Near East*, 32 ff; and below, chapter 4.

11. Hence, as Zeus' order becomes more established , genealogy gives way to narrative. From the emergence of Chaos to the marriage of Cronos and Rhea (116–453) there are 223 lines

of genealogy, 56 of narrative. From here to Zeus' marriage with Themis (453–901), where genealogy takes over again, there are 15 lines of genealogy, 275 of narrative, the remainder being digressions. The narrative of the *Theogony* is thus almost entirely devoted to the story of Zeus' active rise to supremacy. See Suzanne Said, "Les Combats de Zeus et le problème des interpolations dans la *Théogonie* d'Hésiode" *Revue des Études Grecques* 90 (1977): 210; Hamilton, *Architecture*, 15.

12. When Zeus next appears, Cronos is fated to be overthrown both by intelligence: "through the councils of great Zeus" (Διὸς μεγάλου διὰ βουλάς *Th*. 465) and by force: "[Zeus] was soon to overcome him by force and might / And drive him from his honors, and himself rule among the immortals" (ὅ μιν τάχ' ἔμελλε βίῃ καὶ χερσὶ δαμάσσας / τιμῆς ἐξελάαν, ὁ δ' ἐν ἀθανάτοισιν ἀνάξειν *Th*. 490–91). And so, as Cronos vomits up the stone he took for Zeus, he is (somewhat illogically) described as "beaten by the craft and the force of his own son" (νικηθεὶς τέχνῃσι βίηφί τε παιδὸς ἑοῖο *Th*. 496). This is Hesiod's only account of the defeat of Cronos, perhaps because he was himself not entirely comfortable with Zeus' quasi-patricide. See Penglase, *Myths*, 180, for traditions in which Zeus alone overthrows his father.

13. See Arthur W. H. Adkins, "Myth, Philosophy, and Religion in Ancient Greece," in Frank E. Reynolds and David Tracy, eds., *Myth and Philosophy* (Albany: State University of New York Press, 1990), 103 and Arthur W. H. Adkins, "Cosmogony and Order in Ancient Greece," in Robin W. Lovin and Frank E. Reynolds, eds. *Cosmogony and Ethical Order: New Studies in Comparative Ethics* (Chicago: University of Chicago Press, 1985), 53. For the connection between the poems see Grene, "Hesiod," 145; Seth Benardete, "Hesiod's *Works and Days*: A First Reading," *Agon* (1967): 152; Østerud, "Individuality," 28; Jaeger, *Paideia* 1. 65–66; Frederick Will, "Observations on the Conflict of Art and Didacticism in Hesiod," *Symbolae Osloenses* 37 (1961): 5, and, differently, Pucci, *Language*, 74.

14. The most obvious solution to the problem is to claim that the poem has no unity, either because it is the work of several poets or because a single poet was unable to impose a unity upon the disparate material in which he was interested. A. S. F. Gow, "Elpis and Pandora in Hesiod's *Works and Days*," in E. C. Quiggin, ed., *Essays and Studies Presented to William Ridgeway* (Cambridge: Cambridge University Press, 1913), 100 expresses what is still the dominant feeling among scholars in speaking of "the strange collection which has come down to us as the *Works and Days*." See West, 41–42 for a brief survey of the nineteenth-century attitude that "what we have is a compilation from different poems, plus rhapsodes' interpolations," and Welles, "Attitudes," 7 for a more exhaustive bibliography. West's own view (43–59) is that a single poet composed various sections of the poem at different times and then, with moderate success, linked them together. For other views of Hesiod's difficulty in composing see Kurt von Fritz, "Das Hesiodische in den Werken Hesiods," in *Hésiode et son influence*, Entretiens sur l'antiquité classique, 7 (Geneva: Fondation Hardt, 1962), 3–47; Will, "Observations," 5–14; and Rowe, *Essential Hesiod*, 9. See Eric A. Havelock, "Thoughtful Hesiod," *Yale Classical Studies* 20 (1966), 59–72 and Knox, "Work and Justice," 18 for Hesiod perceived as "pre-logical."

15. For the *Works and Days* as a poem in two halves, one on justice and one on farming, see Edward Kennard Rand, "Horatian Urbanity in Hesiod's *Works and Days*," *American Journal of Philology* 32 (1911), 148; Marcel Hofinger, "Le Logos hésiodique des races: Les Travaux et les jours, vers 106 à 201," *L'Antiquité Classique* 50 (1981): 404; Heath, "Didactic Poetry," 245; Gérard Naddaf, "Hésiode, précurseur des cosmogonies grecques de type 'évolutionniste,'" *Revue de l'Histoire des Religions* 203 (1986): 362, n. 84; Knox, "Work and Justice," 21.

For views of the relation of these two halves as justice and work see T. A. Sinclair, *Hesiod: "Works and Days"*, (London: Macmillan, 1932), 10; Detienne, *Crise*, 33, 49; Pucci, *Language*, 32; Jean-Pierre Vernant, *Myth and Thought Among the Greeks* (London: Routledge, 1983), 250; Verdenius, *Commentary*, 87–88; Lamberton, *Hesiod*, 109. Mazon, "Composition," 344, sees a connection in the idea of work. Jaeger, *Paideia*, 1. 70 sees the two halves as about strife and work;

Hamilton, *Architecture*, 53–54 as about Bad and Good Strife. West, 44 ff. sees the second half as a subsequent addition. For a thematic unitarianism see Waltz, *Poème morale*, 20, 214 and Adkins, "Cosmogony," 62. See also Kumaniecki, "Structure," 79–96 and Hamilton, *Architecture*, for additional and more complex ideas of the poem's structure.

16. For Hesiod's use of "key words" for emphasis, and to point out themes and connections see Paul Mazon, *Les Travaux et les Jours* (Paris: Hachette, 1914), 112; Waltz, *Poème morale*, 164; van Groningen, "Composition," 296; Walcot, "Composition," 16. W. J. Verdenius, "Aufbau und Absicht der Erga," in *Hésiode et son influence*, 111–59 and "L'Association des idées comme principe de composition dans Homère, Hésiode, Théognis," *Revue des Études Grecques* 73 (1960): 345–61 as Beye, *Literature*, 105–7, and West, 51, sees Hesiod's connections as based primarily upon an association of ideas. Verdenius sees several central themes—justice, work, due season, usefulness, well-being, divine chastisement, and recompense—as giving a cohesion to the poem, and indicating Hesiod's general train of thought. See Friedrich Solmsen, "The "Days" of the *Works and Days*," *Transactions of the American Philological Association* 94 (1963): 311–12 for a contrary argument. I myself believe that association does not cause, but serves, the arrangement of the *Works and Days*. Repetition is used by Hesiod, as it is by other oral poets, for closing sections in a ring pattern, connecting sections by overlapping lines, pointing to common and underlying themes, and for emphasis.

17. West, 44–47, sees the poem as made up of "heavy units," loosely connected by sections of "free-wheeling."

18. See Kumaniecki, "Structure," 80; Benardete, "Hesiod's *Works and Days*," 150; Hamilton, *Architecture*, 43; Rowe, *Essential Hesiod*, 7; West, 45–59 for Hesiod's sections. For Hesiod's "overlapping" sections see Heber Michel Hays, "Notes on the *Works and Days* of Hesiod" (Ph.D. diss., University of Chicago, 1918), 38. Hoekstra, "L'Élément," 109 , Verdenius, *Commentary*, 382, Mazon, *Les Travaux et les jours*, 93 provide examples.

19. In accordance with their focal points, I refer to the *Works and Days* myth as the "Pandora" myth, the *Theogony* myth as the "Prometheus" myth. See below, chapter 2.

20. Although the myth is told of five γένη or "races," these succeed each other completely in time and so are also, in effect, "ages." For the significance of this see below, chapter 2.

21. See Hans Blumenberg, *Work on Myth*, trans. Robert M. Wallace (Cambridge, Mass: MIT Press, 1985), 306–7.

22. For an excellent analysis of the vision portrayed in these myths see Juha Sihvola, *Decay, Progress, the Good Life?: Hesiod and Protagoras on the Development of Culture*, Commentationes Humanarum Litterarum, no. 89 (Helsinki: Societas Scieniarum Fennica, 1989), 22–48.

23. For Hesiod's inclination towards brief pictures of a scene see Rand, "Urbanity," 161, the tableaux of the Five Ages, or the just and unjust cities. On this section see West, 53. West does not divide sowing into its four component parts although his text indicates three of these divisions. This division leaves twelve blocks of roughly equal length (excepting the descriptions of early fall and winter).

24. Hesiod's advice on agriculture has been viewed as practical and instructive since Aristophanes' *Frogs*: 1030–36. Mazon, "Composition," 346: "A ces leçons de haute morale succèdent des conseils plus pratiques." Frederick Teggart, "The Argument of Hesiod's *Works and Days*," *Journal of the History of Ideas* 8 (1947): 45: "In the *Works and Days*, [Hesiod] formulated precepts for the moral and practical direction of life. The *WD* derives its title from the information brought together for the benefit of men engaged in farming and seafaring. It consists of 828 verses; but before he comes to matters of practical concern, the poet devotes 382 of the 828 lines to the discussion of moral problems." Wade-Gery, "Hesiod," 60: "the poem thenceforward [from line 299] is no longer preoccupied with Justice and Outrage, but is advice to Perses on how to make farming pay." West, 59: "if Hesiod began the written version without envisaging the further prospects which appear after line 380, the inference is that moral sermon and techni-

cal instruction on agriculture had hitherto been separate items in his repertoire." Griffith, "Personality," 60: "From 286 onward, Hesiod's instruction is concerned more with work and farming than with litigation or larger issues of justice or morality. He is now speaking as technical expert." Knox, "Work and Justice," 7, sees the farming section as "some instruction which will help to avoid the irremediable disaster of a crop failure." Rand, "Urbanity," 154, qualifies this view somewhat: "His aim . . . is not *solely* to discuss agricultural and nautical operations, but by selecting typical tasks to point the morals of industry, economy, and social common sense" (italics mine). Sinclair, *Hesiod*, 30 and Mazon, "Composition," 344 also see a moral element in the second half of the poëm as well, carried over from the connection of hard work and justice. For a more recent view see Charles Kanelopoulos, "L'Agriculture d'Hésiode: Techniques et culture," *Éditions de la Maison des Sciences de l'Homme* 15 (1990): 131–58.

25. As pointed out, for example, by Kumaniecki, "Structure," 88–90; Heath, "Didactic Poetry," 255–56; Burford, *Land and Labor*, 103–5. See West, 53 ff. for an amusing list of Hesiod's aberrations, which he attributes to Hesiod's tendency to get sidetracked. West, 52, notices that "[Hesiod] assumes a pupil initially unequipped for anything, without household, oxen, plough, wagon, or even winter clothing. On the other hand, he assumes a general understanding of the purpose and method of ploughing, reaping, threshing, and so forth."

26. An earlier version of this argument appears in my "The Drama of Hesiod's Farm," *Classical Philology* 19 (1996): 45–53.

27. Cato has six chapters (10–15) on tools, listing 80 different items for the vineyard alone (ch.11). Vergil (*Georgics* 2.397–419), with Columella (*De Re Rustica* 5.7.1) and White, *Farming*, 229, see vines as the most labor-intensive product of the farm. See also Isager and Skydsgaard, *Agriculture*, 26–33.

28. E.g. *WD* 515–18, 585–92 and throughout the section on lucky and unlucky days. For animals in ancient agriculture see Isager and Skydsgaard, *Agriculture*, 83–107; Osborne, *Landscape*, 47–52.

29. For the importance of the olive see Columella, *De Re Rustica*, 5.8.1; Isager and Skydsgaard, *Agriculture*, 20, 23; Marie-Claire Amouretti, *Le Pain et l'huile dans la Grèce antique* (Paris: Annales Littéraires de l'Université de Besançon, 1986), 41–45. Hanson, *The Other Greeks*, 96 points to *WD* 522, the only mention of olive oil in the poem, and offers some possible excuses for Hesiod's silence.

30. Hesiod would have broken fallow land in the spring, replowed and sown in fall, and harvested the following spring. See West, 274; White, *Farming*, 173, 176–89; Amouretti, *Pain et l'huile*, 51–75; Osborne, *Landscape*, 40–47; Isager and Skydsgaard, *Agriculture*, 19–26.

31. West, 52: "we are taken methodically through the year to the time of the next ploughing"; Mazon, "Composition," 347–48.

32. *WD* 475–77 and 561–63. Wilamowitz, *Hesiodos' "Erga"*, 106, notes the contradiction, answered by West, 298, and "Miscellaneous Notes on the *Works and Days*," *Philologus* 108 (1964): 167–68. West's assumption that the fall sowing is the "beginning of the cereal cycle" (52) ignores the breaking of fallow land in spring. See also Naddaf, "Précurseur," 349, on the Mesopotamian renewal of the year in spring and Starr, *Growth*, 40. Vergil, in contrast, does begin the farmer's year in the spring, for which see Chapter 3.

33. In contrast, White, *Farming*, 185–88, points out the difficulty and the crucial, although undramatic, importance of threshing, cleaning, sorting, and storing the grain. See also Paul Halstead and Glynis Jones, "Agrarian Economy in the Greek Islands: Time Stress, Scale and Risk," *Journal of Hellenic Studies* 109 (1989): 49.

34. Ironically, the exception is Hesiod, whose father appears to have acquired land either previously unworked or from another farmer. Nicholas F. Jones, "Perses, Work "In Season," and the Purpose of the *Works and Days*," *Classical Journal* 79 (1984): 307–23, notes that Perses' problem is not ignorance but procrastination. Thalia Phillips Howe, "Linear B and Hesiod's

Breadwinners," *Transactions of the American Philological Association* 89 (1958), 45–65, commenting that Hesiod's advice is so painfully obvious that his audience must have been either total idiots or totally inexperienced, argues that agriculture is being newly introduced at this time. Hanson, *The Other Greeks*, 98–100, is one of the few critics to accept Howe's argument. For a refutation see Walcot, *Peasants*, 20–23, who attributes the basic quality of Hesiod's advice to the Greek peasant's love of instruction for its own sake.

35. That the farming section of the *Works and Days* is not didactic becomes obvious if we contrast it to, for example, Cato's *De Agricultura*. Where Hesiod gives us a vivid description of the oxen struggling in harness Cato tells us: "First plow those places which are dry and sandy. Afterwards, the heavier and wetter the spot, the later it should be plowed" (*Ea loca primum arato, quae rudenta harenosaque erunt. Postea uti quaeque gravissima et aquosissima erunt, ita postremo arato* 131). Cato's section on woodcutting describes not the effect of Sirius on men's skin (*WD* 414–21), but the best time to cut particular trees (17). Cato omits the effect of bad weather on the octopus: "In rainy weather look for something inside to do. Do not be idle, rather, clean up. Remember, if nothing is done, there will be expense all the same" (*Per imbrem in villa quaerito quid fieri possit. Ne cessetur, munditias facito. Cogitato, si nihil fiet, nihilo minus sumptum futurum* 39).

Unlike Hesiod, Cato describes which crops to plant in which soils (6), which products are most profitable (1.7), what to do when the oxen fall sick (71), and what one *should* be doing in the winter time: cleaning out the ox stalls (39). In addition, Cato, like Varro, Vergil, Columella, and K. D. White, organizes his works by topic, not by season. Heath demonstrates that Hesiodic poetry is not didactic without attempting to explain what its purpose is, or why it masks itself as didactic. Grene, "Religion," 146, notes: "It does not seem as if Hesiod was really bent on teaching his brother to farm by rules appropriate to farming in Boeotia in the eighth or seventh century B.C."

36. Marked by Hesiod's repetition of λήγει ("leaves off" *WD* 414, 421). As West, 263, points out, "these visible signs might more naturally have been mentioned before τῆμος ἀδηκ(τ)οτάτη πέλεται."

37. To both Vergil and (particularly) Hesiod, a "farmer" is male, just as the vision of human life that farming expresses is paradigmatically, although by no means exclusively, the life of a male citizen. Since this is the case I employ "he" and "him," and "man" and "men" generically when describing either poet's viewpoint.

38. For the impressionistic tone of Hesiod's account of farming see van Groningen, *Composition*, 291; Jaeger, *Paideia*, 1. 72; Kumaniecki, "Structure," 89. West, 252, comments: "A pictorial quality invests even his most technical precepts: by the end, while we may not be much better equipped to run a farm than before, we have a real sense of how it looked and felt at different stages of the year." He does not, however, consider the possibility that this may be deliberate.

39. Otherwise it is difficult to see why one should keep two *different* plows, especially as the spare is intended for the same purpose as the other. See West, 268.

40. Ibid., 269. West explains in reference to the limitations of epic language.

41. The mortar and pestle are for grinding corn, the mallet is for breaking sods, the wagon carries the seed, and the oxen are, as always, for plowing. Notice how Hesiod uses his usual style of composition, through association of ideas to reinforce his dramatic point. Mazon, *Les Travaux et les jours*, 110.

42. In fact, as soon as we abandon the presupposition that this is a farmer's manual, it becomes self-evident that Hesiod's aim is descriptive, and not didactic. Nearly half of the section (95 lines out of *WD* 414–617, 203 lines) describes not a task, but the conditions of the season, the conditions the farmer works under, or how the farmer feels. I include as "descriptive" the lines on fall (414–21), on the crane (448–52), on sowing (467–69), on the harvests

(475–90), on poverty (496–99), on winter (504–35 and 547–56), on the swallow, (564–69), on the snail (571–72), on the dawn (578–81), on the picnic (582–96). As Walcot, "Law", 6, points out: "To call the poem a handbook on farming or a farmer's calendar is to consider only a small part of the complete text. Such a description applies to verses 383–614 alone, a mere 235 out of more than 750 lines, and even from these we must deduct the poet's digressions and particularly his sketches of winter (verses 504–63) and the height of summer (verses 582–96)." It is perhaps significant that no one has ever been able to figure out the dimensions of Hesiod's wagon. See West, 264, N. J. Richardson, Review of *Hesiod: "Works and Days"* by M. L. West, *Journal of Hellenic Studies* 99 (1979): 170, and N. J. Richardson and S. Piggott, "Hesiod's Wagon: Text and Technology," *Journal of Hellenic Studies* 102 (1982): 225–29 for attempts.

43. Similarly, Hesiod's opening with the clearly proverbial Pleiades, as well as the direct injunctions of *WD* 405–10, can only be taken as didactic.

44. Perses disappears between lines 397 and 611, where he is "resurrected" (West, 40) in preparation for the sailing section. See G. Nagy, "Hesiod," 67; van Groningen, *Composition*, 286. For Perses' reappearance at the end of the section, see chapter 6 below. Hesiod disguises Perses' absence from the section as a whole by bringing him, and with him Hesiod's didactic persona, vividly to our mind at both the section's opening and at its close. The tid-bits of information that Hesiod doles out about Perses, the surprising news that he is now reduced to begging for a living (*WD* 393–400) and the account of Perses' and Hesiod's father that occurs early in the sailing section (*WD* 633–40) are strategically placed.

45. West, 3–25, 25– 30, and Walcot, *Near East* are here the primary proponents. See also Griffith, "Personality," 37–63, and Kirk, *Myth*. For the deleterious effect this approach can have on Hesiodic scholarship, see Northrup, "*Theogony*," 7; Millet, "Hesiod," 84–85.

46. See Heath, "Didactic Poetry," 256.

47. The first moment of plowing *is* when you first hear the crane (*WD* 448–50, 458), West 53, 273. The change from the casual τῆμος ἄρ' ὑλοτομεῖν μεμνημένος ὥρια ἔργα ("cut your wood then and remember the timeliness of your work" *WD* 422) to the more urgent φράζεσθαι δ' εὖτ' ἄν . . . δὴ τότε ("Take heed when you hear . . . Then is the time to" *WD* 448, 452) also marks the new urgency.

48. In fall Hesiod moves from the hired plowman (*WD* 441) to slaves: δὴ τότ' ἐφορμηθῆναι, ὁμῶς δμῶές τε καὶ αὐτός ("then drive on your servants and yourself, all of you" *WD* 459) to πρωὶ μάλα σπεύδων ("you [singular] must hurry, to be very early" *WD* 461) to the farmer at the plow. In spring he moves from ἀλλ' ἄρπας τε χαρασσέμεναι καὶ δμῶας ἐγείρειν ("sharpen your blades, and waken your work-people" *WD* 573) to τημοῦτος σπεύδειν καὶ οἴκαδε καρπὸν ἀγινεῖν / ὄρθρου ἀνιστάμενος ("this is the hour of hurry and gather your harvest homewards, / though you [singular] rise before dawn to do it" *WD* 576–77). See West 54, 308–9.

49. For example, West, 273; Solmsen, review, 217.

50. West, 274, thinks πολεῖν is technical for the breaking of fallow land, as νεωμένη. He explains the chronological jump: "What Hesiod *wants* to say now is 'the land you sow should be fallow land which you have ploughed up in the spring and preferably again in the summer" (italics mine). Mazon, *Les Travaux et les jours*, 110, inverts 462 and 463, which does not much help.

51. Grene, "Religion," 158, describes the feeling of the moment as "mythological": "The mythological moment exists when past and present are united, not as in the narrative of history but in already repeated acts—not, as Eliade has it, to control the outcome by repeating the original act, but to participate in an unknowable certainty."

52. West, 278, points out that Hesiod focuses on the peg and strapping because these first take up the strain as the oxen begin to move.

53. I follow the manuscript's τυτθὸς rather than West's τυτθὸν. See West, 278, and Solmsen, review, 218, where he describes the change as "gratuitous." West's point, "there is no earthly

reason why Hesiod should specify a child for the job," nor any guarantee that "the farmer will have exactly one such person at his disposal," is certainly valid, especially given Hesiod's own advice against hiring "a servant with a calf underneath her" (*WD* 604), but explained as above. As West himself points out at 277: "The statement of when to pray develops into a general picture of the scene." Isager and Skydsgaard, *Agriculture*, 52, point out that the "mattock" involved here would not be the one used to break the fallow ("This would be a waste of effort") but a light hoe, such as a boy could wield.

54. Hence, although these lines close the description of the fall sowing, Hesiod refers to the spring (and the dismal harvest first envisioned) as well. See West, 281–82 for the connection to the previous mention of spring and, differently, Mazon, *Les Travaux et les jours*, 117.

55. West, 284, sees this as a "detached thought."

56. Winter occupies *WD* 504–53, 49 lines of the 202 which make up the farmer's year (*WD* 415–617). Mazon, "Composition," 349, and West, 54, see the section on winter as description for its own sake.

57. See Mazon, *Les Travaux et les jours*, 120, and, in contrast, Walcot, "Composition," 54.

58. Hesiod's usual temporal sequence, ὁπότ' . . . τότε δή . . . ("When . . . then . . .) now put to a perverse use, prepares the surprise.

59. From mid-February to mid-May, West, 302. See Pierre Bourdieu, "The Attitude of the Algerian Peasant toward Time" in Julian Pitt-Rivers, ed., *Mediterranean Countrymen: Essays in the Social Anthropology of the Mediterranean* (Paris: Mouton, 1963), 56–69, and J. K. Campbell, *Honour, Family, and Patronage: A Study of Institutions and Moral Values in a Greek Mountain Community* (Oxford: Oxford University Press, 1964), 34, on modern peasants' tendency to measure time in terms of their tasks. See Halstead and Jones, "Agrarian Economy," 47–49 for the "time stress" of the harvest.

60. In contrast to the rushed and paradoxical ὁπότ' ἄν . . . τότε δή σκάφος οὐκέτι οἰνέων ("when . . . then is the time, no longer, for digging the vineyard" *WD* 571, 572) we have ἦμος δὲ . . . τῆμος . . . ἀλλὰ τότ' ἤδη ("but when . . . then . . . but at that time" *WD* 582, 585, 588) which we first saw as ἦμος δὴ . . . δὴ γὰρ τότε . . . τῆμος . . . τῆμος ἄρ' ("but when . . . for then it is . . . then . . . that is the time") at *WD* 414, 417, 420, 422. See Mazon, *Les Travaux et les jours*, 128, and contrast Lamberton, *Hesiod*, 128.

61. Herodotus 1.126. For these sorts of oppositions in a modern peasant calendar, Bourdieu, "Algerian Peasant," 56.

62. West, 309–10, and Mazon, *Les Travaux et les jours*, 132, refuse to believe that Hesiod could heartlessly fire his workman just as winter approaches. This, however, is no time for the other possible reading of the line, hiring *extra* help. See Hugh G. Evelyn-White, *Hesiod, the Homeric Hymns and Homerica*, Loeb Classical Library (Cambridge, Mass.: Harvard University Press, 1914), 47; Grene, "Religion," 154.

63. See Walcot, "Composition," 49, on the Pleiades' role in the ring pattern.

64. Grene, "Religion," 158: "Thus paradoxically the *dike* of farming—that is, the *dike* that expresses in farming the *dike* of the world of man in general—is not a true doctrine or belief, as much as it is the myth of the conjunction of time and event;" Waltz, *Poème morale*, 63: "Mais ce n'est pas tout qui être laborieux: il faut encore savoir déployer à propos son activité, avant tout faire chaque chose en temps;" and White, *Farming*, 115.

NOTES TO CHAPTER 2

1. As we see in *WD* 42 and 47: "For the gods have steadfastly hidden his livelihood from mankind . . . But Zeus in the wrath of his heart hid our living from us" (κρύψαντες γὰρ ἔχουσι

θεοὶ βίον ἀνθρώποισιν· . . . / ἀλλὰ Ζεὺς ἔκρυψε χολωσάμενος φρεσσὶν' ᾗσιν). See Naoko Yam-agata, *Homeric Morality*, Mnemosyne Supplement, no. 131 (Leiden: Brill, 1994), 3–4.

2. I differ here from the wording of Grene's translation in order to bring out the word order of the original.

3. Hesiod links the correspondences to form a chain: A is opposite B, B is opposite C, C is opposite D, D is opposite E, and so on. The end result is the grouping:

$$A \text{ vs. } B >$$
$$< C \text{ vs. } B <$$
$$> C \text{ vs. } D >$$
$$E \text{ vs. } D <$$

where A and C, both opposite to B, are made to seem alike, as are B and D, since both are oppos-ite C, etc. As a logical argument this is a fallacy. As a rhetorical device it is brilliant.

4. See Heath, "Didactic Poetry," 246; Hamilton, *Architecture*, 53–54. These goddesses simply disappear after this introduction, to the extent that, when the goddess Strife happens to come up again, Hesiod mentions only a single goddess (*WD* 804).

5. Incidentally, the rule of keeping a year's worth of grain in stock (*WD* 31) remains rel-evant: Halstead and Jones, "Agrarian Economy," 52–54.

6. For the ambiguity of human life implied by the two kinds of Strife and Hesiod's delib-erate blurring of their realms, see Michael Gagarin's excellent article, "The Ambiguity of *Eris* in the *Works and Days*," in M. Griffith and D. J. Mastronarde, eds., *Cabinet of the Muses: Essays on Classical and Comparative Literature in Honor of Thomas G. Rosenmeyer* (Atlanta: Scholars Press,1990), 173–83, and Pucci, *Language*, 130–32. See also Adkins, *Values*, 34; Verdenius, "L'Association," 350–51. This "doubling" of a single quality is both a Greek and a Hesiodic favorite, one which tends to look for the unity behind opposites in, for example, the single home of Day and Night (*Th.* 748–67). See Richard Garner, *Law and Society in Classical Athens* (New York: St. Martin's Press, 1987), 76; and Lawrence J. Hatab, *Myth and Philosophy: A Contest of Truths* (La Salle, Ill.: Open Court, 1990), 66. As Vernant puts it: "Ever since the Promethean fraud instituted the first sacrificial meal, everything in human life has had its dark shadow and its wrong side . . . There can no longer be happiness without unhappiness, birth without death, abundance without toil, knowledge without ignorance, man without woman, Prometheus with-out Epimetheus." Jean-Pierre Vernant, "Sacrifice in Greek Myths," in Yves Bonnefoy, ed., *Mythologies*, trans. under the direction of Wendy Doniger (Chicago: University of Chicago Press,1991), 1. 423–24.

For Hesiod's overall sense of ambiguity see Michael N. Nagler, "Discourse and Conflict in Hesiod," *Ramus* 21 (1990): 88–90; Vernant, *Myth and Society in Ancient Greece*, trans. Janet Lloyd (New York: Zone Books, 1988), 199–201; Vernant, *Myth and Thought*, 240; Perkell, *Truth*, 9–10. For the modern Greek peasant's rather similar unwillingness to take anything at face value see Walcot, *Peasants*, 57.

7. See Walter F. Otto, *The Homeric Gods: The Spiritual Significance of Greek Religion*, trans. Moses Hadas (New York: Thames and Hudson, 1954), in particular 6, 169–73; Hugh Lloyd-Jones, *The Justice of Zeus*, 2d ed., Sather Classical Lectures (Berkeley: University of California Press,1983), 44; Hatab, *Myth*, 48–50; Walter Burkert, *Greek Religion*, trans. John Raffan (Cam-bridge, Mass.: Harvard University Press, 1985), 125–70, 271–72; Ferguson, *Moral Values*, 80.

For complementary immanent and transcendent concepts of god see Robert Mondi, "Greek Mythic Thought in the Light of the Near East," in Lowell Edmunds, ed., *Approaches to Greek Myth* (Baltimore: Johns Hopkins University Press,1990),172; E. E. Evans-Pritchard, "The Nuer Concept of Spirit in its Relation to the Social Order," 109–26 and "A Problem of Nuer Religious Thought," 127–48 in John Middleton, ed., *Myth and Cosmos: Readings in Mythol-ogy and Symbolism*, American Museum Sourcebooks in American Anthropology (Garden City, N.Y.: Natural History Press, 1967). Theodore H. Gaster, "Myth and Story," in Alan Dundes, ed., *Sacred Narrative: Readings in the Theory of Myth* (Berkeley: University of California Press,1984), 112–13 defines myth as "an expression of the concept that all things can be viewed at once under two aspects—on the one hand, temporal and immediate; on the other, eternal and transcendental."

8. Ferguson, *Moral Values*, 80; Vernant, *Society*, 109–10; Kirk, *Myth*, 175.

9. Even Plato, who blatantly invents myths, regularly presents them as passed down by tradition, as, for example *Republic*, 614b ff., *Meno*, 81b ff., *Gorgias*, 523a ff. This does not mean, however, that Greek myth was either inflexible or canonical, for which see E. F. Beall, "Hesiod's Prometheus and Development in Myth," *Journal of the History of Ideas* 52 (1991): 355–58.

10. I translate ἄρα here as "After all" to bring out Hesiod's change of mind. The particle is not translated in Grene's text.

11. J. D. Denniston, *The Greek Particles* (Oxford: Clarendon Press, 1934), 36: "With the imperfect, especially of εἰμί, denoting that something which has been, and still is, has only just been realized. In such cases Greek tends to stress the past, English the present, existence of the fact." For other (although complimentary) interpretations see Nagler, "Discourse," 87; Bernard Mezzadri, "La Double Éris initiale," *Métis* 4 (1989): 51–60.

12. See Hartmut Erbse, *Untersuchungen zur Funktion der Götter im homerischen Epos* (Berlin: de Gruyter, 1986), 1–5. As E. R. Dodds puts it, "it was detailed factual truth that Hesiod sought from [the Muses], but facts of a new kind, which would enable him to piece together the traditions about the gods and fill the story out with all the necessary names and relationships. Hesiod had a passion for names, and when he thought of a new one, he did not regard it as something he had just invented; he heard it, I think, as something the Muses had given him, and he knew, or hoped that it was "true": *The Greeks and the Irrational*, Sather Classical Lectures (Berkeley: University of California Press,1951), 81. See also Wade-Gery, "Hesiod," 85; Walcot, *Near East*, 50; Kurt Latte, "Hesiods Dichterweihe," *Antike u. Abendland* 2 (1946): 154 ff.; G. Nagy, "Hesiod," 47 and *Mythology*, 8; W. J. Verdenius, "Notes on the Proem of Hesiod's *Theogony*," *Mnemosyne* 25 (1972): 250; Rosenmeyer, "Formula," 306–7; Reynal Sorel, "L'Inconsistance ontologique des hommes et des dieux chez Hésiode," *Revue Philosophique* 170 (1980): 401–2. For a contrary view see Heath, "Didactic Poetry," 259–62.

13. Homer's Aphrodite is the daughter of Zeus and Dione (*Iliad* 5.371, 428). Hesiod justifies his version, that Aphrodite sprang from the genitals of Ouranos, with etymologies. She is "Aphrodite" "because she was raised / In the foam. But also Cytheria, as she touched upon Cythera, / And Cyprus-born, for she was born in famed Cyprus, / And genital-loving, as from genitals she came to the light" (οὕνεκ' ἐν ἀφρῷ / θρέφθη· ἀτὰρ Κυθέρειαν, ὅτι προσέκυρσε Κυθήροις· / Κυπρογενέα δ', ὅτι γέντο περικλύστῳ ἐνὶ Κύπρῳ· / ἠδὲ φιλομμειδέα, ὅτι μηδέων ἐξεφαάνθη *Th.* 197–200).

14. See Nestor-Luis Cordero, "Passé mythique et présent historique chez Hésiode," in Antoine Thivel, ed., *Le Miracle grec* (Nice: Belles Lettres, 1992), 81–88; Edmunds, *Approaches*, 3, 13; and Carlo Brillante, "History and the Historical Interpretation of Myth," 102, in Edmunds: "the legends recounted in the heroic epics were situated in a well-defined past; this past was neither identified nor confused with 'the age of the gods,' which was understood as 'the time of origins' and felt to be profoundly different from the historical world of men." See also William Bascom, "The Forms of Folklore: Prose Narratives," 9–16, and Eric Dardel, "The Mythic," 230–33, both in Dundes, *Sacred Narrative*; M. I. Finley, "Myth, Memory and History," *History and Theory* 4 (1965): 284–89. Solmsen, *Aeschylus*, 21 ff., refers to Hesiod's two layers of reality, the mythic and the immediate, and says at 78: "The two phases of reality have in common, however, the central figure of Zeus. For the Zeus of the heroic epos was in every respect qualified, nay almost destined, to become the symbol and exponent of the world order which embraces all features of Hesiod's experience."

15. Knox, "Work and Justice," 12–13. H. C. Baldry, "Who Invented the Golden Age?," *Classical Quarterly*, n.s., 4 (1973): 91, writes of the myths of the *Works and Days*: "[Hesiod's] purpose is to explain the present condition of man, particularly his need to work." See also van Groningen, *Composition*, 271; Barron and Easterling, "Hesiod," 95; Northrup, "*Theogony*," 7; Wendy Doniger, "Pluralism and Intolerance in Hinduism," in Werner G. Jeanrond and Jennifer L. Rike, eds., *Radical Pluralism and Truth: David Tracy and the Hermeneutics of Religion* (New York: Crossroads, 1991), 222. See Wendy Doniger O'Flaherty, *The Origin of Evil in Hindu Mythology* (Berkeley: University of California Press, 1976), 17–19, and David F. Pocock, "The Anthropology of Time-Reckoning," in Middleton, *Myth and Cosmos*, 312, for the same significance in the Hindu Kali Age: "the Kaliyuga is not homogeneous with the other *yuga*, it is opposed to them, and the radical difference is that it is the age of time which is actually lived."

16. "Miracles," like Athene's delaying the sun on the morning of Odysseus and Penelope's reunion (*Odyssey* 23.241–46), occur, although infrequently, in the Homeric poems, but not in Hesiod's account of human time.

17. Nor is it generally in a results or "shame" culture, which focuses on success rather than moral intention. For a consideration of ancient Greece in these terms see Dodds, *Irrational*, esp. 28–50; Arthur W. H. Adkins, *Merit and Responsibility: A Study in Greek Values* (Oxford: Oxford University Press, 1960; repr., Chicago: University of Chicago Press, 1975), esp. 46–57, 153–68; Lloyd-Jones, *Justice*, 25–26. For modern peasants see David D. Gilmore, ed., *Honor, Shame, and the Unity of the Mediterranean*, American Anthropological Association Special Publication 22 (Washington, D.C., 1987); J. G. Peristiany, ed., *Honour and Shame: The Values of Mediterranean Society* (Chicago: University of Chicago Press, 1966); and Edward C. Banfield, with the assistance of Laura Fasano Banfield, *The Moral Basis of a Backward Society*, Research Center in Economic Development and Cultural Change, University of Chicago (Chicago: Free Press, 1958), 140–43.

A distinction between the practical and the moral does not apply either to Hesiod's myths, his social advice, his religious taboos, or his lucky and unlucky days: Waltz, *Poème moral*, 69; Andrew Robert Burn, *The World of Hesiod: A Study of the Greek Middle Ages* (New York: Dutton, 1937), 78. Martin P. Nilsson, *Greek Piety*, trans. Herbert Jennings Rose (New York: Norton, 1969), 50–51, points to the unity of the moral, practical, and religious in Greek maxims. Jane Ellen Harrison, *Themis: A Study of the Social Origins of Greek Religion*, 2d ed. (Cambridge: Cambridge University Press, 1927), 96, points out the practical focus of the *Works and Days*, particularly in its moral and religious precepts.

The attempt to see Hesiod's advice as either moral or practical ends by classifying the end of the *Works and Days* as "superstitious," the basis of Friedrich Solmsen's rejection of this section in "Days," 293–330. See also the just plain "Erga" of Wilamowitz-Moellendorff. For the contrary argument see West, 346 ff., and, for the unity of "Days" and year, Grene, "Religion," 147; Benardete, "First Reading," 166; Lamberton, *Hesiod*, 133; Mazon, "Composition," 150. On the topic more generally, see Bordieu, "Algerian Peasant," 69 and J. Harrison, *Themis*, 96.

18. See Stephanie Nelson, "Justice and Farming in the *Works and Days*," in Robert T. Louden and Paul Schollmeier, eds., *The Greeks and Us: Essays in Honor of Arthur Adkins* (Chicago: University of Chicago Press, 1996). Heath, "Didactic Poetry," 245–46, points out that justice and work are finally, for Hesiod, "interrelated aspects of a *single* theme" (italics original). See Francis, "Personality," 282 ff., Eric R. Wolf, *Peasants* (Englewood Cliffs, N.J.: Prentice-Hall, 1966), 103–5, and Bourdieu, "Algerian Peasant," 6–59 for the peasant's feeling of immersion in nature and its ethical and social implications. See Isager and Skydsgaard, *Agriculture*, 159–68 and Osborne, *Landscape*, 165–92 for the traditional connection of agriculture and religion, in particular in festivals, and Waltz, *Poème moral*, 86, on religion as pervasive in Hesiod. See Detienne, *Crise*, 63 and R. Redfield, *Peasant*, 27 and 113 for farming as "practical action suffused with

religious feeling" supported by and uniting the practical, moral, and religious, as necessary for economic security, respect from others, and demanded by the gods. On the conflation of economic, social, and religious values among peasants, see Sanders, *Rainbow*, 63; Daryll Forde and Mary Douglas, "Primitive Economics," in Dalton, *Economies*, 16–17; and Manning Nash, "The Organization of Economic Life," in Dalton, *Economies*, 9. As Grene, "Religion," 157–58, puts it: "Farming itself is for [Hesiod] the traditional configuration of man's life—that he may eat, clothe himself, and maintain his social position."

19. Ἀρετή and κακότης may mean "virtue" and "evil," "excellence" and "badness," or "prosperity" and "poverty" for Hesiod. As material success and failure see West, 229; Verdenius, *Commentary*, 145–50; Pearson, *Ethics*, 74; Hamilton, *Architecture*, 61. Elsewhere in Hesiod ἀρετή appears only at *WD* 313 as material success, while κακός and κακότης can refer to either moral or material failure, e.g. *WD* 240, 740 in contrast to *WD* 91, 101. Note also that Hesiod uses the same image, of a hard and easy road, first to contrast wealth and poverty, then to contrast justice and ὕβρις (*WD* 216–18, 287–92), stressing in both that the benefits only appear at the end of the road (*WD* 218, 280, 290–92). For a general Indo-European link between moral and material good, see Bruce Lincoln, *Death, War, and Sacrifice: Studies in Ideology and Practice* (Chicago: University of Chicago Press, 1991), 6. Shirley Darcus Sullivan, "The Psychic Term Νόος in the Poetry of Hesiod," *Glotta* 68 (1990): 77–78, 81–82, points to a connected sense of the importance of perception in one's moral character.

20. See Sihvola, *Decay, Progress*, 42. For a summary of approaches to the Pandora myth, see Vernant, *Myth and Thought*, 237–41; for the Five Ages myth, Peter Smith, "History and the Individual in Hesiod's Myth of Five Races," *Classical World* 74 (1980): 145–53; and for both, Kirk, *Myth*, 172–252.

21. Grene, "Religion," 150.

22. In the *Theogony* Hesiod was concerned with the divine rivalry between Prometheus and Zeus, describing Prometheus' initial challenge of Zeus, Prometheus' final punishment, and Prometheus' release, as well as the creation of women. Here he is concerned with its effect on human beings. Pandora occupies twenty-two lines in the *Theogony* myth (*Th.* 567–89 out of *Th.* 521–616), forty-six in the *Works and Days* version (*WD* 53–89 out of *WD* 47–105), expanded mostly in the fashioning of Pandora, from fourteen to twenty-two lines (*Th.* 570–84, *WD* 60–82). The theft of fire occupies only three lines of the *Works and Days* myth (*WD* 50–52); Prometheus' punishment is never even mentioned.

23. Grene, "Religion," 148: "In the quoted passages the repetition of the word 'hid' and its dramatic placing in the final line not only joins the original punishment, the hiding of the livelihood, to the removal of fire from humanity, but stresses in both cases the depriving and covert nature of this punishment." See also Sihvola, *Decay, Progress*, 40–41; Beye, "Rhythm," 32; Vernant, *Society*, 183–201; Walcot, "Composition," 18–19. Zeus' hiding and Prometheus' theft is also linked by the parallel positions of κρύψε ("he hid" *WD* 50) and ἔκλεψ' ("he stole" *WD* 51). Theft and hiding is particularly emphasized in the *Works and Days* version of the myth. In the *Theogony* Zeus "did not give" fire to human beings (οὐκ ἐδίδου *Th.* 563); in the *Works and Days*, he "hides" it. Compare also Prometheus' theft ἐν κοίλῳ νάρθηκι· δάκεν δ' ἄρα νειόθι θυμὸν / Ζῆν' ὑψιβρεμέτην ("in the narthex stem. And high-thundering Zeus / was bitten in his spirit" *Th.* 567–68) to ἐν κοίλῳ νάρθηκι, λαθὼν Δία τερπικέραυνον (" in the narthex stem, unknown to Zeus / whose joy is in the thunder" *WD* 52).

24. Vernant, "Sacrifice," 423 and *Society*, 187, 197: "for men, desirable things are hidden within evils while evils are sometimes hidden within desirable things and sometimes concealed by their invisibility."

25. In the *Theogony* myth, Zeus' response to Prometheus' theft is to create woman, a "beautiful evil in exchange for good" (καλὸν κακὸν ἀντ' ἀγαθοῖο *Th.* 585). Although the paradox is thoroughly Hesiodic, this is as far as it goes. Woman is "a sheer deception, against which

man has no contrivance" (δόλον αἰπύν, ἀμήχανον ἀνθρώποισιν *Th.* 589) only because whether a man marries or not, evils follow (*Th.* 590–612). In the *Works and Days* Hesiod devises a more complex "sheer deception, against which there is no contrivance" (δόλον αἰπὺν ἀμήχανον *WD* 83).

26. In the *Theogony* woman is made and adorned with clothes, garlands, a veil, and an ingenious crown. In the *Works and Days* the description is doubled, that is, given once as Zeus' command and once in execution. In both, Pandora's lovely outside is contrasted to what is inside: "he bade Hermes the killer of Argos instill in her / the cunning mind of a bitch and a knavish disposition" (ἐν δὲ θέμεν κύνεόν τε νόον καὶ ἐπίκλοπον ἦθος / Ἑρμείην ἤνωγε διάκτορον ἀργειφόντην *WD* 67–68). The contrast of command and execution in Pandora's fashioning may reflect the same internal/external split; see Pucci, *Language*, 86; C. Robert, "Pandora," in Ernst Heitsch, ed., *Hesiod* (Darmstadt: Wissenschaftliche Buchgesellschaft,1966), 354 ff.; West, 161. Penglase, *Greek Myths*, 224–25, points out that in the Near Eastern parallels to this myth the role of Zeus is taken by an "evil god." He and Blumenberg, *Work on Myth*, 303–6, see Hesiod as presenting a "purified" Zeus.

27. Alternatively, because all the gods "gave her a gift." For Pandora's name see West, 164–67. "Giving" as well as "hiding" becomes prominent in the *Works and Days* myth. In the *Theogony* Zeus "brings" woman, unnamed, to the assembly as a "marvel" (*Th.* 585–89). In the *Works and Days* he "gives" her as a "gift," referring to giving six times, five of them in lines 80–89, as opposed to the single reference at *Th.* 561. For the connection of giving and hiding see Vernant, *Society*, 183–201.

28. For the sentiment, see Hesiod on the superiority of the half to the whole (*WD* 40–41) in chapter 5; Thucydides 6.40; the monkey with his fist in the jar; Katherine Olstein, "Pandora and Dike in Hesiod's *Works and Days*," *Emerita* 48 (1980): 295; and Joseph Falaky Nagy, "The Deceptive Gift in Greek Mythology," *Arethusa* 14 (1981): 192–204. For this theme in the Pandora myth in particular, see J. Nagy, 199–201. Pucci, *Language*, 2, 97, points out that the one who is named "All-Giving" is in fact all-taking. Pandora's thieving nature reflects both the appropriate penalty for Prometheus' theft, and Hesiod's general view of women: "One who has trusted a woman has trusted a highway robber" (ὅς δὲ γυναικὶ πέποιθε, πέποιθ' ὅ γε φιλήτῃσιν *WD* 375).

29. The emphatic positions of "consider" (*WD* 86) and the concluding "he knew it" (*WD* 89) point out this contrast, and the nature of human hardship. See also *WD* 293–97; Jensen, "Tradition," 14; Walcot, *Near East*, 60–62; Vandvik, *Prometheus*, 7. In the *Theogony*, Epimetheus was noted, in passing, as the one who accepted woman, but there the detail served simply to reinforce his epithet, "of mistaken wits" (ἁμαρτίνοόν *Th.* 511); the actual acceptance of woman is not described.

30. For Hesiod's inclusion of the jar from another myth see West, 155; Teggart, "Argument," 49; Nilsson, *History*, 184; Walcot, *Near East*, 62. Knox, "Work and Justice," 10, points out that as Pandora could hardly be imagined as carrying a πίθος ("wine-jar") with her, man's evils must have already been on earth, hidden in the jar, for which see also Vernant, "Sacrifice," 423. Hesiod, of course, may not have been quite so literal-minded.

31. See Valdis Leiniers, " ῬΕΛΠΙΣ in Hesiod: *Works and Days* 96," *Philologus* 128 (1984): 6–7.

32. Perhaps the most hotly debated issue of the myth. See, for interpretations most like the following, Peter Walcot, "Pandora's Jar," *Hermes* 89 (1961): 249–51 and W. J. Verdenius, "A 'Hopeless' Line in Hesiod: *Works and Days* 96," *Mnemosyne*, 4th ser., 24 (1971): 225–31. For other interpretations see Mazon, "Composition," 338; Rand, "Urbanity," 136; West, 169–70; Waltz, *Poème moral*, 56–57. For hope as the last *absent* (because still hidden) good, see Sinclair, *"Works and Days"*, 14; Knox, "Work and Justice," 10. Verdenius, "Hopeless," 228 points out, however, that the absence of ἐλπίς does not carry the connotations of our "hopelessness," and

would imply that one does not look to the future rather than that one has no future to look to. It is also worth recalling that Hesiod's interpretation is not necessarily the *original* reason why hope remained in the jar—Hesiod is using the myth, not creating it.

33. Verdenius, "Hopeless," 225–31 and Anna M. Komornicka "L'Elpis hésiodique dans la jarre de Pandore," *Eos* 78 (1990): 63–77 summarize these approaches. Komornicka attributes the ambiguity to a conflation of three separate myths.

34. West, 236, rejecting the idea of a good and a bad hope, prints the infinitive κομίζειν here and at *WD* 317, after *Odyssey* 17.347. On the controversy, see K. J. McKay, "Ambivalent ΑΙΔΩΣ in Hesiod," *American Journal of Philology* 84 (1963): 17–28; Hoekstra, "L'Élément," 99–106; Pearson, *Ethics*, 42; Verdenius, *Commentary*, 160, and "Hopeless," 228, n. 1; Solmsen, review, 220; Sinclair, *"Works and Days"*, 35 and "ΑΙΔΩΣ in Hesiod," *Classical Review* 39 (1925): 147–48; Mazon, *Les Travaux et les jours*, 98.

35. Verdenius, "Hopeless," 227.

36. Sinclair, "ΑΙΔΩΣ," 148: "false hope is hope based on false or insufficient grounds." See also Wilamowitz, *Hesiodos' "Erga"*, 51–52; Hermann Fränkel, *Wege und Form frühgriechischen Denkens* (Munich: Beck, 1960), 332–34; West, 236; Sinclair, *"Works and Days"*, 13–14; K. J. McKay, "Ambivalent," 24–25; and the Athenians' dismissal of ἐλπίς during the Melian dialogue, Thucydides 5.102–3.

37. Verdenius, "Hopeless," 229–30; Leiniers, "'ΕΛΠΙΣ," 1–4. John Myres, "'Ελπίς, ἔλπω, ἔλπομαι, ἐλπιζείν," *Classical Review* 62 (1948): 46, says of ἐλπίς in Homer: "Though 'wishful thinking' is not excluded, purely rational estimation of probability is the normal sense."

38. Walcot, "Pandora's Jar," 249.

39. Walcot, "Pandora's Jar," 250–1; Vernant, *Society*, 200; Vandvik, *Prometheus*, 18–19.

40. Hesiod declares that *any* age would be better than the Iron Age (*WD* 174–76). This does not, I believe, suggest a cyclical view of time, but is merely emphatic, as Hesiod's declaration that he would not have his son just (*WD* 270–71) does not necessarily imply that he is a father. The Indo-European model, however, does tend to take a cyclical view, as O'Flaherty, *Evil*, 18, 38–45. For Hesiod see West, 197; Verdenius, "Aufbau," 133; and *contra*, Vernant, *Thought*, 6–7. For arguments that the myth is cyclical, or alternates between good and bad generations, see Vernant, *Thought*, 3–32; Carl W. Querbach, "Hesiod's Myth of the *Four* Races," *Classical Journal* 81 (1985): 1–12; Walcot, "Composition," 47 and *Near East*, 81–86; E. R. Dodds, *The Ancient Concept of Progress*, (Oxford: Oxford University Press, 1973), 3–4.

41. See O'Flaherty, *Evil*, 13, 22–26: "The Hindu concept of the Golden Age thus lacks any vision of pristine human innocence or the corresponding belief in a separate agency of evil. To the Hindu, the original state of perfection is doomed to a quick extinction from within" (26).

42. For the irreconcilability, although unexplained, see Joseph Fontenrose, "Work, Justice, and Hesiod's Five Ages," *Classical Philology* 69 (1974): 1–2; West, 172; Querbach, "*Four* Races," 9; Arthur W. H. Adkins, *From the Many to the One: A Study of Personality and Views of Human Nature in the Context of Ancient Greek Society, Values, and Beliefs*, Studies in the Humanities, ed. M. Black (Ithaca: Cornell University Press, 1970), 54–55; Smith, "History," 151; Lovejoy and Boas, *Primitivism*, 199. Analyzed as diachronically separate myths, Kurt von Fritz, "Pandora, Prometheus und der Mythos von den Weltaltern," in Heitsch, *Hesiod*, 367–410; Robert Mondi, "The Ascension of Zeus and the Composition of Hesiod's *Theogony*," *Greek, Roman, and Byzantine Studies* 25 (1984): 332. For arguments that the myths are consistent, see Eduard Meyer, "Hesiods Erga und das Gedicht von den fünf Menschengeschlechtern," in Heitsch, *Hesiod*, 471–522; Kirk, *Myth*, 226–29; Lloyd-Jones, *Justice*, 33.

43. Zeus appears always in the first foot, three out of five times as Zeus Kronides, always either "making" or ending a race (*WD* 138, 143, 158, 168, 180). Zeus' metrical and emotional variations in the opening of the Pandora myth (*WD* 47–59) are in striking contrast.

44. See Thomas G. Rosenmeyer, "Hesiod and Historiography (*Erga* 106–210)," *Hermes* 85 (1957): 279; Grene, "Religion," 148–49; Douglas J. Stewart, "Hesiod and History," *Bucknell Review* 18 (1970): 42–49; Adkins, "Cosmogony," 51; Waltz, *Poème moral*, 80; Smith, "History," 151: "The sequence of races unfolds without any notice of choices being made by its characters; their actions and inactions flow spontaneously from their characters rather than from their meeting with external challenges or from their having to choose between alternatives." Knox, "Work and Justice," 11, sees the Iron Age ending when "the genetic clock, so to speak, has run down."

45. Stewart, "History," 46: "[The Silver and Bronze Ages] are destroyed for and *by* their *hybris* towards one another" (emphasis original). See also Lovejoy and Boas, *Primitivism*, 31.

46. Homer assigns Menelaus a place in the Blessed Isles as Zeus' son-in-law. Hesiod does not give even this much justification. Solmsen, review, 217 and Rosenmeyer, "Historiography," 273, would athetize *WD* 166, with the result that *all* of the heroic race ends in the Islands of the Blessed. With West, 192, I find it unlikely that Hesiod would or could deny a tradition as strong as the presence of heroes in Hades, as in, for example, *Odyssey* 11. The emphatic accumulation of μέν and δέ 's points to two alternate fates for the heroes, a distinction more significant than Solmsen's, of the Trojan and Theban cycles.

47. In a line with a strong resonance of Zeus' "hiding" our livelihood, Zeus is said to "hide" the Silver Age, angry at its failure to honor the gods. For the Five Ages myth as explicitly (and the Pandora myth implicitly) describing Zeus' intervention in human life, see Reynal Sorel, "Finalité et origine des hommes chez Hésiode," *Revue de Metaphysique et de Morale* 87 (1982): 24–30; Teggart, "Argument," 53–57 ;and W. J. Verdenius, "Hesiod, *Theogony* 507–616: Some Comments on a Commentary," *Mnemosyne* 24 (1971): 1.

48. See West, 186–87 for the identification with honored, but dead, mortals, and for this reading. I here read θνητοὶ rather than θνητοῖς which is translated by Grene.

49. I read οὐκ ἔσται ("will not be") with the manuscript rather than West's emendation ἐσσεῖται ("will be [in violence]"). The logical difficulty of allowing αἰδώς only, and not δίκη, to be governed by the verb, as also the difficulty with the necessarily late punctuation, is, I think, not as significant as the dramatic delay reinforced by enjambment. Αἰδώς' feat of both not existing and leaving (*WD* 199–200), is matched by Justice at *WD* 220–24. See West, 203 and "Misc. Notes," 161–62; and *contra* Richardson, review, 170. Solmsen, review, 219, points out, in addition, that West's reading must also mean either that "αἰδώς will be," which is the opposite of Hesiod's meaning, or "αἰδώς will be in violence," which is nonsense.

50. Lamberton, *Hesiod*, 120; Welles, "Attitude," 15; Will, "Observations," 7.

51. G. S. Kirk, J. E. Raven, and M. Schofield, *The Presocratic Philosophers: A Critical History with a Selection of Texts*, 2d edn. (Cambridge: Cambridge University Press, 1983)

52. For moral interpretations, see Solmsen, *Aeschylus*, 83–85; Hermann Fränkel, *Early Greek Poetry and Philosophy*, trans. Moses Hadas and James Willis (Oxford: Basil Blackwell, 1975), 134 ff.; Lloyd-Jones, *Justice*, 35; Welles, "Attitude," 15; Stewart, "History," 46–47; Jensen, "Tradition," 18; Kumaniecki, "Structure," 81–82; Will, "Observations," 7–10; Teggart, "Argument," 52: "The races are characterized; judgements are passed upon them; and, as it appears, the judgements fit the deeds attributed to the different kinds of men." Fontenrose, "Work," 10–12, believes that all races after the Golden were intended to work, and were destroyed for not doing so. For nonmoral interpretations, Adkins, *Many*, 53; Smith, "History," 153 ff.; and Lovejoy and Boas, *Primitivism*, 17, who see this as "chronological" rather than "moral" primitivism. Smith, 151–53, provides a summary. West, 49, sees Hesiod as requiring and proposing a myth about hardship, but telling (with some blunders) one of moral degeneration. For a metallic myth that *is* of moral degeneration see Daniel 2:31 ff. and, for other parallels, West, 172–77, and Bruce Lincoln, *Myth, Cosmos, and Society: Indo-European Themes of Creation and Destruction* (Cambridge, Mass.: Harvard University Press, 1986), 217, n. 24.

53. Knox, "Work and Justice," 11. For another view, Welles, "Attitude," 15.

54. The metallic is also the quality underlined in each age. The delayed identification of the Iron Age, νῦν γὰρ δὴ γένος ἐστι σιδήρεον· οὐδέ ποτ᾽ ἦμαρ . . . ("For now indeed is the race of iron . . ." *WD* 176), with its dieresis in the fourth foot, is most emphatic. West, 197; Grene, "Religion," 151; Lovejoy and Boas, *Primitivism*, 30.

55. As Hesiod does not describe a moral degeneration in the races, neither does he point to their lives, their deaths, or their fates after death, as punishment for their sins. As to their deaths, the first generation to die is the blameless Golden Race, which makes it clear that Hesiod is not thinking of an angry god destroying generations of men for their unrighteousness. All of the races die, and are "hidden under the earth" (*WD* 121 = 140 = 156). As to their fates after death, the impious Silver Race dies like the Golden, and, like the Golden, becomes guardian spirits, a better fate than any of the races that follow . The Heroes have better moral natures, but live lives that are worse than the Bronze, having to endure sailing as well as warfare. Half the generation suffers precisely the same fate as the Bronze. There is no indication that it is the less virtuous half. Finally, the fate after death of the Iron Age, morally the worst of all, is never mentioned. The only punishment described in the myth of the Five Ages is the destruction of the Silver Race for impiety (*WD* 137–39). It is explicitly mentioned because, as an exception, it could not be deduced from the overall pattern of the myth. See Victor Goldschmidt, "Théologia," *Revue des Études Grecques* 63 (1950): 20–42; Vernant, *Society*, 61–64; Hofinger, "Logos," 413. In contrast West, 173, concludes that the Bronze Age is worse than the Silver *from* their fate after death.

56. They are never described by any terms of moral approbation. The possible exception "dear to the gods" (*WD* 120) is athetized by West, 181, and, in any case, would probably refer to similarity of life, rather than to moral virtue. This is not to deny that the Golden Race was blameless. They were, but they were because they had no hardships, not vice versa.

57. Lovejoy and Boas, *Primitivism*, 29; West, 185, disagrees.

58. Lamberton's claim, *Hesiod*, 119, that the heroes were "better and more just" than *us* is unconvincing—this is the place where Hesiod describes each race as worse or unlike their predecessor.

59. See West, 172–77; Lovejoy and Boas, *Primitivism*, 25; Fontenrose, "Work," 2–5, etc.

60. As a result, as the generations proceed they come more and more to resemble human life as we know it, Grene, "Religion," 153; Benardete, "First Reading," 158. See also Adkins, *Many*, 50–59; Dodds, *Progress*, 1–25.

61. Hesiod carefully guards against such an interpretation by pointing out that the Heroes on the Blessed Isles are not quite as blessed, even after their lives are over, as the Golden Race was in life. Grain in the Golden Age grew spontaneously (*WD* 116–17); on the Blessed Isles three times a year (*WD* 172–73). The Golden Age lived like gods, free from trouble (*WD* 112–13); the Heroes live only with untroubled hearts (*WD* 170). Finally, only *half* of the heroes are involved. For the return to a Golden Age, Fontenrose, "Work," 15; Stewart, "History," 51. For Hesiod's closure in a ring pattern, Walcot, "Composition," 5. For the same treatment of the just city see chapter 5.

62. The conclusion of most scholars is Fränkel's: "Hesiod could not ignore the Homeric Age" (*Poetry*, 120). In other words, Hesiod put them in because he felt he had to, which seems to beg the question. See, for example, Knox, "Work and Justice," 12.

63. Adkins, "Myth," 104; Fontenrose, "Work," 9–10. See *Iliad* 6.48; 9.366; 23.261 for the Heroes' possession of iron as well as bronze.

64. Even here he does not see any need to establish a continuity of nature which corresponds to the continuity of physical descent. He certainly did not see the people of his own age as demi-gods. See Rosenmeyer, "Historiography," 266; Hofinger, "Logos," 408. Hesiod's failure to describe the creation of the Iron Age is corrected by an interpolator, for which see West, 194–95; Fontenrose, "Work," 9–10.

65. Nilsson, *History*, 184–85: "What Hesiod has created is a mythical history of the development of the human race, the first philosophy of history." It is, however, a *myth* of history, and not history itself: Smith, "History," 149–51; Adkins, *Many*, 56; Stewart, "History," 42–49; Rosenmeyer, "Historiography," 257–85; Beall, "Prometheus," 370–71.

66. The progression is from a purely primitive race, to one much like Homer's Cyclopes, to people like ourselves, with communities and δίκη, but not courts: there is no authority which can decide between Agamemnon and Achilles, and the scene of justice on Achilles' shield (*Iliad* 580 ff.) appears to be voluntary. As M. I. Finley describes the situation, "The defense of right was a purely private matter. He who felt aggrieved had the responsibility to take the necessary steps and the right to choose from among the available methods": *The World of Odysseus*, rev. ed. (New York: Viking, 1978), 111. See also Burn, *World*, 136–40; Lloyd-Jones, *Justice*, 5–7, 26–27; Vernant, *Thought*, 17; Michael Gagarin, "*Dike* in the *Works and Days*," *Classical Philology* 68 (1973): 83; West, 174, 188–90. Bonner and Smith, *Justice*, 11, agree with Hesiod's understanding of the heroic age: "Crimes and criminals were unknown to Homer. The conception of crime as a wrong which was a menace to society was not yet formulated."

67. J. Redfield, "Sparta," 147 points out that "the Greek reading of history is opposite to ours," seeing "a decline from some original perfection where we would see a continuing attempt to adapt political and social structures to a changing environment." Another strain of the myth portrays human beings as growing historically "older", from the childish Silver Age to the gray-haired babies of the future Iron Age, as West, 173–74; Smith, "History," 153–63; Vernant, *Thought*, 20–22.

See O'Flaherty, *Evil*, 32–35 for the regular Indo-European view that civilization is man's downfall. Teggart, "Argument," 77, and Pearson, *Ethics*, 82, who see δίκη as a positive good, see this as real progress. Hesiod's position here is foreshadowed by Prometheus, the god of civilization, who brings man hardship; see Erik Vandvik, "Some Notes on the 'Works' of Hesiod," *Symbolae Osloenses* 24 (1945): 154–63.

68. Translated by Wendy Doniger O'Flaherty, quoted in O'Flaherty, *Evil*, 24.

69. Whatever Hesiod means by being born from ash trees, it is unlike the present, e.g. *Odyssey* 19.163. For other traditions of this sort see West, 187; West, *Th.*,167.

70. Mazon, *Les Travaux et les jours*, 101 sees this as metaphorical. It also appears in the *Statesman*, 274a.

71. Adkins, *Many*, 50–66, esp. 53, and see Lovejoy and Boas, *Primitivism*, 16.

72. See Alexander G. McKay, "Prometheus Then and Now," *Augustan Age* 10 (1990–92): 26–33.

73. Hesiod's Golden Age has no hardship, no hunger, and so no need for agriculture, battles, or wars. Neither is there, apparently, any need for communities or sacrifice—or for justice. There is certainly no need for courts. Hesiod gives no indication that he understands mankind to have degenerated from this condition by the *loss* of any of these aspects of life. The Cyclopes have no respect for the gods, and no need for agriculture, communities, ships, or δίκη (*Odyssey* 9.105–40, 273–79); the people aided by Prometheus also lack sacrifice, ships, agriculture, or community (*PB* 440 ff.); the *Theogony* speaks of a time before human beings had sacrifice (*Th.* 535 ff.). See Sorel, "Finalité", 27; Teggart, "Argument," 53–56; Garner, *Law*, 20; and for δίκη specifically, Sihvola, *Decay, Progress*, 46; Benardete, "First Reading," 158–59; Pearson, *Ethics*, 81; Grene, "Religion," 153: "what Hesiod has to say about Justice belongs specifically to the Age of Iron and to a somewhat new condition existing between Zeus and man." As an Indo-European tendency, Lincoln, *Sacrifice*, 24: "paradise is defined more by *what it is not* than by what it is" (italics original).

74. See Rosenmeyer, "Historiography," 266, and against this view, Hofinger, "Logos," 405, n. 7. West, *Th.*, 188 defines γένος in Hesiod as "order" or "brood."

75. See Adkins, *Many*, 50–66 and especially 53; Rosenmeyer, "Historiography," 279; Grene, "Religion," 148–49; Stewart, "History," 42–49; and Lovejoy and Boas, "Primitivism," 16. As Shivola puts it, *Decay, Progress*, 62, "these conditions [for achieving success and prosperity] are not historically qualified but are determined by the objective and eternal cosmic order established and maintained by Zeus."

76. As Sihvola puts it, *Decay, Progress*, 34: "the main function of Hesiod's historical myths is not to present accounts of the past as such, but through these accounts to express concepts and values which are necessary for understanding and judging the present human condition."

77. An Indian myth seems relevant: "When [people] were frightened of the [newly introduced] fire and asked the king what it was, he replied, 'This fire arises because of the fault of a time that is both harsh and smooth. It does not exist in a period that is altogether harsh nor in one that is altogether smooth.' Then he began to institute social order and laws of conduct and punishment." O'Flaherty, *Evil*, 30.

78. Hence B. F. Perry, "Fable," *Studium Generale* 12 (1959): 19 compares the fable to a gnomic aorist, citing *Iliad* 17.32: "The fool learns after the event" (cf. *WD* 218).

79. For this interpretation of the fable see, primarily, Jensen, "Tradition." As Grene puts it: "If this story is specifically addressed to the kings and the point is helplessness, Zeus has to be the hawk and the kings the victim. This is indeed the drift of the whole passage before and after: 'You kings do not realize that you are in the grip of someone far stronger.'" Also Welles, "Attitude," 17–19; V. A. Rodgers, "Some Thoughts on ΔΙΚΗ," *Classical Quarterly* 21 (1971): 290–91; and Beye, "Rhythm," 35, 39, who, like Grene, support this interpretation without examining it in detail. A more detailed version of this argument appears in my "The Justice of Zeus in Hesiod's Fable of the Hawk and the Nightingale," *Classical Journal* 92 (1997): 235–47. An article that I discovered only after developing this interpretation, by Marie-Christine Leclerc, "L'Épervier et le rossignol d'Hésiode: une fable à double sens," *Revue des Études Grecques* 105 (1992): 37–44, takes a very similar stance.

80. For representative statements of this, the prevailing view see Lloyd Daly, "Hesiod's Fable," *Transactions of the American Philological Association* 92 (1961): 45–51; Heath, "Didactic Poetry," 249–50; Østerud, "Individuality," 21–23; Adkins, *Values*, 30–31; W. Nicolai, *Hesiods Erga* (Heidelberg: C. Winter, 1964), 50–53; Lamberton, *Hesiod*, 120–24; Pucci, *Language*, 63–66. See also West, 204–9; Rowe, *Essential Hesiod*, 132; Walcot, "Law," 20 and *Peasants*, 115; Jaeger, *Paideia*, 1. 68; Kumaniecki, "Structure," 82; Hamilton, *Architecture*, 50, 63; Knox, "Work and Justice," 13.

81. For example, Daly, "Fable," 49; West, 50, 226: Lamberton, *Hesiod*, 124; Hamilton, *Architecture*, 50.

82. See B. F. Perry, "The Origin of the Epimythium," *Transactions of the American Philological Association* 71 (1940): 403: "the great majority of fables from all periods end with a speech by one of the characters; and even when this speech does not take the form of a statement of a general truth, it nevertheless seems always designed to point the moral of the fable." West, 206, 208, points out that Hesiod's opening emphasizes that the hawk's words comprise the point of the story. On the other side see Østerud, "Individuality," 22; and Daly, "Fable," 50: "None of the other details of the fable [other than violence], including its moral, has any significance for Hesiod, for Perses, or the kings."

83. As West, 205 suggests, citing this kind of "subjection of the bad bird by another, higher power" in other fables.

84. Daly, "Fable," 49 explains: "it is Hesiod's way to interrupt himself"; West, 50: "the unsatisfactory story of the hawk and the nightingale is still on his mind"; Lamberton, *Hesiod*, 120: "The fable floats luminously before the mind's eye for sixty lines before the speaker tells us what it means."

85. See Jensen, "Tradition," 21; West, 205. Heath, "Didactic Poetry," 249, sees this "element of the unexpected and paradoxical" as adding force to the correction.

86. Which is how most commentators read the line. See, for example, Østerud, "Individuality," 22; Daly, "Fable," 50; West, 209; Wilamowitz, *Hesiodos' "Erga"*, 64; and Welles, "Attitude," 18, n. 41.

87. ἀλλὰ σύ γ' ἡμετέρης μεμνημένος αἰὲν ἐφετμῆς / ἐργάζεο Πέρση ("But, Perses, do you remember all that I urge—and work" *WD* 298–99) and ἀλλὰ σὺ τῶν μὲν πάμπαν ἔεργ' ἀεσίφρονα θυμόν ("But you, from such acts keep your sinful mind at a distance" *WD* 335) contrast the way Perses should take to that of those who neither understand nor listen, and to the way of those whose injustice is punished by Zeus. West, 209, assuming that *WD* 213 is adversative, cites these instances as similar, without noting the difference in form. *WD* 306 is a similar case, but without the vocative.

88. See Liddell and Scott, 9th ed., s.v. "δέ": "when the speaker turns from one person to another, the voc. stands first, then the pers. Pron. folld. by δέ" and, similarly, Denniston, *Particles*, 189. Although West interprets the phrase adversatively in the fable, he describes the same formula at line 27 (147), "ὦ Πέρση, σὺ δε: the vocative introduces the application of the universal truth to the present situation."

89. On these connections see also Leclerc, "L'Épervier," 41–43. The κρείσσων ("stronger" *WD* 210) that the nightingale resists becomes, just below, the road to justice itself, while the hawk's claim to be ἀρείων ("superior" *WD* 207) echoes Hesiod's repeated description of justice as "better" or "best" (*WD* 19, 36, 279).

90. The ἄλγεα ("miseries" *WD* 211) suffered by the nightingale reflect both the preceding ἄλγεα λυγρά ("baleful miseries" *WD* 200) that human beings suffer when they abandon straight δίκη and the following sufferings that come to kings who try to pervert justice (*WD* 213–66). See Welles, "Attitude," 17, *WD* 133, describing the ἄλγεα of the Silver Age, and *WD* 741. Jensen, "Tradition," 20–22, points out that Hesiod, who does not picture himself as weak, pitiful, or even as "contending against a greater," is not at all similar to the nightingale.

91. For νήπιος see *WD* 40, 131, 218, 286, 397, 456, 633. Jensen, "Tradition," 21 points to Epimetheus as well. Hesiod appears to prefer formulae as keys. Ἄλγεα πάσχει recalls the formulaic ἄλγεα πάσχων. For κρείσσων see e.g. *Iliad* 17.176, and West, 209; for the formulaic νήπιος, and its connection to ἄφρων, see *Iliad* 15. 104: νήπιοι, οἳ Ζηνὶ μενεαίνομεν ἀφρονέοντες ("We are fools who rage against Zeus senselessly") and West, 207–8. For Zeus' power to effect opposites see *Iliad* 20.242, *Th.* 26–28, and, on Hecate, *Th.* 442–43. Whether we see these verbal echoes as a deliberate compositional device, or as the result of composition through association of ideas, they link the fable to Hesiod's basic theme, that those who challenge Zeus suffer for it.

92. Niobe, Arachne, Marsyas, and Tantalus spring immediately to mind.

93. Scholars have almost universally agreed that Hesiod's fable of the hawk and the nightingale is a fable—a traditional story, drawing a general moral, applied to a particular situation. Given Hesiod's general tendency to use traditional material, along with the existence of several other hawk and nightingale fables, it seems most likely that Hesiod adopted rather than invented the fable. The obvious implication is that Hesiod did not *choose* the birds of the fable, but had them given him as part of the fable. Perry, "Fable," cites the hawk and the nightingale as a typical example of the genre (pp. 18, 21). Wendy Doniger ("Myths With and Without Points of View," Surjit Singh Lecture, University of California, Berkeley, October 31, 1994) discusses the way in which the outlines of a traditional story, including, of course, the characters, remain the same while the use the story is put to may vary widely.

In contrast, P. Walcot, who points to the fable's traditional nature in *Near East*, 90, discusses in *Peasants*, 115–16, the reasons for Hesiod's *choice* of these particular birds. West, 204–5 and Daly, "Fable," 46–48, 50–51, believe that Hesiod's failure is due to his inability to make effective use of a pre-existing fable, West missing "the subjection of the bad bird by another, higher power." In contrast see Beye, "Rhythm," 35. For other hawk and nightingale fables, see West, 205.

94. Perry, "Fable," 18 describes a fable as relating "a particular action or series of actions that took place once in the past through the agency of particular characters." West's argument that Hesiod was able to change the bird, but not its epithet (206) is answered by Sinclair, "Works and Days", 25, who also cites D'Arcy Thompson (A Glossary of Greek Birds [Oxford: Clarendon Press, 1895]) on the difficulty of identifying the particular bird intended. The misunderstanding, as well as West's theory that the victim was originally a dove or a thrush, has arisen though a conflation of the fable and the simile, two quite distinct genres. See Perry, "Fable," 18 as opposed to Wilamowitz, Hesiodos' "Erga", 64; Walcot, "Law," 20; West, 206. Hamilton, "Architecture," 63 describes the fable as an "allegory." Adkins, Values, 31 points to the difference between a parable, where "the creatures or objects mentioned are merely symbolic for what is signified" and a fable. Prof. W. R. Johnson first pointed out to me the difference between a fable which is traditional and an allegory created to represent a particular situation.

95. To the extent that the formulaic φρονέουσι καὶ αὐτοῖς ("one they know themselves") means more than "although they are knowing themselves" (Grene) it means not that the kings know that they commit injustice, but (the reason why the fable stings) that they know that Zeus punishes it. At Iliad 1.577 Hephaestus warns Hera about angering Zeus in just these terms. See West, 205–6.

96. As the hare and the tortoise of fable represent, in modern terms, neither timidity nor soup, but only the contrast of speed and slow perseverance. The hawk and nightingale fables cited by West, 205, also contrast power and helplessness.

97. See Odyssey 8.169–73 and Alcinous' and Eumaeus' description of Odysseus as a "singer" at 11.367–69 and 17.514–21, despite the fact that Odysseus must be understood to have spoken in prose. For the general link between song and persuasive speech see F. Solmsen, "The 'Gift' of Speech in Homer and Hesiod," Transactions of the American Philological Association 85 (1954): 4–8; John T. Kirby, "Rhetoric and Poetics in Hesiod," Ramus 21 (1992): 34–60; and Michael Gagarin, "The Poetry of Justice: Hesiod and the Origin of Greek Law," Ramus 21 (1992): 61–78. The reason for the link becomes apparent when we recall that "δίκη" refers primarily to the proposed method of ending disputes without violence rather than to the judgement itself, as Raphael Sealey, The Justice of the Greeks (Ann Arbor: University of Michigan Press, 1994), 101–7.

98. For the kings as poets see Kirby, "Rhetoric"; Marie-Christine Leclerc, "La Parole chez Hésiode," L'Information Littéraire 43 (1991): 3–4; Catherine P. Roth, "The Kings and the Muses in Hesiod's Theogony," Transactions of the American Philological Association 106 (1976): 331–38; J. Duban, "Poets and Kings in the Theogony Invocation," Quaderni Urbinati di Cultura Classica, n.s., 4 (1980): 7–21; Solmsen, "Gift," 6–8 ,13–15; Pucci, Language, 16–21; Østerud, "Individuality," 26–28; and, for the relation of poetry and law in an oral culture, E. A. Havelock, The Greek Concept of Justice: From its Shadow in Homer to its Substance in Plato (Cambridge, Mass.: Harvard University Press, 1978), 4–37 and passim.

99. The unmetrical variant δίκας for μύθους indicates what the scribe expected; Hesiod's usual "straight δίκη" indicates why. For the connection of words and judgements see Pucci, Language, 45–50; Gagarin, "Poetry," 71–76.

100. See G. Nagy, Mythology, 66–67.

101. As Welles (with tongue in cheek) puts it: "the hawk is sinful; he is a brutal and lawless predator who is tormenting an innocent and helpless victim, and a songster at that" ("Attitude,"18).

102. This view is more often noted in authors other than Hesiod, see Burkert, Religion, 130; Arthur W. H. Adkins, Poetic Craft in the Early Greek Elegists (Chicago: University of Chicago

Press, 1985), 158. For Hesiod see Hugh Lloyd-Jones, "Zeus in Aeschylus," *Journal of Hellenic Studies* 76 (1956): 65–66: "What is emphasized in Hesiod, and also in tragedy, is the supremacy of [Zeus'] power and the uselessness of trying to deceive him or in any way resist his will . . . The gods by their laws encourage righteousness among men. But they themselves are not obliged to obey these laws, nor should we be reasonable to expect it." Also (qualified) Beye, "Rhythm," 35–41. More usual is Verdenius, "Notes," 244: "In Hesiod the gods give evil only as punishment."

103. Jensen's interpretation of the fable is softened by the view that mankind, not Zeus, is responsible for the hardship of human life ("Tradition," 15–20).

104. Theognis does not take this tradition as easily, see 205 ff., 731–52, and Adkins, *Craft*, 153–54.

105. See below, chapter 5.

CHAPTER 3

1. Although the *Eclogues* are written against the background of Theocritus, as the *Aeneid* is written against that of Homer, this is the only place where Vergil actually names his model. Farrell, *Tradition*, 27 ff., 157ff., sees this as indicating the end of Vergil's references to Hesiod. As J. Bayet, "Les Premières "Géorgiques" de Virgile (39–37 avant J.-Ch.)," *Revue de Philologie* 56 (1930), 131 ff., 227, though for different reasons, Farrell feels that only the first Georgic is intended to refer to the *Works and Days*. It may be, on the other hand, exactly because the second Georgic begins to move away from a direct modeling on the *Works and Days* that Vergil feels it necessary to be this explicit. See also Dorothea Wender, "From Hesiod to Homer by Way of Rome," *Ramus* 8 (1979): 61–64. Boyle, *Dove*, 36, on the other hand, points to the fervency with which Vergil assumes the Hesiodic mantel, and see A. J. Boyle, "In Medio Caesar: Paradox and Politics in Virgil's *Georgics*," *Ramus* 8 (1979): 83, n. 13 for the importance of Hesiod to the *Georgics*.

"[U]nlike the poems which surround it, the *Georgics* has no single formal or generic model—that is, no author and no work could lay claims, even on the surface, to Vergil's allegiance" (Thomas, "Reference," 173). For the old view, that Vergil modeled the *Georgics* on the *Works and Days* see Rand, *Magical Art*, 179–80, and "Urbanity," 165; W. Y. Sellar, *The Roman Poets of the Augustan Age: Virgil* (Oxford: Oxford University Press, 1908), 175. For the modern view, see Ross, *Elements*, 10; George E. Duckworth, "Vergil's *Georgics* and the Laudes Galli," *American Journal of Philology* 80 (1959): 227; Monica R. Gale, "Man and Beast in Lucretius and the *Georgics*," *Classical Quarterly* 51 (1991): 414–26; Thomas, *Virgil*, 1.6. W. Clausen, "Callimachus and Latin Poetry," *Greece and Rome* 5 (1964): 196, believes that "References to Hesiod in Virgil and Propertius are really references to Callimachus or his conception of Hesiod." A. J. Boyle, "Virgil's Pastoral Echo," *Ramus* 6 (1977): 130–31, n. 12 and Farrell, *Tradition*, 314–18 disagree. As the subject of the *Georgics* is taken to be not farming but philosophy, not Hesiod but Lucretius is seen as its model. The *Georgics* is of course a response to Lucretius, but not to Lucretius rather than Hesiod, just as the poem is philosophical, but not philosophical rather than about farming. For the multiplicity of influences on the *Georgics* see Thomas, *Virgil*, 1.1–11 and Farrell, *Tradition*, 132–34 and passim. For a specific example see José Ignacio García Armendáriz, "Hesíodo y Virgilio: a propósito de nudus ara, sere nudus," *Myrtia* 6 (1991): 71–81.

2. See Lee, *Orpheus*, 131: "Nature herself survives through a balance of opposites, and Virgil's poem is held together by similar tensions. The ebb and flow of feeling from book to book, and especially in the endings of the four books (war/peace/death/renewal) are witness to the alternating currents of destruction and creation in nature herself. What appear to be contra-

dictions between the books are components of Virgil's view of the unresolved tensions of the world."

3. The rough rhythm of 1.150, with its concluding disyllables, and the complete failure of caesura at 1.153, recreate the farmer' sense of constant, harsh, and unrelenting labor.

4. The rushed elisions of the first half of 1.320 contrast with the deliberate destruction of the latter half, and then rush the rhythm back into chaos.

5. In contrast Ross, *Elements*, 121–22, takes this as a reference to Hesiod's lying Muses.

6. In contrast to Hesiod, Vergil begins the farmer's year in spring (Farrell, *Tradition*, 137; Wilkinson, *Survey*, 76). Spring is also the season of the storm and Ceres' festival. Italy, Vergil says, is a land of perpetual spring (*hic ver adsiduum*). The central passages of Books 2, 3, and 4 are, respectively, the praise of spring's fecundity, the sexual frenzy of spring, and the spring rebirth of *bougonia*. In Hippocratic writings the battle of the elements, heat and cold, dry and wet, occurs in spring, and makes the season tempestuous and unsettled, for which see Ross, *Elements*, 165; Peter Connor, "The *Georgics* as Description: Aspects and Qualifications," *Ramus* 8 (1979): 42; Thomas, *Virgil*, 1.215.

7. For works on Vergil's use of allusion see the Preface, n. 7.

8. The effect of the elisions in lines 1.140–43, especially in the last, where the caesura is effectively eliminated, is to hurry mankind into its own destruction.

9. See Patricia A. Johnston, *Vergil's Agricultural Golden Age: A Study of the "Georgics"*, Mnemosyne Supplement no. 60 (Leiden: Brill, 1980), 51, 62, and passim, for the peace of the Golden Age. See also Friedrich Klingner, *Virgils "Georgica"* (Zurich: Artemis, 1963): 119–35.

10. See Sara Mack, *Patterns of Time in Vergil* (Hamden, Conn.: Archon Books, 1978), 18–21 for Vergil's movement from a historical to an archetypical Golden Age.

11. "Overall," as seen above, is important. The first and second Georgics fall into three sections. In both, the central section is the most "Hesiodic", marked by specific references to the *Works and Days*, e.g. 1.160–75, 276–86, 299, 341; 2.176, 401–2, 412–13. In the first Georgic this central section, on due season, is the book's most hopeful section. In the second the central section, on the labor which the vines require, is the bleakest. See also below, chapter 4.

12. Vergil's elision, and consequent avoidance of caesura, similarly carries away the reader.

13. For the complex structure of the *Georgics* see Drew, "Structure," 242–54; Wilkinson, *Survey*, 72 ff.; Perkell, *Truth*, 14; Boyle, "Paradox," 65–67; and, especially, Otis, *Virgil*, 151 ff. and "New Study," 45. William R. Nethercut, "Vergil's *De Rerum Natura*," *Ramus* 2 (1973): 46, points out that Vergil reverses Lucretius' movement from a positive book to a negative one.

14. See Otis, *Virgil*, 153–54 and "New Study," 175; Miles, *Interpretation*, 204.

15. In accordance with the two schools of criticism, there are two schools regarding farming. For the older view, that farming is human life in accordance with nature, see Rand, *Magical Art*, 195; Klingner, "Landlebens," 159–89; Sir James Mountford, "The Architecture of the *Georgics*," *Proceedings of the Virgil Society* 6 (1967): 25–34; Perret, *Truth*, 37; Heitland, *Agricola*, 213ff. For the more current view that the *Georgics* exposes our brutal exploitation of nature see Thomas, *Virgil*, 1.16–24; Ross, *Elements*, 78 ff.; Michael C. J. Putnam, "Italian Vergil and the Idea of Rome," in L. L. Orlin, ed., *Janus: Essays in Ancient and Modern Studies* (Ann Arbor: Center for Coordination of Ancient and Modern Studies, University of Michigan, 1975), 171–200; Putnam, "Achievement," 56; Christine G. Perkell, "A Reading of Virgil's Fourth Georgic," *Phoenix* 32 (1978): 211–21; Boyle, "Paradox," 65–80; Antony Bradley, "Augustan Culture and a Radical Alternative: Vergil's *Georgics*," *Arion* 8 (1969): 347–58.

16. See Boyle, "Introduction," 5; Perkell, *Truth*, 13 ff.; R. S. Conway, *The Vergilian Age* (Cambridge, Mass.: Harvard University Press, 1928), 96–112; Johnson, *Darkness*, 158–59, n. 17; and, with reference to Hesiod, Rosenmeyer, "Historiography," 262. So, on the *Aeneid*, Johnson, *Darkness*, 111: "The two images refuse to merge into a steady whole that will permit us to understand the grounds of their opposition, and, by this understanding, to view them separate

but unified, each a necessary eternal part of the process. Rather, the arcs that should complete the circle, in precise proportion as they seem to near one another, keep swerving off in opposite tangents."

17. I mean here to describe not Rome so much as Rome's vision of itself, one often idealized, and as often presented in self-mockery. George Washington and the cherry tree, Honest Abe returning the penny, MacArthur's "I will return," are not the facts of American history, but they are deeply influential and indicative nonetheless. Cato's description of farming is, of course, the *locus classicus:* "It is true that to obtain money by trade is sometimes more profitable, were it not so hazardous; and likewise money-lending, if it were as honorable. Our ancestors held this view and embodied it in their laws, which required that the thief be punished double, the usurer fourfold. How much less desirable a citizen they considered the usurer than the thief may be judged from this. And when they would praise a good man they praised him thus: 'good farmer,' 'good cultivator.' One so praised was judged to have received the most extensive commendation" (*Est interdum praestare mercaturis rem quaerere, nisi tam periculosum sit, et item fenerari, si tam honestum sit. Maiores nostri sic habuerunt et ita in legibus posiverunt, furem dupli condemnari, feneratorem quadrupli. Quanto peiorem civem existimarint feneratorem quam furem, hinc licet existimare. Et virum bonum quom laudabant, ita laudabant, bonum agricolam bonumque colonum. Amplissime laudari existimabatur qui ita laudabatur: De Agricultura* 1.1). Johnson describes Cato's attitude: "The Roman way was prudence, caution, patience; waiting for the opportunity, careful pacing, slow change, methodical trial and error. If, after the victory over Carthage, Romans began to act like Greeklings, the game was over." W. R. Johnson, "Vergil's Bees: The Ancient Romans' View of Rome," in Annabel Patterson, ed., *Roman Images: Selected Papers from the English Institute, 1982*, n.s., 8 (Baltimore: Johns Hopkins University Press, 1984), 5–6. See also Cato in Cicero's *De Senectute*, Loeb Classical Library (Cambridge, Mass.: Harvard University Press, 1950), 56; Ross, *Elements*, 20; Gordon Williams, *Tradition and Originality in Roman Poetry* (Oxford: Oxford University Press, 1968), 427; L. A. S. Jermyn, "Vergil's Agricultural Lore," *Greece and Rome* 18 (1949): 55; Ferguson, *Moral Values*, 159, 162.

18. Hence the negative treatment of Odysseus in the *Aeneid* and (in Shakespeare's version) the "worthy soldier's" advice to Antony: "O noble Emperor, do not fight by sea, / Trust not to rotten planks ... Let th'Egyptians / And the Phoenicians go a'ducking; we / Have us'd to conquer standing on the earth" (*Antony and Cleopatra* III.vii.61–65). For Cato (*De Agricultura* 1.1) farming is most *pious*, the quintessential Roman virtue.

19. As Horace: "Another generation is now destroyed with civil war / And Rome herself falls to ruin through her own strength." (*Altera iam teritur bellis civilibus aetas, / Suis et ipsa Roma viribus ruit: Epod.* 16.1–2).

20. On Roman attitudes toward farming see, in particular, Ross, *Elements*, 10 ff.; also Farrell, *Tradition*, 254; Gretchen Kromer, "The Didactic Tradition in Vergil's *Georgics*," *Ramus* 8 (1979): 13; R. O. A. M. Lyne, "'Scilicet et Tempus Veniet ...'": Vergil, *Georgics* 1.463–514," in Tony Woodman and David West, eds., *Quality and Pleasure in Latin Poetry* (Cambridge: Cambridge University Press, 1974), 47; Miles, *Interpretation*, 3 ff.; Sellar, *Roman Poets*, 268; G. Williams, *Tradition*, 165, 169; Jasper Griffin, *Virgil* (Oxford: Oxford University Press, 1986), 47.

21. For the decline of the peasant farmer and the rise of the wealthy estate owner see Miles, *Interpretation*, 12–17; Heitland, *Agricola*, 202 ff.; Weber, *Agrarian Sociology*, 322; Toutain, *Economic Life*, 278.

22. See Farrell, *Tradition*, 204–5; G. Williams, *Tradition*, 591–92; M. S. Spurr, "Agriculture and the *Georgics*," *Greece and Rome* 33 (1986): 182; Parry, "Art," 38—despite his view that farming is the "vehicle" for the message of the *Georgics*.

23. For this connection between Hesiod and Vergil, most often with the loss of Hesiod's real concern with farming, see Perkell, *Truth*, 9–10; Boyle, "Introduction," 4; Wilkinson, *Survey*, 60.

24. For an excellent study of Vergil's relation to his Greek models see Brooks Otis, "The Originality of the Aeneid," 27–66 in D.R. Dudley, ed., *Virgil* (London: Routledge,1969).

25. For the *latifundia* as the cutting edge of Augustan agriculture see Heitland, *Agricola*, 153 ff. and White, *Farming*, 336 ff. White, 34–35 (and see 40–41) points out the contrast between the peasant farmer that Cato holds up as a standard and the fact that he, like Varro, writes for an owner of a large estate worked by slaves, and managed by an overseer. A "place in the country," like Horace's Sabine farm, was not, of course, desired for profit, but neither was it seen as the "way of life" of the peasant. See Perkell, *Truth*, 28–29. Boyle, "Introduction," 4 and Wilkinson, *Survey*, 50 ff. point out the archaism; Bayet, "Premières," 232, points out that the farm has been taken from Hesiod. For a contrary opinion see Spurr, "Agriculture," 164–83.

26. In contrast, by the Augustan period grain was primarily provided from outside Italy (Toutain, *Economic Life*, 266; Weber, *Agrarian Sociology*, 323); slaves had replaced yeomen as workers (Weber, 318); and goods were largely purchased rather than made on the farm (Weber, 325).

27. It is unlikely that Vergil adopted this farm in order to try to change Roman agricultural practices. The possibility of reversing a trend that was now entrenched, and that had dominated Roman agriculture since before his birth, could not have appeared more than slight, nor is it likely that Vergil would dedicate seven years of his life to such a project, even if he thought it feasible. L. P. Wilkinson, "The Intention of Virgil's *Georgics*," *Greece and Rome* 19 (1950): 22, points out that Vergil's "poem has gained in universality by his tacit exclusion of the system dominant in his day." Heitland, *Agricola*, 6–8, 133–60 sees the rise of the *latifundia* system as coterminous with the decline of farming, on which see White, *Farming*, 273 and 370–76, 384–412 passim, on the persistence of smaller, traditional farming.

28. Rand, *Magical Art*, 186 points out Vergil's Hesiodic, gnomic, didactic, and personal tone. Note also Vergil's programmatic opening, his invocation of rustic deities, modeled on Varro's farming manual, and his vocabulary, modeled on Lucretius. See Kromer, "Didactic Tradition," 7 and passim, for Vergil's didactic persona as parallel to Hesiod's; Richard F. Thomas, "Prose into Poetry," *Harvard Studies in Classical Philology* 91 (1987): 236 and "Reference," 176 on Vergil's Lucretian vocabulary.

29. On the actual or merely literary reality of the old Corycian see Gabriele Marasco, "Corycius senex (Verg. Georg. 4, 127)," *Rivista di Filologia e di Istruzione Classica* 118 (1990): 402–7 and Richard F. Thomas, "The Old Man Revisited: Memory, Reference and Genre in Virg. *Georg.* 4, 116–48," *Materili e Discussioni per l'Analisi dei Testi Classici* 29 (1990): 35–70.

30. See G. Williams, *Tradition*, 257 on Vergil's use of his own personality to give life to his didactic poem. Wilkinson, *Survey*, 14 sees this technique as adapted from Lucretius. See also Connor, "Description," 53, 55; Francis Muecke, "Poetic Self-consciousness in *Georgics* II," *Ramus* 8 (1979): 87; Vinzenz Buchheit, *Der Anspruch des Dichters in Vergils "Georgica": Dichtertum und Heilsweg* (Darmstadt: Wissenschaftliche Buchgesellschaft, 1972). Slavitt, *Virgil*, 57–66, sees Vergil as pointing here towards his own kind of *labor*.

31. For other models for the *sphragis* see Thomas, *Virgil*, 2.239–41. Vergil's tendencies to follow elaborately poetic passages with prosaic reminders of his didactic purpose, to situate Alexandrianisms incongruously (see the African herdsman's "Spartan dog and Cretan quiver" at 3.345 or the "warlike Spaniard's" attack on the farm at 3.408), and to mock his didactic persona, also serve to emphasize his "poetic" role. It is not an accident that the *Georgics* was for so long seen as a somewhat dull technical treatise enlivened by purple patches; it is an effect Vergil himself creates. See Rand, *Magical Art*, 225; Wilkinson, *Survey*, 88; Jasper Griffin, "Haec Super Arvorum Cultu," *Classical Review*, n.s., 31 (1981): 33 and *Virgil*, 42. For the same technique in the *Eclogues* see Charles Segal, "Vergil's Caelatum Opus: An Interpretation of the Third Eclogue," *American Journal of Philology* 88 (1967): 279–308.

32. Servius declares that this is taken from Cato. See R. A. B. Mynors, *Virgil's "Georgics"* (Oxford: Clarendon Press, 1990): 154.

33. See Parry, "Art," 40 for Vergil's professional delight in the points of a cow; in contrast, Thomas, "Prose," 229. Heitland, *Agricola*, 241, who takes the question seriously, concludes that Vergil probably was not a farmer. Similarly, White, *Farming*, 40–41.

34. The elisions of 476 postpone the caesura, creating a sense of breathless excitement. Compare *De Rerum Natura* 1.924 ff. for the far from agricultural persona Vergil is here adopting.

35. Kromer, "Didactic Tradition," 9 attributes this to Vergil's didactic stance.

36. See Gale, "Man and Beast," 417–18.

37. See Rand, *Magical Art*, 215–16; M. Ruch, "Virgile et le monde des animaux," in Henry Bardon and Raoul Verdière, eds., *Vergiliana: Recherches sur Virgile* (Leiden: Brill, 1971), 322; W. Ward Fowler's introduction in Thomas Fletcher Royds, *The Beasts, Birds and Bees of Virgil: A Naturalist's Handbook to the "Georgics"* (Oxford: Blackwell, 1918), viii, xiii; and Farrell, 330. Otis, "New Study," 43 sees Vergil as a bookish poet, not a naturalist. Vergil's delight in wild nature is unusual in Latin literature, where nature is seen more often seen as hostile and untamed than as unspoiled. See Zoja Pavlovskis, *Man in an Artificial Landscape: The Marvels of Civilization in Imperial Roman Literature*, Mnemosyne Supplement, no. 25, (Leiden: Brill, 1973), 10 and Ross, *Elements*, 20–23 for an overall view.

38. I refer to Vergil's technique by the slight barbarism "personalizing" rather than "humanizing" because his aim is precisely *not* to make animals human, while "personifying" implies that nature is made into something which it is not. For the term used in a different context, see Adkins, "Cosmogony," 64, n. 15. For Vergil's animals as symbols for men, see, for example, Viola G. Stephens, "Like a Wolf on the Fold: Animal Imagery in Vergil," *Illinois Classical Studies* 15 (1990): 107–30; Farrell, *Tradition*, 91; Ross, *Elements*, 149; Putnam, *Earth*, 59–62; Boyle, *Dove*, 59; and, in contrast, W. Liebeschuetz, "Beast and Man in the Third Book of Virgil's Georgics," *Greece and Rome*, 2d ser., 12 (1965): 68 and passim; Bayet, "Premières," 240. David West, "Two Plagues: Virgil, *Georgics* 3.478–566 and Lucretius 6.1090–1286," in David West and Tony Woodman, eds., *Creative Imitation and Latin Literature* (Cambridge: Cambridge University Press, 1979), 80–83, notes Vergil's delight in animals but sees him as anthropomorphizing. In contrast see Otis, *Virgil*, 176 and Konrad Lorenz, *King Solomon's Ring: New Light on Animal Ways*, trans. Marjorie Kerr Wilson (New York: Crowell, 1952), 152: "You think I humanize the animal? Perhaps you do not know that what we are wont to call 'human weakness' is, in reality, nearly always a pre-human factor and one which we have in common with the higher animals? Believe me, I am not mistakenly assigning human properties to animals: on the contrary, I am showing you what an enormous animal inheritance remains in man, to this day."

39. Segal, "Fourth Georgic," 307: "The fundamental theme of Vergil's *Georgics* is the relation of man and nature." Ward W. Briggs, Jr., *Narrative and Simile from the "Georgics" in the "Aeneid"*, Mnemosyne Supplement no. 58 (Leiden: Brill, 1980), 31–52, discusses Vergil's use of the animals of the *Georgics* as similes in the *Aeneid*, a practice that is somewhat circular if the former are merely symbols for human beings.

40. Vergil's most extreme personalization, of the bees of Book 4, is taken largely from Varro, who certainly *was* really describing bees. See below, chapter 5.

41. Briggs, *Narrative*, 103; G. Williams, *Tradition*, 259.

42. Wilkinson, *Survey*, 127; Otis, *Virgil*, 387.

43. See Gerard Manley Hopkins, "Binsey Poplars," for an unambivalent poetic account of the scene.

44. Heitland, *Agricola*, 222 should be given credit for first pointing this out. See also Rand, *Magical Art*, 266; Connor, "Description," 41; in the *Eclogues*, Segal, "Caelatum," 304–8 and, in

contrast, Griffin, *Virgil*, 50. Miles, Interpretation, 62 and passim, builds his thesis on this fact. Don Fowler, "Deviant Focalization in Virgil's *Aeneid*," *Proceedings of the Cambridge Philological Society* 216 (1990): 42–63 points to some of the techniques Vergil uses to achieve this same end in the *Aeneid*.

CHAPTER 4

1. As Hesiod is usually our earliest source for these myths, a caveat should be understood throughout any discussion of the "tradition" within which he is working.

2. The combination and opposition of force and intelligence is a general characteristic of Near Eastern mythology as well as of Greek thought. Robert Mondi finds two distinct patterns of divine kingship in Near Eastern mythology, the ancient patriarch whose rule is characterized primarily by wisdom, as Cronos, the king of the Golden Age, and the young warrior-king, whose supremacy is characterized by force, as Zeus, the young god of thunder : "The influence of the former resides in his wisdom and command of respect; efficacious through verbal utterance rather than physical action, he holds a position of authority in the council of the gods as the ultimate font of cosmic order and is often accorded a judicial function, especially in the settling of disputes between gods . . . The younger god, on the other hand, physically manifest in the weather, is mythologically conceived of as the warrior-king: he is both the victor in the cosmic struggle that brought about the current world order and the executive force through which this order is maintained" (Mondi, "Near East," 173). The first is god in his immanent mode, the second god as transcendent (Mondi, "Near East," 166–68). For Hesiod's Zeus as the "all-conquering son" rather than the good/bad father, see Richard Caldwell, *The Origin of the Gods: A Psychoanalytic Study of Greek Theogonic Myth* (New York: Oxford University Press, 1989), 187–88.

The two aspects of kingship, force and intelligence, are thus opposed. Hesiod, however, unites in Zeus both the god of wisdom and the god of force, and both the immanent and the transcendent views of the divinity: "When we turn to the Greek system, we see the same coalescence of transcendent authority and executive imminence [sic] in the representation of Zeus that emerges from the poetry of both Homer and Hesiod: Zeus is not only the executive deity manifest in atmospheric phenomena, but he is also the guardian of *themis*" (Mondi, "Near East," 173), and "in the Greek mythological tradition *overall* Zeus and Cronos represent two quite different aspects of divine kingship, while the Zeus of Homer and Hesiod is in some ways a coalescence of the two, at the expense of Cronos, in the person of a single universal ruler" (Mondi, "Near East," 167). See also Ana Iriarte, "Savoir et pouvoir de Zeus," *Ítaca* 2 (1986): 9–24; Walcot, *Near East*, 24; Baldry, "Golden Age," 86. By taking from Cronos his traditional cunning, and assigning to him instead a role of brute force, Hesiod transforms Zeus' victory from a victory of young force over ancient wisdom into a victory of the combination of force and intelligence over primeval force.

3. Aeschylus, like Hesiod, seems to have felt that the final confirmation of Zeus' power required a union of force and intelligence, which, for Aeschylus, lay in a reconciliation between Prometheus and Zeus.

4. The binding of Prometheus points out the parallel fates of Prometheus and his brothers, Atlas and Menoitius, who are also suffering for their ὕβρις ("insolence") against Zeus. Like his brothers, Prometheus presents a challenge to Zeus' incipient order. As the decisive third, his return is to be rendered immobile by Zeus' unchallengeable force. Hesiod's ring composition emphasizes the immobility Zeus imposes on the ever-shifting Prometheus (*Th.* 521–22, 615–16), for which see Olstein, "Pandora," 297.

5. Hesiod's digression on women (*Th.* 590–612) might indicate an interest in the effect on man, but it is more likely that Hesiod is using his favorite theme to point out how clever the trick was; whether a man marries, or does not, he is doomed.

6. On the Prometheus episode as a contest of wits see Hamilton, *Architecture*, 32; Vernant, *Society*, 184 and "Sacrifice," 422. Prometheus is the only male god in the *Theogony* other than Zeus who employs craft. He has taken over both the δολίην τέχνην ("guileful device") of Earth (*Th.* 160, 540, 555, 547, 586) and Cronos' epithet ἀγκυλομήτις ("of crafty wiles" *Th.* 546 as *WD* 48). He is also described as ποικίλον αἰολόμητιν ("of shifty, moving wiles" *Th.* 511), ποικιλο-'βουλον ("of shifting counsel" *Th.* 521), πάντων πέρι μήδεα εἰδώς ("above all knowing in wiles" *Th.* 559), and πολύιδριν ("much wise" *Th.* 616). For Prometheus as "the trickster god," see Karl Kerényi, "The Trickster in Relation to Greek Mythology," trans. R. F. C. Hull, commentary in Paul Radin, *The Trickster: A Study in American Indian Mythology* (New York: Philosophical Library, 1956), 173–91; Penglase, *Greek Myths*, 221–26.

7. The "detail" of the stalemate, which, West, *Th.*, 340 sees as pointless, serves to underline the inadequacy of pure force, as also in *Prometheus Bound*, 212–13. Said, "Combats," 194–96 and Marylin B. Arthur, "Cultural Strategies in Hesiod's *Theogony*: Law, Family, Society," *Arethusa* 15 (1982): 76 see the Hundred-Handers themselves as representing the submission of force to intelligence.

8. Zeus bids the Hundred-Handers remember the woes they have escaped "through our counsels" (ἡμετέρας διὰ βουλὰς *Th.* 653). They resolve the difficulty of "our" by taking it as the royal we. What Hesiod attributed to "the cunning of Earth" (Γαίης φραδμοσύνῃσιν *Th.* 626) thus becomes, for the Hundred-Handers, "your shrewdness" (σῇσι δ' ἐπιφροσύνῃσιν *Th.* 658).

9. ἡ δ' ἐντὸς στοναχίζετο Γαῖα πελώρη / στεινομένη ("And she, huge Earth, groaned, / Straitened within" *Th.* 159–60); ἐπεστονάχιζε δὲ γαῖα ("earth groaned at it') *Th.* 843; στονά-χιζε δὲ γαῖα πελώρη ("huge earth groaned" *Th.* 857–88). See Waltz, *Poème moral*, 113; Solmsen, *Aeschylus*, 22–23; Lamberton, *Hesiod*, 72; Mondi, "Near East," 160–61; Adkins, "Myth," 101, and *Values*, 49 (on Solon).

10. Commentators have objected to the anomaly that Earth, who has up until this point been Zeus' ally, should be the mother of his last and greatest adversary. Walcot, *Near East*, 199 and Michael C. Stokes, "Hesiodic and Milesian Cosmogonies I," *Phronesis* 7 (1962), 33 see no reason to assume that Earth is here opposed to Zeus, as she does nothing. See West, *Th.*, 379–83 and Robert Mondi, "The Ascension of Zeus and the Composition of Hesiod's *Theogony*," *Greek, Roman, and Byzantine Studies* 25 (1984): 334 for other views. In fact, Typhoeus' challenge of Zeus is in many ways parallel to Cronos' challenge of Ouranos. Like Cronos (*Th.* 137–38), Typhoeus is the youngest and most terrible son of Earth; his father, Tartarus (given a personal role solely for the purpose of begetting Typhoeus) is the underworld counterpart of Cronos' father Ouranos; and as Cronos is unsuccessfully suppressed inside his mother Earth, Typhoeus is successfully suppressed inside his father Tartarus, as Stokes, "Cosmogonies," 4. West, *Th.*, 23–24 cites a Near Eastern parallel to the necessity that Zeus, in some sense, overcome Earth herself, to which one might add the vision of the *Oresteia*, that male gods have taken over from the primal female goddesses. See Fabienne Blaise, "L'Épisode de Typhée dans la Théogonie d'Hésiode (v. 820–885)," *Revue des Études Grecques* 105 (1992) 349–70, for an excellent account of the place of the episode in the scheme of the *Theogony*.

11. Burkert, *Religion*, 129. Solmsen, *Aeschylus*, 67–68 and 161 finds this interpretation tempting, but as he rejects *Th.* 886–900 is forced to reject it. In contrast see Stokes, "Cosmogonies," 36–37; Jean-Pierre Vernant, "Mètis et les mythes de souveraineté," *Revue de l'Histoire des Religions* 180 (1971): 31–34 and "Theogony and Myths of Sovereignty," in Bonnefoy, *Mythologies*, 1.378; Naddaf, "Précurseur," 355; Adkins, "Cosmogony," 46. Hence Zeus acquires his title, μητίετα, used just below, *Th.* 904

12. Zeus forces the cunning of the mother, here the goddess "most knowing among gods and mortal men" (πλεῖστα θεῶν εἰδυῖαν ἰδὲ θνητῶν ἀνθρώπων *Th.* 887) to work not against him but for him. "But Zeus beforehand put her into his own belly / So that for him might be the goddess' contriving of good and of evil" (ἀλλ' ἄρα μιν Ζεὺς πρόσθεν ἑὴν ἐσκάθετο νηδύν, / ὡς δή οἱ φράσσαιτο θεὰ ἀγαθόν τε κακόν τε *Th.* 899–900). I follow here the manuscript reading: ὡς δή οἱ φράσσαιτο "that she might devise for him," rather than Chrysippus' ὥς οἱ συμφράσσαιτο, "that she might consult with him" or "so that the goddess could advise him of what was good or bad" as West translates (West, *Hesiod*, 29). West, *Th.*, 405 objects to the δή of the manuscript as referring back to a reason Zeus gave Wisdom for swallowing her. Denniston, however, cites this passage as an example of δή in final clauses "describing an ingenious stratagem or device," here Zeus' getting Wisdom to work for him (*Particles*, 232). Hesiod may be more tolerant of the monstrous than Homer, but even he would rebel at the idea of Zeus holding a conference with an adviser lodged in his stomach.

13. West, *Th.*, 401 misses this mythologically logical point in thinking that, since the swallowing did not prevent Athene's birth, it could not prevent the birth of a son. For the pattern, see Walcot, *Near East*, 204; Querbach, "*Four Races*," 10; Arthur, "Strategies," 77; Vernant, "Mètis," 41.

14. See Caldwell, *Origin*, 161–64.

15. As with Cronos, the Hundred-Handers, Typhoeus, and Zeus himself. The tendency to associate force with the male line is particularly notable in Cronos, whom Hesiod has transformed from his traditional role as a god of craft to a god of force. In Hesiod's version, Cronos retains only the title of his famous craftiness. All of his actions in the *Theogony*, which consist primarily of binding other gods and imprisoning them in Tartarus, rely on force rather than on intelligence. The alternative view of Cronos, which associates him, as a god of wisdom, with the Golden Age, is altogether gone. See Mondi, "Near East," 175: "It has long been noted that there is a seemingly irreconcilable break between the Cronos of the succession myth and the Cronos of the golden age," and 166–77; H. S. Versnel, "Greek Myth and Ritual: The Case of Kronos," in Jan Bremmer, ed., *Interpretations of Greek Mythology* (London: Routledge, 1988), 121–52; M. van der Valk, "On the God Cronos," *Greek, Roman, and Byzantine Studies* 26 (1985): 5–11; Edmund R. Leach, "Cronos and Chronos," in William A. Lessa and Evon. Z. Vogt, eds., *Reader in Comparative Religion: An Anthropological Approach*, 4th edn. (New York: Harper and Row, 1979), 224–25; and Mondi, "Near East," 192, n. 26 for a good bibliography.

16. Aside from the castration of Ouranos, the counsel of Earth is responsible for Cronos' swallowing of his children, for the hiding of Zeus *from* Cronos, for the later deception of Cronos, for the recalling of the Hundred-Handers, for the election of Zeus as king, and for the swallowing of Wisdom. See Jean-Pierre Vernant, "Greek Cosmogonic Myths," in Bonnefoy, *Mythologies*, 1.371–72. In an attempt to preserve male dignity Hesiod includes Ouranos with Earth as often as possible, but cannot think of anything for him to do. Hesiod's distrust of female cunning is also apparent in Pandora and in the *Works and Days*: ὃς δὲ γυναικὶ πέποιθε, πέποιθ' ὅ γε φιλήτησιν· ("One who has trusted a woman has trusted a highway robber" *WD* 375). See Mondi, "Near East," 161; Patricia A. Marquardt, "Hesiod's Ambiguous View of Women," *Classical Philology* 77 (1982): 289, and, among modern Greeks, Campbell, *Honour*, 271. At *WD* 245 the formula Γαίης φραδμοσύνῃσιν ("Earth's councils" *Th.* 626, 884, 890) has become Ζηνὸς φραδμοσύνῃσιν ("Zeus' councils"). See Stokes, "Cosmogonies," 4 and 36, n. 70. Arthur, "Strategies," 63–82 describes Zeus' increasing dominance over the male and female elements, respectively, of the *Theogony*.

17. For the Typhoeus episode as another version of the pattern of son challenging father, see Caldwell, *Origin*, 173–4. For the inevitable question of Zeus himself being overthrown, see Blumenberg, *Work on Myth*, 315.

18. Blaise, who describes Typhoeus as an "anti-Zeus" (359–63), declares, "Épisode," 363: "Typhée constitue, en soi, une menace pour l'orginsation du cosmos." Typhoeus' disorder is set in contrast to the order of Tartarus, as guarded by Zeus' deputies, the Hundred-Handers, which immediately precedes the episode. See Lamberton, Hesiod, 88; Will, "Observations," 11; Naddaf, "Precurseur," 352–53; Jean-Pierre Vernant, "Theogony and Myths of Sovereignty," in Bonnefoy, Mythologies, 377: "The last of the children of Gaia, he represents within the organized world a return to the primordial chaos to which all things would revert if he was to triumph." He has been described at Th. 307 as "Terrible, hubristic and with no νόμος" (δεινόν θ' ὑβριστήν τ' ἄνομον θ'). Judging from Hesiod's usual use of νόμος, this seems to mean that Typhoeus has no established "way," which certainly corresponds to Hesiod's description.

19. See Blaise, "Épisode," 368–9. Here, as in the Works and Days, "the gods" and "Zeus" are interchangeable. The lines which describe the disorderly and destructive after-effects of Typhoeus are immediately followed by the settlement of Zeus' supremacy, and his distribution of τιμή among the gods.

20. Mondi, "Near East," 177–87; Penglase, Greek Myths, 189–96; and West, Th., 21–22, 380–81, cite Near Eastern and Greek versions of the story, all of which agree in placing the challenge of Typhoeus or his equivalent after Zeus' establishment as king. Certain difficulties which have been taken as evidence of interpolation, as the doubling of episodes, and the reference to the Titanomachia at Th. 881–82, may have arisen from Hesiod's idiosyncratic placement of the challenge of Typhoeus. See Blaise, "Épisode," 349–70; Said, "Combats," 201–10; Stokes, "Cosmogonies," 33–36; Naddaf, "Précurseur," 348; Cornford, Principium, 220.

21. See Will, "Observations," 11; Naddaf, "Précurseur," 357; van Groningen, Composition, 268; Otto, Gods, 171: "Harmony becomes unity in the person of Zeus, who not only stands above the gods as supreme power and directs great destinies according to his will, but also appears as exponent of divine sway in general, so that it is he who is effective in all and to whom all prayers rise."

22. See also Hesiod's request that the Muses declare ὥς τ' ἄφενος δάσσαντο καὶ ὡς τιμὰς διέλοντο, / ἠδὲ καὶ ὡς τὰ πρῶτα πολύπτυχον ἔσχον Ὄλυμπον ("How their wealth was distributed and their honors divided, / And how at first they held many-folded Olympus" Th. 112–13). The poem the Muses have been asked to sing is, of course, the Theogony itself. See Walcot, "Prooemium," 42–43, for this ring and, for ring-composition in the Theogony overall, "The Text of Hesiod's Theogony and the Hittite Epic of Kumarbi," Classical Quarterly, n.s., 6 (1956): 198–206. Within the outer ring of Proem and Zeus' children Walcot sees two succession myths on either side of the Zeus–Prometheus encounter.

23. The importance of this theme to Hesiod can be seen in the care he takes to have it run throughout the narrative, despite chronology. The honors granted Styx (Th. 389–403), Hecate (Th. 414–52), and Zeus' heroic sons (Th. 270–336) are described not only out of chronological sequence, but even before Zeus' birth.

24. On Zeus' cooptation of the old gods into his new order see Solmsen, Aeschylus, 75; Walcot, "Prooemium," 42; Otto, Gods, 17; van Groningen, Composition, 265; and, on Hecate, Griffith, "Personality," 53. N. O. Brown, Hesiod's "Theogony", Library of Liberal Arts (Indianapolis: Bobbs-Merrill, 1953), 11 points out Hesiod's "systematic concern with showing how Zeus integrates older powers into his new order." Mondi, however, in "Zeus," 334, sees the placement as due to genealogical considerations.

25. Hesiod's desire to coopt the old gods into Zeus' order provides yet another reason for the Typhoeus episode, so that Zeus can have a battle to win single-handedly. See Walcot, "Kumarbi," 205 and Said, "Combats," 208.

26. Iliad 15.185–99; Pindar Olympians 7, 55; Hymn to Hermes, 425 ff. On this theme see Francis MacDonald Cornford, From Religion to Philosophy: A Study in the Origins of Western

Speculation (London: Arnold,1912), 15–29; Hesiod's deliberate avoidance of the expected division is discussed by Hamilton, *Architecture*, 20; Kirk, "Structure," 87; Verdenius, "Proem," 259; Solmsen, *Aeschylus*, 15, n. 31; Robert Mondi, "Tradition and Innovation in Hesiodic Titanomachy," *Transactions of the American Philological Association* 116 (1986): 38. The tradition that Zeus himself achieved his place by lot Hesiod smothers with silence, preferring a guiding, if undemocratic, intelligence to a cosmos assigned by chance. See Adkins, "Cosmogony," 64, n. 11.

27. Hence it is Zeus who receives the emphasis in a line (*Th.* 428) that parallels both the introduction of Hecate above (*Th.* 411–12) and the final lines of the ring pattern: θῆκε δέ μιν Κρονίδης κουροτρόφον, οἳ μετ' ἐκείνην / ὀφθαλμοῖσιν ἴδοντο φάος πολυδερκέος 'Ηοῦς. / οὕτως ἐξ ἀρχῆς κουροτρόφος, αἳ δέ τε τιμαί ("And the son of Cronos made her a nurse of the young, who, afterwards, / Saw with their eyes the light of all-seeing Dawn. Thus was / She from the first a nurse of the young, and these are her honors" *Th.* 450–52). Similarly, Zeus is said to have distributed to Atlas his μοῖρα at *Th.* 520.

28. For the human logic of this equation see Cornford, *Religion*, 16 and Adkins, *Merit*, 20–21, *Values*, 22. West, *Th.*, 180, glosses the gods' τιμάς as their "provinces" or "spheres of influence," clearly akin to their μοῖραι. The connection of αἶσα and μοῖρα with τιμαί, in the formulaic phrase ἔμμορε τιμῆς "to have a μοῖρα of honors," clarifies Hesiod's association of the distribution of honors and the divine order.

29. For the relation of μοῖρα, αἶσα, and τιμή see Yamagata, *Morality*, 95–121; W. Pötscher, "Moira, Themis und τιμή im homerischen Denken," *Wiener Studien* 73 (1960): 5–39.

30. Arthur W. H. Adkins, "Law versus Claims in Early Greek Religious Ethics," *History of Religions* 21 (1982): 222–29.

31. Barron and Easterling, "Hesiod," 96. Hesiod gives the evil abstractions of the *Theogony* their own line of descent, but this seems due more to their negative nature than to a view of them as different in kind.

32. West, *Th.*, 33; Vernant, "Mètis," 29–30.

33. West, 144. In Otto's phrase, *Gods*, 43, Zeus is "the epitome of the divine."

34. At *Th.* 1002 the account of Jason's marriage to Medea, and of the birth and rearing of Medeius, is closed with the phrase "And the mind of great Zeus was accomplished" (μεγάλου δὲ Διὸς νόος ἐξετελεῖτο). Zeus has not previously been mentioned, but the two events which lead to the birth of Medeius, the marriage of Aestes and Idyia which produces Medea, and her abduction by Jason, are both said to be "by the counsel of the gods" (θεῶν βουλῇσιν *Th.* 960, βουλῇσι θεῶν αἰειγενετάων *Th.* 993), a formula which is used nowhere else in the closing genealogies of the *Theogony*. West, 431, suggests that Hesiod implies a great destiny for Medeius, e.g., as ancestor of the Medes.

35. Blumenberg, *Work on Myth*, 31.

36. See *Th.* 73–74, emended by van Lennep from ἀθανάτοις διέταξεν ὁμῶς καὶ ἐπέφραδε τιμάς ("To the immortals he ordained alike and declared out their honors") to ἀθανάτοις διέταξε νόμους καὶ ἐπέφραδε τιμάς ("To the immortals he ordained their ways and declared out their honors"). The emendation is supported by *WD* 276: τόνδε γὰρ ἀνθρώποισι νόμον διέταξε Κρονίων ("For this νόμος the son of Cronos ordained for man"), and refers back to the subject of the Muses song above: πάντων τε νόμους καὶ ἤθεα κεδνὰ / ἀθανάτων ("Of all the immortals, the νόμοι and goodly ways" *Th.* 66–67). It also reflects Hesiod's usual style of doubling both verb and object, e.g., ὥς τ' ἄφενος δάσσαντο καὶ ὡς τιμὰς διέλοντο ("How they shared out their wealth and distributed honors" *Th.* 112). For a defense of the emendation see West, *Th.*, 180, who prints it. Verdenius, "Proem," 249, rejects the emendation and its implicit association of νόμοι and τιμαί.

37. There is little doubt that Hesiod's *Theogony* ended somewhat before ours, although exactly where remains a matter of speculation. As it is extremely unlikely that Hesiod would

have omitted the birth of the gods introduced in the poem's opening lines (*Th.* 13–14), Hesiod's poem must have ended somewhere after 929. West, who alone among scholars doubts 901–29, admits that these lines "even if not worded by Hesiod himself, correspond fairly closely to his intentions" (*Th.* 399). West's arguments against the ending of the *Theogony* as we have it, moreover, generally apply to later lines, the objections to 901–29 resting on two phrases unusual in Hesiod, but admittedly formulaic. See West, *Th.*, 398 for other proposed ending points, all beyond line 928, Northrup, "*Theogony*" for an argument against West's position; and Hamilton, *Architecture*, 96–99. This analysis is based on a Hesiodic text continuing minimally to 929, although I have no objection to a later ending point.

38. Marylin B. Arthur, "The Dream of a World without Women," *Arethusa* 16 (1983): 97 and Solmsen, *Aeschylus*, 65: "The Proem in which [Hesiod] celebrates the wisdom and beneficial influence of the Muses presents a picture of the world order of Zeus as established and existent, the same world order which we see emerge only at the end of the poem." The return also refers us to a sense of time as cyclical, as in the *Works and Days*, rather than linear, as in the narrative of the *Theogony*. See Walcot, "Composition," 9; Beye, *Literature*, 109, 120; Vernant, *Myth and Thought*, 58–59; and Mary Matossian, "The Peasant Way of Life" in Wayne Vucinich, ed., *The Peasant in Nineteenth Century Russia* (Stanford: Stanford University Press, 1968), 40, for a Hesiodic, and peasant, circular sense of time. In contrast, see Naddaf, "Précurseur," 339–64. O'Flaherty, *Evil*, 35–45 and "Pluralism," 222, describes the Hindu sense of linear and circular time.

39. Hence the Proem is a hymn not to Zeus, but to Zeus through his children, the Muses. Zeus, whose only act is begetting the Muses, is introduced with the dance of his children around their father's altar (*Th.* 11–13). He is described once as father of Athene (*Th.* 13) and seven times as the father of the Muses (*Th.* 25, 29, 52, 72, 76, 81,104). P. Friedländer, "Das Proömium von Hesiods Theogonie," in Ernst Heitsch, ed., *Hesiod* (Darmstadt: Wissenschaftliche Buchgesellschaft, 1966), 277–94, points to the Muses' birth, entry to Olympus, and τιμαί as characteristic parts of their hymn. See also William W. Minton, "The Proem-Hymn of Hesiod's *Theogony*," *Transactions of the American Philological Association* 101 (1970): 357–77; and Edward M. Bradley, "The Relevance of the Prooemium to the Design and Meaning of Hesiod's *Theogony*," *Symbolae Osloenses* 41 (1966): 29–47, for the use of the hymn form in the Proem. As Hesiod begins and ends with the Muses, the Muses begin and end with Zeus, "the father of gods and men" (Ζῆνα θεῶν πατέρ' ἠδὲ καὶ ἀνδρῶν *Th.* 47). After the swallowing of Wisdom, Zeus is mentioned by name eleven times. In seven of these cases he is simply the father. In seven other cases Zeus is the understood subject. In all of these he is the father.

40. Zeus' awarding of the greatest honor to the Portioners (Moirai) (*Th.* 904) simply confirms their position as the Portioners of the new order. Zeus gives his daughter Persephone to Hades not as originating but as confirming the act (*Th.* 913–14). He confirms Ariadne's accession to Olympus by making her deathless and unchanging, as the wife of his son Dionysus (*Th.* 949).

41. The role of the Muses as Zeus' intermediaries has been much studied. See E. Bradley, "Prooemium," 34; Patricia A. Marquardt, "The Two Faces of Hesiod's Muse," *Illinois Classical Studies* 7 (1982), 3; Duban, "Invocation," 13; Kurt von Fritz, "Das Proömium der Hesiodischen Theogonie," in Heitsch, *Hesiod*, 295–315.

42. Lloyd-Jones, *Justice*, 49: "we must note how often and how emphatically the gods, and Zeus and Apollo in particular, are identified with order, peace, and harmony, in contrast with the forces of brute strength and violence." See Martin Ostwald, *Nomos and the Beginnings of the Athenian Democracy* (Oxford: Clarendon Press, 1969), 63, for Eunomia as characteristic of Zeus' order, and West, *Th.*, 408 on the Horai and Moirai. For the significance of Zeus' wives and children, Solmsen, *Aeschylus*, 55; Naddaf, "Précurseur," 354; Cornford, *Principium*, 248; G. Nagy, "Hesiod," 60; Walcot, "Prooemium," 43; Northrup, "Personification," 225 and "*Theogony*", 7.

43. It is unlikely that this is a case of either Hesiod or an interpolator nodding. The birth of the Moirai, who are basic in any understanding of Greek religion, is not like the death of a passing warrior—a poet is not likely to forget that he already told this story. Nor, for that matter, is so much as a Nereid's birth ever repeated elsewhere in the *Theogony*. For the two sets of Moirai see West, *Th.*, 408, and Northrup, "Personification," 227, n. 13, summarizing arguments for and against interpolation. Solmsen, *Aeschylus*, 37 suggests that the first Moirai imply "the abandonment of all hope for a rational and moral direction of man's life" and/or a restriction of their role to revenge, while as "daughters of Zeus and Themis . . . the Moirai are agents of a stern but fundamentally just world order. What they give man is beyond repeal (Atropos!) but they give both good and bad."

44. Cornford, *Religion*, 19 sees in the Moirai "the departmental ordering of the world" and the "primary world-order," both moral and physical, which was usurped by Zeus. For other versions of Zeus' association with the Moirai see Nilsson, *History*, 168–72.; Otto, *Gods*, 283.

45. If we accept *WD* 218–19 these lines refer to the Moirai, if not, to the associated Κῆρες. Hesiod's Erinyes are born from the castration of Ouranos (*Th.* 185) and play no further role in the poem. West, *Hesiod*, 9 translates Κῆρας (to whom he thinks *Th.* 220–22 apply) as "Furies," commenting, 65, "literally Dooms, but in function hard to distinguish from the Erinyes of 185." See Solmsen, *Aeschylus*, 88; C. M. Bowra, "A Prayer to the Fates," *Classical Quarterly*, n.s., 8 (1958): 231–40; and Jeannie Carlier, "The Moirai," in Bonnefoy, *Mythologies*, 1.491, for the links between the Moirai and the Furies.

46. West, *Th.*,229: "one's fate is fixed at birth," with citations. See also John Cuthbert Lawson, *Modern Greek Folklore and Ancient Greek Religion: A Study in Survivals* (Cambridge: Cambridge University Press, 1910; reprint, New Hyde Park, N.Y.: University Books, 1964), 121–30 for the belief in Greek rural communities that the Fates visit a newborn child.

47. If we accept lines 219–20 (= 905–6) it is interesting to note that the minor change from βροτοῖσι / γεινομένοισι διδοῦσι to διδοῦσι / θνητοῖς ἀνθρώποισιν has significantly altered the meaning. The repeated phrase, "of good and of evil" (ἀγαθόν τε κακόν τε), is formulaic, but not common in Hesiod. It is consequently notable that the only other time it is used in the *Theogony* is five lines above, of Zeus' swallowing of Wisdom: "But Zeus beforehand put her into his belly / So that for him might be the goddess' contriving of good and of evil" (ἀλλ' ἄρα μιν Ζεὺς πρόσθεν ἑὴν ἐσκάτθετο νηδύν, / ὡς δή οἱ φράσσαιτο θεὰ ἀγαθόν τε κακόν τε *Th.* 899–900).

48. Although both Zeus and Cronos are pictured by Hesiod as youngest sons, in accordance with what West, *Th.*, 204 calls "a favorite motif in folk-lore," outside of the succession myth Hesiod identifies the eldest child as the most significant. For example, the good Strife (*WD* 17–19), Styx (*Th.* 361, 777), the Oceanids important enough to be named (*Th.* 363), Nereus (*Th.* 234–35) and, perhaps, Calliope (see *Phaedrus* 259d and West, *Th.*, 39), are all eldest children. See also the *Shield of Heracles* 259–60); and Solmsen, *Aeschylus*, 24. In the *Iliad* Zeus too is the oldest son (15.201–4). Near Eastern and other parallels, e.g., Jacob and Rachel in Genesis, suggest that Hesiod, in portraying Zeus as the youngest child, is working from an older tradition which outweighed his general inclination to identify the most important child as the eldest, for which see Caldwell, "Theogony," 164. The Seasons' importance also appears in their being born directly after Zeus accession as king, also the basis of Xerxes' claim to the throne (Herodotus 7.2–3).

49. Given the nature of gods, Right, Zeus' second wife, would not naturally be the mother of his first children. Hesiod was unwilling to see Peace, Justice, and Good Order as the children of any mother except Right, but could not, as Pindar did (fr. 10), make Right Zeus' *first* wife, since he sees the swallowing of Wisdom as Zeus' final consolidation of his reign. Hesiod, therefore, has Athene's birth, predicted at *Th.* 895, not occur until *Th.* 924. Athene thus gets to be both the first and last born—like her father before her. Despite the marriages that follow, Hes-

iod marks off *Th.* 886–929 as a separate section by describing Wisdom as Zeus' first wife, and Hera as his last (*Th.* 886, 921).

50. To the extent that the divine triad of the *Works and Days*, Zeus, Justice, and Demeter, could be seen equally well as Zeus, the center of the cosmic order, together with his particular manifestations in justice and in farming. See Waltz, *Poème moral*, 75; Hays, "Notes," 57.

51. See Lloyd-Jones, *Justice*, 160, on Greek religion as neither poly- nor mono-theistic.

52. West opens this paragraph at line 381 although Solmsen, review, 216, Sinclair, "*Works and Days*", 41; and West himself, 254, point out the dramatic opening of the three-word line.

53. Mazon, *Les Travaux et les jours*, 101, points out that each of Hesiod's seasons begins with a celestial sign that reveals to men the order of god. These "natural" gods are far more common in the *Works and Days* than the Olympians are, who are limited to Poseidon (*WD* 665), Apollo and Leto (*WD* 771), and Dionysus (*WD* 614). Hamilton, *Architecture*, 56–57 sees a diminution of the gods' importance in the second half of the *Works and Days*, marked by just this tendency to become meteorological. On the Greek feeling for the divinity of nature see Frisch, *Might*, 189; Otto, *Gods*, 161 ff., 220; Burkert, *Religion*, 174–76. See Nilsson, *Piety*, 186, and Dodds, *Irrational*, 244, for the tendency of such beliefs to linger in the countryside; and Sanders, *Rainbow*, 15; Bourdieu, *Algerian Peasant*, 57; and Lawson, *Survivals*, 89 for modern peasants. See also Walcot, *Peasants*, 20: "The close link in religious belief between ancient and modern Greek is brought vividly home when Friedl, speaking of God as an omnipresent force in the lives of men, remarks that the villagers of Vasilika attribute 'to God, rather than to nature as an abstraction, . . . common physical phenomena,' and then quotes the expression 'God is raining' (Friedl, 78)", quoting Ernestine Friedl, *Vasilika: A Village in Modern Greece* (New York: Holt, Rinehart and Winston, 1962).

54. Also "the holy stream of Ocean" (*WD* 566), "rosy-fingered dawn" (*WD* 610), "the strength of Orion" (*WD* 598, 615, 619), and the carpenter, "the servant of Athene" (*WD* 430).

55. Mazon, *Les Travaux et les jours*, 146; J. Harrison, *Themis*, 97.

56. Francis, "Personality," 283; Detienne, *Crise agraire*, 40.

57. Grene, "Religion," 158: "The landscape includes everything from the warning cry of the cranes, which signals the beginning of plowing, to the watchfulness for the plow beams, which may be worm-eaten, to the struggle, naked, with the toil of harvest, to the picnic afterward." The servant of Athene has his role to play in growing the grain of Demeter; and even Poseidon has his honor among farmers (*WD* 430, 667). See also West, 300, and Adkins, "Ethics," 280. Waltz, *Poème moral*, 107, points out the immediacy of Hesiod's description of nature. See Lawson, *Survivals*, 342 for modern peasants.

58. As they did in life, see Jeannie Carlier, "Orion" and "The Pleiades," in Bonnefoy, *Mythologies*, 1.500–1, 510.

59. The "measures of the sea" are clearly not distances, as in Herodotus 1.47. Nor does Hesiod mention any "rules and formulae known to the expert" (West, 318), or "lois qui régissent l'état de la mer" (Mazon, *Les Travaux et les jours*, 136), although this seems closer to his conception.

60. Hence Hesiod's unusual willingness to discuss a subject of which he has no experience. For less commonplace interpretations of Hesiod's knowledge of the mind of Zeus, see Ralph M. Rosen, "Poetry and Sailing in Hesiod's *Works and Days*," *California Studies in Classical Antiquity* 9 (1990): 99–113; Lamberton, *Hesiod*, 125–26; Walcot, "Law," 7; Jensen, "Tradition," 25–26; Griffith, "Personality," 62. In contrast, West, 55, notices the severe limitations to Hesiod's knowledge: "Hesiod speaks as a confessed landlubber, and he speaks only of what can be seen from the land: loading, launching, returning, laying up for the winter. There is nothing about controlling the vessel at sea or finding direction by the stars."

61. For the "seasonableness" of the Days see van Groningen, *Composition*, 263; Waltz, *Poème moral*, 70; Detienne, *Crise agraire*, 40.

62. Vernant, *Society*, 109; Nilsson, *History*, 171; Burkert, *Religion*, 131; Kirk, *Myth*, 239.

63. Benardete, "First Reading," 164; J. Harrison, *Themis*, 184. See Nilsson, *History*, 121; Burkert, *Religion*, 126; Kirk, *Myth*, 7, for Zeus' role as weather god, and 90, for the chief god as weather god in other cultures. See Sanders, *Rainbow*, 171, for the belief that God regulates the modern Greek peasant's life through the seasons and weather.

63. The contrast of Hesiod's peaceful, peasant ethics and Homer's (archaized) warlike aristocratic code dates back at least as far as *The Contest of Homer and Hesiod*. See R. Redfield, *Peasant*, 112; Adkins, *Merit*, 71–73; Barron and Easterling, "Hesiod," 99; Jaeger, *Paideia*, 1,62, 70–3; Francis, "Personality," 292–93; Detienne, *Crise agraire*, 17; K. McKay, "Ambivalent," 26; Yamagata, *Morality*, 85. A feeling for the importance of honor continues among Greek peasants; see, for example, Campbell, *Honor*, 263–321. Walcot, *Peasants*, 57–65 does not sufficiently allow for the distinction between Hesiod's sense of social status, earned through hard work, and the jealous and violent standards of honor of the Homeric warrior, or of Campbell's modern Greek shepherd, for which see Wolf, *Peasants*, 69; Julian Pitt-Rivers, "Introduction," in Pitt-Rivers, *Countrymen*, 15. Yamagata, 87–88 goes on to point out that, alongside the different societies taken as their points of reference, a large part of the difference between the poets is that Homer speaks from an omniscient, Hesiod from a purely human perspective.

65. See Dodds, *Irrational*, 29; Lloyd-Jones, *Justice*, 4, 36; Adkins, *Merit*, 63: "The maintenance of his *time* is the chief aim of Homeric man and Homeric god; and god, like man, ever fears that it may be diminished." See also Adkins, *Many*, 36. See Martin Nilsson, *Homer and Mycenae* (London: Methuen, 1933; repr., Philadelphia: University of Pennsylvania Press, 1972), 266–72 (page references are to reprint edition); Lloyd-Jones, *Justice*, 6–7; Finley, *Odysseus*, 83, 132–34.

66. See Starr, *Growth*, 49 and J. Redfield, "Sparta," 9–10, on the changing sense of ἀρετή. For the contrast with a farming community Adkins, *Merit*, 255.

67. Waltz, *Poème moral*, 61; Francis, "Personality," 285. On honor among modern peasants, Banfield, *Basis*, 73; Friedl, *Vasilika*, 37.

68. Hesiod speaks of "honor" when he is describing the gods or the relations of human beings and gods. Unlike Homer, he does not use the word of purely human relations. Forms of τιμή are used twenty-five times in the *Theogony* and *Works and Days* in contexts in which the gods are involved, and only three times (*WD* 185,192, 347) in a context of human relations. Two of these occur in the rather epic description of the Iron Age, and the third, *WD* 347, West, 244, glosses: "not 'honour,' as in the Homeric formula ἔμμορε τιμῆς, but probably 'good value'; one can imagine the phrase applied to someone who barters something for something fully as valuable." For some speculations on why τιμή is not more important to Hesiod, see Apostolos N. Athanassakis, "Cattle and Honour in Homer and Hesiod," *Ramus* 21 (1992): 156–86.

69. Libations, *WD* 724–26; sacrifice, *WD* 336–40, 755–56; prayer to Zeus and Demeter, *WD* 465–67. Hesiod's final summation of what is necessary for happiness, *WD* 826–28, mentions not sacrifice, libations, and prayer, but understanding, justice, and hard work. Nilsson's description of Hesiod's religion as "legalistic" (*Piety*, 31–33) misses Hesiod's emphasis. For Hesiod, Zeus' order includes taboos and lucky and unlucky days just as it contains the order of the seasons. What Hesiod emphasizes in both cases is the *knowledge* of the gods' requirements, rather than the propitiation of particular gods.

70. Hence the end of the Silver race, the importance of respecting the sun, the night, and rivers, the need to sacrifice (*WD* 336–40), and the Muses' command (*Th.* 33–35).

71. Hesiod's highest praise, even of Hecate, is that Zeus honors her (*Th.* 411–52). More generally see Beye, *Literature*, 119; Adkins, "Cosmogony," 49; Vernant, *Society*, 103; and van Groningen, *Composition*, 268: "Hésiode est profondément croyant, mais, en sa qualité de bâtisseur de système, l'objet de sa foi est le monde divin comme ensemble, et non point tel ou tel dieu particulier." See also George M. Foster, "Peasant Society and the Image of Limited Good," in

Jack M. Potter, May N. Diaz, and George M. Foster, eds., *Peasant Society: A Reader* (Boston: Little, Brown, 1967), 326.

72. In fact, at 2.325–27 Father Sky (*pater Aether*) has replaced Jupiter in this role.

73. Thomas, *Virgil*, 1.68–73

74. See O'Flaherty, *Evil*, 1–3, on theodicies.

75. See Thomas, *Virgil*, 1.90; Farrell, *Tradition*, 147. The parallel is reinforced by Jupiter's hiding of fire at 1.131, a reference to the Prometheus myth.

76. Many scholars have accepted this, Vergil's initial explanation, as final, not noting Vergil's switch from the Golden to the Iron Age and the violence with which it is accomplished. See, for example, Lovejoy and Boas, *Primitivism*, 370; Rand, *Magical Art*, 202; L. P. Wilkinson, "Virgil's Theodicy," *Classical Quarterly*, n.s., 13 (1963): 75–84; Inez Scott Ryberg, "Vergil's Golden Age," *Transactions of the American Philological Association* 89 (1958): 119–22; Perret, "Georgics," 32–34; Griffin, *Virgil*, 45; Wilkinson, *Survey*, 137 ff; and Eva M. Stehle, "Virgil's *Georgics* and the Threat of Sloth," *Transactions of the American Philological Association* 104 (1974): 347–69. Otis, *Virgil*, 158 ff. sees the theodicy as our connection to nature; Bayet, "Premières," 238, as Vergil's reconciliation of Hesiod's bleak view of farming with Aratus' ideal vision of farming as the just life. For positive views which connect the theodicy with the theme of *labor* throughout the Vergilian corpus, see Annic Loupiac, "Le Labor chez Virgile: essai d'interprétation," *Revue des Études Latines* 70 (1992): 92–106, and Susan Scheinberg Kristol, *"Labor" and "Fortuna" in Vergil's "Aeneid"* (New York: Garland, 1990), 129–37.

For less positive interpretations see Heinrich Altevogt, *"Labor Improbus": Eine Vergilstudie* (Munich: Aschendorff, 1952); Putnam, *Earth*, 30–35; A. La Penna, "Esiodo nella cultura e nella poesia di Virgilio," in *Hésiode et son influence*, 220 ff.; Thomas, *Virgil*, 1.17, 87–93; Miles, *Interpretation*, 79 ff. Vergil's description of the arts neglects to mention the ends at which they are aimed, leaving the reader with a disquieting sense of violence simply begetting violence. Note also the perversity of Vergil's account, where men go hungry in order to learn to fish, rather than vice versa. See Christine G. Perkell, "Vergil's Theodicy Reconsidered," in Bernard, *Virgil at 2000*, 74 and overall for the theodicy's negative side.

77. Perkell, *Truth*, 54.

78. This concept of divinity is also expressed in the gadfly who torments Io earlier in the third Georgic (compare 3.150–53 and 3.551–55), in Mars (1.511), and in Allecto (*Aeneid* 10.761 ff.). See Thomas, *Virgil*, 2.144.

79. Vergil's "And hence are the flocks and the herds, men, all kinds of beasts" (*hinc pecudes, armenta, viros, genus omne ferarum* 4.223) here recalls his earlier descriptions of sex and death: "Each single race on earth, man and beast" (*Omne adeo genus in terris hominumque ferarumque* 3.428) and "And gave over to death all kinds of cattle, all kinds of wild beast" (*et genus omne neci pecudum dedit, omne ferarum* 3.480). See Rand, *Magical Art*, 322–23; R. D. Williams, *Virgil: The "Eclogues" and "Georgics"* (Basingstoke: Macmillan Education, 1979), xii; Parry, "Art," 43–44; and Ruch, "Virgile," 326.

80. See P. Hardie, *Cosmos*, 330; and Dodds, *Irrational*, 247: "The old religious dualism of mind and matter, God and Nature, the soul and the appetites, which rationalist thought had striven to overcome, reasserts itself in fresh forms and with a fresh vigor," and 248: "The adoration of the visible cosmos, and the sense of unity with it which had found expression in early Stoicism, began to be replaced in many minds by a feeling that the physical world—at any rate, the part of it below the moon—is under the sway of evil powers, and that what the soul needs is not unity with it but escape from it."

81. Hence the contrast between Italy, the peaceful land of Saturn, and the Trojans' decent from Jove in *Aeneid* 7 (55–61, 267–91). The etymological oxymoron "Dodona negaret" (1.149) noted by Clifford Weber, "Dodona Reneges: A Neglected Oxymoron in *Georgics* 1.149," *Classical Philology* 86 (1991): 323–27, points to the same contradiction.

82. Otis, "New Study," 47, and see Farrell, *Tradition*, 131–68 for Vergil's allusions to Hesiod and Aratus. Farrell sees the structure of Book 1 as bipartite, reflecting first Hesiod's "Works" and then his "Days."

83. Connor, "Description," 49; Bayet, "Premières," 242.

84. For example, at 1.104–17 the movement from irrigation to drainage is interrupted by two lines (1.111–12) of advice on grazing down the crops. See Rand, *Magical Art*, 205.

85. Otis, "New Study," 51 points out the switch in topics. On Vergil's interest in means and extremes, particularly in balancing the four elements, see K. W. Gransden, review of *Virgil: the "Eclogues and Georgics"*, by R. D. Williams, *Virgil's Poem of the Earth: Studies in the "Georgics"*, by Michael C. J. Putnam, *Narrative and Simile from the "Georgics" in the "Aeneid"*, by Ward W. Briggs, and *Vergil's Agricultural Golden Age: A Study of the "Georgics"*, by Patricia A. Johnston, *Journal of Roman Studies* 72 (1982), 209; Ross, *Elements*, 38–46 and passim; Aya Betensky, "The Farmer's Battles," *Ramus* 8 (1979): 115–16; and Otis, *Virgil*, 164.

86. Eratosthenes is Vergil's direct model here; see Thomas, *Virgil*, 1.107.

87. Despite 1.238 this is Lucretius' (5.200–17) proof that the gods do not care for mankind. See Farrell, *Traditon*, 172 ff.; Thomas, *Virgil*, 1.108–9. Miles, *Interpretation*, 95 accepts the gods' good will at face value

88. Putnam, *Earth*, 6, 59,122. This is a technique Vergil employs often. Here the zones follow a description of how the farmer suits his sowing to the season. An interesting example involving the farmer himself occurs at 3.322–83, where the pastoral Italian shepherd is revealed as standing midway between the ever-wandering African and the immobile Scythian.

89. And which the earth now bears spontaneously, as it once bore grain (1.127–28; 184–85).

90. Turning Hesiod's Ὅρκος, god of Oaths, into the Roman Orcus, god of the underworld, a rather black pun. See Thomas, *Virgil*, 1.115–16; Farrell, 123, for the confusion of the Giants, the Aloidae, and Typhoeus. On the implied violence, Putnam, *Earth*, 145 ff.; Ross, *Elements*, 76; Lyne, "Scilicet," 54.

91. See Farrell, *Tradition*, 219–21; Thomas, *Virgil*, 1.121–22 for the comparison. Briggs, *Narrative*, 83, 93 sees the storm as punishment for man's neglect of the heavens. On the storm's violence Briggs, 85; Revard, "Vergil's *Georgics*," 271. A. G. McKay, "Virgilian Landscape into Art: Poussin, Claude and Turner," in D. R. Dudley, ed., *Virgil* (New York: Basic Books, 1969), 155–57, compares Vergil's image of human frailty in the face of nature's violence to Turner's paintings. On Jupiter see Thomas, *Virgil*, 1.123.

92. Vergil's reassurance: *numquam imprudentibus imber / obfuit* ("Never has a rainstorm / Injured imprudent men" or "Never has a rainstorm / Injured men who were unwarned" 1.373–74) is a double edged sword. Vergil is not declaring that men are never injured by a storm; he is saying that there is always a warning first The destruction—*obfuit* is enjambed for emphasis—happens nonetheless. Mynors, *"Georgics"*, 80, reports attempts to correct the meaning. See also Thomas, *Virgil*, 1.120–21, 131, 149; Putnam, "Achievement," 55; Ross, *Elements*, 89–93.

93. Otis, "New Study," 49; Putnam, *Earth*, 50. Lyne, "Scilicet," 50, 60 points to the repetition of *concurrere*, 1.318 and 489, first of the violence of the storm, then of the violence of civil war, the only two occurrences in the first Georgic. See also Rand, *Magical Art*, 225 and Miles, *Interpretation*, 107.

94. See Lyne, "Scilicet," 58, 62; Bayet, "Premières," 245; Boyle, *Dove*, 52; Gary B. Miles, "Amor and Civilization," *California Studies in Classical Antiquity* 8 (1980): 188; Sellar, *Roman Poets*, 259. Lucretius (2.264 ff.) uses the image of horses starting from the barrier to illustrate the slight hesitation before the will moves the body. In Vergil the hesitation is gone and with it, perhaps, the free will. Hence also the incomprehension of the future farmers of Philippi—such violence cannot be understood (1.491–97).

95. So, on the *Aeneid*, Johnson, *Darkness*, 152: "Since [Vergil] is prevented by his grasp of Epicurus and by the tragic history of his country from giving full allegiance to the concept of the rational cosmos, reified evil refuses to be subordinate to the grand and rational design, insists on its own way, rushes off into the deeper darkness, bearing with it the meaning of history and the dream of rational freedom."

96. Wilkinson, *Survey*, 85. On the abruptness of the transition see Boyle, *Dove*, 47–48, and 54–56 on the second Georgic overall. See also Griffin, *Virgil*, 45–46; Revard, "Vergil's *Georgics*," 265; Miles, *Interpretation*, 132. Harry Berger, "Archaism, Vision, and Revision: Studies in Virgil, Plato, and Milton," *Centennial Review* 11 (1967): 30, in contrast, feels that the abruptness of the transition reveals only the unreality of Book 2.

97. Thomas, at 2.52, reads *voces*. See Thomas, *Virgil*, 1.166; Mynors, "*Georgics*", 107 for this reading. Note also how the rough monosyllables of 2.49 are gradually smoothed into the regular rhythm of 2.51–52, as nature and culture adapt themselves to each other. For a very different view of the relation, see Thomas, "Prose," 253–60.

98. Thomas, *Virgil*, 1.260.

99. Underlined by the repetition of the slow heavy line, *agricola incurvo terram molitus aratro* (1.494), used at the end of Book 1 to describe the amazed farmers of Phillippi. See Wilkinson, "Intention," 23.

100. See Ross, *Elements*, 135; Miles, *Interpretation*, 135.

101. On the change in tone Miles, *Interpretation*, 144–46; Ross, *Elements*, 141–42.

102. See Jenny Strauss Clay, "The Argument of the End of Vergil's Second Georgic," *Philologus* 120 (1976): 234–35

103. For Vergil's deep feeling for nature see A. Bosson, *Études agronomiques sur les "Géorgiques" de Virgile* (Paris: A. Lévy, 1869), ix–x; Sellar, *Roman Poets*, 10–14, 33–35; Elfriede Abbe, *The Plants of Virgil's "Georgics"* (Ithaca: Cornell University Press, 1965), xi; W. Ward Fowler in Royds, *Beasts*, viii–xiii; and, for more recent interpretations, Otis, *Virgil*, 384–89; Wilkinson, *Survey*, 13 ff.; R. D. Williams, *Virgil*, x–xi; Revard, "Vergil's *Georgics*," 262.

For Vergil's "lies," see Perkell, "Reading," 215–16; Thomas, *Virgil*, 1.21, 161, 244–45, and "Prose," 244–46; and, especially, Ross, *Elements*, 105–22. For Vergil's "mistakes," see White, *Farming*, 56; Wilkinson, *Survey*, 235 ff.; Bosson, *Études*, 208, 223; Jermyn, "Agricultural Lore," 209. For Vergil's preferring effect to accuracy, see Farrell, *Tradition*, 330–31. Noricum is landlocked, so Vergil's slaughter of fish, at least, is exaggerated. See Royds, *Beasts*, 23, 26; E. L. Harrison, "The Noric Plague in Vergil's Third Georgic," *Papers of the Liverpool Latin Seminar*, vol. 2: *Virgil and Roman Elegy, Medieval Latin Poetry and Prose, Greek Lyric and Drama*, ed. Francis Cairns (Liverpool: Francis Cairns, 1979), 1–6; Farrell, *Tradition*, 84–94; and D. West's conclusion ("Plagues," 79) that Vergil's plague "is emotionally effective, rhetorically arresting by means of paradox and pathos, and has no regard for historical or scientific truth."

On the bees, see Royds, 66–68; Wilkinson, *Survey*, 179. On the stallion, Royds, 6. Grafting can only occur within the same family of trees. Bees never fight on the wing.

104. Wendy Doniger O'Flaherty, *Asceticism and Eroticism in the Mythology of Siva* (Oxford: Oxford Univesity Press, 1973), 33–39, discusses a similar use of contradictory extremes in Hindu myth.

105. As also with the destroyers of the threshing floor at 1.181–86. See Briggs, *Narrative*, 56; Jermyn, "Agricultural Lore," 59, and "Weather-Signs in Virgil," *Greece and Rome* 20 (1951): 34–35.

106. Perkell, *Truth*, 157.

107. The horse under control introduces the third Georgic (3.17–18) only to succumb to sexual fury at the center of the book (3.266–89, hence Vergil's emphasis on *hippomanes*, "horse-madness" (3.280, 282) and to the madness caused by the plague at the book's end (3.499–514).

CHAPTER 5

1. As in the Near Eastern parallels to the *Theogony*, see Walcot, *Near East*, 55–79. Reynal Sorel, "Finalité et origine des hommes chez Hésiode," *Revue de Metaphysique et de Morale* 87 (1982): 24–30; Naddaf, "Précurseur," 353; and Vernant, *Myth and Thought*, 238 argue that the Prometheus myth is essentially a creation myth, although not presented as such by Hesiod. See Penglase, *Greek Myths*, 197–209 for parallels. In Genesis, of course, the creation of the cosmos culminates in two accounts of the creation of man, corresponding to Mircea Eliade's two types of mythic primordiality, one of cosmic, and one of human origins (see "Cosmogonic Myth and 'Sacred History'," in Dundes, *Sacred Narrative*, 150–51). It is the latter that is missing in Hesiod

2. For example, in the existence of gods such as "Killings-of-Men" (Ἀνδροκτασία *WD* 228) or the honors of Aphrodite which, "from the beginning" (ἐξ ἀρχῆς) were "among men and immortal gods" (ἐν ἀνθρώποισι καὶ ἀθανάτοισι θεοῖσι *Th*. 204).

3. Men appear in the Proem, as victims of the monsters destroyed by the sons of Zeus, in the description of Hecate, in the account of Prometheus, as the passive recipient of evil, as the victims of Sleep and Death, in the description of Tartarus, and, at the end of the *Theogony*, in the intermarriages of gods and mortals. Even Epimetheus' willing acceptance of Pandora, through which, in the *Works and Days*, man willingly embraced his own evil (*WD* 56–58) is suppressed in the *Theogony*. For a contrary view, see Hamilton, *Architecture*, 36–40, and E. Bradley, "Prooemium," 46–47.

4. See Nicole Loraux, "The Origins of Mankind in Greek Myths: Born to Die," in Bonnefoy, *Mythologies*, 1.390–95; Kirk, *Myth*, 105–6, 116–17; West, *Th.*, 173, 221, 306; Cornford, *Principium*, 210, 223–24.

5. For another comparison of these versions of the myth see Teggart, "Argument," 71–73.

6. See Otto, *Gods*, 178–84; and, among peasants, Friedl, *Vasilika*, 76, 85; Banfield, *Basis*, 140–42. For the significance of νήπιος see Susan T. Edmunds, *Homeric Nêpios* (New York: Garland, 1990).

7. Although the Silver Age comes close, even they eventually grow up. They are destroyed by their folly, but are never as utterly helpless as the race Prometheus had to teach not only to break animals, but even to tell one season from another (*PB* 440–70).

8. See *WD* 456; *Th*. 488; *Iliad* 2.38, 5.406, 20.264, 22.445. Hence also *WD* 130 describes the hundred-year-old babies of the Silver Age as νηπίοι.

9. The difficulty lies in the "for" (γάρ) of line 43. Grammatically, and formulaicly, "they do not know ..." (οὐδὲ ἴσασιν ...) elaborates on the judges' mistaken ideas, and "for the gods have hidden ...") explains why these ideas are mistaken: the judges are fools because they do not know that the half is more than the whole, and the evidence that the half *is* more is that the gods have made it hard for man to gain a livelihood. Waltz, *Poème moral*, 128, attributes the γάρ to this pattern; Mazon, *Les Travaux et les jours*, 48, takes it as introducing the myth which follows; Dorothea Wender, *Hesiod and Theognis* (New York: Penguin, 1973), 60, leaves it untranslated. West comments (153), "the logic of the connection leaves something to be desired," and goes on to explain: "[Hesiod's] thoughts have swung away from the kings, back to Perses and the need to work." See also van Groningen, *Composition*, 294.

10. Grene, "Religion," 148: "The proof of the harsh design of the gods lies in Hesiod's awareness of the infinitely greater potentiality of the earth's fertility over what it achieves—because of the inhibition of weather, that is, Zeus." West, 153: "the kings are wrong to uphold your rapacious claims: wealth must be won by work, that is the gods' will." See also Mazon, *Les Travaux et les jours*, 48; Laszlo Versényi, *Man's Measure: A Study of the Greek Image of Man from*

Homer to Sophocles (Albany: State University of New York Press, 1994), 53. Failing to see the significance of farming here, West, 50–51, 226, is forced to conclude that Hesiod has forgotten about the kings in the second half of the poem, when he begins his discourse on agriculture. For a more considered presentation of the same viewpoint. see Jens-Uwe Schmidt, *Adressat und Paraineseform: Zur Intention von Hesiods "Werken und Tagen"*, Hypomnemata 86 (Göttingen: Vandehoeck and Ruprecht, 1986).

11. Cited by West, 152, with other similar proverbs. West also adds a proviso to the mallow and asphodel, 153: "better these than a loaded table that depends on dishonesty." But, as he comments, this is not particularly apt as an address to the kings; *their* choice is not between riches with wickedness and honesty with beggar's fare. See also Mazon, *Les Travaux et les jours*, 45; Knox, "Work and Justice," 8; Gagarin, "Hesiod's Dispute with Perses," *Classical Philology* 104 (1974), 111; Vandvik, *Prometheus*, 17 and "Notes," 149.

12. Which is how Plato understood the proverb, *Republic* 466 b–c. See van Groningen, *Composition*, 294: "c'est à dire qu'une cupidité exagérée entraîne fatalement des conséquences fâcheuses;" Nilsson, *Piety*, 54–57; and, in contrast, Peter Walcot, *Envy and the Greeks: A Study of Human Behaviour* (Warminster, Wilts.: Aris and Phillips, 1978), 23.

13. West, 152–53; Vernant, *Origins*, 70; Job 30:3–4; Aristophanes, *Plutus* 543–44:

> And a jolly hard stone for a pillow you'll own; and, for
>   griddle cakes barley and wheaten,
> Must leaves dry and lean of the radish or e'en sour stalks
>   of the mallow be eaten.

(ἀντὶ δὲ προσκεφαλαίου / λίθον εὐμεγέθη πρὸς τῇ κεφαλῇ· σιτεῖσθαι δ' ἀντὶ μὲν ἄρτων / μαλάχης πτόρθους, ἀντὶ δὲ μάζης φυλλεῖ' ἰσχνῶν ῥαφανίδων) (trans. B. B. Rogers). Theophrastus (*Historia plantarum* 7.7.1–2) discusses mallow under plants which are not cultivated. One can feel confident, at least, that the asphodel in Hades grows wild (*Odyssey* 11.539; 24.13). See also Mazon, *Les Travaux et les jours*, 48; van Groningen, *Composition*, 294. Hanson, *The Other Greeks*, 105, sees mallow and asphodel as simply the workingman's diet.

14. For an interesting study of the gods' punishment of injustice in Homer, see Yamagata, *Morality*, passim, esp. 238–44. Her conclusion, that the gods are primarily concerned with *moira*, human beings with justice, fits nicely into this vision. In contrast, Otto, *Gods*, 257, sees Hesiod's sense of Zeus' justice as the triumph of bourgeois morality.

15. Hesiod assumes Greek conditions, under which any "taking" must be from other human beings. Mallow and asphodel represent what, for Hesiod, one is able to "take" directly from nature. See Versényi, *Man's Measure*, 53; Rand, "Urbanity," 150; Sinclair, *"Works and Days"*, 54; Wilamowitz, *Hesiodos' "Erga"*, 101; Evelyn-White, *Hesiod*, 39; West, 499. On the connection of justice and work, although as two benefits, Sinclair, xxx; Welles, *Attitude*, 21; Østerud, "Individuality," 23; Waltz, *Poème moral*, 54; Heath, "Didactic Poetry," 246; Mazon, "Composition," 335; Detienne, *Crise agraire*, 51–55; Fontenrose, "Work," 7.

16. See also *WD* 279–80 and G. Nagy, "Theognis," 39–40 for the importance of justice worked out over time.

17. See Nagler, "Discourse," 88–90. The idea is not unique to Hesiod, as in the "ancient saying" quoted at Herodotus 7.51: τὸ μὴ ἅμα ἀρχῇ πᾶν τέλος καταφαίνεσθαι ("Not every end shows at its beginning"). For this attitude in Solon, see Richmond Lattimore, "The First Elegy of Solon," *American Journal of Philology* 68 (1947): 166–68.

18. Despite the attraction that the section on justice has had for scholars, West's summary of it is quite accurate: "Dike is good because the gods reward it. Hybris is bad because the gods punish it. Work is good because it brings prosperity, independence, and hence social status. Idleness is bad because it brings want and forces you to beg or turn to crime. Work and righteous-

ness, in short, are what succeed in this world, or in other words, they are what the gods have prescribed for men" (47).

19. See, for example, Theognis 205 ff., 731 ff.; Solon 13.29 ff.; Plato, *Republic* 363d; Adkins, *Merit*, 68–69 and *Craft*, 153–60; Dodds, *Irrational*, 33–35; and West, 238, for other examples.

20. To reclaim a farm which has been run down, or to run down a farm which has been well-tended, takes time, although the latter is (of course) quicker. See Arthur W. H. Adkins, "Ethics and the Breakdown of the Cosmogony in Ancient Greece," in Robin W. Lovin and Frank E. Reynolds, eds., *Cosmogony and Ethical Order: New Studies in Comparative Ethics* (Chicago: University of Chicago Press, 1985), 294, and *Values*, 43–44; West, 278; Verdenius, *Commentary*, 148; and Martin C. Yang, "The Family as a Primary Economic Group," in Dalton, *Economies*, 342. See also Glaukos on the generations of man (*Iliad* 6.145–50).

21. As Pandora evidences, Hesiod does not see the "gifts" of Zeus as an unmixed blessing. Wealth which is a "gift" from Zeus must nonetheless be earned: "Yet easily Zeus will grant large wealth for more than one" (ῥεῖα δέ κεν πλεόνεσσι πόροι Ζεὺς ἄσπετον ὄλβον *WD* 379) because "when more men are at work, there is more work done and the increase / is greater" (πλείων μὲν πλεόνων μελέτη, μείζων δ᾽ ἐπιθήκη *WD* 380). If the goddess Demeter loves you she will fill your barn with grain. She will love you if you work (*WD* 299–301). See Mazon, *Les Travaux et les jours*, 90; Verdenius, *Commentary*, 161: "'god-given' is equivalent to 'lawfully acquired.'" At *WD* 717–18 poverty too is described as a gift of the gods; see Verdenius, *Commentary*, 161 and West, 238. For the same theme in Homer see Adkins, *Merit*, 16; Otto, *Gods*, 184–87.

22. In addition: the Golden Race ἥσυχοι ἔργ᾽ ἐνέμοντο σὺν ἐσθλοῖσιν πολέεσσιν ("At their will / they leisurely did their work in the midst of their many blessings" *WD* 119); in the just city θαλίης δὲ μεμηλότα ἔργα νέμονται ("at their feasts / they eat their land's crops, on which they spent their care" *WD* 231). In the Golden Age ὥστε θεοὶ δ᾽ ἔζωον, ἀκηδέα θυμὸν ἔχοντες / νόσφιν ἄτερ τε πόνου καὶ ὀιζύος· ("They lived like gods, their hearts undisturbed by cares, / without labour, without misery." *WD* 112–13); in the just city θάλλουσι δ᾽ ἀγαθοῖσι διαμπερές ("With all good things, utterly, they prosper" *WD* 236). Contrast also Vergil's Golden Age: Hesiod's sheep bear heavy fleeces; Vergil's bear fleeces already dyed (*Eclogues* 4.42–45); in Vergil's Golden Age honey flows from the trees (*Georgics* 1.131); proverbially hard-working bees make Hesiod's. See Beye, "Rhythm," 41, and, for the just city as the return of the Golden Age, Stewart, 45; Knox, "Work and Justice," 15; Teggart, "Argument," 66.

23. The life of the just city is the positive counterpart to the future Iron Age. As that was the worst, this is the best that life in the Iron Age can be, the condition where people are able to enjoy the goods mingled with our inevitable evils (ἀλλ᾽ ἔμπης καὶ τοῖσι μεμείξεται ἐσθλὰ κακοῖσιν *WD* 179).

24. As Anaximander, fr. 101; Heraclitus, fr. 211 (pp. 107, 193 in Kirk and Raven). See also J. Harrison, *Themis*, 517: "Dike, we have seen, is the way of life of each natural thing, each plant, each animal, each man. It is also the way, the usage, the regular course of that great animal the Universe, the way that is made manifest in the Seasons, in the life and death of vegetation; and when it comes to be seen that these depend on the heavenly bodies, Dike is manifest in the changes of the rising and setting of constellations, in the waxing and waning of the moon and in the daily and yearly courses of the sun"; Cornford, *Religion*, 171, who identifies Dike as "the wheel of Time" and "the wheel of Right"; and J. W. Jones, *Law*, 24–25, 40.

25. It is important, however, to realize that δίκη, for Hesiod, meant not a rigid system of legal codes but a particular "speech act," as Gagarin, "Poetry," 71. For a further distinction between δίκη and "justice," see Yamagata, *Morality*, 61–63.

26. Gagarin, "*Dike* in *WD*," 81, argues that "in the *WD* dike may mean "law," in the sense of a process for the peaceful settlement of disputes, and that in this sense it is generalized and personified and praised as something of definite value to society, but that dike does not apply to

actions outside this narrow area of law and does not have any general moral sense." See also Gagarin, "Archaic," 196, "Blind Justice," 61–78, and, with a focus on orality, "Poetry," 71–76.

For Hesiod's concrete sense of δίκη see, aside from Gagarin, Hays, "Notes," 67; Stewart, "History," 48; Walcot, "Law," 10–13; Pucci, *Language*, 51; Waltz, *Poème moral*, 97. For the argument that "an oral culture is incapable of conceptualizing justice apart from its pragmatic application in day-to-day procedure" (Havelock, *Concept*, 217), hence early Greek δίκη is a "process" rather than a principle, Erik A. Havelock, "Δικαιοσύνη," *Phoenix* 23 (1969): 68, and, on Hesiod in particular, *Concept*, 213, 216–17. For archaic Greek justice as the basis of civilized life rather than a moral code, Pearson, *Ethics*, 43–48, 234, n. 13. For the importance of a shame rather than a guilt culture, Kurt Latte, "Der Rechtsegedanke in archaischen Griechentum," *Antike u. Abendland* 2 (1946): 65. Matthew Dickie, "*Dike* as a Moral Term in Hesiod and Homer," *Classical Philology* 73 (1978): 100, argues, I believe correctly, that δίκη *can* mean justice or righteousness in Hesiod or Homer although "it is more commonly used to mean 'custom' or 'judgement.' " See Dickie, 91–92 and Verdenius, *Commentary*, 10, for a summary of these positions. Rodgers' argument that δίκη *means* that which avoids disaster is answered by Dickie, 100–1. See also Jean Defradas, *Les Thèmes de la propagande delphique* (Paris: C. Klincksiech, 1954), 45–52; and for modern peasants, Campbell, *Honour*, 320–22; Walcot, *Peasants*, 103–4.

27. When Justice is abused she brings evil (*WD* 219–24). Hence the contrast between the just and the unjust city: the unjust city is punished; the just city is not (*WD* 225–47). Hesiod's exhortation to the kings shows them (1) that they cannot escape Zeus' attention, and (2) that consequently they cannot escape his punishment: the gods are near to men and mark their injustice (*WD* 248–51); Zeus has thirty thousand watchers (*WD* 252–55); the goddess Dike reports the unjust mind of men to Zeus (*WD* 256–60), which he punishes accordingly (*WD* 261–64); planning evil brings evil to the planner (*WD* 265–66); and the eye of Zeus sees all, even this δίκη that the kings are now judging (*WD* 267–69). Finally Hesiod explains to Perses that perjury also is punished (*WD* 280–85). End of argument. The exception, *WD* 270–80, will be discussed below.

28. Almost all of Hesiod's images occur elsewhere. For the meeting of the ἐσθλός ("noble") man with ruin see Herodotus 1.32; for the image of two roads, Theognis 910 ff.; West, 229; for the just city, *Odyssey* 19.109 ff., West, 213; for the city at war and the city at peace, *Iliad* 18.490 ff.; for the pursuit of Horkos and our line, *WD* 285, Herodotus 3.86; for Zeus' invisible watchers, *Odyssey* 17.485–87; West, 219. Phoenix' account of the Litae (*Iliad* 9.502 ff.) parallels Hesiod's images of Horkos pursuing crooked δίκαι, of Dike winning at the end of the race, of Dike, clothed formulaically in mist, following behind weeping, and of injured Dike complaining to Zeus. The "eye of Zeus" that sees all (West, 223–24), and the belief that the generations of a perjurer are diminished are both traditional. *WD* 265–66 is a proverb—see West, 222, for parallels. See Sinclair, "*Works and Days*", xxviii; Walcot, "Law," 18–20; Lloyd-Jones, *Justice*, 17. Havelock, *Concept*, 193–217 sees the entire section as derived from Homer.

29. *WD* 712, for which see below. *WD* 9 asks Zeus to straighten the judicial θέμιστες with δίκη; *WD* 239 and 256 describe Zeus' punishment of unjust judges; *WD* 192, perjury in the Iron Age; *WD* 275, 278, and 279 contrast men and animals, preceding a description of perjury; *WD* 213 tells Perses to "listen to δίκη" opening the section as a whole. Of the courts directly, *WD* 36, 39, 124, 217, 219, 220, 221, 225, 249, 250, 254, 262, 264, 269, 275, 283. Δίκαιος is used of the courts at *WD* 190, 217, 226, and 280, of gaining a "greater δίκη," presumably "settlement," at 270 and 271, and non-judicially of the heroes at *WD* 158; ἄδικος is used in a judicial context at *WD* 260 and 272, in a non-judicial context at 334. Gagarin, "*Dike* in *WD*," 87 generalizes: "every use of *dike* in Hesiod belongs to the second area of meaning, 'settlement, legal process.' " Although I disagree with Gagarin overall, he deserves thanks for calling attention to Hesiod's overwhelmingly "legal" sense of δίκη, which is, *pace* Gagarin, in startling contrast to Homer.

30. The offenses of the future Iron Age are followed by the adjective χειροδίκαι ("violent justicers" *WD* 182–89). As the plural adjective cannot belong with the ἕτερος of the next description of sacking cities, it must be taken either on its own, as by West, or as part of the preceding description, as by Evelyn-White, Sinclair, and Wilamowitz, who also bracket the adjective. West, 201, defends the connection by reference to δίκη ("justice") in its general sense: "the repayment of the debt owed to one's parents has a strong connotation of τὸ δίκαιον, what is fair and good."

31. Gagarin, because of this passage, argues that the noun δίκη ("justice") cannot, although the adjective δίκαιος ("just") can, have a moral meaning. "The two areas of meaning are kept separate and there does not seem to be any interaction between them" ("*Dike* in *WD*," 87). Gagarin's etymological argument is based on L. R. Palmer, "The Indo-European Origins of Greek Justice," *Transactions of the Philological Society* (1950): 149–68. Palmer (168), however, quotes Cornford, *Religion*, 172 with approval: "the Greeks believed that there was an order in human affairs which cohered with an order in surrounding nature and derived its sanction from that world order," and points to his own discussion of δίκη ("justice") as a "boundary word" as evidence for this view. Gagarin himself admits that the uses cannot be seen as completely separate, "*Dike* in *WD*," 87 and, retracting his earlier more extreme claim, "Archaic," 188, n. 15.

32. West, 45 describes the passage as "a list of standard outrages guaranteed to incur Zeus' anger"; and see 239–40 for other references to these "classic sins." See also Adkins, *Values*, 20; Dickie, "Moral Term," 97–98; Gagarin, "*Dike* in *WD*," 93. Solmsen, review, 220 does not think that "classic sins" is a strong enough term. See G. Nagy, "Theognis," 39–40, and Heath, "Didactic Poetry," 245 for the relation of specific to universal justice.

33. See *Odyssey* 17.481–87; Herodotus 1.159; and Themistocles in Thucydides 1.136, for historical examples of the importance of protecting suppliants. That there are words of greater approbation does not, of course, change this fact. Hesiod also links both δίκη ("justice") and work to ἀρετή ("excellence") as *WD* 313–16. See Adkins, *Merit*, 70–73.

34. Noun and adjective appear together at *WD* 190–3, 216–18, 225–26, 270–72, 279–81. Only at *WD* 158, in describing the non-judicial justice of the heroic age, does Hesiod use the adjective without the noun.

35. See Aristotle's distinction between justice as complete virtue, or the "lawful," and justice as a specific, primarily economic virtue, not taking more than one's due (*Nicomachean Ethics* 1129a25 ff.). Aristotle points out that it is the being done for "profit" (1130a24 ff.) that characterizes the latter. Hays, "Notes," 58–62, also sees "two strata of ethical sentiment" (60) in Hesiod, one traditional, and one centered on property rights. As Heath, "Didactic Poem," 245, puts it: "δίκη in its restricted sense is for Hesiod an exemplary case for right social behavior in general."

36. For the idea that Zeus operates strictly a court of appeals, see Francis, "Personality," 285; Gagarin, "*Dike* in *WD*," 89, 91; and, in Solon, Gagarin, "*Dike* in Archaic Greek Thought," *Classical Philology* 69 (1974): 191.

37. West, 50–51, 56–57.

38. West, 216, 331 glosses this use of δίκη ("justice") as "atonement"; Mazon, *Les Travaux et les jours*, 143 as "une satisfaction." That this general idea of social relations is connected to δίκη is evident from the definition of δικαιοσύνη ("justice") quoted in the *Republic*: doing good to friends and evil to enemies (332a ff.). See Havelock, "Δικαιοσύνη," 51, 68 and *Concept*, 135; R. Renehan, "Progress in Hesiod," review of *Hesiod: "Works and Days"* by M. L. West, *Journal of Hellenic Studies* 99 (1979), 352–53; Hays, "Notes," 61; Pearson, *Ethics*, 17. See also *Odyssey* 2.74–79 for the justice of paying oneself back.

39. τὸν φιλέοντα φιλεῖν would be better translated "maintain a relationship of reciprocity with one who maintains a relationship of reciprocity with you," which is harder to put into

meter. See Arthur W. H. Adkins, "'Friendship' and 'Self-Sufficiency' in Homer and Aristotle," *Classical Quarterly*, n.s., 13 (1963): 36–39. Verdenius, *Commentary*, 173 points out that "Hes. is concerned with the best way of obtaining something from one's neighbor, not with the other's well-being." Finley, *Odysseus*, 64: "It may be stated as a flat rule of both primitive and archaic society that no one ever gave anything, whether goods or services or honors, without proper recompense . . . The act of giving was, therefore, in an essential sense always the first half of a reciprocal action, the other half of which was a counter-gift."

40. See Sihvola, *Decay, Progress*, 58. In the *Theogony*, the justice of good kings is described as the accomplishment of a "turning back" (μετάτροπα ἔργα) that balances and negates the harm done. Zeus' punishment is a "harsh return in exchange for unjust deeds" (ἔργων ἀντ' ἀδίκων χαλπὴν ἐπέθηκεν ἀμοιβήν WD 334) which "pays back" the good that was snatched, just as in the Pandora myth the evil "gift," Pandora, pays men back for the good they gained from fire (*WD* 55). As the measure which restores the balance, "δίκη" is the punishment, as well as the decision (see *WD* 238–39; Vernant, *Myth and Thought*, 107). Nor is it idiosyncratic of Aristotle, in the *Ethics*, to discuss justice in terms of proportion (1132b20–1134a15). As Aristotle implies, ἴσος, meaning both "equal" and "fair," almost demands that justice be discussed in terms of a balance. As Nilsson, *Piety*, 35 puts it: "For the Greeks justice was the retribution which counters wrong-doing." See also Ferguson, *Moral Values*, 28; Gagarin (who excepts Hesiod), "Dike in *WD*," 93; J. W. Jones, *Law*, 27–28; Rodgers, "Thoughts," 393–94; Havelock, *Concept*, 181, 277–80; Pearson, *Ethics*, 15–17, 88.

41. Hence, Aristotle says, men set up shrines to the Graces in the marketplaces, as a reminder of the importance of reciprocity (*Nicomachean Ethics* 1133a5).

42. See *WD* 303–6, 320–26, 359–60, 393–403, and fragments 70.27 and 204.82; Plato, *Protagoras* 322a–d; Adkins, *Values*, 16; Verdenius, *Commentary*, 114,162; Dickie, "Moral Term," 92–93; Dodds, *Irrational*, 17–18; Pearson, *Ethics*, 40–42; Yamagata, *Morality*, 84, 149–74. For modern peasants, David D. Gilmore, "Honor, Honesty and Shame," in Gilmore, *Honor*, 93; Campbell, *Honour*, 310; Walcot, *Peasants*, 59–60.

43. *Hesiod* (Oxford: Clarendon Press,1970), ed. Friedrich Solmsen, fragments ed. R. Merkelbach and M. L. West. In the *Oresteia* also justice is the balance that demands that a man suffer as he has done (*Choephoroi* 62–7, 306–12).

44. The revelation is intended to surprise, hence Hesiod's sudden switch both in rhythm and from a universal to a particular "you." The surprise is put to dramatic use by the reminder that Perses' failure is what Hesiod has been predicting all along. See Schmidt, *Adressat*, passim; Kumaniecki, "Structure," 86 and Gagarin, "Dispute," 108 in contrast to the usual view that Hesiod's portrait of Perses is simply erratic, e.g., West, 39 ff.; G. Nagy, "Hesiod," 59; Hays, "Notes," 20.

45. See Theophrastus, *Agroikos* 4.11; Francis, "Personality," 298; Waltz, *Poème moral*, 82, 89; Walcot, *Peasants*, 80; Redfield, "Sparta," 151; Millet, "Hesiod," 96–107; Hanson, *The Other Greeks*, 137–41. The strain between competitive and cooperative values studied in Adkins, *Merit*, is well attested in modern peasant communities. See Foster, "Limited Good," 311, and "Peasant Character and Personality," in Potter, *Peasant Society*, 296; Stanley Broder, "Reflections on Honor and Shame," in Gilmore, *Honor*, 122–32; Thomas W. Gallant, *Risk and Survival in Ancient Greece: Reconstructing the Rural Domestic Economy* (Stanford: Stanford university Press, 1991), 143–58.

46. See Foster, "Limited Good," 304–20 for the definitive statement; Millet, "Hesiod," 96–98 applied to Hesiod, and 98–101 for the resulting, and ambiguous, need for reciprocity. Hence people must trust each other, but not too much (*WD* 372): "for a brother / get a witness as well, though you do it with a laugh" (κασιγνήτῳ γελάσας ἐπὶ μάρτυρα θέσθαι WD 371). See also Walcot, *Envy*, 7; Adkins, "Friendship," 44–45; Hanson, *The Other Greeks*, 101–2.

47. West, 249–50 athetizes these lines. For a defense see Verdenius, *Commentary*, 176–77.

48. See Aristotle on the need for individual judgement, *Nicomachean Ethics* 1137a30 ff. For the overall ambiguity of human life for Hesiod, see Gagarin, "Ambiguity," 177–8; Sihvola, *Decay, Progress*, 37, 409–41. Nagler, "Discourse," 85, points out Hesiod's sense that we "walk a tightrope between choices that can lead steeply towards opposite conclusions."

49. For example, *WD* 349–51, 396–97, where Hesiod gives Perses *his* equal measure: " but I shall give you no more, / nor measure out more to you; work, you stupid Perses" (ἐγὼ δέ τοι οὐκ ἐπιδώσω / οὐδ᾽ ἐπιμετρήσω· ἐργάζεο νήπιε Πέρση). For the connection between these key words, propriety, and the various sections of the *Works and Days* see Benardete, "First Reading," 164–68; Richardson, review, 171; van Groningen, *Composition*, 287–88; and, connecting δίκη and propriety, Havelock, *Concept*, 181.

50. See Hanson, *The Other Greeks*, 150–53, 166–78.

51. See *Nicomachean Ethics* 1106b15–25. Hesiod's description of adultery with one's sister-in-law, an "unjust act," as "acting outside the proportion" (παρακαίρια ῥέζων *WD* 329) does not suggest that there is a right time and place for adultery, as Aristotle, *Nicomachean Ethics* 1107a151. Verdenius, *Commentary*, 164 glosses παρακαίρια as "beside the right measure," citing *PB* 507. See Theognis 199; Pindar, *Olympians* 8.24; Solon 13.11; West, 240; and Palmer, "Origins," 153 ff. for numerous other examples. Palmer argues for the etymological connection of δίκη as a "boundary word" to μέτρον, καιρός, and ὅρος and, at 162 ff., for a further connection to αἶσα and μοῖρα, pointing to Hesiod's identification of Dike as one of the Horai (168, n. 1).

52. As Sihvola, *Decay, Progress*, 55: "Hesiod's view seems to be that the immanent structures of the human way of life are enough to bring disastrous results to those who neglect justice." See also Versényi, *Man's Measure*, 52. Gregory Vlastos, "Solonian Justice," *Classical Philology* 41 (1946): 65–83, as Jaeger, *Paideia*, 1.140–41, exaggerates the difference between natural causality in Solon and in Hesiod, dismissing Hesiod's idea of the punishment of injustice as of "the order of magic"(Vlastos, 65) while, nonetheless, admitting that "Hesiod, too, can picture justice in natural terms" (65, n. 6). See also Vernant, *Origins*, 86; Lloyd-Jones, *Justice*, 44; Frisch, *Might*, 29; Gagarin, "Archaic," 196; Walcot, "Law," 17; Mazon, *Les Travaux et les jours*, 79.

53. As Poseidon's charge is the sea and Demeter's the cornfields, the place of Justice, the daughter of Zeus, is the courts. Gagarin, "*Dike* in *WD*," 91–92 fails to see that Dike's μοῖρα is a focus, not a limitation. See J. W. Jones, *Law*, 25–27; Stewart, "History," 42, 48; Walcot, *Peasants*, 108–9. Lloyd-Jones, however, goes somewhat too far in the other direction: "Dike means basically the order of the universe, and in this religion the gods maintain a cosmic order. This they do by working through nature and the human mind, and not by means of extraneous interventions" (*Justice*, 161)

54. Teggart, "Argument," 57 ff. sees this description as extending into the section on δίκη.

55. This and Hesiod's parallel description—χειροδίκαι—are usually interpreted as meaning just this, that there will be no justice, only violence: "their "justice" [will be] force," as Gagarin, "*Dike* in *WD*," 90 translates. See also Verdenius, *Commentary*, 112, 114 and Pearson, *Ethics*, 82–83 for this position.

56. *WD* 238–39 is our first example of δίκη as "punishment." The use is clarified and reinforced by Hesiod's picture of an offended Dike "bringing evil to men" (*WD* 222–24).

57. Which may or may not reflect Hesiod's own experience. Given Thebes' relationship to Thespiae it seems unlikely that Hesiod never encountered violence. See, however, Nussbaum, "Labour," 217–18.

58. The bad Strife, who is introduced as fostering violence, is soon revealed as more crucially the instigator of crooked justice. Elsewhere in the *Works and Days*, violence appears in the past ages, and as above, which make up all the uses of βία ("force") or κράτος ("might") in the *Works and Days*, against innumerable uses in the *Theogony*. The beast one doesn't lose at

WD 348 has probably wandered off, rather than been taken in an armed raid (West, 244); Hesiod's thief is a "day-sleeper," that is, he is a thief, not a robber (*WD* 604–5). Note also Hesiod's statement that violence is for animals; human beings have δίκη. It is hard to imagine Achilles making this distinction.

59. Friedl, *Vasilika*, 31, comments on modern Greek peasants' obsessive fear of theft, and the consequent importance of watchdogs. See also Eumaeus' dogs, *Odyssey* 14.20–39.

60. Knox, "Work and Justice," 16 and Kumaniecki, "Structure," 83, for reasons unexplained, take this line as a ringing declaration of faith. I would prefer to see it as either hesitant or ironic. In any case it is not Hesiod's last word. See Grene, "Religion," 153, and, on the verb tense and construction of the line, West, 225 and West, *Th.*, 323; Verdenius, *Commentary*, 144–45; Sinclair, *"Works and Days"*, 31; Mazon, *Les Travaux et les Jours*, 96. This and the following passage are exceptional in not focusing on the courts, and, apparantly, in not being based on tradition.

61. The qualification is formulaic and all the more serious for being so. See also *WD* 1–9; *Th.* 429 ff. and West, *Th.*, 163; Pucci, *Language*, 87; Grene, "Religion," 158: "any formulation that man makes of Zeus's true designs is lamentably unsure."

62. For this passage seen as a retraction of Hesiod's fable, see above, chapter 2.

63. See Sealey, *Justice*, 102–7. West, 226, comments: "Certainly the emphasis is not on its being God's law, but on its being the norm for men." The emphasis placed on τόνδε reflects the emphatic central position of the anticipated word, νόμος, set off by the caesura. Zeus is named only by his patronymic, unemphatically, at the end of the line. In contrast *WD* 335, where Hesiod's point is that Zeus punishes injustice, places the emphasis on Zeus: τῷ δ' ἤτοι Ζεὺς αὐτὸς ἀγαίεται ("With that man Zeus himself is angry"). See also the contrast with *WD* 239 (= *WD* 229), τοῖς δὲ δίκην Κρονίδης τεκμαίρεται εὐρύοπα Ζεύς ("against them the son of Cronos, loud-voiced Zeus/set as witness of his judgement, Retribution"), where the emphasis is again on Zeus, with the caesura on his patronymic leading to the formulaic second half of the line.

64. For the gods: ἀθανάτοις διέταξε νόμους καὶ ἐπέφραδε τιμάς ("To the immortals he ordained their ways and declared out their honors" *Th.* 73–74), see above, chapter 4. *Nomos* as either a written law or ordinance, or as human convention, opposed to what exists by nature (φύσις) post-date Hesiod, who never uses the word "nature" (φύσις), and who would hardly recognize as a *nomos* Aristotle's example of human convention, the arbitrary decision that the ransom for a prisoner shall be two minae (*Nicomachean Ethics* 1134b20). Hesiod does not distinguish "custom" from "nature" in the sense that what is "natural" is opposed to what is "artificial." It is as "natural" to Hesiod that men have δίκη ("justice") as it is that animals eat one another. That does not mean that nature and culture are the same; that they are not is precisely the point of the passage. See Jaeger, *Paideia*, 1.72–3 and 434, and, for a study of the *Works and Days* in these terms, Østerud, "Individuality".

Ostwald, *Nomos*, 21 (on *WD* 276), argues "That *nomos* does not here bear the sense of 'law' or 'ordinance' which prescribes a certain kind of behaviour but designates the behaviour itself has long been recognized. It is, rather, an order of living, a way of life." West does not agree (*Th.*, 178, 226) although, as Ostwald points out, Ostwald's own "way of life" fits West's interpretation of these passages better than West's "ordinances." Verdenius, "Proem," 248 glosses νόμοι as "manners." See also Cornford, *Religion*, 29 and the pairing of νόμοι and "goodly manners" as West *Th.*, 178: "the epithet shows that ἤθεα here means 'manners' as in Op. 67, 78, 699." See also Verdenius, *Commentary*, 145–46; J. W. Jones, *Law*, 34–36; Waltz, *Poème moral*, 145; Kirk, *Myth*, 178. Ostwald, however, fails to see the inherent connection between Zeus and his order: "The *nomos* of man includes and that of animals excludes *dike*; that it is god-given is only incidental, for the point is that it constitutes a norm followed by any human being who does not wish to degenerate into an animal" (21). Here West's description is better: "Zeus is not so much prescribing to men as providing them with a *nomos* which prescribes to them" (226).

65. The intermediate step is taken by Aratus, *Phaen.* 100–34, to whom 2.536–38 also refers. See Thomas, *Virgil*, 2.249; Hardie, *Cosmos*, 35–36; J. J. L. Smolenaars, "Labour in the Golden Age: A Unifying Theme in Vergil's Poems," *Mnemosyne*, 4th ser., 40 (1987): 395.

66. As Aristotle saw, justice is subordinate to friendship (*Nicomachean Ethics* 1155a23–33). See also Putnam, "Rome," 181; Johnston, *Golden Age*, 6; Perkell, *Truth*, 94; and see *Aeneid* 7.202–4 and 8.319–27 for other connections of peace and justice.

67. For the proem to Book 3 as itself the reconciliation of force and poetry, see Boyle, "Paradox," 74 and *Dove*, 44; Miles, *Interpretation*,170. For the promise of another poem, see Thomas, *Virgil*, 2:36–37; Rand, *Magical Art*, 268; Klingner, "Georgica," 136–42.

68. For various versions of this comparison, see Putnam, *Earth*, 320; Miles, *Interpretation*, 289 ff.; Griffin, *Virgil*, 57; Perkell, *Truth*, 188; Boyle, *Dove*, 45; G. Williams, *Tradition*, 436; Lee, *Orpheus*, passim, esp. 127–29, 132–39.

69. Charles Segal, "Pastoral Realism and the Golden Age: Correspondence and Contrast between Virgil's Third and Fourth Eclogues," *Philologus* 121 (1977): 158–63; Mack, *Time*, 8–11; and, in the *Georgics*, David O. Ross, "The Pastoral in the *Georgics: Si Numquam Fallit Imago*," *Arethusa* 23 (1990): 74–75.

70. For a study of Caesar as a contributor to order, see, for example, Robert M. Wilhelm, "Apollo, Sol and Caesar: Triumph of Order," *Augustan Age* 5 (1986): 60–75. Caesar, of course, also helped *start* the civil war. To say that his role is, in itself, ambivalent is to say nothing new. See Michael Dewar, "Octavian and Orestes in the Finale of the First Georgic," *Classical Quarterly*, n.s., 38 (1980): 563–65; Sellar, *Roman Poets*, 10; Lyne, "Scilicet," 65; Boyle, "Paradox," 73; Putnam, "Rome," 179; Kromer, "Didactic Tradition," 14; and Ronald Syme, *The Roman Revolution* (Oxford: Oxford University Press,1939), esp. 12–62.

71. Otis, *Virgil*, 173; Liebeschuetz, "Beast and Man," 69.

72. See Bosson, *Études*, 383; Mynors, "*Georgics*", 287, who ultimately disagrees; and T. E. Page, *P. Vergilii Maronis: Bucolica et Georgica* (London: Macmillan, 1898), 360.

73. In Book 1, Vergil, unlike Hesiod, describes sowing the crops, but never the harvest. In Book 2, as Bosson, *Études*, 301, points out, Vergil treats vines, but not wine-making. The exception, 1.273–75, leads into the Hesiodic "Days." Thomas, "Prose," 237–38 sees profit, as well as slavery, as topics which offended Vergil's sensibilities.

74. In order to strengthen the effect, Vergil neglects to mention how these kids *are* fed, either from a bucket or after the (not total) milking, Polyphemus' practice (*Odyssey* 9.244–49). See White, *Farming*, 314.

75. Thomas, "Prose," 253. Rand, *Magical Art*, 245, points out that in the second Georgic as well we are being given the *vines'* point of view, not the farmer's.

76. See Mynors, "*Georgics*", 191 and Kromer, "Didactic Tradition," 17 on the transition.

77. See Parry, "Art," 43, the bees, 4.206–9, and the farmer's proverb: "Live as if to die tomorrow; farm as if to live forever."

78. The simile used of the stallion reinforces his personalization. The same device is used in the descriptions of the rival bulls (3.237–41) and the bees (4.96–98). The necessity of discarding old animals is assumed by Cato (*Agr.* 2.7) and, of course, disapproved of by Plutarch (Life of Marcus Cato). Stallions can, in fact, remain at stud up to a very advanced age—it is work animals, not animals at stud, that Cato discards. Vergil may have chosen a stud rather than a work animal in order to connect the theme treated here, death, with the other great theme of the third Georgic, sex.

79. *Turpi* is "ugly" as well as "disgraceful," which softens the blow. For the attempt to read "pity his not disgraceful old age," see Mynors, "*Georgics*", 196; Page, *Bucolica*, 300; and, for a refutation, Thomas, *Virgil*, 2.56–57.

80. Considering that Hesiod's society ate a good deal less meat than Vergil's (as Burford, *Land*, 146), it is surprising that Hesiod does (*WD* 591–92), and Vergil does not, mention animals

raised for food. Wilkinson, *Survey*, 253 is one of few commentators to notice the omission. White, *Farming*, 276–77, believes that few animals (besides pigs) were *raised* for meat.

81. *Nec singula morbi / corpora corripiunt, sed tota aestiva repente, / spemque gregemque simul cunctamque ab origine gentem* ("It is not single bodies / That diseases seize, but suddenly a whole summer's flock / Present and future at once, the whole stock, root and branch" 3.471–73). To the individual sheep, of course, death does seize a single life, her own.

82. See Mynors, *"Georgics"*, 249, vs. Page, *Bucolica*, 328. The sheep's "guilt" parallels the stallion's "base" old age. In both cases Vergil makes the contradiction implicit in the farmer's feelings explicit in his description.

83. Introduced by the surprisingly unsupervised bulls of 219–41. See Miles, "Amor," 177–97; Putnam, *Earth*, 229. E. Harrison, "Noric Plague," 1–66 sees the plague as divine punishment for man's impiety and the suffering of the innocent animals as a reflection of man's guilt. For the integral importance, now universally accepted, of Vergil's "purple patches," see Drew, "Structure," 243.

84. See Miles, *Interpretation*, 190 and "Amor," 180. Peter E. Knox, "Love and Horses in Virgil's *Georgics*," *Eranos* 90 (1992): 43–53, proposes a somewhat less grim picture, while also pointing out the inescapability of sex in the *Georgics*.

85. See Perkell, *Truth*, 116 ff.; Putnam, *Earth*, 218; Mynors, *"Georgics"*, 256; and Otis, *Virgil*, 180, for Vergil's description of the plague as the blackest of parodies, a parody of the Golden Age.

86. Hence, also, the importance of communal celebrations and festivals in Vergil, as opposed to Hesiod, e.g. *Georgics* 1.341–50, 2.380–92 and 527–31. For Hesiod's "individualism," see Hays, "Notes," 62–63.

87. Liebeschuetz, "Beast and Man," 75. For a deeply sympathetic study of much the same dichotomy in the *Aeneid*, which sees not a fundamental split but a relation, simultaneously, of tension and of mutual dependence, see Susan Ford Wiltshire, *Public and Private in Vergil's Aeneid* (Amherst: University of Massachusetts Press, 1989).

88. Rand, *Magical Art*, 307; Kromer, "Didactic Tradition," 18, and contrast the easier transition between Books 2 and 3.

89. For example, the *admiranda tibi levium spectacula rerum / magnanimosque duces* ("Wondrous pageant of a tiny world and / Great-hearted leaders" 4.3–4) that Maecenas, of all men, is asked to admire.

90. Vergil follows Varro's organization, but reverses the position of flocks and herds, so that his animals become progressively smaller and more social. Otis, *Virgil*, 170, 177; Boyle, *Dove*, 67.

91. The surprising metrical pattern of 4.84 may be due to Ennian heroic coloring, see Thomas, *Virgil*, 2:161; Mynors, *"Georgics"*, 270; R. D. Williams, *Virgil*, 205; and compare *Aeneid* 10.9. It certainly creates a sense of conflict.

92. Johnson, *Darkness*, 121–22. Book 24 of the *Iliad* and Milton's "They hand in hand, with wandering steps and slow, / Through Eden took thir solitarie way" sound a similar note.

93. Rand, *Magical Art*, 309; Otis, *Virgil*, 185. Hence the prevalence of *ipsae* ("themselves") in this passage. See Page, *Bucolica*, 350; Otis, *Virgil*, 183; and compare G. 4.215 to 4.110–11. This is one of many explanations of the two parts of Vergil's description, and by no means exclusive. For others see Ross, *Elements*, 188 ff.; Thomas, *Virgil*, 2.175; Miles, *Interpretation*, 252; Boyle, *Dove*, 65 ff.

94. Johnston, *Golden Age*, 90 ff.; Christine G. Perkell, " On the Corycian Gardener of Vergil's Fourth Georgic," *Transactions of the American Philological Association* 111 (1981): 193; Mynors, *"Georgics"*, 279.

95. Hence some commentators find Vergil's bees an ideal, as Edward Coliero, "Allegory in the IVth Georgic," in Bardon and Verdière, *Vergiliana*, 113–23, and others find them repul-

sive, as Griffin, "Haec," 20 and "The Fourth Georgic, Virgil and Rome," *Greece and Rome*, 2d ser., 26 (1979): 64; Connor, "Description," 43–44; Perkell, "Reading," 212–14. This is rather hard on the bees, who are neither ideal nor flawed human beings, but just bees, in some respects similar to men, but in this crucial respect different, as Segal, "Fourth Georgic," 310, points out. Among the bees there is only one point of view: *mens omnibus una est* ("for all a single will" G. 4.212). "The mind in the hive is the collective mind of the whole colony, apart from the queen and the drones—an hereditary, communal intellect evolved through the ages, the sum and total of all bee experience since the world of bees began": Tickner Edwardes, *The Lore of the Honey Bee*, ch. 5, quoted in Royds, *Beasts*, 73. See also Edward O. Wilson, *Sociobiology: The Abridged Edition* (Cambridge, Mass.: Belknap Press, 1975): 194–96 on the genetic identity of bees and 201–3 on their social nature, and Smith Palmer Bovie, "The Image of Ascent-Descent in Vergil's *Georgics*," *American Journal of Philology* 77 (1956): 353; Otis, "New Study," 57; Ruch, "Virgile," 325; Briggs, *Narrative*, 52.

For various interpretations of the bees as trope, see Colin Hardie, *The Georgics: A Transitional Poem*, Third Jackson Knight Memorial Lecture (Abingdon, Oxon.: Abbey Press, 1971), 22; Steele Commager, Introduction, in Commager, *Virgil*, 3; Johnston, *Golden Age*, 90 ff.; Wilkinson, *Survey*, 178; Johnson, "Bees," 13–20. For the bees as human society writ small, see, in particular, Hellfried Dahlmann, "Der Bienenstaat in Vergils *Georgica*," Akademie der Wissenschaft und der Literatur in Mainz, *Abhandlungen der Geistes- und Sozialwissenschaftlichen Classe* 10 (1954): 547–62; Thomas, *Virgil* 1.21, 2.146–47; Ross, *Elements*, 191; Rand, *Magical Art*, 313; Eleanor Winsor Leach, "*Sedes apibus*: From the Georgics to the Aeneid," *Vergilius* 23 (1977), 15; Klingner, "Georgica," 161–94.

96. Vergil's *hinc pecudes, armenta, viros, genus omne ferarum* ("And hence are the flocks and the herds, men, all kinds of beasts" 4.223) recalls, now in a positive vein, his earlier descriptions of sex and death: *Omne adeo genus in terris hominumque ferarumque* ("Each single race on earth, man and beast" 3.428) and *et genus omne neci pecudum dedit, omne ferarum* ("And gave over to death all kinds of cattle, all kinds of wild beast" 3.480).

97. Thomas, *Virgil*, 2.167 sees the old Corycian as the farmer of Book 2, now in the real world. For his similarity to the bees, D. E. Wormell, "*Apibus quanta experientia parcis*: Virgil's *Georgics* 4.1–227" in Bardon and Verdière, *Vergiliana*, 430; Ross, *Elements*, 201–6; Abbe, *Plants*, 90 ff. Davis, "Pastoral," 31 and Perkell, "Corycian," 168 see the gardener as an ideal, Golden Age, figure. See Perkell, 167–68 for other views.

98. W. R. Johnson, "Medea Nunc Sum: The Close of Seneca's Version" 85–101, in Pietro Pucci, ed., *Language and the Tragic Hero: Essays on Greek Tragedy in Honor of Gordon M. Kirkwood* (Atlanta: Scholar's Press, 1988), 90–91; Perkell, "Corycian," 171–72, 177.

99. For the untranslatable Roman implications of the *fasces* see 3.347–48.

100. *Namque aliae victu invigilant et foedere pacto / exercentur agris* ("For some see to the food, and by firm agreement / Work in the fields" 4.158–59). For the identification of Vergil's bees with his farmer, see P. J. Davis, "Vergil's *Georgics* and the Pastoral Ideal," *Ramus* 8 (1979): 29; Dahlmann, "Bienenstaat," 555–56.

101. The farmer moves from a very Roman control of another country's politics, deciding between rival kings: *dede neci; melior vacua sine regnet in aula* ("Put him to death; let the better one reign alone in the palace" 4.90), to personally, and brutally, restraining apian frivolity: *nec magnus prohibere labor: tu regibus alas / eripe* ("Nor is it hard to stop them: take the kings / And tear off their wings" 4.106–7).

102. For this contrast of bees and farmer, see Johnson, "Bees," 15–16.

103. Hence the passage is introduced by a sympathy available to the farmer, once more, because of his similarity to the bees: "But if you fear a harsh winter and would spare their future and pity their crushed spirits and broken fortunes..." (*sin duram metues hiemem parcesque futuro / cont*sosque animos et res misabere fractas* ... 4.239–40).

104. Thomas, *Virgil*, 2.188; Mynors, *"Georgics"*, 286, describes this section as "placatory." ·Most commentators deny that it is the harvest of honey that Vergil is referring to here, seeing the pests as draining the hive. But for Vergil *not* to raise the question of how much honey to remove, as Varro does (3.16.32–35), following Aristotle (*History of Animals* 627a31), would be very surprising. It would also create a rather startling transition from the dangers of pests to the dangers of diseases—the unimportance of the threat. See Putnam, "Achievement," 57 and Mynors, 290, on both sides of the question.

105. G. Williams, *Tradition*, 260; Wilkinson, *Survey*, 121; Perkell, *Truth*, 174. See Perkell, 167 and Sellar, *Roman Poets*, 213 on the inadequacy of Vergil's scientific explanations. Thomas, *Virgil*, 1.135–36 examines Vergil's personalizing of Aratus' weather signs.

106. "Happy the man who has been able to learn the causes of things / And all fear, and inexorable fate / Cast under his feet, and the roar of greedy Hell" (*felix, qui potuit rerum cognoscere causas / atque metus omnis et inexorabile fatum / subiecit pedibus strepitumque Acherontis avari* 2.490–2).

107. For various views of the ultimate division between the personal and the impersonal in Vergil, see P. Hardie, *Cosmos*, 2; Adam Parry, "The Two Voices of Virgil's *Aeneid*," *Arion* 2 (1963), repr. in Commager, *Virgil*, 118, 121 ff. (page references are to the reprint); Nethercut, "*Natura*," 47; Wender, "Resurrection," 433–36; Segal, "Fourth Georgic," 320–23; A. Wankenne, "Aristée et Orphée dans les *Géorgiques*," *Études Classiques*, 24; Kromer, "Didactic Tradition," 15–18; Sellar, *Roman Poets*, 83 and 354.

CHAPTER 6

1. In contrast, see Lamberton, *Hesiod*, 1.127–28.

2. For the complexity of this interrelation, in particular the economic complexity, see Robin Osborne, "Pride and Prejudice, Sense and Substance: Exchange and Society in the Greek City," in John Rich and Andrew Wallace-Hall, eds., *City and Country in the Ancient World* (London: Routledge, 1991), 119–45.

3. See Tityrus on the difference between Rome and the local town (*Eclogues* 1.19–25). A simple word count is also significant. The word *urbs* is used nine times in the *Georgics*, 197 times in the *Aeneid*. The word *oppidum*, used four times in the *Aeneid*, is also used four times in the *Georgics*: 3.401, as below; 4.178, where the little farmer bees have "towns"; 2.156 describes the "so many outstanding cities, so many crowded towns" of Italy; while 2.176, in what is nearly a contradiction in terms, refers to the "Roman towns" (*Romana oppida*) through which Vergil sings the song of Ascra.

4. See Mack, *Time*, 29–30.

5. I invert my usual pattern of considering Hesiod and then Vergil partly in order to end where I began, partly because Hesiod's is the more optimistic vision.

6. For the pairing of Ceres, who aids Jupiter in instituting farming (1.147–49), and Bacchus, see Lucretius (5.14–15); Thomas, *Virgil*, 1.70. The other god of the wild, as opposed to the domesticated, landscape is Pan, god of the *Eclogues*. He too lurks in the background of the *Georgics* (1.17; 2.494; 3.392) and is absent from the *Works and Days*. See the *Hymn to Pan*, and for both Dionysus and Pan, Osborne, *Landscape*, 189–92.

7. The farmer orders his farm as Caesar orders his troops (2.277–84). For Vergil's military metaphors, Betensky, "Battles," 108–19; Boyle, *Dove*, 48, n. 24 and "Paradox," 82, n. 3; Putnam, *Earth*, 14; Buchheit, *Anspruch*, 19–20.

8. Ryberg, "Golden Age," 125. On the farmer's sympathy for nature, Stehle, "Sloth," 367; A. Michel, "Virgile et la politique imperiale: un courtesan ou un philosophe?", in Bardon and

Verdière, *Vergiliana*, 221, 244; Klingner, "Landlebens," 159–89 and *contra* Perkell, *Truth*, 46–52; Clay, "Argument," 239–40. On the need for both violence and veneration see Dorothea Wender, "Resurrection in the Fourth Georgic," *American Journal of Philology* 90 (1969): 431–32.

9. For Gallus, see Segal, "Fourth Georgic," 309; Howard Jacobson, "Aristaeus, Orpheus, and the Laudes Galli," *American Journal of Philology* 105 (1984): 271–300; Griffin, "Fourth Georgic," 75; Drew, "Structure," passim; Duckworth, "Laudes," 234; Robert Coleman, "Gallus, the *Bucolics*, and the Ending of the Fourth Georgic," *American Journal of Philology* 83 (1962): 55–71. As Vergil, who was not easily satisfied, seems to have published the poem as we have it, it appears unnecessary to consider possible earlier versions.

10. D. E. Wormell, "*Apibus quanta experientia parcis*: Virgil's Georgics 4.1–227," in Bardon and Verdière, *Vergiliana*, 432–35; J. Chomarat, "L'Initiation d'Aristée," *Revue des Études Latines* 52 (1974), 189; and Arthur Bernard Cook, "The Bee in Greek Mythology," *Journal of Hellenic Studies* 15 (1895): 10, point to the traditional association of bees with the soul and its rebirth. Christine Perkell, "Vergil's Theodicy Reconsidered," in Bernard, *Virgil at 2000*, 78 and Putnam, "Achievement," 58 see this "rebirth" as itself ambivalent. For another chapter in this debate see T. N. Habinek, "Sacrifice, Society, and Vergil's Ox-born Bees," in M. Griffith and D. J. Mastronarde, eds., *Cabinet of the Muses: Essays on Classical and Comparative Literature in Honor of Thomas G. Rosenmeyer* (Atlanta: Scholars Press, 1990), 209–23; answered by Richard Thomas, "The 'Sacrifice' at the End of the *Georgics*, Aristaeus, and Vergilian Closure," *Classical Philology* 86 (1991): 211–18.

11. An ambiguity suggested again in "tondent" which can mean "graze," as here, but which can also mean "reap" or "mow," as 1. 71, 1.290.

12. The simile of Book 4 also refers us back to the fact of 2.205–11, revealing that, to the nightingale, the completely rational violence of the plowman is no different from the completely irrational violence of Aristaeus. See Thomas, *Virgil*, 1.23–24, 195; Johnston, *Golden Age*, 113; and Boyle, *Dove*, 73, n. 79.

13. Aristaeus is a shepherd (4.317) and a tender of cattle, crops, woods, vines, and bees (4.329–332), all the topics of the *Georgics*, for which see Segal, "Fourth Georgic," 313. Marking the connection between Aristaeus' vision of farming and the theodicy, 1.133 and 4.315, 328 are the only uses of *extundo* in the *Georgics*. See Thomas, *Virgil*, 1.90; Charles Segal, *Orpheus: The Myth of the Poet* (Baltimore: Johns Hopkins University Press, 1989), 81; and for Aristaeus' violence, Perkell, "Theodicy," 77. Perkell, 67–83 points out the links between the theodicy and the *bougonia*. Note also that in the version of the *Odyssey* (8.266–366) told here Mars, not Vulcan (force, not craft), is successful (4.345–46). For Aristaeus as a figure for Octavian (and Orpheus as a figure for Vergil himself) see Lee, *Orpheus*, 132–39.

14. See Segal, "Fourth Georgic," 315–16; Miles, *Interpretation*, 267–69, and contrast Cyrene's horrific warning, 4.405–14, with the adumbrated fact, 4.440–42. Lines 437–38 describing Proteus' weakness stand out as the one alteration in a passage that otherwise follows its Homeric model very closely; Homer's version here is simply ἔπειτα δὲ λέκτο καὶ αὐτός ("When he too had lain down," *Odyssey* 4.451). In the *Odyssey*, Menelaus is also advised to leave off force and let the old man go free after he has changed back to his original shape (*Odyssey* 4.420–24). Cyrene leaves this out (4.411–14). See Pavlovskis, *Man*, 3, 7 for the usual Roman sense that order must be imposed on nature.

15. A. Bradley, "Augustan," 357; Boyle, *Dove*, 70; Chomarat, "Aristée," 202.

16. Contrast the use of this image in the more permanent vision that opens the third Georgic (3.37–39), and see E. A. Havelock, "Xanadu," *Phoenix* 1 (1996), pt. 2, 7.

17. Many commentators seem to have the same difficulty as the Shades. For Orpheus' guilt, see Ross, *Elementa*, 230–31; Otis, *Virgil*, 212; Griffin, "Fourth Georgic," 71; and, more sympathetically, but still with a focus on the "irrationality" of Orpheus' doubt, Miles, "Amor," 192.

18. Wankenne, "Aristée," 26; Boyle, *Dove*, 71, n. 75. Ross, *Elements*, 227–31 sees Orpheus as representing "control of nature through intellectual understanding" (227).

19. The world of Orpheus and his sisters-in-law, the Nymphs, is the world of farming seen as the Golden Age, as in the second Georgic: "and happy is he who knows the farmer's gods / Pan, and old Silvanus, and the sisterhood of Nymphs." (*fortunatus et ille, deos qui novit agrestis / Panaque Silvanumque senem Nymphasque sorores* 2.493–94).

20. Boyle, "Echo," 121–31; Otis, *Virgil*, 201–2. On Orpheus' failure, see Perret, "The Georgics," 30 and, in contrast, Segal, "Fourth Georgic," 317.

21. Contrast the very different mourning of Achilles and Priam in *Iliad* 24.507 ff. and, for a very different view of the simile, Segal, "Fourth Georgic," 316–17.

22. For example, Perkell, "Reading," 215–16. We should also keep in mind that the phrase the "rape of nature" might not have come as readily to Vergil's lips as to our own.

23. Jacobson, "Aristaeus," 280. *At non Cyrene* (4.530) sounds an underlying note of contrast to Proteus' sympathy, as well as a literal resolve to stand by Aristaeus.

24. See Chomarat, "Aristée," 188, and Parry, "Art," 46.

25. Cyrene addresses Aristaeus always as *nate* (4.375, 396, 412, 531 and see 4.375, 416); Vergil may intend us to hear in the repetition the same root as "natura." See Klingner, *Georgica*, 201–11.

26. Vergil emphasizes Aristaeus' access to the inaccessible elements of nature by the contrast with Thetis, who (rather more naturally, especially if Cyrene is "struck with fear," 4.337) goes to Achilles, rather than waiting for him to come to her (*Iliad* 1.357–62).

27. Also reflecting the nightingale's *queritur* and *questibus* (4.512, 515). Segal, *Orpheus*, 73, points out that the allusion to Achilles emphasizes Aristaeus' petulance.

28. Aristaeus is, in fact, a deeply unattractive individual, which may be due more to subconscious antipathy than to conscious intention on Vergil's part. See Perkell, "Reading," 218; Griffin, "Haec," 26; Segal, "Fourth Georgic," 316.

29. Segal, *Orpheus*, 74–76. Vergil conveys the same impression through his use of an impersonal style for Aristaeus, and an empathetic style for Orpheus and Eurydice. See, in particular, Otis, *Virgil*, 195–202; Miles, *Interpretation*, 270; Boyle, *Dove*, 74 n. 81; Klingner, *Georgica*, 222–27.

30. See Griffin, *Virgil*, 56. Francis, "Personality," 289 ff. and Sellar, *Roman Poets*, 47 point out this quality in farmers. Its other side is the "ignorance" which Vergil not only attributes to his farmers, but tacitly counts as one of their blessings. Not to know the evils of the city is also not to know how precarious the farmer's "natural" place may be. For another view, see Clay, "Arguments," passim.

31. Putnam, *Earth*, 10–11.

32. On the ultimate sterility of Orpheus' grief, see Perkell, *Truth*, 85 and Wender, "Resurrection," 433 ff. For another perspective, see Segal, "Fourth Georgic," 78, and *Orpheus*, 77–79.

33. Perkell, *Truth*, 77; Miles, *Interpretation*, 272.

34. See G. Nagy, "Theognis," 38–39 on the boundaries of "ritual correctness" and their link to moral rectitude and above, chapter 4, for Nilsson's view of Hesiod as "legalistic" (*Piety*, 31–33). The modern Greek peasant crosses himself before crossing a river, Lawson, *Survivals*, 160.

35. Hesiod's use of key words such as ὡραῖος and καιρός throughout the sections points to the connection. See Mazon, *Les Travaux et les jours*, 140; Beye, "Rhythm," 30; Burn, *World*, 78; Richardson, review, 171. See also Robert Redfield, *Peasant*, 29–46, 64–88 and *The Primitive World and its Transformations* (Ithaca: Cornell University Press, 1953), 30 ff. and Wolf, *Peasants*, 11 on the peasant's necessary connection to a "big" as well as a "little" world.

36. Hesiod's insistent repetition of the idea of seasonableness has been noted by Beye, *Literature*, 115; Sinclair, *"Works and Days"*, 10, 30; Hays, "Notes," 14, 27; Mazon, "Composition,"

90, 352 ff.; Kumaniecki, "Structure," 90; van Groningen, *Composition*, 287; Waltz, *Poème moral*, 40, 64; Griffith, "Personality," 60–61; and N. Jones, "Perses," overall. Benardete, "First Reading," 166, stresses the importance of words such as ὡραῖος and μέτριος to Hesiod's idea of man's place in the "cosmic framework." Hamilton, *Architecture*, 84, points to an overall movement in the poem from ages to years to months to days.

37. The injunction to "Naked, sow the seed, plow with your oxen, naked, / and, naked, harvest the crop" (*WD* 391–92), adds to the idea of seasonableness the idea of hard work. One strips both because the work is hard, and because the season is warm. See *Georgics* 1.299; Mazon, "Composition," 374; Solmsen, review, 217. See West, 257, and Mazon, *Les Travaux et les jours*, 97 on the parallel precepts.

38. West, 258: "we were told in 42 that it was by the will of the gods that we must work for our living. That they marked out our tasks (229 n.; δια- suggests distribution through the year) is a new idea"; Mazon, *Les Travaux et les jours*, 98.

39. Verdenius, *Commentary*, 182.

40. An exploration of farming in the proper philosophical way, from its first beginnings. See Aristotle's use of *WD* 405 (*Politics* 1252b10) and Plato, *Republic* 358c, 369b. These lines can hardly be intended as instruction for Perses, whose wife, children, and neighbors have just been mentioned. See Mazon, *Les Travaux et les jours*, 99; vs. West, 51–52.

41. Marked by the connection of the key words, μεμνημένος, φυλασσόμενος, φράζεσθαι, etc. (*WD* 404, 422, 448, 491, 561, 616, 623, 641, 688, 694) with ὡραῖος, etc. See Detienne, *Crise agraire*, 43–49 and for the modern peasant, Bourdieu, *Algerian Peasant*, 69.

42. Rosen, "Poetry and Sailing," 105–6. There is perhaps no more vivid example of the difference between Hesiod and Vergil than this. A shift in viewpoint is, for Vergil, a shift in the reality of the experience. For Hesiod, whether we are part of the experience or deliberately divided from it, the experience and its lesson remain exactly the same.

43. Perhaps because it is so odd it has gone largely unnoticed. See G. Nagy, "Theognis," 64–66 for a negative view of sailing, in particular in contrast to farming, and its connection to seasonableness. On the peasant's hostility to the sea, Sanders, *Rainbow*, 43; on his fear of risk, Francis, "Personality," 280. Lamberton, *Hesiod*, 131 sees the contradiction as evidence that Hesiod is a persona.

44. Here Hesiod's seasonal description (familiar from the farming section) leads into "at that very time is when the blasts of all winds rage" (δὴ τότε παντοίων ἀνέμων θυίουσιν ἀῆται *WD* 621), the best time *not* to sail.

45. Griffith, "Personality," 61. Sinclair, *"Works and Days"*, 38, attributes Hesiod's dislike of sailing to his father's bad experiences. On Ascra see West, 317; Richardson, review, 171; *Hésiode et son influence*, 268 ff.; and, for modern peasants' tendency to downgrade their property, Manning Nash, "The Social Context of Economic Change in a Small Society," in Dalton, *Economies*, 534. Richardson, 171, notices that Hesiod's comparison of his journey to Agamemnon's journey to Troy is intended to be humorous. The distance according to modern maps is about half a kilometer, as opposed to West, who gives the distance as 65 meters.

46. As does the fact that this is Hesiod's second start to the section. See West, 55–56, where he notes that Hesiod's autobiography interrupts the argument, and Kumaniecki, "Structure," 89–90. Walcot, *Peasants*, 23, attributes the delay to the Greek peasant's love of talking about himself.

47. West, 55, not making this connection, sees *WD* 643–45 as "isolated." Right measure and due season have already been linked at *WD* 630–32, whose ἐν δέ τε φόρτον / ἄρμενον ἐντύνασθαι ("stow in her a suitable cargo") is explained here. The concept of μέτρον is equally important in farming, see *WD* 436–47, 692–93.

48. The emphatic position of the future verb may also serve to remind us that the gains are still potential. This is, however, a common position for the verb "to be" in Hesiod.

49. These spots are occupied, in Hesiod's description of the farmer's year, by the summer picnic and the sudden jump from vine-pruning to harvest. See Richardson, review, 171.

50. Hesiod's reluctance to admit that there is a season for sailing thus has the effect of Br'er Rabbit's plea not to be thrown into the briar patch. There must be a natural matching of season and task, as Hesiod is forced to admit, even about sailing.

51. This is Hesiod's usual word for robbery, as in χρήματα δ' οὐχ ἁρπακτά· θεόσδοτα πολλὸν ἀμείνω ("Riches are not for grabbing; when God gives them they are far better" WD 320). See Rand, "Urbanity," 153.

52. Mazon, Les Travaux et les jours, 137.

53. As emphasized by Hesiod's opening and closing the year in the fall, by his description of the preparations for fall plowing, his splitting this task into four separate vignettes, his chronological leaps, and his final surprise inclusion of the vintage. See above, chapter 1.

54. See Vernant, "Sacrifice," 422–23.

55. West, 275–76; and for current practices, such as crossing oneself at the commencement of sowing, Campbell, Honour, 341; Sanders, Rainbow, 265; Banfield, Basis, 113.

56. See Benardete, "First Reading," 155; Marquardt, "Women," 290; Mazon, Les Travaux et les jours, 116. That it should be in the context not of unexpected disaster, but of unexpected rescue, not of a divine snake, but of a divine ladder, that Hesiod makes most explicit his belief in the ambiguity of Zeus' order, should perhaps alter our sense of his native pessimism. See Adkins, "Myth," 99 ff.; Vernant, Society, 185; Grene, "Religion," 154–55.

57. George Carlin's "hippy-dippy weather-man" routine, in which he did a year-end summary of the weather—cold at first, with some warmer spells, growing warmer, some rain, until it got very hot, then gradually cooler, finally cold, with eventual scattered snow and freezing—took advantage of the same contradiction.

58. In contrast, modern Greek peasants tend to attribute the regular workings of nature to God, its irregularities to other divinities: Lawson, Survivals, 50 ff. Gagarin, "Ambiguity," 178 points to the same underlying sense in the prologue to the Work and Days: "Hesiod's sense is that Zeus (who here in some sense represents the god and the non-human universe) displays both regular and arbitrary behavior. And the ambiguity and tension in Zeus' behavior are 'emblematic' . . . of the ambiguity and tension in human affairs."

59. Particularly in the Mediterranean, see White, Farming, 173. As Grene, speaking from experience, "Religion," 148: "Getting the right weather at the right time is where the trouble is." Osborne, Landscape, 41, points out the impossibility of following Hesiodic "rules."

60. Lloyd-Jones, Justice, 162, points out that Zeus' will is inscrutable, not irrational. For the feeling that God is "close, real, and not wholly inscrutable" (italics mine), see Friedl, Vasilika, 78; Campbell, Honour, 323. Van Groningen, Composition, 297; Grene, "Religion," 143: "Farming is the way of life that to Hesiod most clearly reveals man's relation to the gods—to Zeus's harshness and unpredictability, but also to whatever general directions of his, regarding time and fitness, in cultivation of the earth and in dealing with family and others, are available to us."

61. In an anecdote that Hesiod would have appreciated, a friend tells me that during his stay in Zaire with the Peace Corps he and his wife were told that the rain would come on the first of September. Correcting his students, he replied, "You mean around the first of September." The reply was, "Oh no, monsieur, the first of September." Sure enough, on the first of September they awoke to the sound of rain on the tin roof. There are no rules for farming, including that one.

62. See Halstead and Jones, "Agrarian Economy," 50, 53; Dalton, Economies, 64; Oscar E. Handlin, "Peasant Origins," in Dalton, 467; Nash, "Social Context," 526; Banfield, Basis, 111; Friedl, Vasilika, 80; and F. G. Friedmann, "The World of 'La Miseria,'" in Potter, Peasant Society, 8.

63. Blumenberg, *Work on Myth*, 30: "This Olympian of Hesiod becomes the epitome of the ordering of human existence. For man must adapt his relationship to reality to the given conditions, rather than following his heterogeneous nature. He does it by necessity in the regulated relationship of work as the fundamental form in which he comes to terms with nature. The trustworthiness of the cosmos and of its lawgiver is shown by the fact that he gives a dependable reality the form of time. One can only do the right thing if there is a right time for it."

BIBLIOGRAPHY

Abbe, Elfriede. *The Plants of Virgil's "Georgics"*. Ithaca: Cornell University Press, 1965.

Adkins, Arthur W. H. *Merit and Responsibility: A Study in Greek Values*. Oxford: Oxford University Press, 1960; repr., Chicago: University of Chicago Press, Midway Reprint, 1975.

———. "'Friendship' and 'Self-Sufficiency' in Homer and Aristotle." *Classical Quarterly*, n.s., 13 (1963): 30–45.

———. *From the Many to the One: A Study of Personality and Views of Human Nature in the Context of Ancient Greek Society, Values, and Beliefs*. Studies in the Humanities, ed. M. Black. Ithaca: Cornell University Press, 1970.

———. *Moral Values and Political Behavior in Ancient Greece: From Homer to the End of the Fifth Century*. New York: Norton, 1972.

———. "Law versus Claims in Early Greek Religious Ethics." *History of Religions* 21 (1982): 222–39.

———. "Cosmogony and Order in Ancient Greece." In Robin W. Lovin and Frank E. Reynolds, eds., *Cosmogony and Ethical Order: New Studies in Comparative Ethics*, 39–66. Chicago: University of Chicago Press, 1985.

———. "Ethics and the Breakdown of the Cosmogony in Ancient Greece." In Robin W. Lovin and Frank E. Reynolds, eds., *Cosmogony and Ethical Order: New Studies in Comparative Ethics*, 279–309. Chicago: University of Chicago Press, 1985.

———. *Poetic Craft in the Early Greek Elegists*. Chicago: University of Chicago Press, 1985.

———. "Myth, Philosophy, and Religion in Ancient Greece." In Frank E. Reynolds and David Tracy, eds., *Myth and Philosophy*, 95–130. Albany: State University of New York Press, 1990.

Altevogt, Heinrich. *"Labor improbus": Eine Vergilstudie*. Munich: Aschendorff, 1952.

Amouretti, Marie-Claire. *Le pain et l'huile dans la Grèce antique*. Paris: Annales Littéraires de l'Université de Besançon, 1986.

Arthur, Marylin B. "Cultural Strategies in Hesiod's *Theogony*: Law, Family, Society." *Arethusa* 15 (1982): 63–82.

———. "The Dream of a World without Women." *Arethusa* 16 (1983): 97–116.

Athanassakis, Apostolos N. "Introduction." *Ramus* 21 (1992): 1–10.

———. "Cattle and Honour in Homer and Hesiod." *Ramus* 21 (1992): 156–86.

Austin, M. M. and P. Vidal-Naquet. *Economic and Social History of Ancient Greece*. Translated by M. M. Austin. Berkeley: University of California Press, 1977.

Baldry, H. C. "Who Invented the Golden Age?" *Classical Quarterly*, n.s., 4 (1973): 83–92.

Banfield, Edward C., with the assistance of Laura Fasano Banfield. *The Moral Basis of a Backward Society*. Research Center in Economic Development and Cultural Change, University of Chicago. Chicago: Free Press, 1958.

Bardon, Henry and Raoul Verdière, eds. *Vergiliana: Recherches sur Virgile*. Leiden: Brill, 1971.

Baroja, Julio Caro. "The City and the Country: Reflections on Some Ancient Commonplaces." In Julian Pitt-Rivers, ed., *Mediterranean Countrymen: Essays in the Social Athropology of the Mediterranean*, 27–38 (Paris: Mouton, 1963).

Barron, J. P. and P. E. Easterling. "Hesiod." In *The Cambridge History of Classical Literature*, 92–105. Cambridge: Cambridge University Press, 1985.

Bayet, J. "Les Premières 'Géorgiques' de Virgile (39–37 avant J.-Ch.)." *Revue de Philologie* 56 (1930): 128–50 and 227–47.

Beall, E. F. "Hesiod's Prometheus and Development in Myth." *Journal of the History of Ideas* 52 (1991): 355–71.

Benardete, Seth. "Hesiod's *Works and Days*: A First Reading." *Agon* (1967): 150–70.

Berger, Harry. "Archaism, Vision, and Revision: Studies in Virgil, Plato, and Milton." *Centennial Review* 11 (1967): 24–52.

Bernard, J. D., ed. *Virgil at 2000: Commemorative Essays on the Poet and his Influence*. New York: Ams Press, 1986.

Betensky, Aya. "The Farmer's Battles." *Ramus* 8 (1979): 108–19.

Beye, Charles Rowan. "The Rhythm of Hesiod's Works and Days." *Harvard Studies in Classical Philology* 76 (1972): 23–43.

———. *Ancient Greek Literature*. Garden City, N.Y.: Doubleday, 1975.

Blaise, Fabienne. "L'Épisode de Typhée dans la Théogonie d'Hésiode (v. 820–885)." *Revue des Études Grecques* 105 (1992): 349–70.

Blumenberg, Hans. *Work on Myth*. Translated by Robert M. Wallace. Cambridge, Mass: MIT Press, 1985.

Boas, George, Arthur O. Lovejoy, and Ronald S. Crane, eds. *A Documentary History of Primitivism and Related Ideas*. Baltimore: Johns Hopkins University Press, 1935.

Bonnefoy, Yves, ed. *Mythologies*. Translated under the direction of Wendy Doniger. Vol. 1. Chicago: University of Chicago Press, 1991.

Bonner, Robert J. and Gertrude Smith. *The Administration of Justice from Homer to Aristotle*. Chicago: University of Chicago Press, 1930.

———. "The Administration of Justice in the Age of Hesiod." *Classical Philology* 40 (1945): 11–23.

Bosson, A. *Études agronomiques sur les "Géorgiques" de Virgile*. Paris: A. Lévy, 1869.

Bourdieu, Pierre. "The Attitude of the Algerian Peasant toward Time." In Julian Pitt-Rivers, ed., *Mediterranean Countrymen*, 55–72 (Paris: Mouton, 1963).

Bovie, Smith Palmer. "The Image of Ascent-Descent in Vergil's Georgics." *American Journal of Philology* 77 (1956): 337–58.

Bowra, C. M. "A Prayer to the Fates." *Classical Quarterly*, n.s., 8 (1958): 231–40.

Boyle, Antony J. "Virgil's Pastoral Echo." *Ramus* 6 (1977): 121–31.

———. "Introduction." *Ramus* 8 (1979): 1–5.

———. "In Medio Caesar: Paradox and Politics in Virgil's Georgics." *Ramus* 8 (1979): 65–86.

————. *The Chaonian Dove: Studies in the "Eclogues," "Georgics," and "Aeneid " of Virgil*. Mnemosyne Supplement, no. 94. Leiden: Brill, 1986.

Bradley, Anthony. "Augustan Culture and a Radical Alternative: Vergil's *Georgics*." *Arion* 8 (1969): 347–58.

Bradley, Edward M. "The Relevance of the Prooemium to the Design and Meaning of Hesiod's *Theogony*." *Symbolae Osloensis* 41 (1966): 29–47.

Bravo, B. "Remarques sur les assises sociales, les formes d'organisation et le terminologie du commerce maritime grec à l'époque archaïque." *Dialogues d'Histoire Ancienne* 3 (1977): 1–59.

Bremmer, Jan, ed. *Interpretations of Greek Mythology*. London: Routledge, 1988.

Briggs, Ward W., Jr. *Narrative and Simile from the "Georgics" in the "Aeneid"*. Mnemosyne Supplement, no. 58. Leiden: Brill,1980.

Buchheit, Vinzenz. *Der Anspruch des Dichters in Vergils "Georgica": Dichtertum und Heilsweg*. Darmstadt: Wissenschaftliche Buchgesellschaft, 1972.

Burck, Erich. "Die Komposition von Virgils Georgica." *Hermes* 64 (1929): 279–321.

Burford, Alison. *Land and Labor in the Greek World*. Baltimore: Johns Hopkins University Press, 1993.

Burford-Cooper, Alison. "The Family Farm in Greece." *Classical Journal* 73 (1977): 162–75.

Burkert, Walter. *Greek Religion*. Translated by John Raffan. Cambridge, Mass.: Harvard University Press, 1985.

Burn, Andrew Robert. *The World of Hesiod: A Study of the Greek Middle Ages*. New York: Dutton, 1937.

Caldwell, Richard S. *Hesiod's Theogony*. Cambridge, Mass.: Focus Classical Library, 1987.

————. *The Origin of the Gods: A Psychoanalytical Study of Greek Theogonic Myth*. New York: Oxford University Press, 1989.

Campbell, J. K. *Honour, Family and Patronage: A Study of Institutions and Moral Values in a Greek Mountain Community*. Oxford: Oxford University Press,1964.

Chomarat, J. "L'Initiation d'Aristée." *Revue des Études Latines* 52 (1974): 185–207.

Claus, David B. "Defining Moral Terms in the *Works and Days*." *Transactions of the American Philological Association* 107 (1977): 73–84.

Clausen, Wendell. "Callimachus and Latin Poetry." *Greece and Rome* 5 (1964): 181–96.

Clay, Jenny Strauss. "The Argument of the End of Vergil's Second Georgic." *Philologus* 120 (1976): 232–45.

Coleman, Robert. "Gallus, the *Bucolics*, and the Ending of the Fourth Georgic." *American Journal of Philology* 83 (1962): 55–71.

Commager, Steele, ed. *Virgil: A Collection of Critical Essays*. Englewood Cliffs, N.J.: Prentice-Hall, 1966.

Connor, Peter. "The *Georgics* as Description: Aspects and Qualifications." *Ramus* 8 (1979): 34–58.

Conte, Gian Biagio. *The Rhetoric of Imitation: Genre and Poetic Memory in Virgil and Other Latin Poets*, ed. Charles Segal. Ithaca: Cornell University Press, 1986.

Conway, R. S. *The Vergilian Age*. Cambridge, Mass.: Harvard University Press, 1928.

Cook, Arthur Bernard. "The Bee in Greek Mythology." *Journal of Hellenic Studies* 15 (1895): 1–24.

Cordero, Nestor-Luìs. "Passé mythique et présent historique chez Hésiode." In Antoine Thivel, ed., *Le Miracle grec*, 81–88. Nice: Belles Lettres, 1992.

Cornford, Francis MacDonald. *From Religion to Philosophy, A Study in the Origins of Western Speculation*. London: Edward Arnold, 1912.

————. *Principium Sapientiae*. Cambridge: Cambridge University Press, 1952.

Dahlmann, Hellfried. "Der Bienenstaat in Vergils *Georgica*." Akademie der Wissenschaft und der Literatur in Mainz, *Abhandlungen der Geistes- und Sozialwissenschaftlichen Classe* 10 (1954): 547–62.

Dalton, George, ed. *Tribal and Peasant Economies: Readings in Economic Anthropology*. Garden City, N.Y.: National History Press, Doubleday, 1967.

Daly, Lloyd. "Hesiod's Fable." *Transactions of the American Philological Association* 92 (1961): 45–51.

Davis, P. J. "Vergil's *Georgics* and the Pastoral Ideal." *Ramus* 8 (1979): 22–33.

Defradas, Jean. *Les Thèmes de la propagande delphique*. Paris: C. Klincksiech, 1954.

Denniston, J. D. *The Greek Particles*. Oxford: Clarendon Press, 1934.

Detienne, Marcel. *Crise agraire et attitude religieuse chez Hésiode*. Collection Latomus, Revue des Études Latines, no. 68. Brussels: Berchem, 1963.

Dewar, Micael. "Octavian and Orestes in the Finale of the First Georgic." *Classical Quarterly*, n.s., 38 (1988): 563–65.

Dickie, Matthew. "*Dike* as a Moral Term in Hesiod and Homer." *Classical Philology* 73 (1978): 91–100.

Diller, H. "Die dichterische Form von Hesiods *Erga*." In Ernst Heitsch, ed., *Hesiod*, 239–74. Darmstadt: Wissenschaftliche Buchgesellschaft, 1962.

Dodds, E. R. *The Greeks and the Irrational*. Sather Classical Lectures. Berkeley: University of California Press, 1951.

———. *The Ancient Concept of Progress*. Oxford: Oxford University Press, 1973.

Doniger, Wendy. [See also O'Flaherty, Wendy Doniger.] "Pluralism and Intolerance in Hinduism." In Werner G. Jeanrond and Jennifer L. Rike, eds., *Radical Pluralism and Truth: David Tracy and the Hermeneutics of Religion*, 215–33. New York: Crossroad, 1991.

———. "Myths With and Without Points of View." Surjat Singh Lecture, University of California, Berkeley, October 31, 1994 (unpublished).

Drew, D. L. "The Structure of Vergil's *Georgics*." *American Journal of Philology* 50 (1929): 242–54.

Duban, Jeffrey M. "Poets and Kings in the *Theogony* Invocation." *Quaderni Urbinati di Cultura Classica*, n.s., 4 (1980): 7–21.

Duckworth, George E. "Vergil's *Georgics* and the Laudes Galli." *American Journal of Philology* 80 (1959): 225–37.

Dundes, Alan, ed. *Sacred Narrative: Readings in the Theory of Myth*. Berkeley: University of California Press,1984.

Edwards, G. P. *The Language of Hesiod in its Traditional Context*. Oxford: Oxford University Press, 1971.

Edmunds, Lowell, ed. *Approaches to Greek Myth*. Baltimore: Johns Hopkins University Press, 1990.

Edmunds, Susan T. *Homeric Nêpios*. New York: Garland, 1990.

Erbse, Hartmut. *Untersuchungen zur Funktion der Götter im homerischen Epos*. Berlin: de Gruyter, 1986.

Evelyn-White, Hugh G. *Hesiod, the Homeric Hymns and Homerica*. Loeb Classical Library. Cambridge, Mass.: Harvard University Press, 1914.

Farrell, Joseph. *Vergil's "Georgics" and the Traditions of Ancient Epic: The Art of Allusion in Literary History*. Oxford: Oxford University Press, 1991.

Ferguson, John. *Moral Values in the Ancient World*. London: Methuen, 1958.

Finley, M. I. "Myth, Memory and History." *History and Theory* 4 (1964): 284–89.

———. *The World of Odysseus*. Revised edn. New York: Viking, 1978.

Fontenrose, Joseph. "Work, Justice, and Hesiod's Five Ages." *Classical Philology* 69 (1974): 1–15.

Forbes, P. B. R. "Hesiod vs. Perseus." *Classical Review* (1970): 82–87.

Forde, Daryll and Mary Douglas. "Primitive Economics." In George Dalton, ed., *Tribal and Peasant Economies: Readings in Economic Anthropology*, 13–28. Garden City, N.Y.: National History Press, Doubleday, 1967.

Foster, George M. "Peasant Society and the Image of Limited Good." In Jack M. Potter, May N. Diaz, and George M. Foster, eds., *Peasant Society: A Reader*, 304–20. Boston: Little, Brown, 1967.

Fowler, Don. "Deviant Focalization in Virgil's *Aeneid*." *Proceedings of the Cambridge Philological Society* 216 (1990): 42–63.

Francis, E. K. L. "The Personality Type of the Peasant According to Hesiod's *Works and Days*: A Culture Case Study." *Rural Sociology* 10 (1945): 275–95.

Fränkel, Hermann. *Early Greek Poetry and Philosophy*. Translated by Moses Hadas and James Willis. Oxford: Blackwell, 1975.

———. *Wege und Form frühgriechischen Denkens: Literarische und philosophiegeschichtliche Studien*. Munich: Beck, 1960.

Friedl, Ernestine. *Vasilika: A Village in Modern Greece*. New York: Holt, Rinehart and Winston, 1962.

Frisch, Hatvig. *Might and Right in Antiquity*. Translated by C. C. Martindale. Copenhagen: Gyldendale, 1949.

Fritz, Kurt von. "ΝΟΟΣ and ΝΟΕΙΝ in the Homeric Poems." *Classical Philology* 38 (1943): 79–93.

———. "Das Hesiodische in den Werken Hesiods." In *Hésiode et son Influence*. Entretiens sur l'antiquité classique, 7: 3–47. Geneva: Fondation Hardt, 1962.

———. "Pandora, Prometheus und der Mythos von den Weltaltern." In Ernst Heitsch, ed., *Hesiod*, 367–410. Darmstadt: Wissenschaftliche Buchgesellschaft, 1966.

Gagarin, Michael. "Blind Justice," review of *The Justice of Zeus*, by Hugh Lloyd-Jones. *Arion*, n.s., 1 (1973): 197–204.

———. "*Dike* in the *Works and Days*." *Classical Philology* 68 (1973): 81–93.

———. "*Dike* in Archaic Greek Thought." *Classical Philology* 69 (1974): 186–97.

———. "Hesiod's Dispute with Perses." *Classical Philology* 69 (1974): 103–11.

———. "The Ambiguity of *Eris* in the *Works and Days*." In M. Griffith and D. J. Mastronarde, eds., *Cabinet of the Muses: Essays on Classical and Comparitive Literature in Honor of Thomas G. Rosenmeyer*, 173–83. Atlanta: Scholars Press, 1990.

———. "The Poetry of Justice: Hesiod and the Origin of Greek Law." *Ramus* 21 (1992): 61–78.

Gale, Monica R. "Man and Beast in Lucretius and the *Georgics*." *Classical Quarterly* 51 (1991): 414–26.

Gallant, Thomas W. *Risk and Survival in Ancient Greece: Reconstructing the Rural Domestic Economy*. Stanford: Stanford University Press, 1991.

García Armendáriz, José Ignacio. "Hesíodo y Virgilio: a propósito de nudus ara, sere nudus." *Myrtia* 6 (1991): 71–81.

Garner, Richard. *Law and Society in Classical Athens*. New York: St. Martin's Press, 1987.

Gilmore, David, ed. *Honor and Shame and the Unity of the Mediterranean*. Special Publication of the American Anthropological Association, no. 22. Washington, D.C.: American Anthropological Association, 1987.

Goldschmidt, Victor. "Théologia." *Revue des Études Grecques* 63 (1950): 20–42.

Gow, A. S. F. "Elpis and Pandora in Hesiod's *Works and Days*." In E. C. Quiggin, ed., *Essays and Studies Presented to William Ridgeway*, 99–109. Cambridge: Cambridge University Press, 1913.

Gransden, K. W. Review of *Virgil: The "Eclogues" and "Georgics,"* by R. D. Williams, *Virgil's Poem of the Earth: Studies in the "Georgics,"* by Michael C. J. Putnam, *Narrative and Simile from the "Georgics" in the "Aeneid,"* by Ward W. Briggs, and *Vergil's Agricultural Golden Age: A Study of the "Georgics,"* by Patricia A. Johnston. *Journal of Roman Studies* 72 (1982): 207–9.

Grene, David. "Hesiod: Religion and Poetry in the *Works and Days*." In Werner G. Jeanrond and Jennifer L. Rike, eds. *Radical Pluralism and Truth: David Tracy and the Hermeneutics of Religion*, 142–58. New York: Crossroad, 1991.

———. Response to "Justice and Farming in the *Works and Days*." In Robert B. Louden and Paul Schollmeier, eds., *The Greeeks and Us: Essays in Honor of Arthur Adkins*, 36–42. Chicago: University of Chicago Press, 1996.

Griffin, Jasper. "The Fourth Georgic, Virgil, and Rome." *Greece and Rome*, 2d. ser., 26 (1979): 61–80.

———. "Haec Super Arvorum Cultu." *Classical Review*, n.s., 31 (1981): 23–57.

———. *Virgil*. Past Masters. Oxford: Oxford University Press,1986.

Griffith, Mark. "Personality in Hesiod." *Classical Antiquity* 2 (1983): 37–65.

Groningen, B. A. van. *Hésiode et Persès*. Amsterdam: Verhandelingen der Konnklijke Nederlandse Akademie van Wetenschappen, 1957.

———. *La Composition littéraire archaïque grecque*. Amsterdam: Verhandelingen der Konnklijke Nederlandse Akademie van Wetenschappen, 1958.

Habinek, T. N. "Sacrifice, Society, and Vergil's Ox-born Bees." In M. Griffith and D. J. Mastronarde, eds., *Cabinet of the Muses: Essays on Classical and Comparative Literature in Honor of Thomas G. Rosenmeyer*. Atlanta: Scholars Press, 1990.

Halstead, Paul. "Traditional and Ancient Rural Economy." *Journal of Hellenic Studies* 107 (1987): 77–87.

Halstead, Paul and Glynis Jones. "Agrarian Economy in the Greek Islands: Time Stress, Scale and Risk." *Journal of Hellenic Studies* 109 (1989): 41–55.

Hamilton, Richard. *The Architecture of Hesiodic Poetry*. AJP Monographs in Classical Philology, ed. Diskin Clay. Baltimore: Johns Hopkins University Press, 1989.

Hanson, Victor Davis. *The Other Greeks*. New York: Free Press, 1995.

Hardie, Colin. *The Georgics: A Transitional Poem*. Third Jackson Knight Memorial Lecture. Abingdon, Oxon.: Abbey Press, 1971.

Hardie, Philip R. *Virgil's Aeneid: Cosmos and Imperium*. Oxford: Clarendon Press, 1986.

Harrison, E. L. "The Noric Plague in Vergil's Third Georgic." In Francis Cairns, ed., *Papers of the Liverpool Latin Seminar: Vergil and Roman Elegy, Medieval Latin Poetry and Prose, Greek Lyric and Drama*, 1–66. Liverpool: Francis Cairns, 1979.

Harrison, Jane Ellen. *Themis: A Study of the Social Origins of Greek Religion*. 2d ed. Cambridge: Cambridge University Press, 1927.

Hatab, Lawrence J. *Myth and Philosophy: A Contest of Truths*. La Salle, Ill.: Open Court, 1990.

Havelock, Erik A. "Virgil's Road to Xanadu." *Phoenix* 1 (1946): 3–18.

———. "Thoughtful Hesiod." *Yale Classical Studies* 20 (1966): 59–72.

———. "Δικαιοσύνη." *Phoenix* 23 (1969): 49–70.

———. *The Greek Concept of Justice: From its Shadow in Homer to its Substance in Plato*. Cambridge, Mass.: Harvard University Press, 1978.

Hays, Heber Michel. "Notes on the *Works and Days* of Hesiod." Ph.D. diss., University of Chicago, 1918.

Heath, Malcolm. "Hesiod's Didactic Poetry." *Classical Quarterly*, n.s., 35 (1985): 245–63.

Heitland, W. E. *Agricola*. Cambridge: Cambridge University Press, 1921.

Heitsch, Ernst, ed. *Hesiod*. Darmstadt: Wissenschaftliche Buchgesellschaft, 1966.

Hésiode et son Influence. Entretiens sur l'antiquité classique 7. Geneva: Fondation Hardt, 1962.

Hirzel, Rudolf. *Themis, Dike und Verwandtes*. Leipzig: S. Hirzel, 1907.

Hoekstra, A. "Hésiode, *Les Travaux et les jours*, 405–407, 317–319, 21–24: L'Élément proverbial et son adaptation." *Mnemosyne*, 4th ser., 3 (1950): 89–114.

———. "Review." *Mnemosyne*, 4th ser., 3 (1950): 406–7.

———. "Hésiode et la tradition orale." *Mnemosyne*, 4th ser., 10 (1967): 193–225.

Hofinger, Marcel. "Le Logos hésiodique des races: *Les Travaux et les jours*, vers 106 à 201." *L'Antiquité Classique* 50 (1981): 404–16.

Howe, Thalia Phillips. "Linear B and Hesiod's Breadwinners." *Transactions of the American Philological Association* 89 (1959): 45–65.

Iriarte, Ana. "Savoir et pouvoir de Zeus." *Ítaca* 2 (1986): 9–24.

Isager, Signe and Jens Erik Skydsgaard. *Ancient Greek Agriculture*. London: Routledge, 1992.

Jacobson, Howard. "Aristaeus, Orpheus, and the Laudes Galli." *American Journal of Philology* 105 (1984): 271–300.

Jaeger, Werner. *Paideia: The Ideals of Greek Culture*, Vol. 1. Translated by Gilbert Highet. 2d edn. New York: Oxford University Press, 1945.

Janko, Richard. *Homer, Hesiod and the Hymns: Diachronic Development in Epic Diction*. Cambridge: Cambridge University Press, 1982.

Jensen, Minna Skafte. "Tradition and Individuality in Hesiod's *Works and Days*." *Classica et Mediaevalia* 27 (1966): 1–27.

Jermyn, L. A. S. "Virgil's Agricultural Lore." *Greece and Rome* 18 (1949): 49–69.

———. "Weather-Signs in Virgil." *Greece and Rome* 20 (1951): 26–37.

Johnson, W. R. *Darkness Visible: A Study of Vergil's "Aeneid"*. Berkeley: University of California Press, 1976.

———. "The Broken World." *Arethusa* 14 (1981): 49–55.

———. "Vergil's Bees: The Ancient Romans' View of Rome." In Annabel Patterson, ed., *Roman Images: Selected Papers from the English Institute, 1982*, 1–22. Baltimore: Johns Hopkins University Press, 1984.

———. "Medea Nunc Sum: The Close of Seneca's Version." In Pietro Pucci, ed., *Language and the Tragic Hero: Essays on Greek Tragedy in Honor of Gordon M. Kirkwood*. Atlanta: Scholar's Press, 1988.

Johnston, Patricia A. *Vergil's Agricultural Golden Age: A Study of the "Georgics"*. Mnemosyne Supplement, no. 60. Leiden: Brill, 1980.

Jones, J. Walter. *The Law and Legal Theory of the Greeks: An Introduction*. Oxford: Clarendon Press, 1956.

Jones, Nicholas F. "Perses, Work "In Season", and the Purpose of the *Works and Days*." *Classical Journal* 79 (1984): 307–23.

Kanelopoulos, Charles. "L'Agriculture d'Hésiode: Techniques et culture." *Éditions de la Maison des Sciences de l'Homme* 15 (1990): 131–58.

Kerényi, Karl. "The Trickster in Relation to Greek Mythology," trans. R. F. C. Hull. In Paul Radin, *The Trickster: A Study in American Indian Mythology*, 173–91. New York: Philosophical Library, 1956.

Kirby, John T. "Rhetoric and Poetics in Hesiod." *Ramus* 21 (1992): 34–60.

Kirk, G. S. "The Structure and Aim of the *Theogony*." In *Hésiode et son Influence*, Entretiens sur l'antiquité classique 7, 68–101. Geneva: Fondation Hardt, 1962.

———. *Myth: Its Meaning and Function in Ancient and Other Cultures*. Sather Classical Lectures. Berkeley: University of California Press, 1970.

Kirk, G. S., J. E. Raven, and M. Schofield. *The Presocratic Philosophers: A Critical History with a Selection of Texts*. 2d edn. Cambridge: Cambridge University Press, 1983.

Klingner, Friedrich. "Über das Lob des Landlebens in Virgils *Georgica*." *Hermes* 66 (1931): 159–89.

———. *Virgils "Georgica"*. Zurich: Artemis, 1963.

Knight, W. F. Jackson. *Roman Vergil*. Rev. edn. Harmondsworth, Middx.: Penguin, 1966.

Knox, Bernard. "Work and Justice in Archaic Greece: Hesiod's *Works and Days*." In *Essays: Ancient and Modern*. Baltimore: Johns Hopkins University Press, 1989.

Knox, Peter E. "Love and Horses in Virgil's *Georgics*." *Eranos* 90 (1992): 43–53.

Komornicka, Anna M. "L'Elpis hésiodique dans la jarre de Pandore." *Eos* 78 (1990): 63–77.

Kristol, Susan Scheinberg. *"Labor" and "Fortuna" in Vergil's "Aeneid"*. New York: Garland, 1990.

Kromer, Gretchen. "The Didactic Tradition in Vergil's *Georgics*." *Ramus* 8 (1979): 7–21.

Kumaniecki, Kasimierz. "The Structure of Hesiod's *Works and Days*." *London University Institute of Classical Studies Bulletin* 10 (1963): 79–96.

Lamberton, Robert. *Hesiod*. Hermes Books, ed. J. Herington. New Haven: Yale University Press, 1988.

Latte, Kurt. "Der Rechtsgedanke in archaischen Greichentum." *Antike u. Abendland* 2 (1946): 63–76.

———. "Hesiods Dichterweihe." *Antike u. Abendland* 2 (1946): 154–63.

Lattimore, Richmond. "The First Elegy of Solon." *American Journal of Philology* 68 (1947): 161–79.

Lawson, John Cuthbert. *Modern Greek Folklore and Ancient Greek Religion: A Study in Survivals*. Cambridge: Cambridge University Press, 1910; repr., New Hyde Park, N.Y.: University Books, 1964.

Leach, Edmund R. "Cronos and Chronos." In William A. Lessa and Evon. Z. Vogt, eds. *Reader in Comparative Religion: An Anthropological Approach*, 241–46. New York: Harper and Row, 1979.

Leach, Eleanor Winsor. "*Sedes apibus*: From the Georgics to the Aeneid." *Vergilius* 23 (1977): 2–16.

Leclerc, Marie-Christine. "La Parole chez Hésiode." *L'Information Littéraire* 43 (1991): 3–4.

———. "L'Épervier et le rossignol d'Hésiode: une fable à double sens." *Revue des Études Grecques* 105 (1992): 37–44.

Lee, M. Owen. *Virgil as Orpheus: A Study of the "Georgics"*. Albany: State University of New York Press, 1996.

Leiniers, Valdis "'ΕΛΠΙΣ in Hesiod: *Work and Days* 96." *Philologus* 128 (1984): 1–8.

Lessa, William A. and Evon. Z. Vogt, eds. *Reader in Comparative Religion: An Anthropological Approach*. 4th edn. New York: Harper and Row, 1979.

Liebeschuetz, W. "Beast and Man in the Third Book of Virgil's *Georgics*." *Greece and Rome*, 2d ser., 12 (1965): 64–77.

Lincoln, Bruce. *Myth, Cosmos, and Society: Indo-European Themes of Creation and Destruction*. Cambridge, Mass.: Harvard University Press, 1986.

———. *Death, War, and Sacrifice: Studies in Ideology and Practice*. Chicago: University of Chicago Press, 1991.

Lloyd-Jones, Hugh. "Zeus in Aeschylus." *Journal of Hellenic Studies* 76 (1956): 55–67.

———. *The Justice of Zeus*. 2d edn. Sather Classical Lectures. Berkeley: University of California Press, 1983.

Lorenz, Konrad. *King Solomon's Ring: New Light on Animal Ways*. Translated by Marjorie Kerr Wilson. New York: Crowell, 1952.

Loupiac, Annic. "Le labor chez Virgile: essai d'interprétation." *Revue des Études Latines* 70 (1992): 92–106.

Lovejoy, Arthur O. and George Boas. *Primitivism and Related Ideas in Antiquity*. Vol. 1 of Arthur O. Lovejoy, George Boas, and Ronald S. Crane, eds., *A Documentary History of Primitivism and Related Ideas*. Baltimore: Johns Hopkins Press, 1935.

Lyne, R. O. A. M. "'Scilicet et Tempus Veniet . . .': Vergil, *Georgics* 1.463–514." In Tony Woodman and David West, eds., *Quality and Pleasure in Latin Poetry*, 47–66. Cambridge: Cambridge University Press, 1974.

Mack, Sara. *Patterns of Time in Vergil*. Hamden, Conn.: Archon, 1978.

Marasco, Gabriele. "Corycius senex (Verg. *Georg.* 4, 127)." *Rivista di filologia e di istruzione classica* 118 (1990): 402–7.

Marquardt, Patricia A. "Hesiod's Ambiguous View of Women." *Classical Philology* 77 (1982): 283–91.

———. "The Two Faces of Hesiod's Muse." *Illinois Classical Studies* 7 (1982): 1–12.

Martin, Richard P. "Hesiod's Metanastic Poetics." *Ramus* 21 (1992): 11–33.

Marx, Leo. *The Machine in the Garden*. Oxford: Oxford University Press, 1964.

Mazon, Paul. "Hésiode: La composition des *Travaux et des jours*." *Revue des Études Anciennes* 14 (1912): 328–55.

———. *Les Travaux et les jours*. Paris: Hachette, 1914.

McKay, Alexander G. "Virgilian Landscape into Art: Poussin, Claude and Turner." In D. R. Dudley, ed., *Virgil*, 139–60. Studies in Latin Literature and its Influence, ed. D. R. Dudley and T. A. Dorey. New York: Basic Books, 1969.

———. "Prometheus Then and Now." *Augustan Age* 10 (1990–92): 26–33.

McKay, K. J. "Ambivalent αἰδώς in Hesiod." *American Journal of Philology* 84 (1963): 17–28.

Mezzadri, Bernard. "La Double Éris initiale." *Métis* 4 (1989): 51–60.

Middleton, John, ed. *Myth and Cosmos: Readings in Mythology and Symbolism*. American Museum Sourcebooks in American Anthropology. Garden City, N.Y.: Natural History Press, 1967.

Michel, A. "Virgile et la politique impériale: Un courtesan ou un philosophe?" In Henry Bardon and Raoul Verdière, eds., *Vergiliana: Recherches sur Virgile*, 212–45. Leiden: Brill, 1971.

Miles, Gary B. "*Georgics* 3.209–294: Amor and Civilization." *California Studies in Classical Antiquity* 8 (1975): 177–97.

———. *Virgil's "Georgics": A New Interpretation*. Berkeley: University of California Press, 1980.

Millet, Paul. "Hesiod and his World." *Cambridge Philological Society Proceedings* 209 (1983): 84–115.

Minton, William W. "The Proem-Hymn of Hesiod's *Theogony*." *Transactions of the American Philological Association* 101 (1970): 357–77.

Mondi, Robert. "The Ascension of Zeus and the Composition of Hesiod's *Theogony*." *Greek, Roman, and Byzantine Studies* 25 (1984): 325–44.

———. "Tradition and Innovation in the Hesiodic Titanomachy." *Transactions of the American Philological Association* 116 (1986): 25–48.

———. "Greek Mythic Thought in the Light of the Near East." In Lowell Edmunds, ed., *Approaches to Greek Myth*, 142–98. Baltimore: Johns Hopkins University Press, 1990.

Mountford, Sir James. "The Architecture of the *Georgics*." *Proceedings of the Virgil Society* 6 (1967): 25–34.

Muecke, Frances. "Poetic Self-Consciousness in *Georgics* II." *Ramus* 8 (1979): 87–107.

Mynors, R. A. B. *Virgil's "Georgics"*. Oxford: Clarendon Press, 1990.

Myres, John. "'Ελπίς, ἔλπω, ἔλπομαι, ἐλπιζείν." *Classical Review* 62 (1948): 46.

Naddaf, Gérard. "Hésiode, précurseur des cosmogonies grecques de type 'évolutionniste.'" *Revue de l'Histoire des Religions* 203 (1986): 339–64.

Nagler, Michael N. "Discourse and Content in Hesiod." *Ramus* 21 (1992): 79–96.

Nagy, Gregory. *The Best of the Achaeans: Concepts of the Hero in Archaic Greek Poetry*. Baltimore: Johns Hopkins University Press, 1979.

———. "Hesiod." In T. J. Luce, ed., *Ancient Writers: Greece and Rome*, 43–73. New York: Scribner's, 1982.

———. "Theognis and Megara: A Poet's Vision of His City." In Thomas J. Figueira and Gregory Nagy, eds., *Theognis of Megara: Poetry and the Polis*, 22–81. Baltimore: Johns Hopkins University Press, 1985.

———. "Authorization and Authorship in the Hesiodic *Theogony*." *Ramus* 21 (1990): 119–30.

———. *Greek Mythology and Poetics*. Ithaca: Cornell University Press, 1990.

———. *Poetry as Performance: Homer and Beyond*. Cambridge: Cambridge University Press, 1996.

Nagy, Joseph Falaky. "The Deceptive Gift in Greek Mythology." *Arethusa* 14 (1981): 191–204.

Nash, Manning. "The Organization of Economic Life." In George Dalton, ed., *Tribal and Peasant Economies: Readings in Economic Antropology*, 3–11. Garden City, N.Y.: National History Press, Doubleday, 1967.

———. "The Social Context of Economic Choice in a Small Society." In George Dalton, ed., *Tribal and Peasant Economies: Readings in Economic Antropology*, 524–38. Garden City, N.Y.: National History Press, Doubleday, 1967.

Nethercut, William R. "Vergil's *De Rerum Natura*." *Ramus* 2 (1973): 41–52.

Nelson, Stephanie A. "The Drama of Hesiod's Farm." *Classical Philology* 19 (1996): 45–53.

———. "Justice and Farming in the *Works and Days*." In Robert T. Louden and Paul Schollmeier, eds., *The Greeks and Us: Essays in Honor of Arthur Adkins*, 17–36. Chicago: University of Chicago Press, 1996.

———. "The Justice of Zeus in Hesiod's Fable of the Hawk and the Nightingale." *Classical Journal* 92 (1997): 237–47.

Nicolai, W. *Hesiods Erga*. Heidelburg: C. Winter, 1964.

Nilsson, Martin P. *A History of Greek Religion*. 2d edn. Translated by F. J. Fielden. Oxford: Oxford University Press, 1949.

———. *Greek Piety*. Translated by Herbert Jennings Rose. New York: Norton, 1969.

———. *Homer and Mycenae*. London: Methuen, 1933; repr., Philadelphia: University of Pennsylvania Press, 1972.

Northrup, Mark. "Hesiodic Personification in Parmenides A37." *Transactions of the American Philological Association* 110 (1980): 223–32.

———. "Where Did the *Theogony* End?" *Symbolae Osloensis* 58 (1983): 7–13.

Notopoulos, James A. "Homer, Hesiod, and the Achaean Heritage of Oral Poetry." *Hesperia* 29 (1960): 177–97.

Nussbaum, G. "Labour and Status in the *Works and Days*." *Classical Quarterly*, n.s., 10 (1960): 213–20.

O'Flaherty, Wendy Doniger. [See also Doniger, Wendy.] *Asceticism and Eroticism in the Mythology of Siva*. Oxford: Oxford University Press, 1973.

———. *The Origin of Evil in Hindu Mythology*. Berkeley: University of California Press, 1976.

Olstein, Katherine. "Pandora and Dike in Hesiod's *Works and Days*." *Emerita* 48 (1980): 295–312.

Osborne, Robin. *Classical Landscape with Figures: The Ancient Greek City and its Countryside*. London: Sheridan House, 1987.

———. "Pride and Prejudice, Sense and Substance: Exchange and Society in the Greek City." In John Rich and Andrew Wallace-Hall, eds., *City and Country in the Ancient World*, 119–45. London: Routeledge, 1991.

Østerud, Svein. "The Individuality of Hesiod." *Hermes* 104 (1976): 13–29.

Ostwald, Martin. *Nomos and the Beginnings of the Athenian Democracy*. Oxford: Clarendon Press, 1969.

Otis, Brooks. *Virgil: A Study in Civilized Poetry*. Oxford: Oxford University Press, 1964.

———. "The Originality of the *Aeneid*." In D. R. Dudley, ed., *Virgil*, 27–66. London: Rouledge, 1969.

———. "A New Study of the Georgics." *Phoenix* 26 (1972): 40–62.

Otto, Walter F. *The Homeric Gods: The Spiritual Significance of Greek Religion*. Translated by Moses Hadas. New York: Thames and Hudson, 1954.

Page, T. E. P. *Vergili Maronis: Bucolica et Georgica*. London: Macmillan, 1898.

Palmer, L. R. "The Indo-European Origins of Greek Justice." *Transactions of the Philological Society* (1950): 149–68.

Parry, Adam. "The Two Voices of Vergil's *Aeneid*." *Arion*, 2 (1963): 66–80.

———. "The Idea of Art in Virgil's *Georgics*." *Arethusa* 5 (1972): 35–52.

Pavlovskis, Zoja. *Man in an Artificial Landscape: The Marvels of Civilization in Imperial Roman Literature*. Mnemosyne Supplement, no. 25. Leiden: Brill, 1973.

Pearson, Lionel. *Popular Ethics in Ancient Greece*. Stanford: Stanford University Press, 1962.

Penglase, Charles. *Greek Myths and Mesopotamia: Parallels and Influences in the Homeric Hymns and Hesiod*. London: Routledge, 1994.

Peristiany, J. G., ed. *Honour and Shame: The Values of Mediterranean Society*. Chicago: University of Chicago Press, 1966.

Perkell, Christine G. "A Reading of Virgil's Fourth Georgic." *Phoenix* 32 (1978): 211–21.

———. "On the Corycian Gardner of Vergil's Fourth Georgic." *Transactions of the American Philological Association* 111 (1981): 167–77.

———. *The Poet's Truth: A Study of the Poet in Virgil's "Georgics"*. Berkeley: University of California Press, 1981.

———. "Vergil's Theodicy Reconsidered." In J. D. Bernard, ed., *Vergil at 2000: Commemorative Essays on the Poet and his Influence*, 67–83. New York: Ams Press, 1986.

Perret, Jacques. "*The Georgics*." In Steele Commager, ed., *Virgil: A Collection of Essays*, 37. Englewood Cliffs, N.J.: Prentice-Hall, 1966.

Perry, B. F. "The Origin of the Epimythium." *Transactions of the American Philological Association* 71 (1940): 391–419.

———. "Fable." *Studium Generale* 12 (1959): 17–37.

Pitt-Rivers, Julian, ed. *Mediterranean Countrymen: Essays in the Social Anthropology of the Mediterranean*. Paris: Mouton, 1963.

Pötscher, W. "Moira, Themis und τιμή im homerischen Denken." *Wiener Studien* 73 (1960): 5–39.

Potter, Jack M., May N. Diaz, and George M. Foster, eds. *Peasant Society: A Reader*. Boston: Little, Brown, 1967.

Pucci, Pietro. *Hesiod and the Language of Poetry*. Baltimore: Johns Hopkins University Press, 1977.

Putnam, Michael C. J. "The Virgilian Achievement." *Arethusa* 5 (1972): 53–70.

———. "Italian Virgil and the Idea of Rome." In L. L. Orlin, ed., *Janus: Essays in Ancient and Modern Studies*, 171–200. Ann Arbor: Center for Coordination of Ancient and Modern Studies, University of Michigan, 1975.

———. *Virgil's Poem of the Earth: Studies in the "Georgics"*. Princeton: Princeton University Press, 1979.

———. *Virgil's "Aeneid": Interpretation and Influence*. Chapel Hill: University of North Carolina Press, 1995.

Querbach, Carl W. "Hesiod's Myth of the *Four* Races." *Classical Journal* 81 (1985): 1–12.

Rand, Edward Kennard. "Horatian Urbanity in Hesiod's *Works and Days*." *American Journal of Philology* 32 (1911): 131–61.

———. *The Magical Art of Virgil*. Cambridge, Mass.: Harvard University Press, 1931; repr. Hamsden, Conn.: Archon, 1966.

Redfield, James M. *Nature and Culture in the Iliad: The Tragedy of Hector*. Chicago: University of Chicago Press, 1975.

———. "The Women of Sparta." *Classical Journal* 73 (1977): 146–61.

Redfield, Robert. *The Primitive World and its Transformations*. Ithaca: Cornell University Press, 1953.

———. *Peasant Society and Culture: An Anthropological Approach to Civilization*. Chicago: University of Chicago Press, 1956.

Renehan, R. "Progress in Hesiod." Review of *Hesiod: "Works and Days"* by M. L. West. *Classical Philology* 75 (1980): 339–58.

Revard, Stella. "Vergil's *Georgics* and *Paradise Lost*: Nature and Human Nature in a Landscape." In J. D. Bernard, ed., *Virgil at 2000: Commemorative Essays on the Poet and his Influence*, 259–80. New York: Ams Press, 1986.

Richardson, N. J. Review of *Hesiod: "Works and Days"* by M. L. West. *Journal of Hellenic Studies* 99 (1979): 169–71.

Richardson, N. J. and S. Piggott. "Hesiod's Waggon: Text and Technology." *Journal of Hellenic Studies* 102 (1982): 225–29.

Roberts, W. Rhys. *The Ancient Boeotians: Their Character and Culture, and their Reputation*. Cambridge: Cambridge University Press, 1895.

Rodgers, V. A. "Some Thoughts on ΔΙΚΗ." *Classical Quarterly* 21 (1971): 289–99.

Rosen, Ralph M. "Poetry and Sailing in Hesiod's *Works and Days*." *California Studies in Classical Antiquity* 9 (1990): 99–113.

Rosenmeyer, Thomas G. "Hesiod and Historiography (*Erga* 106–201)." *Hermes* 85 (1957): 257–85.

———. "The Formula in Early Greek Poetry." *Arion* 4 (1965): 295–311.

Ross, David O. *Virgil's Elements: Physics and Poetry in the "Georgics"*. Princeton: Princeton University Press, 1987.

———. "The Pastoral in the *Georgics*: *Si Numquam Fallit Imago*." *Arethusa* 23 (1990): 59–76.

Roth, Catharine P. "The Kings and the Muses in Hesiod's *Theogony*." *Transactions of the American Philological Association* 106 (1976): 331–38.

Rowe, C. J. *Essential Hesiod: "Theogony" 1–232, 453–733, "Works and Days" 1–307*. Bristol: Bristol Classical Press, 1978.

Royds, Thomas Fletcher. *The Beasts, Birds and Bees of Virgil: A Naturalist's Handbook to the "Georgics"*. Oxford: Blackwell, 1918.

Ruch, M. "Virgile et le monde des animaux." In Henry Bardon and Raoul Verdière, eds., *Vergiliana*, 322–27. Leiden: Brill, 1971.

Ryberg, Inez Scott. "Vergil's Golden Age." *Transactions of the American Philological Association* 89 (1958): 112–31.

Said, Suzanne. "Les Combats de Zeus et le problème des interpolations dans la *Théogonie* d'Hésiode." *Revue des Études Grecques* 90 (1977): 183–210.

Sanders, Irwin T. *Rainbow in the Rock: The People of Rural Greece*. Cambridge, Mass.: Harvard University Press, 1962.

Schmidt, Jens-Uwe. *Adressat und Paraineseform: Zur Intention von Hesiods "Werken und Tagen"*. Hypomnemata 86. Göttingen: Vandenhoeck and Ruprecht, 1986.

Sealey, Raphael. *The Justice of the Greeks*. Ann Arbor: University of Michigan Press, 1994.

Segal, Charles. "Orpheus and the Fourth Georgic: Vergil on Nature and Civilization." *American Journal of Philology* 87 (1966): 307–25.

———. "Vergil's Caelatum Opus: An Interpretation of the Third Eclogue." *American Journal of Philology* 88 (1967): 279–308.

———. "Pastoral Realism and the Golden Age: Correspondence and Contrast between Virgil's Third and Fourth Eclogues." *Philologus* 121 (1977): 158–63.

———. *Interpreting Greek Tragedy: Myth, Poetry, and Text*. Ithaca: Cornell University Press, 1986.

———. *Orpheus: The Myth of the Poet*. Baltimore: Johns Hopkins University Press, 1989.

Sellar, W. Y. *The Roman Poets of the Augustan Age: Virgil*. Oxford: Oxford University Press, 1908; repr., New York: Biblo and Tanner, 1965.

Sihvola, Juha. *Decay, Progress, the Good Life?: Hesiod and Protagoras on the Development of Culture*. Commentationes Humanarum Litterarum, no. 89. Helsinki: Societas Scientiarum Fennica, 1989.

Sinclair, T. A. "ʼΑΙΔΩΣ in Hesiod." *Classical Review* 39 (1925): 147–48.

————. *Hesiod: "Works and Days"*. London: Macmillan, 1932.

Slavitt, David. *Virgil*. New Haven: Yale University Press, 1991.

Smith, Peter. "History and the Individual in Hesiod's Myth of Five Races." *Classical World* 74 (1980): 145–63.

Smolenaars, J. J. L. "Labour in the Golden Age: A Unifying Theme in Vergil's Poems." *Mnemosyne*, 4th ser., 40 (1987): 391–405.

Snell, Bruno. "Die Welt der Götter bei Hesiod." In Ernst Heitsch, ed., *Hesiod*, 708–25. Darmstadt: Wissenschaftliche Buchgesellschaft, 1955.

————. *The Discovery of the Mind*. Translated by T. G. Rosenmeyer. New York: Harper and Row, 1960.

Solmsen, Friedrich. *Hesiod and Aeschylus*. Cornell Studies in Classical Philology. Ithaca: Cornell University Press, 1949.

————. "The 'Gift' of Speech in Homer and Hesiod." *Transactions of the American Philological Association* 85 (1954): 1–15.

————. "The 'Days' of the *Works and Days*." *Transactions of the American Philological Association* 94 (1963): 293–320.

————. Review of *Hesiod: "Works and Days"* by M. L. West. *Gnomon* 52 (1980): 209–22.

Sorel, Reynal. "L'Inconsistance ontologique des hommes et des dieux chez Hésiode." *Revue Philosophique* 170 (1980): 401–12.

————. "Finalité et origine des hommes chez Hésiode." *Revue de Metaphysique et de Morale* 87 (1982): 24–30.

Spofford, Edward W. *The Social Poetry of the "Georgics"*. Monographs in Classical Studies, ed. W. R. Connor. New York: Arno Press, 1981.

Spurr, M. S. "Agriculture and the *Georgics*." *Greece and Rome* 33 (1986): 164–83.

Starr, Chester. *The Economic and Social Growth of Greece 800–500 B.C.* Oxford: Oxford University Press, 1977.

————. "Hesiod." In I. E. S. Edwards, C. T. Gadd, and N. G. L. Hammond, eds., *The Cambridge Ancient History*. 3rd edn. Cambridge: Cambridge University Press, 1982.

Stehle, Eva M. "Virgil's *Georgics* and the Threat of Sloth." *Transactions of the American Philological Association* 104 (1974): 347–69.

Stephens, Viola G. "Like a Wolf on the Fold: Animal Imagery in Vergil." *Illinois Classical Studies* 15 (1990) 107–30.

Stewart, Douglas J. "Hesiod and History." *Bucknell Review* 18 (1970): 37–52.

Stokes, Michael C. "Hesiodic and Milesian Cosmogonies—I." *Phronesis* 7 (1962): 1–37.

Sullivan, Shirley Darcus. "The Psychic Term νόος in the Poetry of Hesiod." *Glotta* 68 (1990): 68–85.

Syme, Ronald. *The Roman Revolution*. Oxford: Oxford University Press, 1939.

Tandy, David W. and Walter C. Neale. *Hesiod's "Works and Days": A Translation and Commentary for the Social Sciences*. Berkeley: University of California Press, 1996.

Teggart, Frederick J. "The Argument of Hesiod's *Works and Days*." *Journal of the History of Ideas* 8 (1974): 45–77.

Thomas, Richard F. "Virgil's *Georgics* and the Art of Reference." *Harvard Studies in Classical Philology* 90 (1986): 171–98.

————. "Prose into Poetry." *Harvard Studies in Classical Philology* 91 (1987): 229–60.

————. *Virgil: "Georgics"*. 2 vols. Cambridge: Cambridge University Press, 1988.

————. "Ideology, Influence, and Future Studies in the *Georgics*." *Vergilius* 36 (1990): 64–73.

————. "The Old Man Revisited: Memory, Reference and Genre in Virg., *Georg.* 4, 116–48." *Materiali e discussioni per l'analisi dei testi classici* 29 (1990): 35–70.

————. "The 'Sacrifice' at the End of the *Georgics*, Aristaeus, and Vergilian Closure." *Classical Philology* 86 (1991): 211–18.

Thompson, Wentworth D'Arcy. *A Glossary of Greek Birds*. Oxford: Clarendon Press, 1895.

Toutain, Jules. *The Economic Life of the Ancient World*. Translated by M. R. Dobie. New York: A. A. Knopf, 1930.

Valk, M. van der. "On the God Cronos." *Greek, Roman and Byzantine Studies* 26 (1985): 5–11.

Vandvik, Erik. *The Prometheus of Hesiod and Aeschylus*. Skrifter utgitt av det Norske Videnskaps-Akademi i Oslo II. Hist.-Filos. Klasse, no. 2. Oslo: Jacob Dybwad, 1942.

———. "Some Notes on the 'Works' of Hesiod." *Symbolae Osloensis* 24 (1945): 154–63.

Verdenius, W. J. "L'Association des idées comme principe de composition dans Homère, Hésiode, Théognis." *Revue des Études Grecques* 73 (1960): 345–61.

———. "Aufbau und Absicht der Erga." In *Hésiode et son Influence*, Entretiens sur l'antiquité classique 7, 111–59. Geneva: Fondation Hardt, 1962.

———. "Hesiod, *Theogony* 507–616: Some Comments on a Commentary." *Mnemosyne* 24 (1971): 1–10.

———. "A 'Hopeless' Line in Hesiod: *Works and Days* 96." *Mnemosyne* 24 (1971): 225–31.

———. "Notes on the Proem of Hesiod's *Theogony*." *Mnemosyne* 25 (1972): 225–60.

———. *A Commentary on Hesiod: "Works and Days," vv. 1–382*. Mnemosyne Supplement, no. 86. Leiden: Brill, 1985.

Vernant, Jean-Pierre. *The Origins of Greek Thought*. Ithaca: Cornell University Press, 1962.

———. "Mètis et les mythes de souveraineté." *Revue de l'Histoire des Religions* 180 (1971): 29–76.

———. *Myth and Thought Among the Greeks*. London: Routledge, 1983.

———. *Myth and Society in Ancient Greece*. Translated by Janet Lloyd. New York: Zone Books, 1988.

———. "Sacrifice in Greek Myths." In Yves Bonnefoy, ed., *Mythologies*, Vol. 1, 423–24. Translated under the direction of Wendy Doniger. Chicago: University of Chicago Press, 1991.

———. "Theogony and Myths of Sovereignty." In Yves Bonnefoy, ed., *Mythologies*, Vol. 1, 375–78. Translated under the direction of Wendy Doniger. Chicago: University of Chicago Press, 1991.

Versényi, Laszlo. *Man's Measure. A Study of the Greek Image of Man from Homer to Sophocles*. Albany: State University of New York Press, 1974.

Versnel, H. S. "Greek Myth and Ritual: The Case of Kronos." In Jan Bremmer, ed., *Interpretations of Greek Mythology*, 121–52. London: Routledge, 1988.

Vlastos, Gregory. "Solonian Justice." *Classical Philology* 41 (1946): 65–83.

Vucinich, Wayne S. *The Peasant in Nineteenth-Century Russia*. Stanford: Stanford University Press, 1968.

Wade-Gery, H. T. "Hesiod." *Phoenix* 3 (1949): 84–90.

Walcot, Peter. "The Text of Hesiod's *Theogony* and the Hittite *Epic of Kumarbi*." *Classical Quarterly*, n.s., 6 (1956): 198–206.

———. "The Problem of the Prooemium of Hesiod's *Theogony*." *Symbolae Osloensis* 33 (1957): 37–45.

———. "The Composition of the *Works and Days*." *Revue des Études Grecques* 74 (1961): 1–19.

———. "Pandora's Jar, *Erga* 83–105." *Hermes* 89 (1961): 249–51.

———. "Hesiod and the Law." *Symbolae Osloensis* 38 (1963): 5–21.

———. *Hesiod and the Near East*. Cardiff: University of Wales Press, 1966.

———. *Greek Peasants, Ancient and Modern: A Comparison of Social and Moral Values*. Manchester: Manchester University Press, 1970.

———. *Envy and the Greeks: A Study of Human Behavior*. Warminster, Wilts.: Aris and Phillips, 1978.

Waltz, Pierre. *Hésiode et son poème moral.* Bibliòtheque des Universités du Midi, Fasc. no. 12. Bordeaux: Feret, 1906.

Wankenne, A. "Aristée et Orphée dans les *Géorgiques.*" *Études Classiques* 38 (1970): 18–29.

Warden, J. R. "The Mind of Zeus." *Journal of the History of Ideas* 32 (1971): 3–14.

Weber, Clifford. "Dodona Reneges: A Neglected Oxymoron in Georgics 1.149." *Classical Philology* 86 (1991): 323–27.

Weber, Max. *The Agrarian Sociology of Ancient Civilizations.* Translated by R. I. Frank. London, NLB, 1909; repr., Atlantic Highlands, N.J.: Humanities Press, 1976.

Welles, C. Bradford. "Hesiod's Attitude toward Labor." *Greek, Roman, and Byzantine Studies* 8 (1967): 5–23.

Wender, Dorothea S. "Resurrection in the Fourth Georgic." *American Journal of Philology* 90 (1969): 424–36.

———. *Hesiod and Theognis.* New York: Penguin, 1973.

———. "From Hesiod to Homer by Way of Rome." *Ramus* 8 (1979): 59–64.

West, David. "Two Plagues: Virgil, *Georgics* 3.478–566 and Lucretius 6.1090–1286." In David West and Tony Woodman, eds., *Creative Imitation and Latin Literature,* 71–88. Cambridge: Cambridge University Press, 1979.

West, M. L. "Miscellaneous Notes on the *Works and Days.*" *Philologus* 108 (1964): 157–73.

———. *Hesiod: "Theogony".* Oxford: Clarendon Press, 1966.

———. *Hesiod: "Works and Days".* Oxford: Clarendon Press, 1978.

———. *Hesiod: "Theogony", "Works and Days".* Oxford: Oxford University Press, 1988.

White, K. D. *Roman Farming.* Ithaca: Cornell University Press, 1970.

Wilamowitz-Moellendorff, Ulrich von. *Hesiodos' "Erga".* Berlin: Weidmannsche Buchhandlung, 1928.

Wilhelm, Robert M. "Apollo, Sol and Caesar: Triumph of Order." *Augustan Age* 5 (1986): 60–75.

Wilkinson, L. P. "The Intention of Virgil's *Georgics.*" *Greece and Rome* 19 (1950): 19–28.

———. "Virgil's Theodicy." *Classical Quarterly,* n.s., 13 (1963): 75–84.

———. *The "Georgics" of Virgil: A Critical Survey.* Cambridge: Cambridge University Press, 1969.

Will, Frederick. "Observations on the Conflict of Art and Didacticism in Hesiod." *Symbolae Osloenses* 37 (1961): 5–14.

Williams, Gordon. *Tradition and Originality in Roman Poetry.* Oxford: Oxford University Press, 1968.

Williams, R. D. *Virgil: The "Eclogues" and "Georgics".* Basingstoke: Macmillan Education, 1979.

Wilson, Edward O. *Sociobiology: The Abridged Edition.* Cambridge, Mass.: Belknap Press, 1975.

Wiltshire, Susan Ford. *Public and Private in Vergil's Aeneid.* Amherst: University of Massachussetts Press, 1989.

Wissowa, Georg. "Das Prooemium von Vergils *Georgica.*" *Hermes* 52 (1917): 92–104.

Wolf, Eric R. *Peasants.* Englewood Cliffs, N.J.: Prentice-Hall, 1966.

Wormell, D. E. "*Apibus quanta experientis parcis:* Virgil's Georgics 4.1–227." In Henry Bardon and Raoul Verdière, eds., *Vergiliana: Recherches sur Virgile,* 429–35. Leiden: Brill, 1971.

Wuilleumier, P. "Virgile et le vieillard de Tarente." *Revue des Études Latines* 8 (1930): 325–40.

Yamagata, Naoko. *Homeric Morality.* Mnemosyne Supplement, no. 131. Leiden: Brill, 1994.

INDEX

Aeneid, 92, 122, 199 n. 18, 211 n. 81, 222
 n. 66
  Aeneas in, 82, 91
  ambiguity in, 213 n. 95, 223 n. 91
  and the *Georgics*, 115, 116, 211 n. 78
Aeschylus, 75, 99, 106, 125–26
agora. See marketplace
allusion
  to the *Eclogues*, 140
  to the *Iliad*, 115
  to the *Odyssey*, 156–57
  to the *Works and Days*, 85–87, 119, 121,
    139–40, 155–56, 198 n. 11
  See also Georgics
ambiguity, 59–61, 63, 64–67, 88, 125–26,
  130–35, 168–69, 229 n. 56
animals
  of fable, 78–80, 195–96 n. 93
  in the *Georgics*, 94–97, 141–45, 201 n. 38
  in the *Works and Days*, 36, 108–9, 137–38
Aphrodite, 62, 104, 105–6, 108, 186 n. 13
Aratus, 114, 212 n. 82, 222 n. 65, 224 n. 105
Aristaeus, 87, 111, 155–62, 226 n. 13
Aristophanes, 5, 180 n. 24, 215 n. 13
Aristotle, 221 n. 64, 222 n. 66
  and the *Georgics*, 225 n. 104
  on justice, 218 n. 35, 219 nn. 40–41

and the *Works and Days*, 133, 220 n. 51,
  228 n. 40
Ascra, 33, 35, 38, 152–53, 165
Athene, 100–1, 106, 107, 187 n. 16, 208
  n. 49, 209 n. 57
Augustus. *See* Octavian

Bacchae, 155
Bacchus, 111, 117, 118, 120, 121–22, 155,
  162, 225 n. 6
balance, 133–34, 136, 219 n. 40
  of good and evil, 48, 106–7, 163, 167
  of the seasons, 56, 57–58, 83
bees, 141, 146–51, 154, 160, 213 n. 103
  personalized, 222 n. 70, 223–24 n. 95
  self-destruction, 116, 122
  social order, 112, 147–49, 161
bougonia, 157, 160, 226 n. 13

Caesar. *See* Octavian
Callimachus, 197 n. 1
Cato, 89, 181 n. 26, 182 n. 35, 199 n. 17,
  222 n. 70
Ceres, 84–85, 111, 118, 155, 225 n. 6
Chaos, 45, 104
chiasmus, 60
Cincinnatus, 89

cities, 34–36, 73–76, 82, 152–54, 225 n. 3.
    See also Ascra; Rome
Columella, 181 n. 29, 182 n. 35
Corycian gardener, 93, 123, 141, 148–50
Cronos, 44–46, 99, 113, 179 n. 12, 202 n. 2,
    203 n. 10, 204 n. 15
Cyme, 33, 34, 38

Darwin, 162–63
days, lucky and unlucky, 47, 108, 109,
    113–14, 115, 163, 210 n. 69
death, 143–46, 150–51, 155–62, 211 n. 79,
    222 n. 73
    See also sex
deception, 64–67, 134–35, 168–69.
    See also ambiguity
Demeter, 103, 104, 108, 109, 111,
    209 nn. 50, 57, 216 n. 21
didactic poetry
    in the *Georgics*, 92–93, 200 n. 28
    in the *Works and Days*, 51–53, 57–58,
        182 nn. 35–42, 183 n. 43
Dionysus, 108, 155, 209 n. 53
disease, 66–67, 112, 116, 122, 144–45,
    150–51
due season, 48, 108, 163–69, 230 n. 63

Earth (*Gaia*), 44–46, 99–102, 104, 108, 111,
    203 n. 10, 204 n. 16
Eclogues, 91, 92, 93, 140, 155, 216 n. 22,
    225 nn. 3, 6
economics, 35–36, 131, 133–34, 175 n. 12,
    218 n. 35.
    See also profit; trade
epic, 41, 44, 130–31, 210 n. 68
Epicurean, 148–49
Epimetheus, 65–66, 67, 128
Escher, M. C., 169
Euboea, 33
Eurydice, 157–59
evil, 68, 71, 112, 168–69, 188 n. 19,
    190 n. 41

fable, Hesiod's, 47, 77–81, 195–96 nn. 93–94
fallow land, 50, 181 nn. 30–32, 183 n. 50
falsehoods, Vergil's, 122–23
farming, 73, 126–27, 152–54, 163–70
    and due season, 134–35, 168–69
    farmer as male, 182 n. 37
    in the *Georgics*, 82–88, 198 n. 15

Hesiod's farm, 36
    manual on farming, 49–50, 57–58
    as microcosm, 51, 141, 154, 163, 169
    and nature, 118, 123–24, 154
    profit, 141–43, 149, 161
    and religion, 187–88 n. 18
    Roman, 88–91
    in the *Works and Days*, 36–39, 48–58,
        109–10, 138
Fates (*Moirai*). *See* Portioners
festivals, 33, 114, 118, 121, 123
Five Ages, 48, 64, 68–77, 114, 125, 138,
    180 n. 20
    Heroes in the, 71–74, 191 n. 46, 192 nn.
        55, 61
    Iron Age in the, 72, 76, 192 n. 55
    Silver Age in the, 69–70, 71, 74–75,
        136
force and intelligence, 202 n. 2
    in the *Georgics*, 112–13, 115–17, 123–24,
        138–40, 155
    in the *Works and Days*, 46, 99–102, 105,
        106
fool (*nepios*), 126, 128
    See also intelligence
formulae, 108, 196 n. 95, 221 nn. 61–63

Gaia. *See* Earth
genealogy, 44–46, 101, 105, 207 n. 39,
    208 n. 48
Georgics, 122–23, 163
    contrast to the *Works and Days*, 91–97,
        113–15
    reference to the *Works and Days*, 85–87,
        119, 121, 139–40, 155–56, 198 n. 11
    structure, 82–84, 87–88
God, 98–124, 150
    abstract gods, 45–46, 103–4, 136
    immanent and transcendent, 61–63, 105,
        185 n. 7, 202 n. 2
    Stoic, 147–48
Golden Age, 74–75, 180 n. 41
    in the *Georgics*, 85–88, 111–13, 114,
        118–19, 124, 138, 145, 155
    in the *Works and Days*, 64, 68–69, 129,
        192 n. 55, 193 n. 73, 204 n. 15
grafting. *See* trees

harvest, 50, 55, 56, 165–68, 222 n. 73
Hecate, 103, 105, 210 n. 71

Herodotus, 35, 127, 173 n. 1, 208 n. 48,
    215 n. 17, 217 n. 28, 218 n. 33
    on Homer and Hesiod, 5, 6
Heroes, 45, 68, 71–74, 110
Hesiod, 5–7, 32–33, 165
    existence, 36–40
    and Perses, 133–34
hiding, 64–67, 168, 188 n. 23, 189 n. 27,
    191 n. 47
Hippocratic writings, 198 n. 6
history, 62, 72–74, 193 n. 65
    Roman, 88–89
holidays. *See* festivals
Homer, 5–7, 31, 33–34, 41–42, 73–7
    contrast to Hesiod, 6–7, 39, 52–53, 110,
    210 n. 63
honor (*time*), 43, 102–4, 109, 110, 210
    nn. 63–68
hope (*elpis*), 66–67, 190 nn. 34–37
Horace, 199 n. 19, 200 n. 25
Hundred-Handers, 99–100, 103, 203 n. 7,
    205 n. 18
Hymn to Hermes (Homeric Hymn to
    Mercury), 133
Hymn to the Muses. *See* Proem to the
    Theogony

Iliad, 34, 35, 42,
    and the *Georgics*, 223 n. 92, 227 nn. 21,
    26–27
    and the *Works and Days*, 193 n. 66,
    216 n. 20, 217 n. 28
indignation (*nemesis*), 69, 133–34, 136
individual, 111, 144–51, 158–59
intelligence, 111, 115–17, 162
    perception (*noos*), 43, 48, 63, 99, 110,
    112, 125–30, 163–65
    understanding, 112, 123, 155
Iron Age
    in the *Georgics*, 85–87, 111–12, 114,
    118–19, 124, 138–39, 155–56
    in the *Works and Days*, 70, 72, 76,
    136–37, 210 n. 68

jealousy (*pthonos*), 127
Jupiter, 85–87, 111–13, 115, 118, 121–22,
    140, 150
just city, 129
justice (*dike*), 34–35, 47, 63, 69–70, 174 n. 9,
    196 n. 97.

in the Five Ages, 74–76, 193 n. 66
in the *Georgics*, 138–40, 141–45
as a goddess, 104, 109, 111, 136, 138, 209
    n. 50, 220 n. 53
legal sense of, 130–31, 138, 216–17
    nn. 25–26, 217 n. 29, 218 n. 33
as reciprocity, 132–35, 219 n. 40
in the *Works and Days*, 127–28, 130–34,
    135–38
and Zeus, 81–82, 128–29
See also work

kairos. See proportion
key words, 43, 47, 79, 135, 180 n. 16,
    227 n. 35, 228 n. 41
    due season, 47, 52–53, 107–10
    measure, 47, 134–35
    perception (*noos*) 47, 125–30
kings, 34–35, 80, 130, 196 n. 98
    apian, 146–47, 148, 224 n. 101
    gift-gobbling, 77, 79, 126
    just, 35, 80, 219 n. 40
kouros, 169

latifundia, 82, 90, 89–92, 200 nn. 25–27
Lucretius, 92, 151, 197 n. 1, 200 nn. 28–30,
    212 nn. 87, 94, 225 n. 6

Maecenas, 93, 223 n. 89
mallow and asphodel, 127, 215 nn. 13–15
marketplace (*agora*), 35, 60, 110, 115, 153
measure, 48, 134–5
    See also key words
Metis. See Wisdom
Moirai. See Portioners
monsters
    in the *Theogony*, 45, 101, 103
    in the *Georgics*, 115
moral
    ethical, as opposed to practical, 63,
    187 n. 17, 188 n. 19
    of the fable, 77–78, 80, 192 n. 52
    interpretations of the Five Ages myth,
    70–71, 191 n. 52, 192 nn. 55–56
Mount Helicon, 33
Muses, 33, 80, 104, 105, 205 n. 22, 207 n. 39
Mycenaean Age, 33
myth, 48, 61–62, 102, 155–56, 183 n. 51,
    186–87 n. 7
    mythic time, 62, 72–73, 187 n. 15

nature, 61–62, 88, 152–54
    alienation from man, 113, 123–24, 151
    and Aristaeus and Orpheus, 156–62
    as erratic/extreme 101, 111–13, 113–17,
        145
    in the *Georgics*, 83–85, 87–88, 95–97,
        141
    and God, 98, 107–9, 135–36
    human nature, 74–76, 138, 154, 192
        n. 64
    Roman view, 90, 201 n. 38
    in the *Works and Days*, 152–53, 221
        n. 64
nemesis. *See* indignation
Night, 45, 103
nomos (rule), 102, 137–38, 164, 221 nn.
    63–64

Octavian, 88, 93, 111, 154, 222 n. 70
    and Vergil 87, 138–40, 155
    and the *Georgics*, 122
octopus, 49, 95
Odysseus, 53, 89, 177 n. 19, 199 n. 18
Odyssey, 37, 193 n. 73, 196 n. 97, 215 n. 13
    and the *Georgics*, 156, 226 nn. 13–14
    justice in, 217 n. 28, 218 nn. 33, 38
    and the *Works and Days*, 42, 187 n. 16,
        221 n. 59, 222 n. 74
olives, 36, 49, 121–22
Olympians, 44–45, 101, 104, 105, 209
    n. 53
oral tradition, 34, 35, 196 n. 98
order of Zeus, 45, 47–88, 51, 62, 104–7,
    107–10, 167–68
Oresteia, 106, 203 n. 10
Orpheus, 87, 122, 155–62, 173 n. 1
Ouranos (Sky), 44–46, 203 n. 10, 204 n. 16

Pan, 225 n. 6
Pandora (All-giving), 65, 188 n. 22, 216
    n. 21
    myth of, 48, 59, 64–67, 68, 70, 168
peasant, 219 n. 45, 227 n. 35
    Hesiod as, 37–39, 109, 175 n. 10, 210
        n. 63
    sees farming as a way of life, 90–92, 175
        n. 10
    vision of the world, 134, 229 n. 58
perception (*noos*). *See* intelligence; key
    words

Perses, 47, 50, 67, 78–79, 128, 133–34
    as dramatic device, 52, 164–65, 219 n. 44
    and Hesiod, 59–60, 67, 139
    inconsistancies of, 38, 177 n. 21, 183
        n. 44, 28 n. 40
    and lawsuit, 32–33, 44, 130–31
persona, 37–39, 228 n. 43
personalization, 94–97, 123, 133–34, 150,
    159–60, 201 n. 38, 222 n. 70
perspective. *See* point of view
plague. *See* disease
Plato, 38, 63, 76, 193 n. 70, 216 n. 19, 218
    n. 38, 228 n. 40
Pleiades, 57, 98, 108–9, 163–64, 183 n. 43
plowing and sowing
    in the *Georgics*, 83–84, 96–97, 114, 156
    in the *Works and Days*, 52–55, 57, 109,
        165–68
poetry
    in the *Georgics*, 155, 161
    oral, 41–44,
    and Vergil, 93–94, 138–40, 157–60
    in the *Works and Days*, 38–39, 80, 165
point of view, 94, 95–97, 141, 143, 147–51,
    228 n. 42
portion (*moira*), 43, 103–4, 133, 206 n. 28
Portioners (*Moirai*), 45, 103, 105, 106–7,
    208 nn. 43–5
Poseidon, 81, 103, 109, 209 nn. 53–57
Proem to the *Theogony*, 43, 79, 102, 105,
    207 n. 39
profit, 218 n. 35
    in the *Georgics*, 141–43, 149, 222 n. 73
    in the *Works and Days*, 166
    See also economics; trade
Prometheus, 81, 188 n. 22, 193 n. 67
    in Aeschylus, 99–100, 125–26, 202 n. 3
    in the *Theogony*, 43, 202 n. 4, 203 n. 6
    in the *Works and Days*, 64–65, 67, 108,
        111
Prometheus Bound, 75, 99, 125–26, 193 n. 73,
    202 n. 3, 203 n. 7
proportion (*kairos*) 135, 219 n. 40
Proteus, 156–57, 159, 160–61

reciprocity, 132–35, 218–19 nn. 39–41
repetition, 43–44, 72, 195 nn. 85–91
right (*themis*), 103, 106, 202 n. 2, 208 n. 49
ring composition, 43, 66, 72, 102, 202 n. 4,
    205 n. 22

Rome, 82–83, 88–91, 91–92, 119, 153–54,
   199 n. 17.
   See also war
Romulus (and Remus), 89, 154

sailing, 36, 89, 110, 165–67, 177 n. 23
Saturn, 86–87, 112–13, 211 n. 81
seasons (*horai*), 105, 107–9, 168–69
   due season, 135
   and farming, 49–50, 51–52, 57–58, 121
   Peace, Justice, Good Order, 105, 106–7,
      208 n. 48
   in Vergil, 92, 114
   See also key words
Servius, 144
sex, 116, 122, 145, 211 n. 79, 222 n. 78
   See also death
shame (*aidos*), 69, 133, 134, 136, 191 n. 49
Sirius, 51, 108, 109
Sky. *See* Ouranos
slaves
   in the *Georgics*, 199 nn. 25–26, 222 n. 73
   in the *Works and Days*, 54, 152, 183 n. 48,
      184 n. 62
sowing. *See* plowing
sphragis, 93, 200 n. 31
spring, 181 n. 32
   in the *Georgics*, 85, 120, 122, 160, 198
      n. 6
   in the *Works and Days*, 50, 54–55, 56,
      165–66, 168
Strife (*Eris*), 67, 76, 77, 109, 128, 134
   goddesses, 47, 48, 59–61, 185 nn. 4–6,
      208 n. 48

Tartarus, 101, 103, 104, 203 n. 10, 204 n. 15,
   205 n. 18
Themistocles, 89
Theocritus, 91
theodicy, 85–86, 111, 115, 124, 149–50,
   211 n. 76, 226 n. 13
Theogony, 31–33, 37, 72, 98–107, 125–126,
   154
   good kings in, 35, 80, 135
   structure of, 44–46, 206–7 n. 37
   and *Works and Days*, 46–47, 66
   and Zeus, 43, 53, 61, 98–103, 105–7
threshing, 49, 56–57, 181 n. 33
Tisiphone, 112
Titanomachia, 99–100

Titans, 44–46, 100, 102–3, 125
trade, 36, 90–92, 133, 141–43, 153–54, 167
   See also economics; profit
trees and grafting, 87, 117, 119, 121, 122,
   213 n. 103
Typhoeus, 46, 100–2, 117, 203 n. 10, 204–5
   nn. 17–18
   in the *Georgics*, 115, 212 n. 90

understanding. *See* intelligence

Varro, 111, 122, 182 n. 35, 223 n. 90, 225
   n. 24
Vergil, 88–89, 159, 200 n. 27
   and Octavian, 87, 138–40, 155
   as poet, 92–94, 139–40
vignettes, 42–43, 49, 51, 54–55, 108, 109,
   114, 119, 229 n. 53
vines
   in the *Georgics*, 119–21
   in the *Work and Days*, 36, 49, 52, 56–57,
      166
violence, 111–12, 113, 121, 133, 138–46
   of Aristaeus, 156–57, 160
   of nature, 115–17, 145
   in the *Works and Days*, 136, 220–21
      n. 58

war
   in the *Georgics*, 118–19, 140, 154
   in Homer, 110
   in the *Work and Days*, 89–91, 116–17
weather
   god, 102, 202 n. 2
   signs, 108, 112, 114, 115–17, 119,
      123–24, 150–51
Wisdom (*Metis*), 46, 99, 100–1, 106, 208
   n. 49
wisdom literature, 6, 52–53
work (*ergon*, *labor*)
   in the *Georgics*, 118, 121, 147–50
   and justice 47–48, 126–29, 137–38
   in the *Works and Days*, 60, 110, 138,
      164
Works and Days, 37–39, 163, 179 n. 14
   composition, 46–48, 182 n. 41
   not a farming manual, 48–50, 57–58, 182
      n. 42

Xenophon, 39, 177 n. 19

Zeus, 59, 109–10, 111, 112, 137–38
   and honors, 102–4, 109–10
   as immanent, 61–63, 70, 104–5
   and justice 61, 77–79, 81, 127–29,
     135–37

   and nature, 51, 62, 74–76, 98, 135–36,
     168–70
   the order of Zeus, 47–48, 104–5
   in the *Theogony*, 43, 44–46, 61, 98–108
   uniting force and intelligence, 46, 202 n. 2